M. E. Saltykov, photograph from late 1850s

Saltykov

The Golovlyov Family

Translated by SAMUEL D. CIORAN

Mikhail Evgrafovich Saltykov (1826-1889)
The Golovlyov Family.
Translation by Samuel Cioran,
Introduction by Carl. R. Proffer,
Copyright © 1977 by Ardis.
ISBN 0-88233-209-0 (cloth)
ISBN 0-88233-210-4 (paperback)
Library of Congress Catalogue Card No. 76-57547.

Published by Ardis, 2901 Heatherway,
Ann Arbor, Michigan 48104
Manufactured by McNaughton & Gunn,
Ann Arbor, Michigan.

CONTENTS

ACKNOWLEDGEMENT

My kind thanks to Miss Pat Goodall, secretary of the Department of Russian at McMaster University, for her unflagging energy in typing and retyping the manuscript of this translation.

—S.D. Cioran

Mikhail Evgrafovich Saltykov
(N. Shchedrin)

A Chronology

1826   Born in Spas-Ugol of the Tver (now Kalinin) Province. His father was from the old, but not wealthy, gentry; his mother from a rich Muscovite merchant family.

1826-35   Childhood spent on family estate in Spas-Ugol.

1838   A pupil at the exclusive lyceum in Tsarskoe Selo near Petersburg where children of prominent citizens received education.

1844   Finishes lyceum and assumes a civil service position in the War Ministry. Begins collaboration with leading journals, writing reviews for *Notes of the Fatherland* and *The Contemporary*.

1847-48   Publishes first two novellas, "Contradictions" (1847) and "A Muddled Affair" (1848). Authorities displeased and Saltykov exiled to Vyatka in April of 1848. Spends almost seven years in exile, but allowed to carry on various duties as a civil servant.

1855   Death of Nicholas I. Saltykov pardoned and allowed to return to Petersburg. Takes up literary activity once again.

1856   Marries E.A. Boltina, daughter of the vice-governor of Vyatka. Serves as an official in the Ministry of Internal Affairs until 1858.

1856-57   Publishes *Provincial Sketches* under the pseudonym of N. Shchedrin, attacking Russian serfdom and bureaucracy with biting satire. Hailed by the social critics, Chernyshevsky and Dobrolyubov.

1858-62   Serves as vice-governor first in Ryazan and then in Tver. In 1862 forced into early retirement because of his contentious views.

1863   Gathers together stories written over past few years and issues them under the title of *Innocent Tales* and *Satire in Prose*. The same year he is invited by Nekrasov to join the journal *The Contemporary* where he works as an editor and feature writer. But leaves journal after a few years because of disagreements.

1865-68   Re-enters civil service and serves in various provincial centers. But the continued publication of his satirical attacks on his superiors convinces government to retire him once and for all.

1869   Publishes *Letters on the Province* and *Signs of the Time*, both of which reflect on the aftermath of the abolition of serfdom which had taken place in 1861.

1868-84   Co-editor of *Notes of the Fatherland.*

1869-70   Publication of *The History of a Town*, a provincial satire aimed at local officialdom in the mythical town of "Glupov" (i.e. "Stupid-ville").

1871-76   Publication of *Pompadours and Pompadouresses* (1863-1874), *Diary of a Provincial in St. Petersburg* (1872), *Gentlemen of Tashkent* (1869-72), all of which deal with topical satire.

1874-75   Publication of *Well-Meant Speeches* in *Notes of the Fatherland.*

1875-80   The appearance of *The Golovlyov Family.*

1877-83   Publication of more topical satire in the works *The Sanctuary of Mon-Repos* (1878-79), *A Contemporary Idyll* (1877-83) and *Letters to Auntie* (1881-82).

1878-84   After death of Nekrasov in 1878, Saltykov-Shchedrin edits *Notes of the Fatherland* by himself. Journal closed in 1884 by authorities, particularly because of Saltykov-Shchedrin's own writings.

1883-84   *Tales from Poshekhonie* appears with sketches of provincial life among peasants and gentry.

1885   Begins publishing in *The European Herald* and *The Russian Record*. Increasing bouts of illness.

1882-86   Publication of *Fairy Tales.*

1887-89   *Olden Times in Poshekonie*, in which he portrays life on a provincial estate just before the abolition of serfdom; based on his own reminiscences.

1889   Dies in St. Petersburg.

Saltykov, watercolor by unknown
artist, late 1850s

Photograph of Saltykov, late 1860s

SALTYKOV AND THE RUSSIAN NOVEL

I

The Golovlyov Family is one of world literature's most depressing books. Of course, Russian prose is not fabled for its lev-
ity, but Saltykov's grim world is something special even among
Russia's chronicles of provincial rot. In the idiocies which Saltykov describes, and in his invective, there is humor which gives the
reader respite; but it is what we now call black humor. The Golovlyov estate is good burial ground, and Saltykov's central character has a flair for doom. Historically, satire and death have gone
together; one of the old Irish satirists' main functions was to
rhyme rats to death, and in his way Saltykov tried to do the same
thing. His rather cheerless life was devoted to the exposé of social
evils. His attacks on tyranny, backwardness, sloth and inertia
helped make him a favorite of Russian radicals from his own day
to the present. Indeed, history has made a rather odd full circle,
and Saltykov's work has acquired new relevance; nowadays he is a
favorite of members of the liberal intelligentsia, who believe that
the character types and abuses of power which Saltykov described
are basically the same as those in Soviet Russia.

Saltykov came from the reasonably wealthy provincial gentry
which he excoriates in many of his sketches. The Saltykov clan
was old nobility, and marriage into the family of Peter the Great
helped to enrich it. Catherine the Great asserted that a Saltykov
was Tsar Paul I's real father. Various Saltykovs had at least periph-
eral relation to Russian literary society. Our Mikhail Saltykov was
the next to the last of eight children, and his family life is strongly
reflected in *The Golovlyov Family*. His mother, Olga, a formidable
woman, as can be seen from her photograph, was the prototype
for Arina Petrovna (Saltykov started writing the sketches for *The
Golovlyov Family* a few months after his mother died), his elder

ix

Saltykov's mother, Olga,
photograph from 1860s

Painting by unknown artist
of Saltykov's mother, 1860s

brother the model for Judas.

In Saltykov's childhood years, he was an excellent student, one of a few chosen to attend the Tsarskoe Selo lyceum. Many of his classmates—and Saltykov himself—would become high-ranking government officials—ministers, governors, ambassadors. His literary interests developed early, and may explain his mediocre performance in most of the lyceum classes. He was considered his class's heir to Pushkin (the lyceum's most famous graduate) and his first published poem, "The Lyre," appeared in the *Library for Reading* when he was only fifteen. A few other poems were published in *The Contemporary,* and he wrote reviews for major periodicals in the mid-1840s.

St. Petersburg was an ideal place for an intelligent young man to develop a social consciousness in the Forties, when Saltykov worked as an official in the War Ministry. It was a period when literature, social and political matters were discussed intensely, and they were considered related problems. As Saltykov wrote:

Everybody knows that in 1840 Russian literature, and with it all youth, divided itself into two camps, the Westerners and the Slavophiles.

At that moment I had just left the university; my spirit was formed in the school of Belinsky, and quite naturally I enrolled in the Westerners' camp. But instead of joining the larger faction of this group, which had taken upon itself to popularize the gifts of German philosophy, which alone was then exercising an influence on literature, I entered a little circle, obscure and as yet unknown, which turned its glance instinctively toward France, to await the light from her. Assuredly it was not the France of Louis-Philippe and of Guizot which fascinated us, but the France of Saint-Simon, of Cabet, of Fourier, of Louis Blanc, and especially the France of George Sand!

From that France emanated faith in humanity and confidence that the golden age, far from being behind us, was yet to come. In short, every aspiration toward what is great and generous and an overflowing love for everything human came from her.

To be sure, we were living in Russia, or rather in St. Petersburg; there we pursued our occupations, wrote letters to our relatives in the provinces, frequented pothouses, gathered for discussions—but our real life, our intellectual and moral life, was actually spent in France.

Russia, in our eyes, represented a land plunged in a dense fog—where everything had become tangled, and where even so simple a thing as the publication of a *Collection of Russian Proverbs* seemed a strange and suspect enterprise to be frowned upon. But France seemed to us as clear as day, in spite of the excisions and blackouts which the censor inflicted on the periodicals

Photograph of Saltykov's wife, Elizaveta
Apollonovna, 1870s

Lithograph of Vyatka in 1856

which came to us from abroad. . . . In France . . . everything seemed just beginning, and this beginning seemed to have been going on for half a century. . . .

I am sure that out of a hundred of us, eighty-nine at least had never set foot in France. . . . Our enthusiasm was at its height in 1848. We followed with palpitating emotion the last years of the reign of Louis-Philippe, and with unwearying transports read over and over the *History of a Decade* of Louis Blanc. . . . Not one among us exhibited that bovine indifference which has become, under a repressive regime, the distinctive sign of the cultivated classes in Russia.[1]

Saltykov moved in very advanced company. In addition to Belinsky and the critic Valerian Maikov, his acquaintances included, for a short time, Petrashevsky. The main interest of Petrashevsky's circle was utopian socialism, but his group was smashed by the secret police in 1848, and its most famous—and most regretful—member, Dostoevsky, was sent to Siberia. As it happened, Dostoevsky and Saltykov became life-long literary and political enemies. The coincidence of the French Revolution of 1848 with the publication of Saltykov's own story "A Confused Affair"— which had sufficient comment on the lack of social justice—earned Saltykov several years of administrative exile in Vyatka. His return to Petersburg came a couple of years before Dostoevsky's.

Saltykov's first years in Vyatka were not unproductive. His official chores and travels while based there provided material to last any satirist for many years. He continued his reading of French books, and even translated part of De Toqueville's *Democracy in America*. And after serving as her tutor and writing a short history of Russia for her, Saltykov—at thirty—married the lovely seventeen-year-old daughter of his superior, the vice-governor of Vyatka. Saltykov's mother's letters from this period are very funny and much in the style of Arina Petrovna: "I consider the girl frivolous, spoiled, and capricious, but I'm not going to answer for this sin, I hope the Lord won't blame me, even though I've given my blessing"(May 30, 1856). One of her major concerns is the logistical problem of delivering two large ikons, tokens of her blessing, to Mikhail. As it turned out, Saltykov's mother was right about the girl, but at the time Saltykov didn't want to hear any of this. And four years after his wedding, Saltykov himself became a vice-governor—first of Ryazan, then Tver.

Liberalization following the death of Tsar Nicholas I allowed

Saltykov to return to the capital in 1855. The long career of writing under the pseudonym N. Shchedrin began with *Provincial Sketches* (1856-57), published in Katkov's liberal magazine *The Russian Herald*. During much of Saltykov's life his civil service and writing careers alternated. He was the only major nineteenth century writer to hold really high government offices. He was known for his honesty and his temper, particularly when dealing with government corruption. Dealers, bribetakers, and speculators found him an inflexible foe. One has to admire a person who not only talked and wrote about Russia's problems but did something about them in a practical, everyday way. Among Russian writers and theoreticians this was singular behavior. The list of Saltykov's accomplishments is long and honorable, but not as long as the list of his plans, because he was often thwarted by bureaucrats with vested interests. As one might expect of a satirist, he had little faith in systems and parties, but his sympathies were close enough to the radicals in Russia to make him a saint to Soviet commentators (although he is rebuked for believing meaningful change could be achieved through liberal reformist measures).

On leaving his government post in Tver in 1862, he wanted to unite all democratic parties in one new journal to be called *Russian Truth* (a typically Russian title), but the government would not license the new periodical, so at the invitation of the influential civic poet Nikolai Nekrasov, he became an editor of *The Contemporary*. Though founded by Pushkin, at this time *The Contemporary* had become the main organ of the radicals.

This was the period of Saltykov's most violent polemic with Dostoevsky. Dostoevsky and his brother had founded two rather unsuccessful journals—*Time* (1861-63), and *The Epoch* (1863-64). Saltykov considered Dostoevksy's socio-political ideas reactionary and his *Notes from the Underground* (*The Epoch,* 1864), a sick joke. A vicious exchange of satires followed: Saltykov lampooned Dostoevsky in his "dramatic fable" *The Swallows*; Dostoevsky retaliated with "Mr. Shchedrin, or, Schism among the Nihilists," with *The Contemporary*, by a small phonetic adjustment, turned into *The Opportunist* and with Shchedrin into "Mr. Munificent."[2] Echoes of this battle run through the works of both writers, including *Crime and Punishment, The Idiot, The Devils,* and finally *The Brothers Karamazov,* in which Dostoevsky digs at Saltykov by having Madame Khokhlakova write an ecstatic letter to Mr.

An 1864 caricature showing the typical reader of *The Moscow News* and the typical reader of Dostoevsky's *The Epoch*. Below: caricature on the polemics between radical journals on topics such as 'progress,' 'nihilism,' and 'female emancipation,' represented as frogs.

Shchedrin. Saltykov, who had just knocked Dostoevsky's Pushkin Speech, got in the last word with a nice rejoinder about Father Karamazov.

The Epoch was closed in 1864, while The Contemporary survived for another two years. But the more militant radicals (especially Pisarev in his Russian Word) considered Saltykov too soft. Even the editorial board of The Contemporary had its doubts about Saltykov; he was insufficiently supportive of old Chernyshevsky ideas and dared to make criticisms of Chernyshevsky's programmatic novel What Is To Be Done. As a result of all this, Saltykov left The Contemporary in 1864 and returned to government work.

The next four years saw Saltykov become Director of the Financial Department in a series of provinces, a post that led to new clashes within the system and eventually he was forced into retirement with civilian rank equivalent to general in the army, but —by order of the Tsar—no right to ever again hold a government post.

In September 1868 he became the fiction editor of the last bastion of radical thought, the journal Notes of the Fatherland. (Nekrasov was general editor and poetry editor.) It was a popular journal with a peak circulation of about ten thousand, very high by Russian standards. For the next sixteen years, virtually all of Saltykov's hundreds of stories, sketches, essays and provincial reportage were first published in Notes of the Fatherland. And as I. P. Foote writes:

As an editor, Saltykov showed the same qualities which had led to his success in the civil service—energy, efficiency, and scrupulous professional standards: qualities which gained him the affection and loyalty of his colleagues and subordinates, despite the fierceness of his manner and the irascibility of his temper. His dedication to Notes of the Fatherland was complete. His private life was inconspicuous: he did not move much in society, nor did he associate out of hours with his journalistic colleagues. He had a small number of friends— neither radicals nor literary men—with whom he dined and played cards.[3]

It was immediately after his forced retirement that Saltykov published The History of a Town—undoubtedly his best-known work after The Golovlyov Family. It is a viciously satirical history of Russia, designed to ridicule the totalitarian incompetence of his own day. A series of extravagantly brutal and obtuse governors

Top: 'The Storm,' a caricature on the destruction of
the May 1874 issue of *Notes of the Fatherland*.
Right: Saltykov holding the map of the city of Glupov
(Stupidville). Below: 1941 Soviet poster entitled
'Saltykov's satire in the battle against Fascism. One
of the tyrants from *The History of a Town* is likened
to Hitler. A famous 1951 satirical magazine cover has
Saltykov standing disapprovingly behind caricatures of
Harry Truman, capitalist generals, and KKK members.

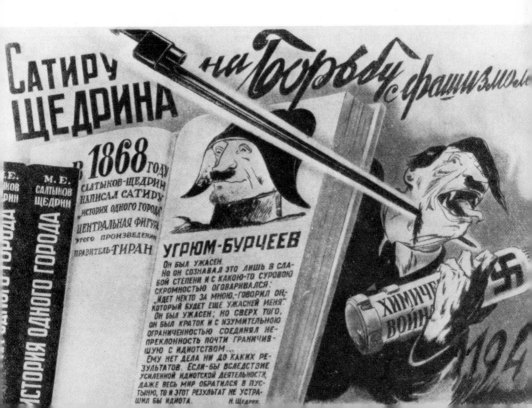

controls the fate of the town, which Saltykov bluntly calls "Stupidville"; their bizarre schemes are reminiscent of Porfiry Golovlyov's preposterous litigations and fantasy potato crops. Maurice Baring wrote of *The History of a Town*:

The various phases Russia had gone through are touched off; the mania for regulations, the formalism, the official red-tape, the persecution of independent thought, and the oppression of original thinkers and writers; the ultimate ideal is that introduced by the last ruler of Glupov (the history lasts from 1731 to 1826), of turning the country into barracks and reducing everyone and everything to one level. . . .[4]

The History of a Town is so highly allusive, so rooted in Russian realia and Russian history, that it has not enjoyed a reputation in translation—but it is a classic which is part of the education of every literate Russian.

Saltykov's publicistic writings in this important period range omnivorously over all aspects of Russia's social and political life.[5] He ridiculed both reactionaries, such as Dostoevsky, and fairweather liberals; and his tone became increasingly bitter in the seventies. This was true in spite of the difficulties presented by increasingly punitive censorship, and for painful periods Saltykov bore the editorial burdens of *Notes of the Fatherland* singlehandedly. The journal was probably more important as a social force than as a purely literary one. The writers whom Salytkov supported when he was a fiction editor were largely third-raters, and a list of their names—Zlatovratsky, Blagoveshchensky, Sleptsov, Novodvorsky, Uspensky—shows how forgotten they are today. Saltykov's battles with the censors were endless; the physical arrest of No. 5 in 1874 (see caricature on page xvii) was one celebrated case. Saltykov wrote later:

Oh, this writer's craft! It's not just torture, it's absolute spiritual hell. Drop by drop the writer's blood oozes out before he gets to the printer's press. What haven't they done to me! They cut me up, chopped me to bits, distorted me, and totally banned me, announcing publicly that I am pernicious, pernicious, pernicious!

In 1882 Saltykov's co-editor, Mikhailovsky, the leading populist critic, was banished from St. Petersburg; and in early 1884 an important staff member was arrested. Finally, in April 1884, after

Turgenev in 1875, oil painting

Saltykov, early 1870s, photograph

receiving a statute-limited third official warning from the censors, the *Notes of the Fatherland* was closed permanently.

During his last years Saltykov published in liberal periodicals —*European Herald* and *The Russian Record*. His famous *Fairytales* (1882-86) appeared here. These were the supposed summit of Saltykov's famous "Aesopian language"—though the allegories were so transparent that the censors immediately banned any cheap mass publication of them. ("How One Muzhik Fed Two Generals" is the most often translated of these tales.) His later works include the collection of sketches *Beyond the Frontier* (1880-81), an irascible reaction to his various trips in Western Europe, notably in 1875-76 when he went abroad for his health—and began *The Golovlyov Family*. In Paris he met Turgenev, who introduced him to Flaubert, Zola, and the rest of French literary society. His relation to Turgenev was ambiguous, to say the least. His letters to Nekrasov in 1875 and 1876 vary in their treatment of Turgenev from restrained gratitude (after all, Turgenev was helping him) to outright hostility. Turgenev will not give a candid description of his next novel (May 3, 1876), Turgenev is "a liar and a hypocrite" (May 11, 1876). But later, at his own request, Saltykov would be buried beside Turgenev in St. Petersburg.

Among the unhappy aspects of Saltykov's later life were the enervating domestic quarrels. His beautiful wife's concerns were militantly unintellectual ("I hear nothing but 'give money.' My wife hates me and laughs at me."). Biographers do not give a satisfactory picture of their life together—which was strange if for no other reason than the fact that they were childless for sixteen years, and then had a son in 1872 and a daughter in 1873. Popular Soviet biographies turn the family into monsters, but this does not fit with Saltykov's last, tender, fatherly letter to his son.

Saltykov's health was very poor during the last two decades of his life. A series of painful illnesses led him to contemplate suicide. He went from famous doctor to famous doctor, but was only frustrated by conflicting diagnoses. He suffered hallucinations in 1885, and for long periods was either unable to work or wrote, by habit, almost automatically. After the publication of *Olden Times in Poshekhonie*, the final disintegration began, and when visitors came Saltykov said, "Tell them I'm busy dying." His misery ended in April 1889.

II

Saltykov played a significant role in the greatest flowering of Russian prose, two prodigious decades (1860-80) when every major work of Tolstoy, Turgenev, Dostoevsky, and Goncharov appeared—along with excellent prose by Pisemsky and Leskov which suffers only in comparison to such extraordinary writers as Tolstoy. The end of that age is clearly marked out: Tolstoy's "conversion" changed his writing dramatically in 1880-81, and in the 1880s all of the writers named above died.

Like most of them, Saltykov began publishing in the mid-1840s when Russia had only one prose satirist—Gogol. Both as a satirist and as a "province" writer Gogol is Saltykov's closest precursor. The portrayal of vegetable existence in the Russian countryside begins with Gogol's stories, particularly "Old-World Landowners" and "The Tale of How Ivan Ivanovich Quarrelled with Ivan Nikiforovich" (1835, *Mirgorod*). *Dead Souls* (1842) is the most polished, rounded, and insane version of this world; but while Gogol's vision has its dark spots of death and brutality, he is basically a Horatian satirist. His eye contains a twinkle, not fire. Saltykov's satire is Juvenalian. That radiant, exalted laughter that Gogol regarded as the satirist's goal when pointing out folly is of no interest to the author of *The Golovlyov Family*. Saltykov's implacable anger is probably one reason why craftsmanship is less evident in his work than in Gogol's *Dead Souls*, which was carefully planned and written, laboriously and repeatedly revised over a period of several years. The final text is a miracle of style, a true "poem" (as Gogol subtitled it in letters which overwhelmed the actual title) with everything in its place. *The Golovlyov Family* began almost by chance—as a short sketch in another book. The writing is uneven from section to section, and as noted by even the friendliest of critics, Saltykov's colleague Mikhailovsky, it contains a number of verbose and repetitious passages.

But both Gogol and Saltykov created eponymous characters. All Russians know them and use their characters' names as nicknames; in polemical writing such allusions have become commonplace. For that matter, Saltykov even borrowed a number of Gogol's characters for his own works; thus he has Nozdrev as the editor of a newspaper called *Garbage*. But the similarities between the

Top left: Nekrasov, 1850s lithograph. Top right: Dostoevsky, 1847 drawing.
Bottom left: Gogol in 1845, daguerreotype. Bottom right: Goncharov, 1859 lithograph.

two writers are not just the result of Saltykov actively borrowing from Gogol, as he probably borrowed from the miser Plyushkin in *Dead Souls* for Judas in *The Golovlyov Family*. Some devices are used almost universally by satirists. These include irony or sarcasm, fantasy, and what satire scholars call "reduction" (presenting the least attractive, lowest possible aspects of something, and oversimplifying). While there are exceptions, the characters of both Gogol and Saltykov tend to be seen externally, tend to lack psychological depth. Wyndham Lewis said that "satire is the art of the outside." Thus we will have to look hard to find examples of either interior monologue or narrated monologue (indirect speech), devices which are typical of the psychological character portraits of Tolstoy and Dostoevsky. Self-analysis is very untypical of Gogol's or Saltykov's characters.[6] Saltykov relies much less on physical description for his characters than does Gogol, but both "reduce" their people—Gogol reduces Sobakevich to a bear whose furniture says "I am Sobakevich too," and Saltykov reduces Judas to a hypocrite whose every action is hypocritical. Mitigating traits and motives are usually omitted. In short, their characters are caricatures which have a semblance of life, even if they are more like animals or puppets than those round characters E.M. Forster discusses. They create powerful illusions of life by creating types—national types from the Russian point of view, but types which others recognize as universal.

Many critics have pointed out works which are prominent in the genealogy of *The Golovlyov Family*. Among these are Dostoevsky's *The Village of Stepanchikovo (The Friend of the Family)*, Goncharov's *Oblomov*, and in a reverse sense, Aksakov's *A Family Chronicle*. The negative hero of Dostoevsky's short novel—Foma Fomich Opiskin—is Russian literature's best known hypocrite before Judas. It is a curious fact that Opiskin is partly modelled on the real-life Gogol—Gogol in his later, most eccentric and evangelical stage. Opiskin tyrannizes an entire provincial family; his unctuous speeches, sham religion, and fake purity are tools he uses to control others and acquire the best food and most comfortable room for himself. Dostoevsky's comedy is lighter—the world he describes is sillier, free of the death that is Golovlyovo. But there is a direct line between Opiskin and Judas, and from them both to their descendent, Peredonov, the paranoiac protagonist of Sologub's turn-of-the-century novel *The Petty Demon*.

In his descriptions of Russian provincial life, particularly family life in the provinces, Saltykov contributes to a fecund Russian tradition. Gogol's humanoid vegetables have already been noted. The section called "Oblomov's Dream" in Goncharov's great novel is also important. The "dream," which is actually a sociological essay in the form of a fantasy, shows how Oblomov, a Faust of inertia, is the product of environmental determination. No literary character was more discussed in the early 1860s than Oblomov. "What is Oblomovism?" asked the radical critic Dobrolyubov in his famous essay, and one could make a case for saying, "Add a drop of venom to Oblomovism, and you get Golovlyovism." The dream presents Oblomov's childhood—provincial life flowing on peacefully and monotonously forever in the bosom of the family, petty gentry life with no purpose, no work, no wit, no culture, no excitement. Consumption and discussion of food are the main activities; procreation, so far as we know, is painless, passionless and automatic. Life is so close to death that when natural death comes it is hardly noticed. Everything is ritualized. Oblomov's controlling fantasy is to recapture this land of milk and honey, in ideal form; but the world he unconsciously creates in St. Petersburg is a degraded substitute. The parallels with the world of Golovlyovo are obvious. Judas's idle fantasies are crazier and crueler versions of Oblomov's self-absorbed day-dreams. Meal-times organize their lives. Oblomov goes to seed, ending up in the care of a plump lower-class woman who plies him with food as indefatigably and abundantly as a baby-food factory. He takes her body too and has an illegitimate heir. Judas does the same, though in a much less pretty way (he packs off the bastard to the foundling home). What is natural in *Oblomov* becomes nasty in *The Golovlyov Family*. But the authors agree that character is determined mainly by environment.[7]

Goncharov obviously had lasting sympathy for the life of the old-world landowners, because he portrayed it in loving detail in his other main novels as well—*A Common Story* and *The Precipice*. The same can be said of Sergei Aksakov, whose charming book *A Family Chronicle* is another of the landlord landmarks which Saltykov had to have in mind when writing *The Golovlyov Family*. *A Family Chronicle*, like *The Golovlyov Family*, began as one sketch, which then developed into a series of sketches based on the lives of two generations of gentry characters. Both focus first on an extremely energetic figure who brings the family to its apogee of power. In both cases the sketches were only later brought together under one title. Aksakov's book presents the thinly-disguised history of his own family, notably his grandfather and father. The life he describes has many features in common with Goncharov's world, especially when he chronicles everyday routine. Again there is a metronomic monotony of Homeric meals and naps. Some of the characters are very strong and self-willed, especially Aksakov's grandfather. He shares some characteristics with Arina Petrovna; his treatment of peasants can be cruel and just as capricious, but on the whole he is a benevolent and dynamic patriarch. Aksakov's view of the old days is at the opposite (positive) pole from Saltykov's. The lyrical passages in *A Family Chronicle* outweigh the few gloomy scenes, and virtue almost always triumphs. Aksakov's grandfatherly approbation of life on the estates was precisely the kind of "reactionary" Slavophile view of serfdom which Saltykov loathed. In *The Golovlyov Family* he is candidly didactic in his presentation of the other view of gentry life. Gogol was too lighthearted (and in fact turned out to be an advocate of serfdom). Aksakov, Goncharov, and Turgenev approved it; Tolstoy approved it in *War and Peace* and other works. Saltykov wanted to *destroy* it, and all sympathy for it.

Students of Russian literature should be aware that the decay of the gentry family and the realm of provincial mire which Saltykov describes with such fury has its literary tradition after Saltykov as well. Chekhov ventures into this milieu in several of his stories. Alexei Remizov often describes it, and Ivan Bunin's *The Dry Valley* is considered a masterpiece of this tradition. Zamyatin makes it even more grotesque and animal in his *The Provinces (Uezdnoe)*. Perhaps the best known Soviet work in this tradition is Pilnyak's *The Naked Year*, where again humor and gloom go hand in hand. In a strangely lyrical way, the provincial prose of Soviet writer Andrei Platonov was strongly influenced by Saltykov; his is a particularly bleak and bovine world.

Its original aspects notwithstanding, *The Golovlyov Family* is typical not only of the traditions of Russian satire, but of the Russian novel as a whole. While generalizations are very dangerous, because of the inevitable exceptions, a few can be made about the great Russian novels of the last century. They tend to be basically static; there is little movement, the main setting is limited. There is little adventure (there is no Russian *Moby Dick*, nor even a worthy imitator of Sir Walter Scott). The Russian novel is not cosmopolitan; foreign travel is not important, and there is nothing comparable to Defoe, Stevenson, James or Kipling. Instead, the typical Russian novel presents an estate, a town, a few streets within a city—or, in our century, a prison camp (the ultimate analogue of the estates of older novels). The great Russian picaresque—*Dead Souls*—covers no more than thirty or forty miles.

Even the fields of action for Russian novel characters are limited; what the social scientists call "upward mobility" scarcely exists, which is one reason for the paucity of Russian novels of education and success. Seldom do we see the process by which a character works to achieve excellence, fame, power, or wealth. Another reason for this, and in this *The Golovlyov Family* is typical, is that the characters of Russian novels don't *do* anything. In a slave society with a slave mentality hardly anyone has a real job or profession, and it would be hard to learn how to do anything, except mow hay, from a nineteenth-century Russian novel. Saltykov himself insists on this in *The Golovlyov Family*.

The classical Russian novel is also overwhelmingly *adult*. There is no Oliver Twist or David Copperfield, Huck Finn or Tom Sawyer. More curious is the fact that the great nineteenth-century novels provide no great stories of love. (Saltykov's world is innocent of elementary loyalty, never mind friendship or love, and he loathed romantic plots.) The couples in *War and Peace* get together by default; Anna Karenina and Vronsky are hardly Romeo and Juliet; Bazarov and Odintsova turn emotional dynamite into formaldehyde; Dmitri and Grushenka's relationship is spoiled by metaphysical exertion, Oblomov and Olga's by too much lassitude and not enough longitude. It is not until the twentieth century, with Grigory and Aksinya (in *The Quiet Don*) or Zhivago and Lara that one can automatically name great love stories.

Finally, *The Golovlyov Family* resembles many other Russian novels in its humor. Humor often results from vile bodies and behavior. The characters are physically repulsive, and what they do is so unthinkably terrible that sometimes we pass into the realm of the ridiculous. There is also invective and humor resulting from the characters' ignorance, but there is no real wit. In fact, it has been argued that the Russian novel generally lacks wit—something one generally associates with skeptical and playful minds.[8]

The Russians tend to preach instead of play. Russia has no works of wit comparable to *Pride and Prejudice* or *Tristram Shandy*—instead it has didacticism from Gogol and Tolstoy to the present day, and with his authorial lectures Saltykov fits in this tradition. Saltykov even makes lack of wit a novelistic virtue—Arina and Judas have absolutely no sense of humor, and this is one of the most frightening things about them. It is symptomatic that while one can easily name other Russian literary characters who are devoid of humor (let alone wit)—Plyushkin, Opiskin, Smerdyakov, Belikov ("The Man in a Case"), Peredonov—there are no famous witty characters in Russian prose. Even if we do not mention the eighteenth century or the Romantic period, when, partly under the influence of dandyism, wit was especially prized in English literature, the witty writers of the English-language prose tradition, including Thackeray, Butler, Shaw, Wilde, or Ambrose Bierce, have no Russian rivals. To mount an old oxymoron, Russians like to be serious about their humor.

III

While I have referred to *The Golovlyov Family* as a novel, it did not begin as a novel, and Saltykov himself declined to call it a novel.[9] The first of the seven sections which comprise the work was originally published under the title "A Family Court" as the fifteenth sketch in a loose collection called *Well-Meant Speeches*. By force of the circumstances of his life and journalistic career, Saltykov's books were usually made up of shorter pieces which he published serially. His favorite genre was the "ocherk" (sketch), a kind of factual reportage, but sometimes with elements of the short story—including invented "typical" characters and dialogue. Characters tended to wander from one piece to the next or even from book to book. Thus Arina Petrovna, Judas and a few lesser characters also appear in other works by Saltykov.

"A Family Court's" publication in *Notes of the Fatherland* (October 1875) was met with enthusiastic letters from Nekrasov, praise by Goncharov, and by Turgenev, who on October 28 wrote to Saltykov in Nice:

Yesterday I got the October issue of *Notes of the Fatherland*, and of course immediately read "A Family Court," with which I was extremely pleased. The characters are all drawn strongly and accurately: I won't even single out the character of the mother, which is so typical—and this isn't its first appearance in your work—she is apparently taken alive—from real life. But particularly good is the character of the alcoholic and lost "blockhead." It is so good that one can't help wondering why instead of sketches Saltykov doesn't write a sizable novel with a grouping of characters and events, a guiding idea, and a broad treatment? To this one may reply that others, to some extent, write novels and stories—but no one else does what Saltykov does. However that may be, I liked "A Family Court" very much and am waiting patiently for a continuation—a description of the deeds of "little Judas."[10]

Though he still did not call it a novel, Saltykov did reluctantly heed the exhortations of his fellow writers to continue. He wrote three more sections, also included in the miscellany *Well-Meant Speeches*, and judging by the title, "The Family Windup," he intended to stop there. Then in 1876, after completing preparation of the book publication of *Well-Meant Speeches*, he returned to the family again and wrote "Forsaken" as a separate work. Then he *again* came back to the subject (apologizing in a footnote to his readers for having to repeat one episode) and wrote "Forbidden Family Joys." The final section—"The Reckoning"—came only in 1880, after a four-year break, and for this Saltykov used part of another unfinished story. In the first separate book edition Saltykov made a number of changes; the order of the penultimate and antepenultimate sections was reversed; he interpolated new passages in three sections, and made major cuts in sections one, four, and five. Discarding his first title *(Episodes from the History of a Family)*, he finally settled on *Gospoda Golovlyovy ("The Golovlyov Family" or "The Golovlyovs")*. This manner of working though not completely without precedent, is rather unusual. Saltykov generally disapproved of conventional novels, partly because of their neatly contrived plots. He also insisted that a love intrigue as the unifying core was artificial and a sign that the author was avoiding serious social problems. The same was true of more narrow family novels. K.N. Grigoryan notes that in "Old Folks' Grief" Saltykov says:

I know my story is reaching the culmination point, after which a catastrophe must follow, and then its natural resolution. Real artists, belle-lettrists, do precisely this: first they gradually tie together the strands of the intrigue, then slowly untie them. Thus it is natural that the reader should expect the same from me, that I should marry Kashirin or make him a drunkard, and finally kill him off. However, I intend to do nothing of the kind. In the first place I am not an artist and cannot "make up things" from my head; and in the second place my hero is an old man.[11]

Given all this it is not surprising that plot as such is not terribly important in *The Golovlyov Family*. But if we except Dostoevsky, for whom intrigue, mystery, and surprise are vital, the same can be said of most well known nineteenth-century novels. "What happens next" is not their driving force.

The great strength of the Russian novel in the last century is characterization. And Saltykov's characters have made *The Golovlyov Family* a lasting book. The theme of the decline of the land-owning class is central to the novel, but without the characters we would not read the book today. The matriarch, Arina Petrovna, was created before Saltykov even had an idea that her son would become the dominant figure of a larger family chronicle.

In many ways the two main characters are similar. Both are acquisitive and miserly. They make the same excuses when their sons die ("disobeyed his parents"), and both come to be haunted by these deaths; they both use religion as a tool and muse on retiring to the monasteries of Zagorsk; they both love the process of calculation (she likes to be alone during these fantasies—and even as a boy he sneaks into the room, fascinated by the activity); there are some similarities in their language. Judas and Arina, like other members of the family as well, reach a period when much of their time is spent isolated in their dusty quarters, overcome by flights of imagination in the dark. Mother and son both experience something like awareness and pangs of conscience near the end of their life. They both play-act, though Judas does so far more consistently (for Judas, Saltykov continually refers to "playing a part," "performance," "pretending," and "acting"). Of course, Arina Petrovna is far more practical than Judas; her legal campaigns are usually successful, while his are so petty and frivolous that they are failures. The special relation between the two goes from birth to death—Judas's delivery being the only easy one she had (as if even as a foetus he was being careful not to draw attention to his true character), and Judas's death coming in his attempt to repent at her grave.

Judas's language, and even his name, cannot be adequately translated. His real name is Porfiry, but in the family, in addition to nicknames such as "Candid Boy," he is called *Yudushka–krovopivushka*. Yudushka (translated by Mr. Cioran as "little Judas") is a diminutive and actually *not* the exact equivalent of "Judas" in the Bible (in which sense the English is less subtle). "Krovopivushka" (little bloodsucker) is another diminutive which nicely rhymes with "Yudushka." Invective is the most elementary form of satire, and Russian critics often praise Saltykov for his facility in inventing vicious nicknames for his characters.

As we see in *The Golovlyov Family*, individualization of language was also Saltykov's forte. Porfiry's voice is instantly recognizable—a putrid mass of pieties and proverbs which overwhelm his listeners. He uses cloying diminutives for everything, and while usually in Russian diminutives signify affection and tenderness, his overuse makes them repulsive. It is part of his sanctimonious style to make up diminutives which are never used in Russian—he reduces even God ("Bog") to a ridiculous form—"nice itty-bitty godlet" (Bozhen'ka"). His handy adages are accompanied by the repeated gestures: folding of the hands, eyes turned to heaven, tears produced on cue. (When Arina dies he tells such a beautiful lie that he weeps.) As the narrator tells us, Judas is a twaddler and tangler, never going straight to the point.

Porfiry is grotesquely serious and hypocritical. His favorite device is to combine a throat-cutting with some minor present—some tobacco to Stepan, a parting chicken to Petya, a new shawl for his mistress to make up for sending their baby to doom in a foundling home. His lies never end. His slobbering lust is directed toward those who are easy game. His wife is so unimportant in his life that she is never described (an impossible omission for most novelists). And his logic is so perverse that even in the case of Yevraxeya's pregnancy where it would seem there is no way he can deny guilt—the crime of fornication—he weasels out of it, by blaming the baby ("naughty little Volodya").

Saltykov was a proudly tendentious writer, so he draws an unambiguous portrait. The narrator makes generalizations and draws conclusions for the reader. Aside from similes comparing Judas to a snake, the narrator's "digressions" are the most obvious manifestation of this trend. The section on "unconscious hypocrites" (pp. 94-97) is the most famous of these. Saltykov apparently interpolated it after several reviewers had called Porfiry a Russian Tartuffe. Saltykov argues at great length that he is not that kind of *conscious*, French hypocrite.

The narrator also tells us that Golovlyovo was death itself. The sections often end with the death of a character as the estate exerts its fatal attraction on a series of family members. Stepan knows he is going back to his coffin (he recalls a disfavored uncle who ate from a dog's bowl and an aunt who died of "abstinence"). For Judas the world is a dead thing (he is always appearing out of darkness); he is said to have a knack for death, and is even called a coffin. There is a sense of doom about the house, and in the end the dead torment Judas. Various scholars have noted that death is natural at the end of satirical works. One theory holds that satire originated in fertility rites in which the satirist was a scapegoat or *pharmakos* who was executed after ritual beating on the genitals. In later satire and comedy a ritual of expulsion or conversion, near the end, often replaces death (think of the end of *Dead Souls* with the Prosecutor's death and the expulsion of Chichikov, Zamyatin's *We* with its wholesale death and surgical "conversions," or Bulgakov's satirical works). In a sense, Saltykov combines the motifs of conversion, expulsion, and death.

Because of the censors, Saltykov could not be totally candid in his explanation of the doom hanging over such families. His repeated assertions that idleness, inability to work, and drink were the three causes do not really go to the heart of the matter. His exhortations about the need to have a goal and "direction," the need to work, are reasonable, but not very specific. What he says on a variety of topical themes does give us a clearer idea of what he thinks is wrong with society. —Alcohol is obviously one of the major problems; several Golovlyovs ride the bottle to oblivion. Descriptions of that "luminous void" occur in several different sections of the novel. The "woman question" is treated mainly through the stories of Anninka and Lyubinka, who are described in a somewhat more conventional—almost sentimentally moralistic —way than the other characters. The theme of religion appears in a variety of ways, from the prayers of Judas to the brief picture of the impoverished and therefore obsequious village priest. There cannot be much spirituality in a world inhabited by people such as the Golovlyovs, but again, think of the differences if Dostoevsky or Tolstoy had described this world. The problem of the peasantry is not in the foreground, but it is always there implicitly—emancipation occurs in the course of the novel. Saltykov portrays the peasants very sympathetically, but not idealistically. We know what he thinks of Judas's assertion that God ordained this social order and put everyone in his place (an echo of Gogol's *Selected Passages from a Correspondence with Friends*, where he tells the landowner to show the serfs the place in the Bible where it says as much). The house serfs are most visible, especially the women, and what can one say of a life (like Ulita's) where the best memories are those of giving enemas to two generations of Golovlyovs? As usual in Saltykov, humor results from reduction, and only the Victorian restrictions of his time prevented the descriptions of Golovlyovo from being more openly scatological.[12]

Saltykov has still not found his critics. Gogol has been passed from school to school for thirteen decades, thoroughly worked over by the nineteenth-century radicals, the religious quacks of the Symbolist period, Freudians, structuralists, sociologists, and specialists interested in everything, including both ends of his alimentary canal ("Food in Gogol"—"Was Gogol a Homosexual?"). Even Bulgakov, who regarded Saltykov as his teacher, who is the most important satirical writer after Saltykov, and whose main works were unpublished until ten years ago, has been written about by representatives of many different critical sects. That Saltykov's works have not had this kind of appeal is somewhat puzzling. With his allegories and large-scale character types, it is easy to see how a myth-critic could fit him into archetypical schemes; even a Freudian novice could work Oedipal themes out of the autobiographical elements in *The Golovlyov Family* ("Saltykov and his Mother"), and the Tartu University school could draw complex diagrams to show how *The Golovlyov Family* is that most wonderful of all things, a "unified whole." While I am afraid these particular remarks may be prophetic, it is time that Saltykov stopped being the exclusive property of critics whose primary concerns are sociological or historical. As the reader of *The Golovlyov Family* will see—with considerable pleasure—Saltykov's prose has much more to offer than that.

Carl R. Proffer
University of Michigan

NOTES TO "SALTYKOV AND THE RUSSIAN NOVEL"

1. Saltykov wrote this in *Beyond the Frontier*, quoted in Nikander Strelsky, *Saltykov and the Russian Squire* (New York, 1940), pp. 22-23.

2. Much of the material in this polemic has been translated by Ralph Matlaw in his edition of F. Dostoevsky, *Notes from Underground* (New York: Dutton paper edition, 1960), pp. 201-229. There is a very good Soviet monograph on the life-long relations of the two writers: S. Borshchevskii, *Shchedrin i Dostoevskii* (Moscow, 1956), 390 pp.

3. I.P. Foote, "Introduction" to M.E. Saltykov-Shchedrin, *Selected Satirical Writings* (Oxford, 1977), p. 5 (This is a Russian-language reader.)

4. Hon. Maurice Baring, *An Outline of Russian Literature* (London, 1933), pp. 186-87.

5. Most of Saltykov's work remains untranslated, but a good short description of the problems he wrote about can be found in I.P. Foote's introduction and notes to the Russian-language reader mentioned above, in Note 3.

6. One of the standard critical problems in *The Golovlyov Family* is the ending and whether or not Porfiry's growing awareness and ultimate self-destruction are motivated sufficiently. I think it is reasonable to argue that what happens is conceivable, but I don't think one can use the early sections of the novel to argue it is predictable, or even probable. There are a few glimmerings of awareness perhaps, but these passages are even less telling than, for example, the three or four cases of interior thought in Chichikov in *Dead Souls*. In general Chichikov and Porfiry live in caricature worlds where it is rather odd even to discuss realistic psychological motivation. The rather sudden change in Porfiry has its analogue in the Chichikov of the unfinished Part II of *Dead Souls*, a Chichikov whom Gogol makes capable of self-awareness and pangs of conscience. Readers seem to be virtually unanimous in not accepting Gogol's new approach to character. It was simply inconsistent.

7. Contrast Dostoevsky, who persistently ridiculed this as an obvious oversimplification (in *Crime and Punishment* and elsewhere). In turn, Saltykov criticized Dostoevsky for psychological excesses, searching in the "will" and the irrational for motivations. Saltykov's more socialist view is one of the important reasons that shallow men such as Gorky warned against reading Dostoevsky, while praising Saltykov—so that in Stalin's time the Soviet national (Lenin) library was surmounted by statues of all the writers considered great, including Saltykov, but not Dostoevsky.

8. See D.J. Richards, "Wit and Worship—Two Impulses in Modern Russian Literature," *Russian Literature Triquarterly*, No. 14 (Winter 1976), pp. 7-19. The obvious exceptions to this generalization come in the early 19th century, and mainly in poetry rather than prose—Pushkin, Griboedov, Krylov, and to some extent Lermontov in *A Hero of Our Time*. In the 20th century the obvious exceptions are Nabokov and Zamyatin. In between the two periods one has Kozma Prutkov, but still this does not really touch on prose fiction. One can point to the epigram as a poetic genre in which Russians have shown great wit; on the other hand in place of the clever limerick of English tradition, Russian poetry now has the crude and vulgar *chastushka*.

9. Russian writers have often had individualistic attitudes toward the genre of their works. Thus Pushkin called *Eugene Onegin* a "novel in verse." Gogol called *Dead Souls* a "poem," Lermontov's *A Hero of Our Time* was originally a series of short stories, Dostoevsky often referred to himself as a poet and to his prose as poems rather than novels, Tolstoy insisted that *War and Peace* was not a novel, but what he wanted to say

on the subject in the form in which he said it. By the way it can be mentioned that scholars who write on satire generally agree that long works are usually not exclusively satirical, but contain a mixture of other elements or genres, such as the novel of manners, socio-political tracts, etc. Indeed, the very word "satire" derives from a word meaning "hash" or "mixture."

10. To give an idea of simultaneous literary events: Turgenev was serving as the intermediary between Saltykov and French writers, including Zola and E. de Goncourt, discussing purchasing Russian rights to their novels. In November 1875 a new installment of Dostoevsky's *A Raw Youth* was published, and Turgenev reacted by writing to Saltykov about the superiority of Goncourt's novel *La fille Elisa*, called Dostoevsky's novel "chaos: God, what sour junk, hospital stench and mumbling that no one needs, psychological somersaults!" This was only a few days after Saltykov wrote to Annenkov after reading *Manette Salomon*, commenting scatologically: "I conceived hate for Zola and the Goncourts—all these [. . .] who can't even [. . .]. Excuse me for putting it this way. Dickens and Rabelais put us face to face with living characters, but these pitiful [. . .] feed us psychology. They must be hellishly industrious. They don't eat or drink—they just write. . . . They're not novelists, they're filth-making [. . .]." The censored words are omitted from the Soviet edition of Saltykov's letters.

11. K.N. Grigor'ian, *Roman M.E. Saltykova-Shchedrina 'Gospoda Golovlevy'* (Moscow: AN, 1962), p. 17.

12. In general, incidentally, Saltykov had a rather scatological turn of mind—particularly, as we have seen, when criticizing other writers; and in another country or time he would no doubt have resorted to the ancient satirical device of reduction to bodily functions—for anal personalities such as the Golovlyovs this would be perfect. Russian satirical prose has traditionally been very sparing in Rabelaisian detail, though there are a few examples in Gogol, Dostoevsky ("The Crocodile"), and in the twentieth century it became somewhat more common: *We*, for example, ends in a public toilet, and Nabokov's Russian novels contain numerous passages in this vein.

THE GOLOVLYOV FAMILY

A FAMILY COURT

One day Anton Vasilyev, the bailiff of a distant patrimonial estate, had finished his report to his lady, Arina Petrovna Golovlyov, about his journey to Moscow to collect the quit-rents from the serfs living there on passports; and although he had already received permission from her to proceed to the servants' quarters, he suddenly became mysteriously rooted to the spot, as though there were some further business he could not make up his mind to report.

Arina Petrovna, who could interpret thoroughly not only the slightest gestures of her people, but their secret thoughts as well, immediately became disturbed.

"Is there something else?" she asked, gazing intently at the bailiff.

"That's all, mistress," Anton Vasilyev said, attempting to avoid the issue.

"Don't lie! There's something else! I can see it from your eyes!"

Nonetheless, Anton Vasilyev could not bring himself to answer and continued to shift from foot to foot.

"Speak up, what further business did you bring?" Arina Petrovna shouted at him imperiously. "Speak up! Stop wriggling about... you turn-coat!"

Arina Petrovna loved to give nicknames to the people who made up her administrative and domestic staff. She called Anton Vasilyev a "turncoat" not because in fact he had been guilty of perfidy, but rather because he had a loose tongue. The estate which he ran was centered around an important trading village containing a large number of taverns. Anton Vasilyev was fond of drinking tea in taverns and boasting of the omnipotence of his lady, and in the course of doing so he would unconsciously blab. Since Anna Petrovna was constantly involved in various lawsuits, it happened more often than not that the talkativeness of this trusted person would reveal the lady's military stratagems before they could be executed.

"Actually, there is something..." Anton Vasilyev muttered at last.

"What? What is it?" Arina Petrovna became agitated.

Being an imperious woman, and moreover one deeply endowed with a creative imagination, she instantly sketched for herself a picture of all possible conflicts and oppositions and immediately assimilated this idea to such a degree that she grew pale and leapt up from her chair.

"Stepan Vladimirych has sold the house in Moscow..." reported the bailiff haltingly.

"What's that?"

"He sold it, mistress."

"Why? How? Don't beat about the bush! Speak up!"

"Because of debts... so one should think! Everyone knows that people aren't about to sell because of good deeds."

"It must have been the police who sold it? The magistrates?"

"That's the way it must have been. They say the house went for eight thousand at the auction."

Arina Petrovna sank heavily into the chair and stared fixedly out the window. For the first few moments this news seemed to deprive her of consciousness. If she had been told that Stepan Vladimirych had killed someone, that the Golovlyov peasants had rebelled and refused to work for the lady or that serfdom had collapsed, she would have been shocked to a lesser degree. Her lips were moving, her eyes gazed somewhere off into the distance but she said nothing. She did not even notice at this moment the girl Dunyasha dashing headlong past the window, covering something with her apron, and then suddenly, catching sight of her mistress, turn around on the spot and walk quietly back (at another time such an action would have occasioned a proper investigation). Finally, however, she came to her senses and pronounced:

"A fine thing!"

There again followed several moments of ominous silence.

"So you say the police sold the house for eight thousand?" she questioned him again.

"That's right."

"This was the blessing bestowed on him by his parents! A fine one he is... the scoundrel!"

Arina Petrovna felt that in view of the news she had just received she had to make an immediate decision but could not think of anything because her thoughts were wandering confusedly in completely opposing directions. On the one hand she was thinking: "The police sold it! But they couldn't have sold it in an instant! No doubt there had been an inventory, an appraisal and an announcement of auction? They had sold it for eight thousand, when only two years before she had put out twelve thousand with her own hands if she had paid a kopeck! If she had known she herself might have bought it at the auction for eight thousand! On the other hand, the thought also came to her: "The police sold it for eight thousand! But this was his parents' blessing! The scoundrel! For eight thousand he gave up his parents' blessing!"

"Who told you?" she asked finally, eventually coming to the conclusion that the house had been sold and, consequently, any thought of purchasing it at a cheap price was lost to her forever.

"Ivan Mikhailov, the tavern owner, told me."

"And why didn't he warn me beforehand?"

"He must have been afraid."

"Afraid! I'll show him: 'afraid' is he! Summon him from Moscow and as soon as he appears, off to the military recruiting center to shave his head! Afraid!"

4

Although serfdom was already waning, it still existed. More than once it had fallen to the lot of Anton Vasilyev to hear the most eccentric orders from his lady, but her latest decision was so unexpected that it made even him feel somewhat awkward. He involuntarily recollected his nickname of "turncoat" at this moment. Ivan Mikhailov was a sturdy peasant and one could not imagine that any misfortune might befall him. Moreover, he was his friend and the godfather of his child—and suddenly he was off to the army, thanks simply to the fact that he, Anton Vasilyev, like a turncoat, had not been able to restrain his tongue!

"Forgive... Ivan Mikhailov!" he was about to intercede.

"Off with you... you conniver!" Arina Petrovna screamed at him, but in such a tone that he did not even consider persisting in any further defense of Ivan Mikahilov.

But before continuing my story, I would request the reader to become more intimately acquainted with Arina Petrovna Golovylov and her family situation.

* * *

Arina Petrovna was a woman of about sixty, but still active and accustomed to living entirely as she pleased. She was an ominous figure. She ran the extensive Golovlyov estate singlehandedly and unhindered. Her existence was solitary, thrifty, almost miserly, she did not keep up friendships with the neighbors, maintained amicable relationships with the local authorities, and from the children she demanded such obedience to herself that at every step they would ask themselves, "What would mummy say about this?" In general she possessed a nature that was independent, inflexible and somewhat contrary, all of which, incidentally, was promoted in no small measure by the fact that in the entire Golovlyov clan there was not a single person from whom she might have encountered any opposition. Her husband was a frivolous and bibulous man (Arina Petrovna was fond of saying of herself that she was neither a widow nor a married woman). Some of the children were serving in Petersburg, others took after the father and as "disgraced" children were not allowed to have anything to do with family matters. It was under these circumstances that Arina Petrovna from early on felt herself isolated so that quite frankly she became quite unaccustomed to any family life, although the word "family" did not disappear from her speech and from appearances all her actions were ruled exclusively by her unceasing concern for the organization of family matters.

From his very youth the head of the family, Vladimir Mikhailych Golovlyov, had been known for his disorderly and mischievous nature, and for Arina Petrovna, who was always distinguished by her seriousness and business ability, he did not represent anything attractive. He led an idle and pointless life, more often than not locking himself in his study, imitating the noises of starlings, roosters and so forth, and occupying himself with the composition of so-called "free verse." In moments of emotional effusion he boasted that he was a friend of Barkov[1] and that the latter apparently had even given him his blessing while on his death-bed. Arina Petrovna was immediately disaffected by the verse of her husband, calling it smut and buffoonery, and since Vladimir Mikhailych had married expressly for the purpose of always having a handy listener for his poems, it was understandable that disagreements would not be long in forthcoming. Gradually waxing and increasing in violence, these disagreements ended, for the wife, in a complete and scornful indifference towards her buffoon-husband, and for the husband, in the most heart-felt hatred for his wife, a hatred which, however, contained a substantial element of cowardice. The husband called the wife a "witch" and a "devil"; the wife called the husband a "windmill" and a "stringless balalaika." With this relationship they still carried on their co-habitation for forty-odd years and never once did it occur to one or the other that such a life had anything unnatural about it. Not only did Vladimir Mikhalych's mischievousness not abate with time's passage, but it assumed an even more nasty character. His poetic exercises in the Barkovian manner aside, he took to drink and was fond of waylaying kitchen maids in the corridor. At first Arina Petrovna reacted to this fresh pastime of her husband squeamishly and even with worry (here it was a matter of a challenge to her accustomed practice of authority rather than any question of forthright jealousy), but subsequently she turned a blind eye to it and simply took care to insure that those disgusting girls did not take the master any herb vodka. From that time forth, once she had declared to herself that her husband was no longer her companion, she concentrated all her attention exclusively on one object: the enlargement of the Golovlyov estate, and to be sure, in the course of her forty-year married life she managed to increase her holdings tenfold. With amazing patience and farsightedness she kept watch over villages distant and near, made secret inquiries into the relationships of their landowners to the trustee council and as certain as snow in winter she would appear at the auctions. In the whirl of this fanatical hunt for acquisitions, Vladimir Mikhailych retreated ever farther into the background and in the end grew totally reclusive. At the moment when this story begins, he was already a decrepit old man who could barely leave his bed and when on a rare occasion he did emerge from his bedroom, it was simply in order to stick his head through his wife's half-opened door to shout: "Devil!"—and then disappear once again.

Arina Petrovna was not much more fortunate with her children. She had too much of an independent nature, a bachelor's nature, so to speak, for her to see the children as anything more than an unnecessary burden. She could only breathe freely when she was alone with her accounts and domestic enterprises, when no one would interfere in her business conversations with bailiffs, overseers, housekeepers and so forth. In her eyes the children were one of those fatalistic situations in life which she did not feel she had any right to protest against; but nonetheless they did not touch a single chord of her inner being which was totally dedicated to the innumerable details of everyday living. There were four children: three sons and a daughter. She did not even care to speak about the oldest son and the daughter; she was more or less indifferent to the youngest son and only the third son, little Porfiry, well, it was not that she loved him exactly, but rather seemed to fear him.

Stepan Vladimirych, the eldest son, with whom the present story for the most part is concerned, was known in the family by the names of Styopka-the-dunce and Styopka-the-troublemaker. Very early in life he had been relegated to the category of those "in disfavor" and from his childhood he had performed a role in the household that was in between that of an outcast and a jester. Unfortunately, he was a gifted fellow who all too readily and quickly absorbed the impressions exerted by his surroundings. From his father he inherited an inexhaustible mischievousness, from his mother the ability to discern quickly people's weaknesses. Thanks to the former quality he quickly became his father's favorite, which only intensified his mother's dislike of him. Frequently during Arina Petrovna's absences on domestic affairs, the father and his stripling son would retire into the study which was adorned with a portrait of Barkov, read poetry of an unrestrained content, and gossip, their victim often being the "witch," that is, Arina Petrovna. But it was as though the "witch" could sense what they were up to. She would come driving noiselessly up to the veranda, tip-toe to the study door and eavesdrop on the mirthful conversations. Thereupon an immediate and vicious beating would ensue for Styopka-the-dunce. But Styopka did not subside; he was insensitive to both the blows and admonishments, and within half an hour he had returned to his former tricks. He would cut up the maid Anyuta's kerchief, or pop flies into sleepy Vasyatka's mouth, or betake himself to the kitchen and pinch pies there (Arina Petrovna, for reasons of economy, kept the children half starved), which, incidentally, he would immediately share with his brothers.

"You ought to be killed!" Arina Petrovna constantly repeated to him, "I'll kill you and not have to answer for it! Even the Tsar wouldn't punish me for doing it!"

This constantly humiliation did not pass without effect in this easygoing nature that quickly forgot. It did not lead to embitterment or protest, but created a servile nature which degenerated into buffoonery, knowing no sense of measure and devoid of all prudence. Such personalities willingly fall victim to any influence and can become anything at all: drunkards, beggars, clowns, and even criminals...

At the age of twenty Stepan Golovlyov completed his studies in of the Moscow high schools and entered the university. But his student years were

7

bitter ones. In the first place, his mother gave him only precisely enough money to prevent his perishing from hunger; secondly, he did not manifest the slightest impulse to work, but instead he harbored an accursed giftedness which expressed itself primarily in his ability for mimicking; thirdly, he was constantly tormented by the need for company and could not bear to remain alone with himself for a moment. Consequently he assumed the easy role of a sponger and *pique-assiette* and, thanks to his inclination for any manner of nonsense, he soon became the favorite of the more affluent students. But these students, while admitting him into their midst, nonetheless realized that he was not their peer, that he was just a clown and that was precisely what his reputation consisted of. Once he reached this level it was natural for him to be drawn ever lower, so that by the end of the fourth year he had made a complete fool of himself. However, thanks to his ability to grasp quickly and remember what he had heard, he did well on his examinations and was awarded a candidate's degree.

When he turned up before his mother with his diploma, Arina Petrovna merely shrugged her shoulders and muttered, "Amazing!" After detaining him for a month in the village she sent him off to Petersburg, assigning him an allowance of one hundred paper rubles per month. Then began the endless wanderings around government ministries and offices. He did not enjoy any patronage, nor did he have the least inclination to make his own way. The frivolous mind of the young man had become so unaccustomed to any concentration that even bureaucratic tasks such as memoranda and extracts from business affairs proved to be beyond his powers. Golovlyov struggled for four years in Petersburg and finally had to admit to himself that any hope of raising himself about the rank of an office clerk did not exist. In response to his complaints Arina Petrovna wrote a threatening letter which began with the words, "I was already convinced of this beforehand" and ended with an order to proceed to Moscow. There, in the committee of her favorite serfs, it was decided to assign Styopka-the-dunce to the provincial legal court and place him under the superivison of a lawyer who had from time immemorial acted for the Golovlyovs on business matters. What Stepan Vladimirych did and how he conducted himself in the provincial legal court remained unknown, but after three years he was no longer there. Then Arina Petrovna resolved on a desperate measure: she "threw her son a sop," which incidentally at the same time was also supposed to represent the "blessing" bestowed on him by his parents. This sop consisted of a house in Moscow for which Arina Petrovna paid twelve thousand rubles.

For the first time in his life Stepan Golovlyov breathed easily. The house promised to bring one thousand rubles in silver as income, and compared with the past this sum represented something in the way of genuine prosperity for him. He kissed his mama's hand ecstatically ("Now, now, just mind, you dunce, don't expect anything more!"—muttered Arina Petrovna

8

during all this) and he promised to justify the favor which had been bestowed upon him. But alas! He was so little used to dealing with money, he understood so badly the ways of life itself, that the fabulous yearly sum of a thousand rubles did not last for long. In some four or five years he went completely bankrupt and was only too happy to join up as a substitute in the militia which was being organized at that time. The militia, incidentally, only got as far as Kharkov when peace was declared and Golovlyov returned to Moscow once again. By that time his house had already been sold. He wore a militiaman's uniform, one, however, that was rather shabby, and a pair of high boots, and in his pocket he had one hundred rubles. He turned to speculation with the money, that is, he began to play cards and lost everything in a short while. Then he set about making the rounds of his mother's well-to-do peasants living in Moscow by their own means. He would eat at the place of one, at another's he would beg a pound of tobacco, at a third's he would borrow a trifling sum. But finally the moment arrived when he, so to speak, came to his senses, face to face with a blank wall. He was approaching forty and he was compelled to admit that he had no strength left to go on existing as a tramp. There remained but one path—to return to Golovlyovo.

Next to Stepan Vladimirych the oldest member of the Golovlyov family was a daughter, Anna Vladimirovna, of whom Arina Petrovna also did not care to speak.

The fact was the Arina Petrovna had designs for Annushka, but Annushka not only failed to justify her hopes, but instead she caused a scandal throughout the entire district. When the daughter left the institute Arina Petrovna settled her in the village in the hopes of making a gratuitous domestic secretary and book-keeper out of her, but instead of this, one fine night Annushka ran off from Golovlyovo with a cornet named Ulanov and married him.

"So, without their parents' blessings, like dogs, they got married!" Arina Petrovna complained over this incident. "At least the wretched fellow took her to the altar! Someone else might have taken advantage of her and then disappeared! You might just as soon whistle as hope to find him!"

Arina Petrovna acted just as decisively with this daughter as she had with her disfavored son: she up and "threw her a sop." She awarded her a sum of five thousand and a miserable hamlet of thirty serfs with a decrepit estate where the wind whistled through all the windows and there was not a single sound plank. In about two years' time the young people had exhausted the sum of money and the cornet ran off, no one knew where, leaving Anna Vladimirovna with twin daughters: Anninka and Lyubinka. Then Anna Vladimirovna passed away in three months and, like it or not, Arina Petrovna had to provide shelter for the orphans in her own home. This she did, placing the tots in the wing under the care of the one-eyed old hag, Palashka.

"God has many mercies," she said in view of this situation. "The orphans, God knows, won't eat much and they'll be a comfort to me in my old age! God took one daughter away and gave two in return!"

But at the same time she wrote to her son Porfiry Vladimirych: "Your sister died just as wantonly as she had lived, casting her two brats on my neck..."

However cynical the observation may seem, in all righteousness it must be admitted that neither of these incidents when "sops were thrown" caused any damage to Arina Petrovna's finances, but indirectly even aided in an expansion of the Golovlyov estate by decreasing the number of share-holders. For Arina Petrovna was a woman of strict principles, and once she had "thrown a sop" she then considered all her responsibilities finished as far as the disgraced children were concerned. Even in considering her orphaned grand-children she never entertained the thought that in time she would have to share anything with them. She simply attempted to squeeze as much as possible out of the small estate which she had presented to Anna Vladimirov-na and lay aside the proceeds with the trustees' council. Here she would say:

"There, I'm putting a little money aside for the orphans, and whatever they cost me for food and expenses I won't take away from them! God will obviously reward me for my generosity!"

Finally, the youngest children, Porfiry and Pavel Vladimirych, were serving in Petersburg: the former in the Civil Service, the other in the military. Porfiry was married, whereas Pavel was a bachelor.

Porfiry Vladimirych was known in his family by three names: little Judas, the bloodsucker, and the goody-goody. Stepan-the-dunce had given him these names when he was still a child. From his earliest years he had been fond of cuddling up to his darling sweet mama, kissing her furtively on her dear little shoulder and sometimes indulging in a little tattle-taling. Soundlessly he would open his mama's door, soundlessly steal into a corner, sit down and then as though entranced he would not take his eyes off his mama while she was writing or immersed in her accounts. But even then Arina Petrovna reacted with a certain suspicion to this filial toadying. And then that unwavering gaze fixed on her seemed enigmatic, and she could not ascertain for herself precisely what it exuded, whether it was poison or filial respect.

"I just can't comprehend what there is in his eyes," she mused to herself at times, "he looks as though, well, as though he is about to fashion a noose. Just as though he's oozing poison and coaxing you on!"

Hereupon she would recall the significant details of the time when she was still carrying Porfiry. At that time there lived in the house a certain pious and clairvoyant old man who was called old Porfisha the blessed and to whom she would always turn when she wished to foresee anything in the future. And lo, this very same old man, when asked whether she would give birth soon, and whether God would give her a son or a daughter, he gave her no direct answer but crowed three times like a cock and then immediately intoned: "A cockerel, a cockerel! He has sharpened his claws! The cock crows, threatens the hen; the hen goes cluck, cluck, cluck, but too late for her!"

And that was all. But three days later (there it was, he had crowed three times!) she gave birth to a son (correct again, a little cockerel it was!) whom she called Porfiry in honor of the old clairvoayant...

The first half of the prophecy had been fulfilled, but what could have been meant by the mysterious words: "the hen goes cluck, cluck, cluck, but too late for her!"? Arina Petrovna would muse over this as she peered at little Porfisha from under her hand while he sat in his corner staring at her with his enigmatic gaze.

But little Porfisha would continue sitting meekly and silently by himself, still staring at her, staring so intently that his wide-open and unblinking eyes would twitch with a tear. It was as though he had divined the doubts stirring in his mother's heart and was acting with such calculation that the most nagging suspicion would have to declare itself disarmed in the face of his meekness. Even at the risk of annoying his mother he was constantly hovering around her as though to say, "Look at me! I'm not hiding anything! I'm all obedience and devotion, and what's more, an obedience born not only of fear but of conscience as well." However strong the feeling of certainty was within her that little Porfisha, the sneak, was simply fawning while all the time his eyes were fashioning a noose, she could not resist such selflessness. Involuntarily her hand would seek out the best piece on her plate to give to her affectionate son despite the fact that a single look from this same son would provoke a vague fear of something enigmatic and evil within her heart.

The brother, Pavel Vladimirych, presented a complete opposite to Porfiry Vladimirych. He was the utmost personification of a human being lacking in any enterprise whatsoever. Even as a child he had not manifested the slightest inclination either for study, games or social intercourse, prefering to live by himself, aloof from people. He was accustomed to skulking in a corner, where he would pout and begin to fantasize. He would imagine that he had eaten too much oatmeal and because of this his legs had gotten ever so skinny and he could not do his lessons. Or that he was not Pavel, the son of a landowner, but Davydka the shepherd, that a large outgrowth had sprung up on his forehead like Davydka's, and that he was cracking a whip and not doing his lessons. Arina Petrovna would keep looking at him and her maternal heart would seethe furiously.

"What's the matter with you, you're like a mouse turning up its nose at the oatmeal!" she would scream at him, unable to restrain herself, "or are you still full of poison! It's bad enough that you never come up to your mother and say give me a hug, mama dear!"

Little Pavlusha would abandon his corner and slowly, as though someone were poking him from behind, go up to his mother.

11

"Mama," he would repeat in a deep voice that seemed unnatural in a child, "give me a hug, mama dear!"

"Get away from you...you sneak! You think you can skulk off in a corner and I won't know what's going on? I can see right through you, sweetie! All your plans and designs are as plain as day to me!"

Just as slowly as before Pavel would turn about and skulk off to his corner.

The years passed and out of Pavel Vladimirych there gradually emerged the kind of apathetic and enigmatically sullen personality which ultimately gives rise to a man devoid of all enterprise. Perhaps he was kind, but he performed no kindness for the benefit of others. Perhaps he was not stupid either, but during his entire life he did not perform a single clever act. He was hospitable, but no one was gratified at his hospitality. He was fond of squandering money but no useful or pleasant result was ever achieved for anyone through this squandering. He never insulted anyone, but no one ever counted this in his favor. He was honorable, yet no one was heard to say how honorably Pavel Golovlyov had acted on such and such an occasion! The crowning touch was that often he was snappish with his mother, and yet at the same time feared her like death itself. I repeat: he was a sullen man, but inactivity was at the root of his sullenness, and nothing more.

When they had grown up, the difference in the characters of both brothers was expressed even more distinctly in their relationship to their mother. Every week little Judas was prompt in sending his mummy a generous epistle in which he expansively informed her about the details of Petersburg life, and in the most exquisite phrases assured her of his unselfish filial devotion. Pavel wrote letters which were infrequent, terse and at times even mysterious, as though he had extracted every word with pincers out of himself. But Porfiry Vladimirych would write his mother in the following way: "I have received such and such an amount of money for such and such a period, my inestimable friend, mama, from your faithful peasant Yerofeev, and for sending me the aforementioned sum to be used for my keep, in accordance with your wishes, I offer you my most heart-felt gratitude, and I kiss your hands with unfeigned filial devotion. There is only one thing that causes me grief and which torments me with doubt: are you not overburdening your most precious health with your unceasing solicitude not only for the needs but the whims as well of your children?! I don't know about my brother, but I..." and so on. For his part, Pavel would express himself on the same occasion in the following way: "Dearest parent, I have received such and such an amount of money for such and such a period, and according to my calculations, I still have six and a half rubles owing me, which sum I beg you most respectfully to forgive me requesting." When Arina Petrovna sent reprimands to the children for their prodigality (this happened often, although there were no serious reasons for doing so), then Porfisha would always submit humbly

12

to these comments and write: "I know, dearest friend, mama, that you are carrying an unbearable burden for our sakes, your unworthy children, I know that very frequently our behavior does not justify your maternal solicitude on our behalf, and what is worse, with that characteristic human fraility we even forget this fact, for which I offer you the sincerest filial apology, hoping with time to divest myself of this sin and to be more cautious in the uses of the money which you have sent, mama, my priceless friend, for my keep and other expenses." However, Pavel would respond in the following manner: "Dearest parent! Although you have not had to pay any of my debts yet, I accept without challenge your calling me a wastrel, whereby I beg you to accept my sincerest assurance." The two brothers responded differently even to Arina Petrovna's letter bearing the news of the death of their sister, Anna Vladimirovna. Porfiry Vladimirych wrote: "The news about the death of my sister and kind companion of my youth, Anna Vladimirovna, was a grievous shock to my heart, and the grief is increased by the thought that you, dearest mama, are being sent a new cross to bear in the personages of the two orphan-infants. Was it not enough that you, our common benefactress who denies all things to herself without sparing her health has concentrated all her efforts on providing her family not only with the necessities but with luxuries as well? Truly, one must grumble at times despite oneself and even though it may be sinful. In my opinion the only recourse for you, my friend, in the present situation, is to recall as often as possible what Christ himself had to endure." On the other hand, Pavel wrote: "I have received the news about the death of my sister, who was the victim of an untimely death. In general I hope that the Almighty will console her in His refuge, although even this is not certain."

Arina Petrovna reread her sons' letters and kept attempting to guess which of them would be her nemesis. She would read Porfiry Vladimirych's letter and it would seem to her that he was that very nemesis.

"My, how he does write! The way he twists his tongue!" she would exclaim, "it was no accident that Styopka-the-dunce gave him the name of little Judas! There's not a single sincere word! He just lies and lies! And this 'dear friend, mama stuff,' and all that about my burdens and my crosses...he doesn't feel a single bit of it!"

Then she would turn to Pavel Vladimirych's letter and again she would imagine that this one would be her future nemesis.

"So stupid, but just look how he gets back at his mother so sneakily!—'Whereby I beg you to accept my sincerest assurance...' —Mercies alive! Just wait, I'll show you the meaning of 'accept my sincerest assurance'! I'll throw you a sop like I did Styopka-the-dunce, then you'll see what I make of your 'assurance'!"

At the end of it all a genuinely tragic wail burst forth from her maternal breast:

"And for whom am I saving up all this lot! For whom am I putting it all aside! I don't get enough sleep at nights, I don't get enough to eat... For whom?!"

Such was the family situation of the Golovlyovs at the moment when the bailiff Anton Vasilyev reported to Arina Petrovna on Styopka-the-dunce's squandering of the "sop she had thrown," which in view of its cheap sale was already beginning to take on an ambiguous significance as a "parental blessing."

* * *

Arina Petrovna was sitting in her bedroom, unable to pull herself together. Something was stirring within her that she could not put a finger on. Was some miraculous appearance of sympathy for her worthless son playing its part here, or was it still nothing more than an unadorned sense of her authority having been offended that was evident here? Not even an experienced psychologist could have determined it, so rapidly were her inner feelings and sensations growing confused. Finally, out of this general multitude of accumulated nothings there emerged most clearly the apprehension that she would be saddled with that "worthless son" once again.

"Anyuta has laden me with her pups, and now there's the dunce as well," she calculated thoughtfully.

She sat for a long time like this, without saying a single word and just staring out the window at a single point. Dinner was served, but she hardly touched it. They came to ask whether the master could please have some vodka. Without even looking she threw the key to the storeroom over. After dinner she disappeared into the chapel, ordered all the ikons to be lit, and then locked herself in, having directed beforehand that the bathhouse be stoked up. These were all signs which proved beyond a doubt that the mistress "was in a fury" and consequently everything in the house suddenly fell as silent as death itself. The maids walked about on their tip-toes. The housekeeper Akulina was running around like one possessed: jam-making had been arranged for after dinner, and now that the time had come, the berries had been cleaned and were now ready, but there was no order from the mistress either to proceed or to stop. The gardener, Matvey, showed up asking whether it was time to pick the peaches, but he was greeted with such hushing sounds in the maids' quarters that he beat a hasty retreat.

After praying to God and taking a bath in the bathhouse, Arina Petrovna felt somewhat pacified, and once again demanded Anton Vasilyev's appearance.

"Well, what is the dunce doing now?" she asked.

"Moscow is a big city and you couldn't cover it all in a year!"

"But I suppose one has to eat and drink?"

"He makes the rounds of his peasants to feed himself. He eats with some of them and begs ten kopeks worth of tobacco from others."

"And just who has given them permission to do so?"

"Mercy, mistress! How could the peasants take offense! They give to strangers who have nothing, how could they refuse their own masters!"

"Just wait, I'll show them...the almsgivers! I'll send the dunce back to the ancestral estate to you, and you will all support him at your own expense!"

"Whatever your command is, mistress."

"What? What did you say?"

"I said, whatever your command is, mistress. If you so order it, we'll feed him!"

"Precisely, you'll feed him! Mind what you say and don't speak any nonsense!"

Silence. But it was not for nothing that Anton Vasilyev had been given the name of turncoat by the mistress. He could not bear it any longer and again began to shuffle about on the spot, just itching to report something.

"He's quite a trickster!" he pronounced finally, "people say that when he returned from the regiment he had one hundred rubles with him. A hundred rubles isn't a lot, but he might have been able to manage with them for a while..."

"Well?"

"He thought he could fix things up a bit, but he got mixed up in some shady business..."

"Go on, stop beating around the bush!"

"Seems he took it to the German club. He thought he'd find a fool there to clean up on playing cards, well-ll, instead he met someone smarter than himself. He tried to skip out but was caught, they say, in the hall. He was fleeced of all his money!"

"I suppose he got a good drubbing as well?"

"That as well. The next day he went to Ivan Mikhailych and told the whole story himself. The most amazing thing was that he was laughing and cheerful! As though they had given him a little pat on the head!"

"Wouldn't mean a thing to him! Just don't let him come into my sight!"

"One would imagine that he will show up."

"What are you saying! I won't let him through the door!"

"There's nothing else but for him to show up!" repeated Anton Vasilyev, "and Ivan Mikahilych said that he himself let it slip out: 'Enough's enough!' he said, 'I'll go to the old lady and live on bread and water!' Yes, mistress, as far as that goes, he spoke the truth, and there's nowhere for him to go but here. He can't hang around his peasants in Moscow for long. He needs clothes and a rest..."

This was precisely what Arina Petrovna had been afraid of, this was the

15

very heart of that murky notion which had been tormenting her unconsciously. Yes, he would show up, there was nowhere for him to go any more.
It could not be avoided! He would be here, eternally before her eyes, accursed, unworthy, lost! Why had she thrown him a sop earlier? She had
thought that once he had received "what was coming to him," he would disappear into eternity, but, no, here he was springing up again! He would come,
he would make demands, he would be an eyesore with his miserable appearance. And his demands would have to be satisfied, because he was a rude person prepared to cause any manner of disorder. You could not hide *him* under
lock and key; *he* was capable of showing up even before strangers together
with other rabble, he was capable of causing a row, of running to the neighbors and telling them all the secrets about the affairs of the Golovlyovs. Perhaps send him to the Suzdal Monastery? But who knows, to be sure, whether
the Suzdal Monastery still exists, and whether in fact it exists in order to lib-
erate afflicted parents from the sight of obstinate children? People said that
there was the insane asylum...but really, the insane asylum, well, how could
you ever get him there, this forty-year-old stallion? In short, Arina Petrovna
was completely at a loss with the thought of the adversities which were
threatening to upset her peaceful existence with the arrival of Styopka-the-
dunce.

"I'll send him to you in the ancestral estate! You feed him at your own
expense!" she threatened the bailiff, "not at the expense of the estate, but at
your very own!"

"But why, mistress?"

"So you won't go on cawing. Caw! Caw! 'There's nothing else but for
him to show up'... get out of my sight, away with you... you crow!"

Anton Vasilyev was about to make a turn to the left, but Arina Petrovna stopped him again.

"Stop! Wait! So it's true that he's preparing the ground for his return to
Golovlyovo?" she asked.

"Am I about to lie, mistress! Truly he said: 'I'll go to the old lady to
eat bread and water'!"

"I'll just show him then what kind of bread the old lady has laid up for
him!"

"What does it matter, mistress, he won't be living with you for long!"

"What do you mean?"

"You see, he's got a very bad cough...he's always clutching at the left
side of his chest... He won't last long!"

"Those are the very ones, my dear, that live even longer! He'll outlive
all the rest of us! So he coughs, what does it matter to him, the long-legged
stallion! Well, we'll see about that. Now go, I have arrangements to make."

Arina Petrovna spent all evening in thought and then finally she made
up her mind: to summon a family council to decide the fate of the dunce.

Such constitutional procedures were not part of her nature, but this time she decided to withdraw from her despotic customs in order to protect herself behind a family-wide decision from the good people's censure. In any event, she did not doubt the outcome of the forthcoming consultation and for that reason it was with a light heart that she sat down to the letters whereby Profiry and Pavel Vladimirych were directed to appear in Golovlyovo without delay.

* * *

While all of this was transpiring, the perpetrator of all the commotion, Stepan-the-dunce, was already making his way towards Golovlyovo from Moscow. At the Rogozhaya Station in Moscow he boarded one of the so-called "diligences" in which at one time in the past, indeed even now in a few places, small businessmen and trading peasants would ride as they made their way homeward for a vacation. The "diligence" was travelling in the direction of Vladimir and the same compassionate tavern-keeper, Ivanych, was taking Stepan Vladimirych along at his own expense, having booked a place for him and paying for his victuals for the duration of the journey.

"Now, Stepan Vladimirych, this is what you should do: get out at the turning in the road, continue on foot, just the way you are in that outfit and show up before your mama looking like that," Ivan Mikhailych deliberated with him.

"Good, good," agreed Stepan Vladimirych as well. "It's not far from the turning, only fifteen versts to cover on foot! I can whip that off in no time! All covered with dirt and mud, that's the way I'll show up!"

"Your mama will take one look at you in that outfit and perhaps she'll take pity on you!"

"Of course she will! How could she not take pity! My mother is after all a kindly old lady!"

Stepan Golovlyov was not yet forty, but to look at, one would put him at not less than fifty. Life had ruined him to such a degree that there remained no sign of the fact that he was the son of a member of the gentry, not the slightest trace of the fact that he had once been to the university and had been exposed to the arts and sciences. He was an extremely tall, unkempt, practically unwashed fellow, skinny from insufficient nourishment, his chest caved in, his arms rake-like. His face was bloated, his hair and beard were dishevelled and heavily streaked with grey, his voice was loud but cracked and hoarse, his eyes bulging and enflamed, partly from an excessive indulgence in vodka, partly from being constantly exposed to the wind. He wore an ancient, grey, threadbare uniform whose epaulets had been ripped off and sold to be melted down for the precious metal in them. On his feet were rusty red top-boots, worn out and patched. From underneath his gaping military jacket a shirt was visible that was almost black, as though it had been smeared with soot, a

17

shirt which he himself called a "flea-bag," with genuinely military cynicism. He would peer out sullenly from under his eyebrows, but this sullenness did not express any inner dissatisfaction, but rather was the consequence of some sort of vague apprehension that any moment now he would perish, like a worm, from hunger.

He talked incessantly, jumping disconnectedly from one subject to another. He talked while Ivan Mikhailych was listening to him as well as when the latter dozed off to the music of his words. He felt terribly uncomfortable sitting there. Four people were crammed inside this "diligence" and consequently he was forced to sit with his feet tucked up, which in the course of three or four versts created an unbearable pain in his knees. Nonetheless, despite the pain, he spoke incessantly. Clouds of dust streamed in through the side openings of the carriage. From time to time the sun's slanting rays crept through, and suddenly the interior of the diligence would be scorched as though by flames, but he still went on talking.

"Yessir, I've knocked about some in my grievous time," he would relate, "now it's time to step aside! After all, I'm not going to eat her out of house and home, surely she can find a crust of bread for me! What do you think about that, Ivan Mikhailych?"

"Your mama's got a lot of crusts!"

"Only they're not for me, is that what you're trying to tell me? Yes, old friend, she has a pile of loot, a whole pile of it, but she'd begrudge me five kopeks! But then the old witch has always hated me! But now things will be different! There's nothing more to be gotten out of me, and I'm ready to take her on! If she thinks of chasing me out, I won't go! If you say she won't give me anything to eat, then I'll take it myself! Yessir, I've served the fatherland, and now everyone is obliged to help me out! There's only one thing I'm afraid of: she won't give me any tobacco—damnation!"

"That's right, it looks as though you'll have to say goodbye to tobacco."

"I'll grab hold of the bailiff! Maybe that bald-headed old devil will give his master some!"

"Sure, why shouldn't he do that! But suppose that mama of yours forbids the bailiff?"

"Well, then I'm really done for. There's only one luxury that I have left of my former munificence, and that's tobacco! Brother, when I was in the money I used to smoke a quarter of Zhukov tobacco a day!"

"Then you'll have to say goodbye to vodka as well!"

"That's damnable too! Vodka's even beneficial for my health, it breaks up the phlegm. Brother, when we were marching to Sevastopol and still hadn't reached Serpukhov, each of the lads had finished off a bucket of vodka."

"I bet you were really soused?"

18

"I don't remember. It seems as though we must have been. Brother, I went right as far as Kharkov, but for the life of me I can't remember a thing. I only remember that we marched through villages and through towns, and also that in Tula a government contractor gave us a speech. The scoundrel was all in tears! Yes, our holy Mother Russia had to drown her sorrows during that miserable time! What with all those suppliers, contractors, receivers, —God alone preserved her!"

"And your mama made herself a nice profit out of it as well. More than half the soldiers from our estate didn't return home, so for each one, they say, a certificate of military compensation was ordered to be issued. Each of these certificates is worth more than four hundred rubles when cashed in."

"Yes, brother, our mother is a clever one! She should have been made a minister and not spent her time skimming froth off jam in Golovlyovo! You know what! She was unjust to me, she wronged me, but I still respect her! She's smart as the devil, that's the main thing! If it weren't for her where would we be now? We would have had only Golovlyovo with a hundred and fifty serfs! But just look at the damned pile she's accumulated!"

"Your brothers will be well-heeled!"

"Sure they will. But I'll be left standing, that's for certain! Yes, brother, I'm down the drain! But my brothers will be rich, especially the bloodsucker. That one could worm his way into anybody's soul. Anyway, he'll finish off the old witch sooner or later. He'll suck all the money and estate right out of her, I can tell these things ahead of time! But Pavel, my brother, there's a man who's all heart! He'll send me some tobacco on the sly, you just wait and see! As soon as I get to Golovlyovo, I'll drop him a line right away, saying such and such, kind brother, help me out! My God, now if I were rich!"

"What would you do?"

"In the first place, I'd cover you in riches..."

"Why me! Look after yourself, I'm satisfied, thanks to your mother's good graces."

"No, not that way, brother, *attendez!*—I'd make you commander-in-chief of all the estates! Yes, friend, you fed and gave shelter to a serviceman and I thank you! If it weren't for you, I'd be trudging along on my own pins right now, back to the home of my ancestors! And I'd slap your freedom on you right now and open up all my treasures before you—eat, drink and be merry! What did you think I'd do, old friend?"

"No, don't worry about me, master. What else would you do if you were rich?"

"In the second place, I'd find myself a little sweetie. In Kursk I went to a service at the Church of Our Lady and there I saw one... ah, what a fine little sweetie she was! Believe it or not, she couldn't stand still for a single minute!"

"Maybe she wouldn't have wanted to be your sweetie?"

19

"And what's money for! What's filthy lucre for! If a hundred thousand is too little, then take two hundred! Brother, when it's a question of money for me, I don't begrudge a thing as long as I can enioy my pleasure! To tell the truth, I sent my corporal with three silver rubles to slip her, but the little cheat asked for five!"

"I suppose you didn't happen to have five?"

"I don't know what to say myself, brother. I tell you it's all as though it happened in a dream. Maybe she even came to me, but I forgot. I can't remember a thing for the whole two months I spent on the road! I don't suppose that's ever happened to you?"

But Ivan Mikhailych was silent. Stepan Vladimirych glanced at him and confirmed that his travelling companion's head was nodding rhythmically and whenever his nose almost touched his knees he would give an awkward start and then begin to nod in rhythm again.

"So-o!" he said, "you've already been rocked off to sleep! Want to take it easy. You've gotten fat, brother, on those tavern snacks and victuals! But there's no sleep in me! No sleep whatsoever, and that's all there is to it! Maybe I could iust play a little trick. Maybe some fruit of the vine..."

Golovlyov looked around and made sure that all the other passengers were asleep. The head of the merchant sitting beside him was thumping against the transom, but he kept on sleeping. His face had gotten all shiny, as though covered with lacquer, and flies were hanging around his mouth.

"What if I popped all these flies down his trap—my, I bet he'd think the sky had caved in!" Golovlyov was struck suddenly by this happy thought, and he was about to edge up to the merchant with his hand to put this plan into operation, but mid-way he thought of something else and stopped.

"No, enough fooling around. That'll do! Sleep, friends, and get your rest! Meanwhile I...where did he stick that bottle? Oh, ho! Here you are, my sweet! Come to papa! Have mer-cy, O Lord, on Thy-y pe-e-ople!" he sang softly, pulling the vessel from the canvas bag fastened to the side of the carriage and pressing the opening to his mouth. "There now, that'll do. I feel warm. Or should I have another? No, that's good enough...there's still another twenty versts to the station, and I'll still have time for a swig...or maybe I should have another? Ah, damn it anyway, this vodka! Just lay eyes on a bottle and it lures you on! Drinking is damnable, but you can't get by without drinking, or you won't sleep! If only sleep would flatten me out, damn it!"

He took a few more swigs from the bottle and stuffed the bottle back into its former place, and then he began to fill his pipe.

"Marvellous," he said, "first we had a drink, and now we'll have our pipe! She won't give me any tobacco, the old witch, she won't, he was right about that. Will she feed me? Some scraps, I suppose, she'll send from the table! God! We had some money and now it's gone! There was a man and now he's gone! That's the way it all goes in this world. There you are today, stuffed, drunk, indulging yourself, having a puff on your pipe... 'But, man, where will you be tomorrow?' But I ought to have a bite of something. You go on drinking like a leaky barrel, but you don't have a bite to eat along the way. The doctors say that drinking is good for you if you have a proper bite to eat, like the most holy Father Smaragd said when we were passing through Kromy! But forget about that now, and see if we can get hold of some food. I seem to recall that he put a sausage and three French loaves in that bag! He must have begrudged buying caviar! Just look at the way he sleeps, the songs he plays with his nose! I suppose he buried the provisions underneath himself!"

He rummaged around and turned up nothing.

"Ivan Mikhailych! Hey, Ivan Mikhailych!" he cried.

Ivan Mikhailvch awoke and for a moment it seemed he was at a loss to understand how he came to be sitting opposite the gentleman.

"I must have been just dropping off to sleep!" he said finally.

"It doesn't matter, friend, sleep! I just wanted to ask where we hid the bag with the provisions?"

"You feel like eating? But I imagine you'll need a drink beforehand!"

"You've got something there. Where have you got the bottle?"

After taking a drink, Stepan Vladimirych reached for the sausage which proved to be as hard as stone, salty as salt itself, and encased in such a tough skin that it was necessary to use a knife to pierce it.

"Some white fish would have gone well now," he said.

"Forgive me, master, I completely forgot it. All morning long I kept thinking about it, and I even told my wife to remind me about the white fish, and the devil went and made me forget!"

"Never mind, we'll eat some of the sausage. When we were in the campaign we didn't even have this to eat. My papa told me a story about how one Englishman made a wager with another Englishman that he would eat a dead cat, and he ate it!"

"Phew... he ate it?"

"He did. But he was sick afterwards! However, he cured himself with rum. He downed two bottles at one go and was in tip-top shape afterwards. And then there was another Englishman who made a wager that he would live on nothing but sugar for a whole year."

"Did he win?"

"No, two days before the year was up he kicked the bucket! And what about you, won't you have a snort of vodka?"

"I've never touched the stuff."

"You only swill tea? That's not good, brother. That'll make your belly grow. What's more, you have to be careful with tea. If you drink a cup you should top it off with a little glass of vodka. Tea causes phlegm to build up but vodka loosens it. What about it?"

"I don't know. You people are educated, you'd know better."

21

"Precisely. When we were in the campaign we never bothered with your teas and coffees. But vodka, that was a sacred business. Unscrew the canteen, pour it out, take a drink—and away you go! They drove us hard in those days, so hard that I went ten days without washing!"

"You certainly had a lot to bear, master!"

"Maybe I did, maybe I didn't, but just you try truding along the highway on foot! On the way there it wasn't bad at all. People gave us things, fed us dinner and all the wine we wanted. But on the way back all of the honor ceased!"

Golovlyov chewed the sausage with difficulty and finally managed to swallow a piece.

"Brother, the sausage is a bit salty!" he said, "but anyway I'm not fussy! My mother is not about to treat me to any delicacies, a plate of cabbage soup and a bowl of porridge, and that's that!"

"God is merciful! Maybe she'll spare you a meatpie on holidays."

"I wouldn't count on it. Neither vodka nor tobacco, you were right there. They say she's taken a fancy to playing cards nowadays, I wonder if that's true? She might invite me to play and treat me to tea. But as far as the rest is concerned, forget it, brother!"

They stopped at a station for four hours to feed the horses. Golovlyov managed to polish off the bottle, and then he was stricken with a powerful hunger. The passengers disappeared into the hut and set themselves down to eat. After taking a stroll around the couryard, peering into the backyards and the horse stalls, scaring the pigeons and even attempting to sleep, Stepan Vladimirych finally came to the conclusion that the best thing for him would be to follow the other passengers into the hut. There, on the table, cabbage soup was already steaming, while off to the side, on a wooden tray, lay an enormous chunk of beef which Ivan Mikhailych was cutting up into smaller pieces. Golovlyov sat down off to the side, lit his pipe, and for a long time had no idea of how to set about satisfying his hunger.

"*Bon appetite,* gentlemen!" he said finally, "the cabbage soup there seems nice and thick."

"It's not bad," replied Ivan Mikahilych, "you ought to have ordered some, master!"

"No, I was just commenting on it, I'm not hungry."

"Not hungry! You only ate a piece of sausage and the accursed stuff only makes one's belly feel emptier. Have a bite! Here I'll tell them to lay a table for you on the side. Eat, and here's to your health! Madam! Lay the gentleman a table on the side, that's right!"

The passengers set about their food in silence, only exchanging looks among themselves in an enigmatic silence. Golovlyov guessed that they had "seen through" him, although he had impudently played the part of the gentleman during the entire journey and had called Ivan Mikhailych his treasurer. He knitted his brows and the tobacco smoke welled up out of his mouth.

He was about to refuse the food, but hunger's demands were so insistent that he threw himself almost rapaciously on the bowl of cabbage soup set before him and devoured it in an instant. With his hunger satisfied, self-confidence returned, and as though it were quite within the order of things, he turned to Ivan Mikhailvch and said, "Well, my good treasurer, you take care of the bill for me and I'll go off to the hayloft to have a chat with Mr. Sandman!"

Swaggering along, he made his way to the barn and this time, with his stomach full, he slept like a lord. At five o'clock he was on his feet again. Seeing that the horses were standing by the empty stalls and rubbing their noses against the edges, he began to rouse the driver.

"The scoundrel is having a good snore," he cried, "and we're in a hurry, but he's having pleasant dreams!"

This continued in this vein until the station where the road branched off to Golovlyovo. It was only at this point that Stepan grew somewhat timid. He was clearly losing heart, and he fell silent. Now it was Ivan Mikhailych's turn to cheer him up and persuade him that above all he should discard his pipe.

"Master, when you get near the estate, throw the pipe in the nettles! You'll find it afterwards."

Finally the horses which were to carry Ivan Mikhailych further were ready. The moment of parting had come.

"Farewell, brother!" said Stepan Vladimirych in a trembling voice as he kissed Ivan Mikhailych, "she'll devour me!"

"God is merciful! Don't you let yourself get too frightened!"

"She'll devour me!" repeated Stepan Vladimirych with such certainty that Ivan Mikhailych looked down despite himself.

Having said this, Golovlyov turned abruptly in the direction of the country lane and set out on foot, leaning on a dry stick that he had broken off a tree beforehand.

Ivan Mikhailych watched him go for a short while, and then he rushed off in pursuit.

"I just thought of something, master!" he said, overtaking him, "when I was cleaning your uniform earlier I found three silver rubles in the side pocket. Don't lose them again!"

Stepan Vladimirych was visibly shaken and did not know how to act under the circumstances. Finally he gave Ivan Mikhailych his hand and said through his tears: "I understand...it's tobacco money for an old soldier..I thank you! As far as what I said about her devouring me, kind friend, just remember my words—she will devour me!"

For the last time Golovlyov turned in the direction of the country lane, and in less than five minutes his gray military cap was bobbing far off in the distance, first disappearing and then suddenly reappearing out of the thickets in the undergrowth of the woods. The hour was still early, just approaching six o'clock and the golden mist of morning was drifting over the country lane, barely admitting the rays of the sun, which was just emerging on the horizon. The grass glistened. The air was saturated with the scent of pines, mushrooms and berries. The road zigzagged through the depressions where countless flocks of birds were madly chirping. But Stepan Vladimirych noticed nothing of this. All frivolous thought had suddenly deserted him, and he was proceeding as though to the Last Judgement. A single thought filled his entire soul to overflowing: in three or four more hours he would go no further. He recalled his former life in Golovlyovo and it seemed to him that the doors of a damp vault were opening up before him, that as soon as he crossed the threshold of these doors, they would slam shut and then all would be finished. He recalled other details as well, ones which did not directly affect him, but which doubtlessly characterized the mores of Golovlyovo.

There was his Uncle Mikhail Petrovich (who was known locally as Mishka-the-troublemaker) who also belonged to the category of "the disgraced" and whom grandfather Pyotr Ivanych had banished to his daughter in Golovlyovo where he lived in the servants' quarters, eating out of the same bowl as the dog Tresorka. Then there was Aunt Vera Mikhailovna, who lived on charity in the Golovlyovo home with her brother Vladimir Mikhailych, and who had died "from abstinence" because Arina Petrovna had reproached her for every bite she took from the table, and for every stick of wood which was used to heat her room. Approximately the same experience lay in store for him. Through his mind flashed an endless series of sunless days drowning in some yawning, gray abyss, and he involuntarily closed his eyes. From this day forth he would be one-to-one with this evil old woman who was not really evil, but rather insensate in her despotic apathy. This old woman would devour him, she would devour him not through torture but through obliviousness. There would be no one to exchange a word with, no place to run, she would be omnipresent, despotic, benumbing and scornful. The thought of this inevitable future filled his whole being so completely with grief that he stopped beside a tree and beat his head several times against it. All of his life, which had been filled with affectation, idleness and buffoonery, was suddenly illuminated in his mind's eye. He was now proceeding to Golovlyovo, and he knew what awaited him there, and yet all the same he was going and could not prevent himself from doing so. There was no other course open to him. The very least of men could have done something for himself, could have earned his own bread, but he alone *could do nothing*. This thought, as though for the first time, had dawned on him. Even earlier he had had occasion to think of the future and outline all manner of possibilities for himself, but these had always been possibilities of idle pleasure and never any possibilities of work. And now he was faced with retribution for the madness which had engulfed his past. It was a bitter retribution which found expression in the single phrase: "She will devour me!"

It was about ten o'clock in the morning when the white steeple of Golovlyovo appeared beyond the forest.

Stepan Vladimirych's face turned pale, his hands began to tremble. He removed his cap and crossed himself. He recalled the Biblical parable of the prodigal son returning home, but he immediately realized that any application of such thoughts to himself represented sheer delusion. Finally his eyes discovered the boundary pole standing beside the road, and he knew that he was on Golovlyovo soil, that despicable soil which had given despicable birth to him, had reared him to be despised, had sent him despised to the four corners of the earth and now, still despised, was once again receiving him into its bosom. The sun was already high in the sky and was mercilessly scorching the endless fields of Golovlyovo. But he grew more and more pale and felt as though he were coming down with a fever.

Finally he reached the churchyard and here his nerve totally deserted him. The manorial house looked so peaceful from behind the trees, as though nothing out of the ordinary were taking place inside. However, the sight of it had the effect of a Medusa's head on him. He imagined his coffin there. "Coffin! Coffin! Coffin!" he repeated unconsciously to himself. And he could not bring himself to proceed directly to the house, instead he first dropped in on the priest and sent him to announce his arrival and to learn whether his mama would receive him.

The sight of him aroused the sympathy of the priest's wife, and she bustled about making an omelette for him. The village lads crowded around him and gazed at the master in amazement. The peasants passing by silently removed their hats and took a curious peek at him. Some old house servant even came running up and begged to kiss the master's hand. Everyone understood that the despised son was here before them, the one who had arrived at this despicable spot, who had come once and for all and that there was no departing from here other than being carried feet first to the churchyard. Everyone felt ill-at-ease and pitied him.

Finally the priest came and said that "mama is ready to receive" Stepan Vladimirych. In ten minutes he was already *there*. Arina Petrovna greeted him with solemn severity and took him in from head to foot with an icy glance. But she did not indulge in any useless reproaches. Nor did she admit him into the main building, but met him in the entry to the maids' quarters and took her leave of him there, after directing that the young master be conducted to his papa by way of another entry. The old man was dozing in bed, covered with a white sheet and wearing a white night-cap, dressed all in white, just like a corpse. On seeing him the old man awoke and fell into an idiotic laugh.

"How about that, dearie! You've fallen into the old witch's clutches!" he cried, while Stepan Vladimirych kissed his hand. Then he cried like a cock, began to laugh once again and repeated several times in a row: "She'll gobble you up, she'll gobble you up!"

25

"She'll gobble you up!" resounded echoingly in his heart.

His premonitions were justified. He was placed in a separate room of the wing where the estate office was also located. He was fetched underwear made of homespun linen and his papa's ancient housecoat which he immediately wrapped himself up in. The doors of the vault swung open, admitted him, and swung shut.

There ensued a series of dreary, monotonous days, one after the other drowning in the gray, yawning abyss of time. Arina Petrovna never admitted him into her presence. Nor was he allowed in to see his father. About three days later, the bailiff, Phinogey Ipatich, announced to him, on behalf of his mother, that the "conditions" consisted of him receiving his food and clothing, and in addition to these a pound of Faller's tobacco per month. He listened to his mama's resolution and merely noted: "Just look at the old woman! She's sniffed out the fact that Zhukov tobacco costs two rubles and Faller's only a ruble ninety—and so she's withholding a mere ten kopeks a month! No doubt she's about to spend it in alms on some beggar at my expense!"

The symptoms of moral sobriety which were beginning to manifest themselves during the hours when he was approaching Golovlyovo by way of the country lane had once again receded somewhere. A frivolousness intruded upon his manner once again and, together with this, a reconciliation with his "mama's will." The future, hopeless and inescapable, which had once flashed through his mind and filled him with apprehension, became enveloped in mist more and more with each day, and finally, ceased to exist entirely. In its place there emerged the daily round in all its mocking unadornment, and it emerged with such impudence and weariness that it entirely filled all his thoughts, all his being. After all, what part could any thought of the future play when the course of all of life had already been immutably resolved even in the slightest details by the mind of Arina Petrovna?

For whole days on end he paced back and forth in his isolated room, never taking the pipe from his mouth and humming some snatches of songs whereby church melodies unexpectedly alternated with off-color ones, and vice versa. When the estate clerk was present in the office, he woud drop in on him and count up the revenue received by Arina Petrovna.

"And where does she stuff all this pile of loot!" he wondered as he counted up a figure that was in excess of eighty thousand paper rubles, "she's not so wonderfully generous that she sends it to my brothers, and she herself lives a niggardly life, she feeds father on salted meat... In the bank! She must be putting it in the bank!"

Sometimes Phinogey Ipatich arrived at the office with the quit-rents himself, and then the very money which set Stepan Vladimirych's eyes blazing would be distributed over the office table in packets.

"Imagine wasting all that loot!" he exclaimed, "and it all goes to

26

stuffing her! She wouldn't think of splitting a little packet with her son! There you go, my poor suffering son! That's for your drink and tobacco."

Thereupon would begin the endless and utterly cynical conversations with Yakov the clerk about how to soften his mother's heart so that she might show him a little sympathy.

"In Moscow I knew a citizen," related Golovlyov, "who knew a 'word'. Whenever his mother did not feel like giving him any money, he would just say this 'word'. And it would cause her to become all contorted, her arms, feet—in short, everything!"

"He must have cast some kind of evil spell on her!" surmised Yakov the clerk.

"Well, whatever it was, but it's the absolute truth that there is such a 'word'. Then there was another fellow who said to take a live frog and at the stroke of midnight put it in an ant-hill. By morning the ants will have eaten it up and only the bones will remain. Take these bones and as long as they are in your pocket, whatever you ask on any woman, she won't be able to refuse you."

"Well, then, it could be done right now!"

"You see, brother, you have to put a curse on yourself first! If it weren't for that I'd have the old witch dancing to my tune like an imp!"

Whole hours were spent in conversation of this sort, but all the same no means could be found. Everything meant either having to lay a curse on oneself, or selling one's soul to the devil. Consequently, nothing else remained but to live according to "mama's conditions," adjusting them by means of a few arbitrary extortions from the village heads on every single one of whom Stepan Vladimirych imposed tribute for his own purposes, in the form of tobacco, tea and sugar. He was fed extremely badly. As a rule, he was brought the remains of his mama's dinner, but since Arina Petrovna's moderation bordered on miserliness, of course very little fell to his lot. It was particularly painful for him because since alcohol had become a forbidden fruit, his appetite grew rapidly. He was hungry from morn till night and could think of nothing but how he might eat his fill. He would lie in wait for the times when his mama was resting, run into the kitchen, take a peek even in the servants' quarters and go rummaging up anything wherever he could find it. He would sit for periods by the open window, waiting to see whether someone would come travelling past. If any of the peasants from the estate passed by, he would stop them and impose a tribute on them—of an egg, a cheese cake and so forth.

At the very first meeting Arina Petrovna in brief words had laid bare to him the entire program of his life-style: "For the time being, go ahead and live!" she had said, "Here's a nook for you in the office, you'll receive food and drink from my table, as for the rest,—no sense in getting upset, dearie! I never cared for delicacies and I'm not about to do so for your benefit.

Your brothers will arrive any time now, and whatever conditions they advise between themselves for you, that will be the way I'll treat you. I don't care to take the sin on myself, whatever your brothers decide, so shall it be!"

So now he was waiting impatiently for the arrival of his brothers. However, meantime he did not even consider what influence this arrival might have on his fate to come (apparently he had decided that it was not even worth considering), but he simply tried to guess whether his brother Pavel would bring him any tobacco and if so exactly how much.

"Maybe he'll throw a little coin my way!" he added thoughtfully, "Porfishka the bloodsucker won't give me anything, but Pavel...I'll say to him: 'come on, brother, give an old soldier something for a drink...' and he'll give it. How could he refuse?"

He did not notice the passage of time. It was that manner of absolute idleness, however, which he did not find wearisome. Only in the evenings did he find it monotonous, because the estate clerk would leave around eight o'clock for home, and Arina Petrovna did not pass out any candles for him, for the reason that he could pace back and forth in his room without candles. But he soon got used to this, and even grew fond of the darkness, because in the darkness his imagination had far greater play and would carry him far away from hateful Golovlyovo. One thing caused him anxiety though: his heart was acting up and fluttering somehow strangely in his chest, in particular when he would lie down to sleep. At times he would leap up from his bed as though distraught, and run around the room clutching the left side of his chest with his hand.

"God, what if I drop dead!" he would think, "no, I won't drop dead! And yet..."

But when one morning the estate clerk secretly informed him that his brothers had arrived, he shuddered involuntarily and changed complexion. Something childlike was suddenly aroused within him. He wanted to run quickly into the house to see how they were dressed, what beds were assigned to them and whether they had the kind of travelling necessaries he had seen with his army captain. He wanted to listen to what they would say to mama, to spy on what they would be given for dinner. In short, he wanted once again to take part in that life which had discarded him so resolutely, he wanted to rush to his mother's feet, beg her forgiveness and then amid the rejoicing, if you please, to partake of the fatted calf. Everything was still quiet in the house, but he had already run down to the cook in the kitchen and learned what he been ordered for dinner. For the first course there was fresh cabbage soup, a small pot of it, and yesterday's soup had been ordered reheated; the second course consisted of a portion of salted meat each, two pairs of cutlets on the side, and for the main course there was mutton with four snipe on the side. For dessert there was a raspberry pie with cream.

"Yesterday's soup, the salt meat and the mutton, that, brother, is for me, the disgraced son!" he said to the cook, "I imagine I won't be given any of the pie!"

"That will be as your mama decides, sir."

"God! There was a time when I ate snipe! I ate it, brother! Once, with Lieutenant Greykin I even made a wager that I could eat fifteen snipe in a row, and I won! The only thing was that afterwards I couldn't look at them without aversion—for an entire month!"

"But now you could eat them again?"

"She won't give me any! And why should she begrudge it! Snipe is a wild bird, you don't have to feed it nor look after it. It makes its own living! Both the snipe and the mutton cost nothing, but just you watch! The old witch knows that snipe tastes better than mutton, and she won't give me any! What's ordered for breakfast?"

"Liver has been ordered, mushrooms in sour cream, fruit cakes..."

"Could you send me a nice little fruit cake...please try, brother!"

"I'll give it a try. This is what you should do, sir. Later, when your brothers are sitting down to breakfast, send the estate clerk over here. He'll sneak you a couple of fruit cakes under his coat."

Stepan Vladimirych waited the whole morning long to see whether his brothers would come, but they did not. Finally, at about eleven o'clock, the estate clerk brought the two promised fruit cakes and reported that the brothers had now completed their breakfast and had locked themselves up with mama in the bedroom.

* * *

Arina Petrovna had greeted her sons solemnly, despondent with grief. Two maids supported her by the arms; gray locks of her hair straggled out beneath her white bonnet, her head was downcast and bobbed from side to side, her feet barely dragging along. In general she loved to play the part of the venerable and grief-stricken mother in the eyes of her children, and on such occasions she dragged her feet with difficulty and demanded that the maids support her by the arms. Styopka-the-dunce called such solemn receptions a "bishop's mass," and mother was the "lady bishop," and the maids, Polka and Yulka, were the "lady bishop's staff bearers." But since it was already two o'clock in the morning, the encounter took place without any exchange of words. She silently offered her hand to be kissed by the children, silently exchanged kisses with them, made the sign of the cross over them, and when Porfiry Vladimirych expressed his readiness to chat with his dearest friend and mother for the remainder of the night, she waved her hand and said:

"Off with you! Rest from your journey! This is not the time for talk, tomorrow we'll talk."

The following day, in the morning, both sons made their way to kiss their papa's hand, but papa would not give them his hand. He lay on his bed with his eyes closed when the children entered and cried, "You've come to judge the publican, have you?... Out of here you pharisees... Out!"

29

Nonetheless Porfiry Vladimirych emerged from his papa's study upset and covered in tears, whereas Pavel Vladimirych, like a "true graven idol," was merely picking his nose.

"He's not in a good way, dearest friend, mama! Goodness, not good at all!" exclaimed Porfiry Vladimirych, flinging himself into his mother's arms.

"Is he really that weak today?"

"Unbelievably weak, unbelievably so! He's not long for this world!"

"Well, he'll manage for a while yet!"

"No, dearest, no! Though your life has never been particularly filled with joy, just think of all the blows you've suffered at once...truly, it's even a wonder you have the strength to bear all these tribulations!"

"What's to be done, my friend, one must bear them if that is the will of God! You know that it is written in the Scriptures: bear ye one another's burdens. And lo, the Father has chosen me to bear the burden of our family."

Arina Petrovna screwed up her eyes even: it seemed only to clear to her that everyone had things ready-made for them, that all their cares were removed, whereas she alone labored without respite the whole day through and bore the burdens for others.

"Yes, my friend!" she said after a moment's silence, "it's been pretty difficult for me in my old age! I've scraped and scrounged for the children on my own, it's time for me to take a rest! Would you believe it—four thousand serfs! To have to take care of a crowd like that at my age! Keeping an eye out for everything! Making sure of everything! The comings and the goings! Even with these bailiffs and overseers of ours, if you don't watch it they won't look you straight in the eye! They'll have one eye on you and the other is pointing off at the woods! The people themselves are so untrustworthy! Well, and what about you?" she suddenly broke off and addressed Pavel, "Just picking your nose?"

"What am I supposed to say!" snapped Pavel Vladimirych, disturbed during the climax of his preoccupation.

"What! You could at least show a little pity for your father!"

"Who cares about father! Father is the same as always! He's been like that for ten years! You're always picking on me!"

"Why should I be picking on you, my friend, I'm your mother! Look at Porfisha here! He knows how to show affection and pity, just as a kind son should, but you don't care to go out of your way to even look at your mother, you keep giving sidelong glances and frowning just as though she isn't your mother but your enemy instead! Be kind enough not to snap back!"

"But what am I supposed..."

"Stop! Be quiet for a minute! Let your mother get a word in! Don't you remember what it says in the Gospels: honor thy mother and thy father and blessed thou shalt be...perhaps you don't care to have any 'blessing' for yourself?"

Pavel Vladimirych said nothing and looked at his mother with uncomprehending eyes.

"There, you see, you say nothing," continued Arina Petrovna, "you must feel the prick of conscience yourself. Well, God be with you! For the sake of this joyous reunion, let's leave this conversation. God, my friend, sees all, and I, goodness, how long I've been able to see right through you! My goodness, kiddies, kiddies! Remember your mother when she'll be lying in her grave, remember—but then it will be too late!"

"Mama!" interrupted Porfiry Vladimirych, "stop these dark thoughts! Stop!"

"Everyone must die, my friend!" pronounced Arina Petrovna sententiously, "these are not dark thoughts, but the most, one might say... divine! I'm growing feeble, kiddies, goodness, how feeble I'm growing! There's nothing left of my former self—only weakness and decrepitude! Even those godless maids of mine have noticed it, and they don't care a whit for me! For each word of mine they reply with two! A word of mine brings ten from them! I have only one threat I can hold over their heads, that I'll complain to the young masters! That will silence them sometimes!"

Tea was served, then breakfast, and all the while Arina Petrovna kept complaining and fussing over herself. After breakfast she invited her sons into her bedroom.

When the door had been locked with a key, Arina Petrovna immediately got down to the business which had brought about this council of her sons.

"The dunce has turned up, you know!" she began.

"We heard, mama, we heard!" responded Porfiry Vladimirych with that mixture of semi-irony and semi-expansiveness coming from a man who has just eaten his fill.

"He has turned up as though he has made something of himself, as though it were quite natural. However much I slaved and suffered, he thought that his poor old mother would always find a crust of bread for him! How much hatred I've seen in him my whole life! How much suffering I've had to endure because of his buffoonery and chicanery! What burdens I had to assume in those days when I had to grease palms to find him a position! And it's all like water off a duck's back! Finally I racked and racked my brains, and I thought, Lord! If he doesn't want to look out for himself, must I ruin my own life because of that long-legged dunce! Wait, I thought, I'll throw him a sop, maybe he'll latch on to it and gradually make something of himself! And so I tossed it to him. I myself searched out a house for him, with my very own hands, down to the last kopek, I put out twelve thousand silver rubles for it! And what happened? Not even three years went by and there he is hanging around my neck once again! How long will I have to endure these outrages?"

Porfisha cast his eyes to the ceiling and shook his head sadly, as though to say: "Alas! Worries! Worries! And our dear friend, mama, must be upset so! People could all be sitting there peacefully, minding their own business, and there wouldn't be any of this and mama wouldn't get angry... Alas! Worries! Worries!" But Arina Petrovna, being a woman who could not bear to have the flow of her thoughts interrupted by anything whatsoever, did not like Porfiry's action.

"No, you just stop wagging your head," she said, "you listen first! How was I to know that he would toss his parental blessing on the trash pile like some cleanly picked bone? How was I to sense, if you please, that I wouldn't sleep nights, wouldn't eat, while he cared not a whit! It was as though he up and bought a toy at the market, grew tired of it and tossed it out the window! That was his parental blessing!"

"Oh, mama! What a thing to do! What a thing to do!" Porfiry Vladimirych was about to begin, but Arina Petrovna stopped him again.

"Stop! Just wait! When I tell you to, then you can speak your mind! And even if he had only forewarned me, the scoundrel! I'm to blame, he could have said, mama, what happened was... I couldn't control myself! If I had known in time I could have bought the house for a trifle! If that worthless son did not know how to make use of it, let the other worthy children take advantage of it! Without a lie, you realize, that house would bear interest at the rate of fifteen percent a year! Maybe I would have tossed him another thousand for charity's sake! But, no chance! Here I sit, completely in the dark, and he's already disposed of it! I put out twelve thousand with my own hands for that house, and he let it go for eight thousand at the auction!"

"And the main thing, mama, is that he acted so basely with his parental blessing!" Porfiry Vladimirych hastily interpolated, as though fearing that his mama would interrupt him again.

"That too, my friend, that too. I haven't got any money to waste, dearie. I didn't get my hands on that money for a song and a dance, but only through sweat and tears. How did I obtain that fortune? When I married your papa, he only had Golovlyovo with its hundred odd serfs, and here and there, far away, twenty and thirty serfs—about a hundred and fifty all told! And I myself had nothing at all! And just you look what a collection I built up with those resources! Four thousand serfs—there's no hiding them! And do you think I can take them to the grave with me! Do you think it was easy for me getting these four thousand serfs? No, my dear friend, it wasn't easy, it certainly wasn't, you couldn't sleep at nights, you kept tossing and turning over how to handle this piece of business cleverly, so that no one would get a whiff of it beforehand! So no one would beat you to it, so you wouldn't spend a kopek more than you had to! And what didn't I try! Through mud and impassable roads, and sheer ice—I tasted it all! It's only recently that I've begun to allow myself the luxury of riding in a proper carriage. At first, however, a peasant cart would do, a flimsy covering stretched over it, a pair of nags hitched up and off I would trot to Moscow! Trotting along I would keep thinking: what if someone beats me to buying the estate! Once in Moscow you would stop at lodgings in the Rogozhskaya District, smelly and filthy—I had to endure it all, my friends! I would begrudge spending ten kopeks for a cab and so on my own two feet I would trudge from Rogozhskaya to Solyanka! Even the watchmen would be amazed: 'Madame, they would say, you are young and well-off, and yet you allow yourself so many burdens!' But I just kept quiet and bore it all. The first time I had, all in all, thirty thousand paper rubles—from your papa's scattered pieces of land, I had sold about 100 serfs, and with that amount, believe it or not, I set out to buy a thousand serfs! I had a service sung at the Iverskaya Church and then I set out for Solyanka to try my luck. And what do you know! It was as though the Holy Virgin had seen my bitter tears and singled out the estate for me! And a miracle it was: when over and above the government mortgage I bid thirty thousand, it was as though the auction were suddenly cut off! Before, everyone had been making a racket and arguing, then all of a sudden they ceased bidding and all around it became every so quiet. Then the auctioneer stood up and congratulated me, and I couldn't understand what was happening! The lawyer was there, Ivan Nikolaich, he came up to me and said congratulations, Madame, and there I was standing just like a wooden post! And you see how great is God's mercy! Just think, if in the midst of my ecstasy someone had mischievously cried thirty-five thousand!—then, if you please, I would have unconsciously bid forty thousand! And where would I have found the money?!"

Arina Petrovna had often related this epos of her first steps in the arena of acquisition to her children, but apparently it had not yet lost its novelty in their eyes. Porfiry Vladimirych would listen to his mama, alternately smiling, then sighing and then rolling his eyes, then lowering them according to the nature of the troubles his mother had gone through. Pavel Vladimirych even grew wide-eyed like a child to whom a familiar but every fascinating tale is being told.

"And I suppose you think that your mother achieved all these things without any effort!" continued Arina Petrovna, "No, my friends! A pimple doesn't pop up on your nose for nothing: after the first purchase I lay in a fever for six weeks! So now you judge: what am I supposed to do after all these, one might say, tribulations, when I see my hard-earned money, for whatever reason, tossed on the trash pile!"

A moment's silence ensued. Porfiry Vladimirych was ready to rend his garments asunder, but feared that there would not be anyone in the village who could repair them. As soon as the "tale" of the acquisition was concluded, Pavel Vladimirych immediately sank back and his face assumed its normal apathetic expression.

"This is why I have summoned you," Arina Petrovna began once again, "judge between me and him, the villain! Whatever you say, so shall it be! If you condemn him, he will be the guilty one, if you condemn me, I shall be the guilty one. Only I'm not about to let that villain get the best of me!" she added quite unexpectedly.

Porfiry Vladimirych sensed that his star was rising, and he burst into song like a nightingale. Yet, like the genuine bloodsucker that he was, he did not proceed directly to the question, but began with circumlocutions.

"If you will allow me, dearest friend, mama, to express my opinion," he said, "then here it is in a few words: children are bound to obey their parents, to follow blindly their behests, to console them in their old age and that's all there is to it. What are children, dear mama? Children are the loving creatures in which everything, beginning with their very persons and ending with the smallest rags which they wear on their bodies,—all of this belongs to their parents. Therefore, parents can judge their children, but the children can never judge their parents. The responsibility of children is to honor and not to judge. You tell us: judge between me and him! That is magnanimous, dear mama, mag-nan-i-mous! But can we even think of such a thing without terror, we, who from the very day of our birth are blessed by you from head to foot? If it be your will, but this would be sacrilege and not a judgement! This would be such sacrilege, such sacrilege..."

"Stop! Wait! If you're saying that you can't judge me, then vindicate me and condemn him!" Arina Petrovna interrupted him after listening and not being able to surmise what trap was being prepared in Porfishka the bloodsucker's mind.

"No, sweet mama, I cannot do that either! Or, it would be better to say, I neither dare, nor do I have the right. Neither to vindicate, nor to condemn—all in all I cannot judge. You, mother, you alone know how to act with us, your children. Reward us according to our services. If we have transgressed, then punish us. Our business is to submit and not to criticize. Even if you found yourself forced to transgress, in a moment of parental wrath, the bounds of righteousness, even then we would not dare to grumble, because the ways of Providence are undisclosed to us. Who knows? Perhaps that is the way it should be! The same is true here: brother Stepan has acted basely, one might even say, evilly, but only you alone can determine the degree of retribution which he deserves!"

"In other words, you refuse? You're saying, extricate yourself, dear mama, as best you can!"

"Oh, mama, mama! You're not committing any sin! Goodness me! I'm saying that whatever be your pleasure in resolving the fate of brother Stepan, then let it be, but you, alas, what evil thoughts you suspect me of!"

"Fine! And what about you?" Arina Petrovna turned to Pavel Vladimirych.

"What am I supposed to say! Would you really listen to me?" began

34

Pavel Vladimirych as though half-asleep, but then he unexpectedly gained courage and continued: "Everyone knows he's guilty... tear him to pieces... pound him to dust... everyone knows what's in store for him... what do I care!"

Having muttered these disconnected words he stopped and gazed at his mother with his mouth wide open, as though he himself could not believe his own ears.

"Well, dearie, we'll deal with you later!" she cut him off coldly, "I can see that you want to follow in Stepan's footsteps... Alas, make no mistake, my friend! You'll repent later, and then it'll be too late!"

"What did I do! I didn't mean anything!.. I'm only saying do whatever you want! What's so disrespectful in that?" Pavel Vladimirych surrendered.

"Later, my friend, we'll have a talk with you later. You think that because you're an officer you can't be kept in check! You can, my dear, ah, believe me, you can! So this means that both of you refuse to pass judgement?"

"I, dear mama..."

"Me too. What can I say! As far as I'm concerned, cut him to pieces if you please..."

"Just keep quiet, for Christ's sake... What a heartless son you are!" (Arina Petrovna recalled that she had the right to say "good-for-nothing," but for the sake of this joyful reunion, she restrained herself.) "But if you are both refusing, then I am being forced to pass judgement on him myself. Then this will be my decision: I shall try to treat him kindly once again. I'll give him papa's small Vologda estate, I'll have a small building erected and let him then live by himself like a beggar at the expense of the peasants!"

Although Porfiry Vladimirych had refused to pass judgement on his brother, his mother's generosity so struck him that he could not restrain himself from pointing out to her the dangerous consequences which would ensue as a result of this announced measure.

"Mama!" he exclaimed, "you are more than magnanimous! You see before you an act which is...well, the most base, evil act...and suddenly all is forgotten, all is forgiven! Mag-ni-fi-cent! But forgive me... I fear, my dearest, for you! Judge me as you will, but in your position...I would not have acted in this fashion!"

"For what reason?"

"I don't know... Perhaps I don't have that magnanimity in me...that, so to speak, maternal instinct... But it keeps occurring to me—what if brother Stepan, with his characteristic depravity, treats this second parental blessing precisely the same as the first?"

As it turned out, however, Arina Petrovna had already given this consideration, but at the same time there existed yet another undisclosed thought which now had to be disclosed.

"After all, the Vologda estate is your papa's very own," she said through her teeth, "sooner or later a portion of papa's estate will have to be

35

turned over to Stepan."

"I understand that, dear friend, mama..."

"But if you understand, then you must understand as well that once the Vologda estate is turned over to him, it is possible to demand a pledge from him that he has no further claims on papa's holdings and is satisfied on all accounts?"

"I understand that as well, dearest mama. But then you would be committing a gross error, because of your kindness! You should have demanded a pledge from him at the time when you bought him the Moscow house, stating that he had no further claims on his father's holdings!"

"What could I do! I never even considered it!"

"At that time he would have signed any paper whatsoever in his delirium! But you, because of your kindness...alas, what a mistake it was! Such a mistake! Such a mistake!"

"All you say is alas, alas, all the time! You should have said your 'alases' at the right time. Now you are prepared to put all the blame on your mother's head, but at the slightest mention of business, you suddenly disappear! By the way, it's not the paper that's important. I could get a piece of paper from him right now. I don't imagine your papa is about to die right now, and for the time being the dunce has to be fed. If he won't give us the paper, we can show him the door and tell him to wait until his papa dies! No, all the same I wish to know whether you like the idea of me handing over the Vologda estate to him?"

"He'll squander it, dearie! He squandered the house and he'll squander the estate!"

"If he squanders it then let him blame himself!"

"You know he'll come to you then!"

"Not a chance! I won't let him cross the threshold! I won't even send a crust of bread or drop of water out to him, the hateful wretch! And people won't condemn me for it and God won't punish me. There you are, I'll say, you wasted the house, you wasted the estate. What am I, his serf, to have to work and slave all my life to care for him alone? You know I have other children!"

"Nonetheless he'll have to come to you. He's pretty brazen, you know dearest mama!"

"I tell you, I won't let him cross the threshold! You just keep chattering like a magpie: 'he'll come, he'll come' — but I won't let him in!"

Arina Petrovna fell silent and stared out the window. She herself had a vague premonition that the miserable little Vologda estate would only free her temporarily from this "despised son," that ultimately he would squander it too, and then he would come to her again and that, *because she was a mother, she would not be able* to refuse him a nook; but the thought that her nemesis would remain with her forever, that even when he was shoved off into the office he would haunt her mind every second like a ghost—she was so oppressed by this thought that her entire body began to shake involuntarily.

"Never!" she cried at last, striking her fist on the table and leaping up from her chair.

Porfiry Vladimirych looked at his sweet friend, mama, and mournfully shook his head in a rhythmic way.

"But just look at you gettting angry, mama!" he said at last, in such a wheedling voice—as if he were about the tickle her sides.

"You think I should start dancing, do you?"

"Ala-as! But what does it say in the Scriptures about patience? Arm thy soul with patience! With patience, that's what! Do you think that God does not see? No, He sees everything, dearest friend, mama! Perhaps we suspect nothing and we sit here planning every which way, but up there He has made up his mind, saying, here now, I'll just put her to the test! Ala-as! And I thought, mama, that you were such a good girl!"

But Arina Petrovna understood full well that Porfishka-the-bloodsucker was merely fashioning a noose, and so she became truly angry.

"Are you trying to make a mockery out of me" she screamed at him, "his mother is talking about business and he's clowning around! Stop beating around the bush! Tell me straight what you're thinking! Do you want to leave him hanging on your mother's neck in Golovlyovo?"

"Precisely, mama, if you are merciful. Leave him in the same situation he's in now and demand a paper from him on the question of his inheritance."

"So...so...I knew that would be your advice. Fine. Let's suppose that we do as you say. However unbearable it will be for me to continually see my nemesis here beside me, well, it's obvious that no one will take pity on me. I was young and I bore my cross, and now in my old age I can look forward to bearing my cross even longer. Let's agree on this for the moment, and now we'll talk about something else. As long as papa and I are alive, he'll live in Golovlyovo, and he won't starve to death. But what about afterwards?"

"Mama, my friend! Why such dark thoughts?"

"What difference does it make what shade they are, all the same the question has to be considered. If we both drop dead, what will happen to him then?"

"Mama! Do you really have no confidence in us, your children? Weren't we raised according to your rules?"

Porfiry Vladimirych gave her one of those enigmatic looks which always flustered her.

"He's fashioning his noose!" resounded the echo in her heart.

"Mama, it will give me great joy to help the poor fellow! A rich man needs nothing! Christ preserve him! A rich man has all he needs! But a poor man—you know what Christ said about the poor man!"

37

Porfiry Vladimirych arose and kissed his mother's hand.

"Mama! Allow me to make a present of two pounds of tobacco to my brother!" he begged.

Arina Petrovna did not respond. She looked at him and thought: would he really be that much of a bloodsucker to chase his own brother out into the street?

"Well, do what you think best! If it must be in Golovlyovo, then let him live in Golovlyovo!" she said finally, "You've encircled me! You've trapped me! You started with 'mama, do as you please!' and then by the end you have nonetheless forced me to dance to your tune! But just you listen to me now! He's my nemesis, all my life he has tormented and shamed me, and finally he has committed an outrage with his parental blessing; but all the same, if you chase him out of the house or force him to go out into the world, you will not receive my blessing! No, no, no! Now both of you go to him! I imagine his eyes are popping out of their sockets trying to get a look at you!"

The sons left, but Arina Petrovna stood by the window and watched them as they crossed the main courtyard to the estate office without exchanging a word. Porfisha was continuously taking off his cap and crossing himself, first to the church gleaming whitely in the distance, then to the chapel, then to the wooden post to which a cup for receiving alms was fastened. Pavlusha, apparently, could not tear his eyes off his new boots, on the toes of which the sun's rays were glistening brightly.

"—And for whom have I scraped and saved! I didn't get enough sleep at night, I didn't get enough to eat... For whom?" —The wail burst forth out of her breast.

* * *

The brothers departed. The Golovlyovo house became deserted. Arina Petrovna set about her domestic chores with increased zeal. The clatter of the cooks' knives died out in the kitchen, but then activity doubled in the office, in the barns, storage shed and cellars. The laying in of the summer harvest neared its end. Jam-making, salting, preserving continued. The winter supplies poured in, and from all the estates the women sent their share-in-kind by the cartloads: dried mushrooms, berries, eggs, vegetables, etc. All of this was weighed up, accepted and added to the supplies of former years. It was not by chance that the mistress of Golovlyovo had an entire series of cellars, storage sheds and barns constructed. They were all filled to bursting and more than a little of their contents was spoiled, making it impossible to get at them because of the obnoxious smell. At the end of the summer all of these goods were sorted through and that portion which proved to be beyond hope was sent to the servants' kitchen.

"The pickles are still good, just a little slimy on the outside and a little smelly, but let the servants have a treat," said Arina Petrovna as she gave orders for one tub and the other.

Stepan Vladimirych came amazingly to grips with his new position. At times he had a passionate desire to "have a snort," "to drink himself silly" and in general "to let himself go" (as we shall see later, he even had money for this), but he restrained himself stoically, as though calculating that the right time had not come yet. For the time being he was busy every instant, because he was taking a lively and bustling part in the process of harvesting, rejoicing and grieving unselfishly at the successes and failures of the Golovlyovo parsimony. In a fit of frenzy he would dash from the office to the cellars in his housecoat alone, without a hat, hiding from his mother behind all possible trees and gateways which cluttered up the main courtyard (incidentally, Arina Petrovna noticed him more than once in this state, and her parent's heart would begin to seethe with the desire to give Styopka-the-dunce a good tongue-lashing, but on further consideration, she decided to ignore him), and there, with feverish impatience, he watched the carts being unloaded, the jars, cans, tubs being brought from the house and all of this being sorted, and then finally disappearing in the yawning abyss of cellars and storage sheds. In the majority of cases he remained satisfied.

"Two cartloads of brown mushrooms were brought today from Dubrovino—there they are, brother, the brown mushrooms!" he informed the estate clerk in ecstasy, "And we were beginning to think that we would have to go without them this winter! Thank you, thank you, Dubrovina people! Fine fellows, those Dubrovino people! They've saved our skins!"

Or:

"Today mother gave the order to catch carp in the pond—fine old fellows they were too! More than a foot long some of them were! We'll be eating carp for sure all this week!"

However, sometimes he was filled with grief.

"The pickles, brother, they didn't turn out today! Tough and spotted they are, not a decent pickle among them, so that's that! Looks like we'll have to feed on last year's, but this year's will go straight to the servants' kitchen, they're not good for anything else!"

But in general he was not happy with Arina Petrovna's domestic organization.

"What a lot of good things she's let spoil, it's a pity! Today they kept dragging it out, salt meat, fish, pickles, and she directed that it all be sent to the servants' kitchen! Is that the way to do it? Is that the way to manage a household? She wastes the fresh supplies and won't touch them until all the old spoilage has been eaten!"

Arina Petrovna's confidence that she could demand any paper she wanted from Styopka-the-dunce without difficulty was completely justified. Not only did he sign all the papers sent him by his mother without protest, but he even boasted that same evening to the estate clerk:

"Today I didn't do anything but sign papers, brother. I gave up my claim to everything—I'm clean now! Not a kopek to my name, not a thing left now, nor is there likely to be any at any time in the future! I've set the old girl's mind at rest!"

He parted with his brothers on friendly terms, and he was in rapture over the fact that he now had a full supply of tobacco. Of course he could not restrain himself from calling Porfisha a bloodsucker and little Judas, but these expressions went unnoticed in the flood of chatter, wherein a single connected thought could not have been detected. Upon taking leave the brothers grew generous, and even gave him some money, Porfiry Vladimirych qualifying his gift with the following words:

"If you should feel the need of oil for your ikon lamp or care to buy a candle for the altar, then you'll have the money to do so! There you go, brother! Lead a calm and peaceful existence, and mama will be pleased and you will find peace and we'll all be happy and joyful. You know mother is kind, my friend!"

"Yes, yes, she is kind," agreed Stepan Vladimirych, "only she does feed me salted meat that's spoiled!"

"And who is to blame? Who dishonored their parental blessing! You have only yourself to blame, you lost a fine little piece of property yourself! And what a fine piece it was: a most suitable, marvellous and generous property! Now if you had acted less freely and easily, you would be eating roast beef and veal, and you could have ordered a nice little sauce. And you would have had plenty of everything, potatoes, cabbage, peas. Isn't that right, brother, what I'm saying?"

If Arina Petrovna had heard this dialogue, she no doubt would not have been able to restrain herself from saying: "He's off and running!" But Styopka-the-dunce was fortunate in the fact that his ear, so to speak, was deaf to any extraneous speech. Little Judas could talk as much as he wanted and be entirely certain that none of his words would have any effect.

In short, Stepan Vladimirych gave his brothers a friendly send-off and then with no small self-satisfaction showed Yakov, the country clerk, two twenty-five ruble notes which turned up in his hand after the parting.

"Now, brother, I'm fixed up for a while!" he said, "we have tobacco, tea and sugar have been taken care of, only alcohol is lacking, but all we have to do is ask, and we'll have it too! Anyway, I'll have to hang on a bit, I don't have the time right now, I have to run off to the cellar! If you don't keep your eye on every crumb, they'll steal you blind! She saw me, the old witch, she saw me, brother, once when I was sneaking along the wall by the servants' kitchen! She was standing by the window, looking at me, I bet, and thinking: 'That's why I'm missing some of the pickles!'"

But then finally October made its appearance out-of-doors: the rain poured down, the road grew dark and became impassable. There was nowhere for Stepan Vladimirych to go because he had on his feet only papa's worn-out shoes, and on his back was papa's old housecoat. Unable to go out, he sat by the window in his room, gazing through the double glazing of the window at the peasant village drowning in the mire. There, in the midst of the gray mists of autumn, like dark specks, people flitted by nimbly, people whom the summer harvent had not managed to exhaust yet. The harvest had not been curtailed, but had merely taken on a new appearance, wherein the radiant colors of summer had been replaced by the unending gloom of autumn. The grain-drying sheds were still smoking past midnight, the swish of threshing flails, with their wearying rhythm, echoed through the whole area. In the estate barns threshing was going on too, while in the office there was talk that the great bulk of the mistress's grain would not be taken care of much before Lent. Everything looked gloomy, drowsy, everything exuded an oppressiveness. The doors of the office were no longer wide open as in summer, and inside the same building hung a grayish mist from the drying sheepskins that had been soaked.

It was difficult to say what impression the picture of the country amid the autumn labor had on Stepan Vladimirych, and even whether he was aware of the harvest continuing in the midst of the muddy morass beneath the unceasing downpour of rain. But it was certain that the gray, eternally weeping heavens of autumn did oppress him. It seemed as though the sky were suspended directly over his head and threatened to drown him in the gaping troughs of earth. He had nothing else to do but look out the window and follow the ponderous masses of clouds. Beginning in the morning, when the light barely began to glimmer, the entire horizon would be thickly covered with clouds. The clouds stood there as though frozen, bewitched. An hour would pass, then another and a third, but they would still be standing in the same places, nor could one even notice the least change in their coloration or their shape. One cloud which lay lower than the others and loomed more darkly had preserved for a long while now its tattered form (looking just like a priest in a cassock with outspread arms) clearly delineated against the whitish background of higher clouds. Even now, at midday, it preserved that very same shape. The right hand, to be sure, had become somewhat shorter, whereas the left one had become formlessly distended and the rain was pouring out of it, pouring out of it in such a fashion that a darker, almost black, streak stood out more distinctly against the dark background of the sky's horizon. Farther on was another cloud which a while before had hung suspended like an enormous shaggy clump over the neighboring village of Naglovka and seemed as though it were threatening to crush it, and now it was suspended in the very same shaggy clump in the same place, but had stretched its paws downward as though it were about to pounce any moment. Clouds, nothing but clouds and more clouds, that's the way it was all day long. Around five o'clock, after dinner, a metamorphosis took place: the surrounding area gradually became increasingly enveloped in mist until finally it completely disappeared. At first the clouds would disappear and dissolve into a uniform black shroud. Then the woods would disappear somewhere together with Naglovka. Thereupon the church would sink from sight along with the chapel, the nearby peasant village, the orchard, and only that eye which had followed with concentration the process of these mysterious vansihings could still distinguish the manorial house standing a stone's throw away. It was already quite dark in the room. In the office it was still twilight, the lamps were not lit. All that remained was to pace back and forth, endlessly back and forth. A sickly weariness paralysed his mind. Despite his idleness, he could feel through his entire body an inexpressible languor that defied diagnosis. A single thought squirmed, gnawed and oppressed, and this thought was: a coffin! a coffin! a coffin! Those specks which had been flitting past for some time against the dark background of mud near the village barns, they were not oppressed by this thought and they did not perish beneath the burden of despondency and weariness. If they were not exactly wrestling with the heavens, then at least they were struggling, they were attempting to build something up, to protect it, to maintain it. Whether it was worth the effort for them to protect and to maintain what they had built up and for which they knocked themselves out day and night, this thought never occured to him, but he was conscious of the fact that even these nameless specks stood immeasurably higher than he himself, that he could not struggle, that he had nothing to protect, nor anything to maintain.

He spent the evenings in the office because Arina Petrovna, as before, did not issue any candles for him. Several times he had requested, through the bailiff, to have boots and a sheepskin sent, but he was told that no boots had been set aside for him, and now that the frosts would soon begin, he would be issued felt boots instead. Apparently, Arina Petrovna intended to carry out her program to the letter: to maintain this despicable son at such a level that he would at least not die from hunger. At first he cursed his mother, but then it was as though he forgot about her. At first he would recollect something, then he would cease to do so. Even the light of the candles lit in the office became hateful for him and he would then lock himself up in his own room so as to be alone in the darkness. Before him lay a single recourse which he still feared for the time being, but which attracted him irresistably to itself. This recourse was to drink and to forget. To forget profoundly, irrevocably, to plunge into the waves of obliviousness to such a degree that it would be impossible to extricate himself. Everything drew him in this direction: his disorderly habits of the past, his enforced idleness at the present time, his sick constitution with its choking cough, with that unbearable, unexpected shortness of breath that came without warning and was accompanied by ever-increasing palpitations of the heart. Finally, he could resist no longer.

"Today, brother, we'll have to put a bottle aside for the night," he said to the country clerk in a voice which boded no good.

That bottle initiated with itself an entire series of new bottles, and from that time on he got properly drunk every night. At nine o'clock, when the light had been extinguished in the office and people had departed to their lairs, he placed the bottle of vodka that had been put especially aside on the table together with a piece of black bread heavily sprinkled with salt. He did not reach for the vodka immediately, but it was as though he were stealing up on it. All around him the world was plunged into a deep slumber. Only mice were rustling behind the wallpaper which had come unstuck from the walls and the clock in the office continued its tiresome ticking. Removing his housecoat and wearing his shirt alone, he rambled back and forth in the overheated room, and from time to time he would stop, go up to the table, fumble around in the darkness for the bottle and then once again resume his pacing. He drank the first glassfuls to the accompaniment of humorous toasts, sensually imbibing the burning liquid. But little by little the beating of his heart quickened, his head grew enflamed and his tongue began to mutter something disconnected. His dulled imagination strove to create some images, his deadened memory attempted to penetrate into the realm of the past, but the images emerged all in tatters, totally senseless, and the past did not respond with a single recollection, be it bitter or sweet, as though between itself and the present moment a solid wall had arisen once and for all. Before him was merely the present in the form of a tightly locked dungeon wherein any idea of time or of space had vanished without a trace. The room, the stove, three windows in the exterior wall, a squeaky wooden bed with a worn-out, thin mattress on it, a table with a bottle on it—his mind could not encompass any other horizons. But in proportion to the disappearance of the contents of the bottle, in proportion to the inflammation of his head, even this miserable sensation of the present receded beyond his control. The muttering which at first had possessed at least some kind of form, finally disintegrated completely. The pupils of his eyes, striving to distinguish outlines in the gloom, became grotesquely distended. Even the gloom itself finally disappeared and in its place appeared an expanse that was filled with a phosphorescent gleam. This was an infinite void, lifeless, which did not respond with a single living sound, ominously radiant. It followed on his heels, was there at each about-face in his pacing. Neither the walls, nor the windows, nothing existed. This gleaming void alone stretched out before him. He became terrified. He had to suppress within himself the sensation of reality to such a degree that even this void would not exist. A further effort of will—and he achieved his goal. His benumbed body was being borne on legs that pitched from one side to the other, his breast emitted not a muttering, but a hoarse rasping sound.

It was as though life itself had ceased. He was overcome by a strange insensateness that, bearing in intself all the signs of conscious life, at the same time doubtless pointed to the presence of some peculair kind of life which had developed independently of any external conditions whatsoever. Moan after moan burst forth from his breast, but they did not disrupt the dreamlike state in the least. This organic malady continued its devastating work without apparently occasioning any physical pain.

In the morning he awoke with the light, and grief, disgust and hatred awoke with his as well. It was a hatred unaccompanied by any desire for protest, a hatred that seemed inexplicable and without specific object, a hatred without definite shape. His bloodshot eyes fastened senselessly first on one object and then another with a gaze that was protracted and unwavering. His hands and legs were trembling. At first his heart would cease to beat as though it had collapsed, then it would start to pound so forcefully that his hand clutched involuntarily at his breast. Not a single thought, not a single desire. Before his eyes was the stove and his mind was so consumed with this image that it could not take in any other impressions. Then the window replaced the stove and there was nothing but a window, a window, a window... He had need of nothing, nothing, he had need of absolutely nothing. He packed his pipe and lit it mechanically and once again it slipped unsmoked from his hands. His tongue was muttering something, but apparently only out of habit. The best thing was to sit and say nothing, say nothing and stare at a single point, It would have felt good to become intoxicated at that moment. It would have felt good to raise the temperature of his organism so as to sense the presence of life if only for a moment, but during the daytime vodka could not be bought for love or money. He would have to wait until nighttime in order to plunge into those moments of ecstasy when the earth disappeared from underfoot and in place of the four hateful walls there would appear before his eyes that boundless shimmering void.

Arina Petrovna did not have the slightest idea of how the "dunce" was passing his time in the office. That fortuitious moment of sympathy which had flitted past in her conversation with Porfishka-the-bloodsucker had been extinguished instantly, so that she did not even take notice. As far as she was concerned, there was not even any systematic action on her part, only a mere obliviousness. She even lost sight of the fact that beside her, in the office, there was a creature living to whom she was related by blood, a creature who perhaps was wasting away with a longing for life. She had fallen almost mechanically into a rut in life which she had invested with an unchanging content and consequently she expected that others would have to do the same as she had. It never occurred to her that the very nature of life's content changed in accordance with the variety of conditions underlying it, and that ultimately for some (with her included in the number) this

44

content represented something preferred, something voluntarily chosen, while for others it was hateful and involuntary. Therefore, although the bailiff gave her frequent reports to the effect that Stepan Vladimirych "was not well," these reports went in one ear and out the other without leaving any impression in her mind. The most she could do was to respond with the stereotyped phrase:

"He'll get his second breath and outlive both you and me! What's it to him, the long-legged stallion! So he's coughing! Some people cough for thirty years in a row and it's just like water off a duck's back!"

Nonetheless, one morning when she was informed that Stepan Vladimirych had disappeared from Golovlyovo during the night, she suddenly came to her senses. She immediately sent the entire house to search for him and personally participated in the hunt, beginning with an examination of the room in which this despicable son had been living. The first thing that struck her was the bottle standing on the table with some liquid still lapping at the bottom. In the general uproar no one had thought of removing it.

"And what is this?" she asked as though not comprehending.

"Must have... been passing the time," replied the bailiff, hemming and hawing.

"Who gave it to him?" she began but then sputtered as she suppressed her wrath and continued the examination.

The room was filthy, black, so slimy that even she, as one who did not admit to any demands for comfort, felt uncomfortable. The ceiling was all sooty, the wallpaper was split on the walls and in many places hung in shreds; the window sills were black beneath a thick layer of tobacco ash, the pillows were strewn on the floor which was covered with a sticky filth; on the bed lay a crumpled sheet all gray from dirt ground into it. The double glazing in one window frame had been removed or, more accurately, ripped out and the window itself had been left open: apparently the despicable son had disappeared via this route. Arina Petrovna glanced instinctively at the out-of-doors and her fright was redoubled. Outside it was already the beginning of November, but autumn had been particularly long-lived this year and the frosts had not yet come. Both the road and the fields loomed all black, soaked and impassable. How had he crossed them and where had he gone? Then she recollected that he wore nothing other than a housecoat and slippers and one of the latter had been found beneath the window, and that all that night, to make things worse, the rain had fallen ceaselessly.

"It's been a fair time since I was in your room, dearie!" she whispered, inhaling some disgusting mixture of cheap alcohol, bad tobacco and sour sheepskins instead of air.

She stood by the window staring at the denuded horizon in mute raptness the whole day through while her people were rummaging through the woods. All this scandal because of the dunce! It seemed like an ugly

45

dream to her. Earlier she had said that he should be sent to the Vologda estate, but no, that accursed little Judas had fawned: "Let him stay in Golovlyovo, dear Mama!" And now I have to put up with him! He could have lived there out of sight however he wished, and Christ be with him! She had done her part, she had thrown him a sop and then a second! Even if he had squandered the second, well, there's no getting angry, Lord! Not even God could have filled that insatiable belly! And everything would have been nice and peaceful for us, but now, this was a fine trick to pull! You might as well whistle in the wind as look for him in the woods! It'll be pure luck if he's brought home alive. What can you expect of an alcoholic other than he'll end up in a noose before you know it! His mother doesn't get enough sleep at night, she doesn't eat enough, and there he goes, a fine way to do it—he takes it into his head to hang himself. It would have been worse if he had not been given enough to eat and drink, if he had been wasted with work, but what does he do, he knocks about the whole day in his room like some disorderly animal, he eats and drinks, eats and drinks! Anyone else in his place could not have thanked his mother enough, but he goes and hangs himself—that's the way my sweet little son repays his debts!

But this time Arina Petrovna's presuppositions concerning the dunce's violent death were not justified. Towards evening a carriage drawn by a pair of peasant horses appeared within sight of Golovlyovo and delivered the fugitive to the office. He had been found in a semi-conscious condition, all bruised, scratched, his face blue and swollen. It turned out that during the night he had gone as far as the Dubrovino estate which stood at a distance of some twenty versts from Golovlyovo.

He slept for a whole twenty-four hours afterwards and awoke only the following day. As was his custom he began to pace back and forth in the room, but he did not touch his pipe, it was as though he had forgotten about it, and he did not respond to any questions with a single word. For her part, Arina Petrovna was so upset that she almost had him transfered from the office to the manorial house, but then she calmed down and once again left the dunce in the office, giving orders to scrub and clean his room, change the bed linen, hang curtains on the windows and so on. The following evening, when she was informed that Stepan Vladimirych had awakened, she had him summoned to the house for tea and she even searched for affectionate words for their discussion.

"Now, why were you leaving your mother," she began, "do you know how much you upset your mother? It's a good thing that Papa didn't know anything about it, what would have happened to him in his condition?"

But Stepan Vladimirych, apparently, remained indifferent to his mother's affection and stared with glassy, unblinking eyes at a tallow candle, as though watching the melting wax form around the wick.

46

"Ach, my silly little, little fool!" Arina Petrovna continued in a tone that was increasingly affectionate, "you ought to have considered what rumors you might have stirred up about your mother! She has her detractors, you know—God Almighty! And who knows what they might prefabricate! They might say that I didn't feed you, or I didn't clothe you...Ach, my silly little, little fool!"

The same silence and the same unblinking, senseless stare fixed on a single point.

"And what did you find so terrible here with your mother? You have clothing and food—praise be to the Lord! And you're nice and cozy...what more could one ask for! If you're bored, then don't be angry, my friend, that's life in the country for you! We don't have parties and balls, and we all sit in our corners and become bored! I'd be happy to kick up my heels and sing some songs, but just take a look out the window and you don't even have any desire to go to the Lord's house in this downpour!"

Arina Petrovna stopped in the expectation that the dunce might at least grunt. But it was as though the dunce had turned to stone. Her heart began by-and-by to seethe, yet she still managed to restrain herself.

"If you were dissatisfied with anything—perhaps there wasn't enough food, or because of the linen in your room,—surely you could have discussed it frankly with your mother? Mama, you could have said, dearest, order some nice liver or have them prepare some nice cheese cakes over there, would your mother really have denied you a bite? Or even a little drink. If you had felt like a little drink, well, Christ be with you! A glass or two, do you think your mama would begrudge it? But what do you do? You're not ashamed to ask a serf, but you can't bring yourself to ask you mother!"

But all these words of coaxing were in vain. Stepan Vladimirych not only was not moved (Arina Petrovna had hoped that he would kiss her hand) nor displayed any remorse, but seemingly did not even hear.

From this time forth he fell absolutely silent. He walked about his room for entire days on end, his forehead sullenly furrowed, moving his lips and experiencing no fatigue. From time to time he would stop as though wishing to express something, but he could not find the words. Apparently, he had not lost the abiblity to think; but impressions were retained in his brain with such feebleness that he would forget them immediately. For this reason his failure to discover the requisite word did not even cause him a sense of impatience. Arina Petrovna, for her part, thought that he would certainly set fire to the house.

"He's quiet for the entire day!" she would say, "the dunce must be thinking about something while he's silent! Just you mark my word, he'll put the torch to the house."

But the dunce was simply not thinking at all. It seemed as though he

47

were totally immersed in an unrelieved gloom wherein there was no place either for reality or fantasy alike. His brain did produce something, but this something did not have any relationship either to the past or to the present or to the future. It was as though a black cloud had enveloped him from head to foot, and he was absorbed in it and in it alone, following its imagined fluctuations and from time to time shuddering and making as though to defend himself from this cloud. In this mysterious cloud the entire physical and mental world became submerged for him...

In December of that same year Porfiry Vladimirych received a letter from Arina Petrovna with the following contents:

"Yesterday morning we were overtaken by a new affliction visited on us by the Lord. My son and your brother, Stepan, passed away. The evening before he had been completely well and had even taken his supper, but then the following morning he was found dead in his bed—such is the transient nature of this life! And it was even more grievous to a mother's heart in that he departed this vain world without a word of farewell in order to proceed to the unknown realm.

"Let this serve as a lesson to us all: whosoever neglects his family ties must always expect this kind of end for himself. The failure experienced in this life, and an early death, as well as eternal torments in the world to come —all of these issue from the same source. For, however wise and illustrious we might be, if we do not honor our parents, then both our wisdom and illustriousness will be turned into naught. Such are the rules which must be affirmed by every person living in this world, and in addition to this, the serfs are bound to honor their masters.

"Incidentally, despite this, all respects were paid in full to the dearly departed, as befits a son. A shroud was ordered from Moscow and the funeral was conducted by the archimandrite, whom you know, and together with all the priests. Masses and requiems are being conducted even to this very day, as is fitting and in accord with Christian tradition. I feel sorry for my son, but I dare not complain, nor do I advise you to do so, my children. For who can have knowledge of these things? We may be weeping here while his soul is rejoicing in Heaven!"

GOOD RELATIVES

It was a hot midday in July. At the Dubrovina estate it was as though all life had ceased. Not only the idle, but the working folk as well, had dispersed to their corners and were lying in the shade. The dogs were stretched out beneath the overhanging branches of the enormous willow standing in the center of the main courtyard, and one could hear them snapping their teeth at the flies while half asleep. Even the trees stood there subdued and motionless, seemingly in anguish. All the windows in both the manorial house and the servants' quarters were wide open. The heat descended from above in a scorching wave. The earth, covered with short scorched grass, was aflame. The implacable light oppressed the area with a golden haze so that it became difficult to distinguish objects, including the manor house, which formerly had been painted gray and now had faded, and the small garden in front of the house and the birch grove separated from the house by the road leading up to the house and the pond and the peasant village and the rye field which began just beyond the village boundary. Everything was submerged in the shimmering haze. All odors, from the fragrance of the blossoming lindens to the stench of the barnyard, hovered in the air like a dense cloud. There was not a sound. From the kitchen alone came the intermittent clatter of the cooks' knives, presaging the inevitable cold soup and cutlets for dinner.

Mute agitation reigned within the master's house. The old mistress and two young girls were sitting in the dining room. They did not touch the knitting which lay abandoned on the table and seemed frozen in expectation. In the maids' quarters two women were busy preparing mustard plasters and compresses, and the measured tinkling of spoons, sounding like the chirruping of crickets, pierced the general torpor. The maids moved cautiously on bare feet along the corridor, running up and down the stairs from the upper floors to their quarters and back. From time to time a cry resounded from up above: "Where are those mustard plasters! Have you fallen asleep there?" and immediately afterwards a maid would come flying out of the servants' quarters like an arrow. Finally the scraping of heavy steps could be heard on the staircase and a regimental doctor came into the dining room. The doctor was tall, broad in the shoulders, with powerful, rosy cheeks which were bursting with health. His voice was clear, his step firm, his eyes bright and cheerful, his lips full and fleshy, he had an open look about him. This was a bon-vivant in the full sense of the word, despite his fifty years, a bon-vivant who even earlier had never passed up an opportunity for any drinking session or any feast, nor was he apt to for a long time yet. He was dressed in his summer uniform and, quite smartly, in a picque jacket of extraordinary whiteness, graced with bright embossed buttons. He came in, smacking his lips and clucking his tongue.

"Tell you what, dearie, bring us some nice vodka and a bite to eat!" he stopped in the doorway leading into the corridor and gave his order.

49

"Well, how is he?" asked the old mistress anxiously.

"God's mercy knows no limit, Arina Petrovna!" replied the doctor.

"What do you mean? In other words..."

"Precisely. He'll drag on for another two or three days and then, that's that!"

The doctor made a significant gesture with his hand and under his breath he hummed: *"Headlong, headlong, headlong he'll fly!"*

"How could it be? The doctors have been treating him and treating him —and then suddenly!"

"What doctors?"

"Our country doctor, and then the city doctor came too."

"Doctors!! If they had administered a proper cupping a month ago, he'd be fine now!"

"Is there really nothing that can be done?"

"I already said that God's mercy knows no limit, and there's nothing more I can add."

"But maybe it will work?"

"What will work?"

"These mustard plasters you're using now..."

"Maybe."

A woman in a black dress and black kerchief brought in a tray with a carafe of vodka and two plates with sausage and caviar. With her appearance conversation ceased. The doctor poured himself a glass, held it up to the light and clucked his tongue.

"Your health, mama!" he said, turning to the old mistress and downing the vodka.

"Your health, batyushka!"

"This is the very stuff which is causing Pavel Vladimirych's downfall in the prime of life, this vodka here!" said the doctor, wincing with pleasure and stabbing his fork into a round of sausage.

"Yes, a lot of people meet their doom through it."

"Not everyone can take this liquid—that's why! But since we can handle it, then we'll have another! Your health, madame!"

"Go ahead and eat! It won't bother you!"

"No, it won't! My lungs, kidneys, liver and spleen are all in order! Now then! Here's what I want you to do," he turned to the woman in the black dress who was lingering by the threshold as though listening in on the masters' conversation, "what have you made for dinner today?"

"Cold soup, cutlets, and roast chicken," replied the woman, with just a hint of a sour smile.

"Do you have any salt fish?"

"But of course we do, sir! There are several kinds of sturgeon... There's plenty of fish to be had!"

"Then tell them to make us a fish stew with sturgeon for dinner...with a

50

piece of it, understand, and the fatter the better! What's your name, Ulitush-ka or something?"

"People call me Ulita, sir."

"All right, be quick about it, Ulitushka!"

Ulitushka left. A heavy silence reigned for a moment. Arina Petrovna arose from her place and glanced out the door to make sure Ulitushka was gone.

"Did you talk to him about the orphans, Andrei Osipych?" she asked the doctor.

"I did."

"Well, what happened?"

"The same thing. He said that as soon as he gets better he'll write out his last will and testament."

An even heavier silence reigned in the room. The girls picked up their embroidery from the table and they began to make one stitch after the other with noticeably trembling hands. Arina Petrovna was sighing with something approaching despair. The doctor paced about the room whistling "Head over heels!.."

"You should have had a proper talk with him!"

"What more could I have said, I did tell him that he would be a scoundrel if he didn't make provision for the orphan girls. Yes, mama, you pulled a real boner there! If you had only called me a month ago I would have administered a cupping to him and I could have made a proper attempt over the will... But now everything will certainly go to little Judas, the legal heir!"

"Grandmother! What's going to happen," complained the older of the two girls in a voice bordering on tears, "what is this uncle doing to us?"

"I don't know, darling, I don't know. I don't even know about myself. I'm here today, but tomorrow I have no idea where I'll be... Perhaps it may be God's will that I'll be passing the night in some miserable barn or in some peasant's hut!"

"Lord! How stupid this uncle is!" exclaimed the younger of the girls.

"You, young lady, you had better put a rein on your tongue!" noted the doctor, adding as he turned to Arina Petrovna, "What about yourself, mama! You ought to try and persuade him yourself!"

"No, no, no! He won't have it! He doesn't even want to see me. The other day I was about to go in to him, and he said, 'Come to see me off or something'?"

"I think that all of this must be Ulitushka's doing...she's turned him against us."

"Yes! She's the one! And she reports everything to little Judas-blood-sucker! People say he keeps his horses harnessed all day long just in case his brother starts to fade! And just imagine, the other day she even made a list of the furniture, dishes and sundry effects, in case, she said, anything disappeared! She wants to make us out as thieves!"

"You should deal with her in the army fashion... Head over heels, you know, head over heels..."

But the doctor did not have the time to expand on his opinion when a maid came running into the room all flustered and cried in a frightened voice:

"Quick, the master! The master is calling for the doctor!"

* * *

The family which appears on stage in the present tale is already known to us. The old mistress is none other than Arina Petrovna Golovlyov; the dying owner of the Dubrovina estate is her son, Pavel Vladimirych; finally, the two girls, Anninka and Lyubinka, are the daughters of the deceased Anna Vladimirovna Ulanov, the very same person whom Arina Petrovna at one time had "tossed a sop." No more than ten years have passed since the time we last saw them, but the situations of the principal characters have changed so much that no trace remains of those artificial ties thanks to which the Golovlyov family represented something in the manner of an unassailable fortress. The family monolith, erected by the inexhaustible hands of Arina Petrovna, had disintegrated, but disintegrated so imperceptibly that without even under-standing herself how it had happened, she had become a party to and even prime mover in the disintegration, whose true inspiration had been, natural-ly, little Porfishka-the-bloodsucker.

From the unchecked and obstreperous mistress of the Golovlyov es-tates Arina Petrovna had turned into a modest dependent in the home of her younger son; she had become an idle dependent who had no voice whatsoever in the domestic affairs. Her head was no longer erect, her back was hunched, her eyes had grown dull, her walk was lifeless, the former impetuosity of movement had disappeared. For want of something to do she had taken up knitting in her old age, but she could not even manage the knitting because her mind was constantly wandering off somewhere—where?—she herself could not always make out, but in any event it was not on the knitting needles. She would sit and knit for a few minutes, and then suddenly her hands would sink of their own accord, her head would fall back on the chair, and she would begin to reminisce. She would reminisce, reminisce, until her entire elderly being would be overpowered by that slumber of old age. Or she would arise and begin to wander about the rooms, always in search of something, looking in everywhere, just like a woman who had held the keys all her life and could not comprehend where and how she had mislaid them.

The first blow to Arina Petrovna's despotism had been delivered not so much by the abolition of serfdom as by the preparations which had preceded abolition. At first the simple rumors, then the meetings of landowners with all their speeches, then the provincial committees, then the drafting commis-sions—all of this had been so exhausting and had sown much discord. Arina Petrovna's mind, and, moreover, her vivid imagination, had sketched out all kinds of nonsense to her. Suddenly it was a matter of the following kind of question: "What am I going to call Agashka? I suppose I'll have to say, dearest Agashka, or maybe even use her full name, Agafya Fyodorovna!" Then she would imagine that she was walking through the empty house and her servants were gathered in the servants' quarters and stuffing themselves with food! They would stuff themselves until they couldn't eat any more, and then they would throw the leftovers under the table! Then it would seem to her that she would take a peek into the cellar and there were her servants Yulka and Feshka stuffing and stuffing their cheeks! She wanted to reprimand them for stuffing themselves so! But she choked, "What can you say to them now! Now they're free, and you can't use the law against them!"

However insignificant all this nonsense was, nonetheless, it gave gradual rise to an entire fantastic reality which absorbed all of a person into it and completely paralysed his ability to act. It seemed as though Arina Petrovna suddenly dropped the reins of government from her hands, and in the course of the two years she did nothing but exclaim from morning till night:

"If only it were settled, one way or the other! But no! There's the first summons for discussion! Then there's the second summons! Neither heaven nor hell!"

At this time amid the dissolution of all the committees, Vladimir Mikhailych died. He died reconciled, at peace, having renounced the poet Barkov and all that business. His final words had been the following:

"I thank the Lord that He has not permitted me to appear before Him side by side with the serfs!"

These words had been deeply imprinted in Arina Petrovna's impressionable soul, and the death of her husband, together with the phantasmagoria of the future, suffused the entire Golovlyov way of life with an atmosphere of despair. It was as though the ancient Golovlyov house, together with its occupants, was about to die altogether.

From the various complaints spilling out of Arina Petrovna's letters, Porfiry Vladimirych surmised, with amazing perceptiveness, the confusion reigning in the plans of Arina Petrovna. No longer did Arina Petrovna admonish or proselytize in her letters, but more and more she put her trust in the help of God, "Who, in view of today's faint belief, does not abandon even the serfs, much less those who with their charity have been the most trustworthy support for the church and its greatest adornment." Little Judas instinctively understood that if his mama were beginning to put her trust in God, then this signified that a certain flaw was lurking in her being. Moreover, he took advantage of this flaw with his typically cunning dexterity.

Just before the very end to the business of emancipation, he paid an unexpected visit to Golovlyovo and found Arina Petrovna grieving, practically in torment.

"What's happening? How can it be? What are they saying in St. Petersburg?" These were her first questions on concluding their mutual greetings.

Porfisha sat silently with downcast eyes.

"No, you just imagine yourself in my position!" continued Arina Petrovna, comprehending from her son's silence that the worst was to be expected, "now I have thirty of those no-good hussies sitting in the maids' quarters—what am I supposed to do with them? If they stay here at my expense, how am I going to feed them? Right now I have a little cabbage, a few potatoes and some bread in sufficient quantity and we'll manage to keep ourselves going! If we run out of potatoes I'll have some cabbage boiled up; if there's no cabbage then I'll make do with pickles! But then I myself will have to run off to the market for everything and pay for everything with money, buy things and give it away—where am I going to provide for all of this crowd!"

Porfisha looked his dear mama right in the eye and smiled bitterly as a sign of sympathy.

"What if they let them loose in every direction: just run along, they'll say, and keep your wits about you!—Well, I just don't know. I don't! I just don't know what's going to become of all this!"

Porfisha grinned as though this "what's going to become of all this" seemed quite funny to him indeed.

"No, don't you laugh, my friend! This business is so serious, so serious that only the Lord can put some sense into them, and then maybe... Of myself I might say that after all I'm not some leftover, somehow or other I have to be taken care of too. What should I do? After all, what kind of upbringing have we had? Just dancing and singing and receiving guests—what am I going to do without those hussies of mine? I can't serve, I can't clean up, I can't cook for myself. You know, I just can't do anything for myself!"

"God is merciful, mama!"

"He was merciful, my friend, but not now! Merciful, yes, He was merciful, but according to a scale: when we were good the Lord rewarded us; but now we've become bad—well, you can't complain! What I'm thinking now is whether I should give everything up while there's still time. Really! I'll build myself a little hut near your papa's grave, and I'll manage to get along!"

Porfiry Vladimirych perked up his ears. Spittle appeared on his lips.

"But who would run the estates?" he objected cautiously, as though tossing out the bait.

"Don't be angry, but all of you can run them! Thanks be to God, I have scraped and saved! I shouldn't have to bear the whole burden alone..."

It was as though Arina Petrovna had suddenly taken a false step and she raised her head. Her eyes filled with the grinning, slavering face of little Judas, which seemed to be all covered with oil, all suffused with some kind of inner carnivorous reflection.

"You're not about to bury me yet!" she remarked drily, "Isn't it a bit early, dearie! Make no mistake!"

In this way the whole business ended in a stand-off the first time. But there are conversations which once they are begun cannot be terminated. Within a few hours Arina Petrovna had once again returned to the interrupted conversation.

"I'll go to the St. Sergius Monastery of the Holy Trinity," she daydreamed, "I'll divide up the estate, buy a little house nearby and spend the rest of my life there!"

But Porfiry Vladimirych, having learned from his earlier experience, kept silent this time.

"Last year when your dearly departed papa was still alive," Arina Petrovna continued to daydream, "I was sitting in my bedroom alone and suddenly I thought I heard something whispering to me: go to the miracle-worker, go to the miracle-worker, go to the miracle-worker!... and it was repeated three times! And so, you see, I turned around and there was no one there. But then I start thinking that after all I have just had a vision! Well then, I say, if my faith is pleasing to the Lord, then I am ready! And no sooner do I say this when suddenly there is such a sweet fragrance in the room! Such a sweet fragrance spilling forth! Naturally, I immediately had my things packed and I was already on the road by evening!"

Tears had even begun to well up in Arina Petrovna's eyes. Little Judas took advantage of the situation to kiss his mama's hand and then even took the liberty of putting his arm around her waist.

"You are such a wonderful person!" he said, "goodness, me! It's so wonderful if one can live in harmony with the Lord! If one prays to God then He will come to that person's aid. That's how it is, dear mama."

"Wait a minute! I haven't finished telling everything! The following evening I arrive at the church and I go directly to the saint. And there is an evening mass being performed: singing, candles burning, fragrance from the censers—and I can't tell where I am, on heaven or earth! I went from the mass to the father superior, Ion, and I say: 'My goodness, your reverence, it is beautiful beyond words in your church today!' And he says to me: 'That's because, Madame, Father Avvakum received a vision at the evening mass! He was just clasping his hands to pray when he looked and right up in the cupola there was a light and a dove was gazing down at him!'— From that time I made a decision, come what may, that I would spend the end of my life in the St. Sergius Monastery of the Holy Trinity!"

"But who will take care of us? Who will look out for your children? Alas, mama, mama!"

"Well, you're not children now and you can fend for yourselves! But I'm going off with Annushka's orphans to the miracle-worker and live out my days under his wing!"

This frivolous conversation continued for several days. Arina Petrovna, on a number of occasions, made the boldest propositions, retracted them and then issued them anew, but finally, things reached the point where there was no turning back. When barely half a year had elapsed since little Judas'

55

visit the state of affairs was as follows: Arina Petrovna neither departed for St. Sergius Monastery of the Holy Trinity nor settled in a little house beside her husband's grave, but divided the estate, retaining only the capital for herself. The result of the division was that Profiry Vladimirych received the better part whereas Pavel Vladimirych received the worst.

* * *

Arina Petrovna remained, as before, in Golovlyovo, and naturally the usual family farce was not to be avoided. Little Judas spilled tears and begged his kind friend, mama, to manage his estate as she saw fit, to take the income from the estate and invest it according to her own discretion, "...and I'll be satisfied with whatever you pass on to me from the income dearie, even be it a small amount." On the other hand, Pavel thanked his mother coldly ("just as though he wanted to bite me"), immediately resigned his commission ("He went ahead without his mother's blessing, like a person possessed, and ran off on his own!") and settled in Dubrovino.

A blindness settled on Arina Petrovna from this time on. That inner image of Porfishka-the-bloodsucker that she had once perceived with such rare insight, suddenly became shrouded in mist. Seemingly, she no longer understood anything other than the fact that she continued to live in Golovlyovo and still did not have to give an account of herself to anyone, all this despite the fact that emancipation had taken place and she had divided up the estate. Right there, close at hand, was living her other son, but what difference did it make! At a time when Porfisha entrusted himself and his family to his mama's discretion, Pavel not only did not consult with her, but even seemed to talk to her through his teeth whenever they met!

The more befogged her reason became, the more her heart seethed with zeal on behalf of her affectionate son. Porfiry Vladimirych demanded nothing of her, for she herself fulfilled all his desires. Little by little, she began to discover shortcomings in the boundaries of the Golovlyovo holdings. At such and such a place someone else's land cut into their property—it would be a good idea to buy up that land. In such and such a place one could set up a separate little farm, but there was not enough meadow land, yet close at hand there was some meadow land for sale—goodness, what a fine piece of meadow it was too! Arina Petrovna became over-enthusiastic in her role as mother, as well as landlady, wishing to show off all her abilities to her affectionate son. But Porfiry Vladimirych seemed to have encased himself within an impenetrable shell. In vain did Arina Petrovna tempt him with the purchases. To all her suggestions to purchase such and such a piece of woods, or such and such a meadow, he invariably replied: "Dearest friend, mama, I am satisfied with what you, in your kindness, have seen fit to give me."

These responses merely incited Arina Petrovna. Enthused on the one hand with her managerial responsibilities, on the other hand with her imagined polemics with that "scoundrel Pavlushka," who was living nearby and did not care to even acknowledge her, she completely lost all conception of her genuine relation to Golovlyovo. Her earlier fervor for acquisition possessed her entire being with renewed force, but now the purchases were made not for her own benefit, but for that of her favorite son. The Golovlyovo estate grew, expanded and flourished.

And lo, at that very moment when Arina Petrovna's capital had decreased to the point where it had become practically impossible to live off the interest deriving from it, little Judas forwarded to her, in a most respectful letter, an entire pile of bookkeeping forms which she must in the future make use of for her management in compiling the annual accounts. Here, side by side with the major items of the estate, stood: raspberries, gooseberries, mushrooms and so forth. For each account there was a specific compilation consisting of approximately the following:

> For 18—the total number of raspberry bushes 00
> Additional plants newly planted 00
> Berries collected from above mentioned
>   total . . . . . . 00 kilos 00 grams
>   Of this total amount:
> Used by you, dearest mama . . . . . 00 kilos 00 grams
> Used for the preparation of jam for the house of His
>   Excellency Porfiry Vladimirych . 00 kilos 00 grams
> Given to the lad X as a reward for good
>   behavior . . . . 00 kilos 00 grams
> Sold to the peasants for a special
>   treat . . . . . . 00 kilos 00 grams
> Spoiled for want of buyers and various other
>   reasons . . . . . 00 kilos 00 grams

NOTE: In the event that the harvest for the reported year is less than that of the previous year, then there must be appended the reasons why, such as drought, too much rain, hail, etc.

Arina Petrovna produced a deep groan. In the first place, she was struck by little Judas' miserliness: she had never even heard of gooseberries entering into the accounting of income in Golovlyovo, but apparently he was going to insist on it with even greater reason. Secondly, she understood quite well that all these forms were nothing less than a set of regulations binding her hand and foot.

The business terminated in an extended and argumentative correspondence. Insulted and unyielding, Arina Petrovna moved to Dubrovino, whereas Porfiry Vladimirych thereupon retired and settled in Golovlyovo.

From that time forth, for the old woman there began a series of somber days devoted to enforced idleness. As a man not given to action, Pavel Vladimirych was particularly fault-finding with his mother. He took her in willingly enough, that is, he took responsibility for feeding her and his orphaned nieces, but only on two conditions: firstly, she was not to come and see him on the upper floors, and secondly, she was not to interfere in the management of the household affairs. The latter condition upset Arina Petrovna particularly. Everything in Pavel Vladimirych's household was managed first of all by the keeper-of-the-keys, Ulitushka, that malicious woman who had been found out to be carrying on a secret correspondence with the bloodsucker, Porfishka; and secondly, the father's former valet, Kiryushka, who had no idea about agriculture whatsoever and daily lectured Pavel Vladimirych in an arrogant fashion. Both stole shamelessly. How many times had Arina Petrovna's heart ached to see the plundering that reigned in the house! How many times had she longed to warn him, to open her son's eyes about the tea, sugar and butter! All of these disappeared in enormous quantities, and Ulitushka repeatedly, in no way inhibited by the presence of the old mistress, would stuff whole handfuls of sugar into pockets before her very eyes. Arina Petrovna saw all of this and had to stand by as a silent witness to the pillaging. For all she had to do was barely open her mouth to point something out when Pavel Vladimirych would pounce on her immediately:

"Mama!" he would say, "there should only be one person managing the house! I'm not making it up, that's the way everyone does it. I know that my directions are stupid, but so be it! Your directions are clever, well, let them be clever! You're clever, even very clever, but all the same, little Judas left you without a place to rest your head!"

To top all of this off, Arina Petrovna made a terrifying discovery: Pavel Vladimirych drank. This passion had eaten away at him stealthily, thanks to the monotony of life in the country, and finally resulted in that frightening development which had to lead to the inevitable conclusion. At first, when the mother had settled in the house he had still exhibited some conscience. Fairly frequently he would come down from the upper floors and chat with his mother. Noting how his tongue got tangled up, Arina Petrovna had thought for a long while that this was a result of his stupidity. She did not care for it when he came "to have a chat," and she considered these conversations extremely oppressive. In fact, he was constantly coming out with absurd complaints. First it was because there had been no rain for weeks on end, then suddenly it was because there was such a downpour it seemed the heavens had caved in; or the beetles had taken over all the trees in the garden and stripped them; then the moles had torn up all the fields. All of this provided an inexhaustible source of complaints. He would come down from upstairs, sit down across from his mother and begin:

"The clouds are passing us by, is Golovlyovo that far? Yesterday the bloodsucker had a proper downpour! But we had nothing! Those clouds keep passing by and passing by, and hardly a drop on our land!"

Or: "What a downpour! The rye has just begun to bud, and wouldn't you know it, it starts pouring! Half the hay is already spoiled, and it keeps coming down! Is Golovlyovo that far! The bloodsucker has long since gathered in everything from the fields, and here we are just sitting and sitting! We'll have to feed the cattle rotten hay this winter!"

Arina Petrovna would just go on keeping her silence as she listened to these foolish words, but sometimes she could bear it no longer and would speak out: "You shouldn't be sitting there with your arms folded!"

She would barely get this out when Pavel Vladimirych would get furious.

"And just what would you order me to do? Send the rain over to Golovlyovo or something?"

"No, not that, but in general..."

"No, you just go ahead and say what you think I should do. Not 'in general,' but precisely... Should I change the climate for you? In Golovlyovo they needed some rain and they got it; if they don't need it, then there isn't any! And everything grows there too... But here everything's the opposite! We'll just see what you have to say when there's nothing to eat!"

"It must be God's will..."

"So now you're saying it must be God's will! That's the explanation you have for your 'in general'!"

Sometimes it went as far as Pavel Vladimirych feeling that his property was a burden to him.

"Why was I given only Dubrovino," he complained, "what's so special about it?"

"What's the matter with Dubrovino as an estate! The soil is good, there's plenty of everything... And what can you be thinking about?!"

"I'm thinking that nowadays there's no need whatsoever to own property! Money—that's the thing! You can take money, put it in your pocket and off you go with it! But property..."

"And why is this such a special time that people shouldn't have property?"

"It's a special time because you don't read the newspapers and I do. Nowadays the lawyers are going about everywhere, understand? If a lawyer finds out that you have property, he'll start hovering about!"

"Why is he going to hover around you if you have the proper documents?"

"He'll hover around just like the others. Or take the bloodsucker Porfishka, he'll hire a lawyer and the lawyer will send you one subpoena after another!"

"What are you talking about! I don't expect that this is a land without laws!"

59

"That's just the reason they'll send the subpoenas, because it's not a land without laws. An uncle of my friend Gorlopyatov died, and like a fool he accepted the inheritance! The inheritance turned out to be worth a kopeck and the debts amounted to a hundred thousand rubles—all in falsified promissory notes. This is the third year in a row they've been prosecuting him. At first they took away his uncle's estate, and then they sold his own at an auction! That's property for you!"

"Is there really a law like that?"

"If there wasn't, they wouldn't have sold it. To be sure, there's every kind of law. All laws are accessible to the person with no conscience; but the person with conscience will find all laws closed to him. Just go and find it in a book!"

Arina Petrovna always gave way in this arguments. More than once she was seized with a longing to scream: "Disappear from my sight, you scoundrel!" But she would think and think, and then remain silent. She would simply whisper to herself, "Lord! What kind of monsters have I given birth to! The one is a bloodsucker, the other some kind of innocent! What have I been scraping and saving for! I went without sleep at night, I didn't get enough to eat...and for whom?"

The more Pavel Vladimirych gave in to hard drinking, the more fantastic and the more, so to speak, abrupt, became his conversations. Finally Arina Petrovna began to notice that there was something wrong. For example, in the morning a full carafe of vodka would be in the cupboard in the dining room, but by dinner there would not be a single drop left. Or she would be sitting in the living room and she would hear a mysterious creaking coming from the dining room near the cherished cupboard. She would cry, "Who's there?" and she would hear someone's footsteps disappearing quickly but cautiously in the direction of upstairs.

"Heavens! Do you realize that he drinks?" she once asked Ulitushka.

"He is passing the time," she replied with a poisonous smile.

Convinced that his mother had seen through him, Pavel Vladimirych finally gave up standing on ceremony. One fine morning the cupboard disappeared completely from the dining room, and to Arina Petrovna's question as to where it had gone, Ulitushka replied, "He had it taken upstairs. He'll be able to pass the time more comfortably up there."

In fact, the carafes succeeded one another with amazing speed. Cut off by himself, Pavel Vladimirych came to loathe the company of living people, and he created for himself a special fantastic reality. This was a complete and stupidly heroic novel, with transformations, disappearances and sudden riches, a novel whose major protagonists were Pavel Vladimirych and Porfishka-the-bloodsucker. Not even he himself was completely aware of how deeply embedded in himself his hatred for Porfishka was. He detested him with all his thoughts, with every fiber of his being, he detested him unremittingly, every minute of the day. The vile image would pass before his eyes as though alive, and in his ears resounded the whimpering, hypocritical prattling of little Judas, a prattling wherein echoed a kind of dry, almost distant malice for every living thing that did not submit to the set of rules created by a long history of hypocrisy. Pavel Vladimirych drank and reminisced. He recalled all the insults and humiliations he had had to bear due to little Judas's pretensions to being the head of the house. In particular, however, he recalled the divisions of the estate, he totaled up every kopeck, compared every clod of earth and—detested him. In his imagination, fired by alcohol, entire dramas were created in which all manner of wrongs figured and in which he, Pavel, now appeared as the perpetrator, and not little Judas. First he pretended that he had won two hundred thousand rubles and had gone to inform Porfishka about it (there would be an entire scene with dialogues), and Porfishka's face would be all distorted with envy. Then he would pretend that a grandfather had died (again a scene with dialogues although there was no such grandfather at all), and had left him a million rubles, whereas Porfishka had gotten nothing. Then he would pretend that he had gained the means of becoming invisible, and therefore was able to inflict such filthy tricks on Porfishka that he would begin to wail. He was inexhaustible in making up these tricks, and an inane laughter would deafen the upstairs for a long period, to the pleasure of Ulitushka, hastening to inform the brother Porfiry Vladimirych about the goings-on.

He detested little Judas and at the same time he was afraid of him. He knew that little Judas' eyes oozed an enchanting poison, that his voice, serpent-like, would creep into your soul and paralyze a person's will. Consequently, he steadfastly refused to meet him. Sometimes the bloodsucker would come to Dubrovino to kiss his dear mama's hand (he had driven her out of the house, but had not curtailed his display of respect), then Pavel Vladimirych would lock the upstairs with a key and sit the whole time behind a locked door while little Judas chatted with mama.

The days passed by in this fashion until finally Pavel Vladimirych woke up to find himself face to face with a fatal illness.

* * *

The doctor spent the night "for appearances' sake" and early the following day left for the city. On leaving Dubrovino he said straight out that the invalid had no more than two days to live, and that it was too late now to think about any "arrangements," because he was incapable even of writing his name correctly.

"He'll just sign 'scribbles' for you, and then you'll never make it past the lawcourts," he added, "you know that even though little Judas has a great deal of respect for his mother, he'll nonetheless start an inquiry into forgery and if they send his nice mama off to parts not so distant, he'll simply have a mass sung to accompany her on her way!"

61

Arina Petrovna walked around the whole morning as though in a fog. She attempted to pray—would God not tell her what to do?—but no prayer came to mind, even her tongue seemed paralyzed. She would begin: "Have mercy on me, Lord, according to Thy great mercy," and suddenly without knowing how she would end up with "Deliver me from the evil one." "Cleanse me! Cleanse me!"—her tongue babbled mechanically, and her mind would lose track of everything. First she would take a peek upstairs, then she would go down into the cellar ("What a lot of good things there had been in the autumn—and they've filched it all!"), then she would begin to recollect something, far, far away. Everything seemed somehow shadowy, and there were people in these shadows, a lot of people, and they were all bestirring themselves, striving, scrimping and saving. *Blessed is the man... blessed is the man... like incense... teach me... teach me...* But here her tongue would gradually relax, her eyes would gaze at the ikons without seeing them. Her mouth was wide open, her arms folded at her waist, and she would stand completely motionless, as though frozen.

Finally she sat down and began to weep. The tears poured so from those bedimmed eyes along the ancient withered cheeks, collecting in the furrows of wrinkles and dripping on the soiled collar of her old cotton blouse. There was something bitter, full of despair, and at the same time impotently stubborn in all of this. Old age and weakness and the helplessness of the situation—all this, it seemed, beckoned her to death as to the only consoling exit, yet at the same time her past intruded with its despotism, self-sufficiency and freedom, and the recollections of this past seemed to take hold of her so firmly and drag her down to the ground. "If only I could die!" flashed through her head, but in an instant the same words were replaced by others: "Only to live!" She thought neither about little Judas nor her dying son, it was as though both had ceased to exist for her. She thought of no one, accused no one, complained about no one; she even forgot whether she had capital and whether it was sufficient to take care of her in her old age. Her entire being was gripped by anguish, a mortal anguish. She felt sick! She felt bitter! This was the sole explanation she could have given for her tears. These tears came from afar; drop after drop they had been stored up from the very moment when she had departed from Golovlyovo and settled in Dubrovino. She was prepared for everything that lay before her now, she had been expecting it and had foreseen it all, but somehow she had never imagined with such clarity that the end would come to what she had anticipated and foreseen. And now this end was at hand, an end that was filled with anguish and hopeless loneliness. All her life she had been organizing things, she had wasted herself on something, and now it turned out that she had wasted herself over a spectre. All her life the word "family" had not disappeared from her lips. In the name of the family she had punished some and rewarded others. In the name of the family she had subjected herself to deprivations, she had tormented herself, she had deformed her entire life—and suddenly it turned out that she had no family at all!

"Lord! Is it really the same for everybody!" the thought kept whirling about in her head.

She sat there with her head resting on her hand with her tear-stained face turned to the rising sun as though saying to it: "You see!" She did not complain, nor did she curse, but merely sobbed quietly as though choking on her tears. At the same time her heart grieved:

"There is no one! No one! No one! No one! No one!"
But then her tears dried. Washing her face she wandered about aimlessly in the dining room, but here she was besieged by the girls with fresh complaints which seemed particularly importunate this time.

"What's going to happen, grandmother! Will we really be left with nothing?" Anninka lamented.

"What a stupid uncle he is!" Lyubinka seconded her.

Around midday Arina Petrovna resolved to gain entry to her dying son. Carefully, hardly making a sound with her feet, she mounted the staircase and felt around in the darkness for the doors leading to his rooms. The upstairs were enveloped in shadow; the windows had been curtained with green blinds through which the light barely penetrated. The stale air in the rooms was saturated with a repulsive mixture of diverse odors consisting of berries, compresses, icon-lamp oil, and those particular evil smells whose presence spoke of sickness and death. There were two rooms altogether. In the first sat Ulitushka sorting berries and viciously waving at the flies which were hovering in a noisy throng over the piles of gooseberries and impudently settling on her nose and lips. Through the half-opened door of the neighboring room came an incessant, dry, hesitant cough which was occasionally interrupted by painful expectoration. Arina Petrovna stopped undecidedly, peering into the shadows as though waiting to see how Ulitushka would react to her appearance. But Ulitushka did not even budge as though she were quite certain that any attempt to influence the patient would meet with failure. An angry expression merely flitted over her lips and Arina Petrovna thought she heard the word "devil" pronounced in a whisper.

"Would you go downstairs, dearie!" Arina Petrovna turned to Ulitushka.

"That's a good one!" snapped Ulitushka.

"Pavel Vladimirych and I have to talk. Off you go!"

"Mercy me, madame, how can I leave him here? What if something suddenly happened, there would be no one to fetch something or clean up."

"What's going on there?" came the hollow sound from the bedroom.

"Tell Ulitushka to leave, my friend. I have to talk to you about something."

Arina Petrovna acted with such insistence this time that she gained the victory. She crossed herself and entered the room. By the inside wall furthest from the windows, stood the bed of the patient. He was lying on his back, was covered with a white blanket and almost unconsciously puffing on a cigarette. Despite the tobacco smoke, the flies were besieging him so cruelly that he was waving first the one and then the other hand uninterruptedly around his face. His arms were feeble and emaciated and were of almost identical narrowness from the hand to the shoulder. His head seemed to cling hopelessly to the pillow, his face and his entire body burned in a dry fever. His large, round eyes were deeply sunken and roamed about aimlessly as though searching for something. His nose had become elongated and pinched, his mouth half-open. He did not cough but breathed so forcibly that it seemed as though all his vital energy was concentrated in his chest.

"Well, then, how are you feeling today?" asked Arina Petrovna, sinking into a chair at his feet.

"All right... tomorrow... I mean today... when did I have that medicine?"

"You had the medicine today."

"Well, that means, tomorrow..."

The patient began to toss and turn as though making an effort to remember the word.

"You'll be able to get up?" Arina Petrovna suggested, "God willing, my friend, God willing!"

Both fell silent for a moment. Arina Petrovna wanted to say something, but in order to do so she would have to strike up a conversation first. This was precisely what she had always found so difficult to do when she found herself face to face with Pavel Vladimirych.

"Is little Judas...alive?" the patient himself finally asked.

"What could be wrong with him! He's getting along just fine."

"I expect he's thinking: my little brother's going to die and with God's help I'll end up with his estate as well!"

"We're all going to die sometime and the estates will go to the legal heirs."

"But not to the bloodsucker. I'll throw mine to the dogs before I let him have it!"

An excellent opportunity had emerged: Pavel Vladimirych himself had broached the topic. Arina Petrovna did not linger in taking advantage of the situation.

"You should be thinking about it, my friend!" she said almost as though in passing, without looking at her son and just examining her hands against the light as though they comprised the principal object of her attention at that moment.

"What do you mean 'about it'?"

"About what you'll do if you don't want your estate to go to your brother..."

The patient was silent. Only his eyes widened unnaturally and his face grew redder and redder.

"Perhaps, my friend, you might take into consideration that you have some orphaned nieces—what means have they got? And your mother as well..." continued Arina Petrovna.

"Didn't you manage to leave everything to little Judas?"

"Whatever happened... I know that I have myself to blame... After all, not even God knows was trespasses... I too thought that my son... And you don't have to remind your mother about this."

Silence.

"Come now, say at least something!"

"Are you getting ready to bury me so soon?"

"Not bury you, but all the same... Other Christians do it... Not everybody's going to die right now, but in general..."

"There it is, that 'in general'! You're always saying 'in general'! Do you think I can't see!"

"What do you see, my friend?"

"I can see that you take me for a fool! Just suppose that I am a fool, well then let me be a fool! Why are you coming to a fool? Don't bother coming and don't pester me!"

"I'm not pestering you. In general I just wanted to say... That every man's life is fated to end..."

"Well, then, you can just wait!"

Arina Petrovna bowed her head and pondered. She could see well enough that her business was not going well, but the hopelessness of the future tormented her to such a point that even the obviousness of the situation could not convince her of the futility of further attempts.

"I don't know why you hate me!" she uttered at last.

"Not at all... I don't... not at all! I even... Mercy! You raised us all in such a way..."

He said this impetuously, choking. In the sound of his voice could be distinguished a strained and simultaneously triumphant laughter. Sparks appeared in his eyes; his shoulders and legs were trembling nervously.

"Perhaps, in fact, I was guilty in some way, if so, then forgive me now, for Christ's sake!"

Arina Petrovna arose and bowed down, touching the floor with her hand. Pavel Vladimirych closed his eyes and did not answer.

"Let us suppose that as far as the land is concerned... For sure in your present condition there's nothing to think about as far as making arrangements is concerned... Porfiry is the legal heir, well let the land go to him... However, the movable property and the capital, what about them?" Arina Petrovna resolved to come to the point directly.

Pavel Vladimirych shuddered but remained silent. Quite possibly at the mention of the word "capital" he was not considering the insinuations of Arina Petrovna, but simply: here it was September outside, it was time to receive the interest... sixty-seven thousand and six hundred multiplied by five and then divided by two—how much would that be?

"Perhaps you're thinking that I'm hoping for your death, if so, don't believe it, my friend! You just go on living and I won't have to suffer any sorrow, old woman that I am! What do I need! I'm warm and well fed in your house and even if I feel like something extra special, I have everything! I'm only saying this because it is a Christian custom that in expectation of the future life..."

Arina Petrovna halted as though seeking the appropriate words.

"To take care of one's own people," she concluded, looking out the window.

Pavel Vladimirych lay motionless and coughed quietly, not indicating with a single movement whether he had heard or not. Apparently he was fed up with the moral lessons of his mother.

"Capital can be transferred from hand to hand while one is alive," Arina Petrovna began, as though casually throwing out the suggestion and once again began to examine her hands against the light.

The patient shuddered ever so gently, but Arina Petrovna did not notice and continued:

"Capital, my friend, can be legally transferred as far as the law is concerned. Thus it is an acquirable item: it was there yesterday, today— it's gone. And no one can ask for an account of it. Whomever I wish to give it to, I can do so."

Pavel Vladimirych suddenly burst out in what seemed malicious laughter.

"You should remember the business with Palochkin," he hissed, "he too passed the capital 'from hand to hand' to his wife and she ran off with her lover!"

"My friend, I don't have any lovers!"

"Then you'll run off without a lover and take the capital!"

"You don't understand what I'm saying!"

"I don't understand you in the least... You spread the word through the entire world that I was a fool, well, that's just what I am! And let me be a fool! Just look at the fast one you've thought up—take the capital out of their hands and give it away! And what am I suppose to do, would you have me go off to a monastery to save my soul and watch from there how you'll manage my capital?"

All of this he fired off in a single volley, maliciously and angrily, and then collapsed completely. For at least four hours afterwards he coughed with all his might so that it was even amazing that this pitiful human skeleton still contained so much strength. Finally he caught his breath and closed his eyes.

Arina Petrovna was looking all about distractedly. Up until now she had continued to have some kind of belief, but now she was finally convinced that any fresh attempt to convince the dying man could only hasten the day of little Judas' triumph. Little Judas flashed before her eyes. There he was walking after the coffin, now he was giving his brother the final kiss of Judas and two vile little tears oozed out of his eyes. Then the coffin was being lowered into the earth: "Farewell-l-l, brother!" Little Judas exclaimed, his lips twitching, his eyes rolling heavenward, and attempting to give his voice a tone of anguish and then immediately afterwards half-turning to Ulitushka and saying: "Now don't you forget to take the funeral rice-pudding home with you! And put it on a nice clean tablecloth... we'll pay our respects to my brother at home again! Then the funeral supper came to an end as well during which little Judas spoke tirelessly with the priest about the virtues of the deceased and received complete confirmation of his praises from the priest. "Alas, brother! brother! You did not care to remain with us!" he exclaimed, emerging from behind the table and extending his hand out, palm downward, for a plessing from the priest. Then, finally, praise be to God, everyone had eaten his fill and even had his sleep after dinner. Little Judas made the proprietary rounds of the rooms of the house, noted various things and entered them into the inventory, and from time to time would glance suspiciously at his mother if he experienced doubt about something.

All of these inevitable scenes of the future flashed before Arina Petrovna's eyes. And as though alive, the oily and penetrating voice of little Judas addressing her rang in her ears:

"Do you recall, mama, that my brother had some gold cuff links...such pretty ones they were, he used to wear them on holidays... now wherever did those cuff links go... I can't even imagine!"

* * *

Arina Petrovna did not even manage to go downstairs before a carriage drawn by four horses appeared on the hill by the Dubrovino church. In the rear seat of the carriage, sat Porfiry Golovlyov, hatless, and making the sign of the cross at the church. Opposite him sat his two sons, Petenka and Volodenka. Arina Petrovna's heart began to pound furiously: "The old fox has caught the smell of death!" she thought to herself. The young girls lost their courage as well and huddled helpless around their grandmother. In the house, which had up until now been quiet, there arose a great furor. Doors were banged, people started to run, cries resounded: "The master is coming! The master is coming!" and the entire population of the house spilled out onto the veranda. Some were crossing themselves, others were simply standing there in an expectant attitude, but everyone was apparently aware of the fact that what had been going on in Dubrovino up until the present time was merely temporary, that only now would the true, genuine state of affairs commence with the real master at the head. Many of the old house servants had been given a monthly allowance under the "former" master. Many maintained their cattle on the master's hay, owned gardens and in general lived "freely", Naturally everyone was interested in the question as to whether the "new" master would let the old customs rest or replace them with new ones from the Golovlyovo estate.

Meanwhile little Judas had arrived and concluded from the greeting accorded him that things were approaching an end in Dubrovino. Taking his time he descended from the carriage, brushed aside the house servants who had come rushing up to kiss the master's hand, then folded his hands piously and slowly began to pick his way up the stairs uttering a prayer in a whisper. His face bore simultaneously an expression of grief and firm submission. As a person he was grief-stricken; as a Christian he did not dare to complain. He was praying for "heavenly intervention," but most of all he put his trust in and submitted to the will of Providence. His sons followed after him in a pair. Volodenka was mimicking his father, that is, he folded his hands together, rolled his eyes upward and moved his lips; Petenka was enjoying the performance given by his brother. A cortege of the house servants followed after them in a silent crowd.

Little Judas kissed his mama's hand, then her lips, then her hand once again; then he put his arm around his dear friend's waist and uttered, as he shook his head sadly:

"You are all disheartened! It's not good, my friend! Alas, it's not good! You should ask yourself what God would say to this? —He would say: 'In my wisdom I arrange all things for the best, yet she complains!' Alas, mama, mama!"

Then he exchanged kisses with both of his nieces and with that same captivating air of kinship in his voice he said:

"As for you, you little magpies, why all these tears! I don't care for it at all! Now you just go ahead and smile and have done with it!"

He stamped his feet at them, or more accurately, he pretended to stamp, but really was joking affably.

"Take a look at me!" he continued, "as his brother I am grieving! Perhaps I have shed a tear more than once... I feel sorry for my brother, even to the point of tears... So you burst into tears, but then you come to your senses: what is God for! Surely God knows better than we the whys and wherefores? If you think about it in this fashion, you'll cheer up. That's the way everyone should act! You too, mama, and you, my little nieces, you too... and everyone!" he turned to a servant. "Take a look at me, the way I'm going about like a fine fellow!"

With the same fascination he showed the "fine fellow" in himself, that is, he straightened up, put one foot forward, puffed out his chest and tossed his head back. Everyone smiled, but with a kind of bitterness as though everyone was saying to himself: "Now the spider is off spinning his web!"

Finishing the performance in the reception room, little Judas proceeded to the dining room and kissed his mama's hand once again.

"Now, now, dear friend, mama!" he said, sitting down on the couch, "and now it's brother Pavel too..."

"Yes, Pavel too..." responded Arina Petrovna softly.

"My, my...and rather early at that! Very early! After all, mama, although I'm being cheerful, in my heart I too...am grieving deeply, yes deeply, over my brother! My brother didn't love me, most definitely he did not, perhaps that's the reason God sent him this affliction!"

"At times like these you should forget about that! Old differences should be set aside..."

"Mama, I have long since forgotten about them! I was merely saying that my brother didn't love me, and for what reason I don't know! I think I tried everything...directly and indirectly, I said 'buddy' and 'dear brother'—but he would back off from me and that was that! And God decided to time things on His own schedule!"

"I'm telling you not to talk about such things! The man is on his last legs!"

"Yes, mama, it's a great mystery, death is! You never know the hour or the day, that's the kind of mystery it is! Here's a person making plans, thinking away how high, yes, how high he stands, that he's beyond the reach of anything, and then all at once, in a single instant, God upsets all his illusions. He could, if he wishes, because of our sins, foreclose on us, mark my word, those sins are inscribed in the Book of Life. And, mama, you can't erase quickly from this Book what's been written there!"

"I expect that repentance will still be accepted!"

"I hope so! With all my heart I do hope so, for my brother's sake! He didn't love me, but I hope so for him! I wish good for everyone! Both the ones who hate and do wrong—for everyone! He was unjust to me, that's why God visited this illness on him, God and not me! Mama, is he suffering a great deal?"

"So-so... It's not too bad. The doctor was here, he even held out some hope," Arina Petrovna lied.

"Well, that's good then! It's all right, my friend! Don't upset yourself! Maybe he'll get his second wind! Here we are distressed over him and complaining of our Maker, while he may be sitting up nice and quiet in his bed and thanking God for healing him!"

Little Judas was so pleased with this idea that he even giggled softly.

"Mama, you see I've come to visit with you for a while," he went on, as though disclosing a pleasant surprise to his mama, "there's nothing for it, dearie...for the sake of the family! Anything can happen...my brother, you know...I should console and advise and take care of things...you'll permit me, won't you?"

"What permission can I give! I'm a guest here myself!"

"Well, then this is what we'll do, dearie. Since today is Friday, if you're agreeable, have a little Lenten fare prepared for dinner. Some nice salted fish, mushrooms, cabbage—you know I don't require much! Meanwhile, like a

69

good family man...I'll just skip upstairs to see my brother. Maybe I'll still be in time. I'll do something beneficial for his soul rather than his body. In his situation, if you please, the soul is more important. Mama, we can set the body right with potions and poultices, but a more essential medicine is required for the soul."

Arina Petrovna did not object. The thought of the inevitability of the "end" gripped her entire being to such a degree that she heard and looked upon everything transpiring around her in a kind of daze. She watched little Judas arising from the couch with a groan, hunching himself over and dragging his feet (he loved to feign weakness once in a while: it seemed to him to be more respectable). She thought that the sudden appearance of the bloodsucker upstairs would profoundly upset the patient and maybe even hasten the denouement; but in the aftermath of that day's agitation she was overcome with such a fatigue that she felt as though she were in a dream.

While this was going on, Pavel Vladimirych found himself in an indescribable state of trepidation. He lay upstairs quite alone and at the same time heard the unusual commotion in the house. Each slamming of the doors, every step in the corridor had a mysterious ring to it. For a while he called with all his might, but finally convinced that his shouts were of no avail, he gathered all his strength, raised himself up in bed and began to listen carefully. After the general running back and forth, after the noisy sound of voices a deadly silence suddenly descended. Something unknown and terrifying began to encroach on him from all sides. Through the lowered curtains the light was penetrating into the room in such a miserly fashion, and with the ikon-lamp burning in the corner before the ikon, the shadows filling the room seemed even darker and thicker. He stared into that mysterious corner as though for the first time he was struck by something in that profoundness. The ikon in its gilded frame with the lamp's rays reflecting directly off it, loomed up out of the darkness with an amazing clarity as though it were something alive. On the ceiling a flickering circle undulated, flaring up and then fading in time to the waxing and waning of the flame in the lamp. A semi-darkness reigned close to the floor and against this backdrop shadows were flickering. On the same wall, near the illuminated corner, hung a housecoat, over which bands of light and darkness trembled, making it seem as if the coat were moving. Pavel Vladimirych peered and peered and he imagined that over there, in that corner, everything had suddenly been put in motion. Isolation, helplessness, the deathly silence—and in the midst of all this gloom a whole throng of shadows. It seemed to him that these shadows were coming nearer and nearer and nearer... In indescribable terror, his eyes bulging and his mouth agape, he peered into the mysterious corner and could not cry out, only moan. His moaning was deep and broken, just like howling. He did not hear the creaking of the stairs, nor the cautious shuffling of footsteps in the outer room and then suddenly beside his bed the odious figure of little Judas loomed up. He imagined that little Judas had issued forth from there, from out of the gloom which had just been stirring so mysteriously before his eyes. And he imagined that there were still more and more shadows, shadows, shadows without end! Drawing nearer and nearer...

"What? Where did you come from? Who let you in?" he cried instinctively as he fell back on his pillow.

Little Judas stood beside the bed, peering at the patient and shaking his head grievously.

"Does it hurt much?" he asked, giving his voice that tone of unctiousness which was in his power alone to express.

Pavel Vladimirych was silent and with uncomprehending eyes he was staring at him as though attempting to understand. Meanwhile, little Judas had gone up to the ikon, bowed down on his knees, said a prayer, performed three bows to the earth, arisen and once again appeared beside the bed.

"Now, brother, arise! God has sent His mercy!" he said, sitting down in a chair, his tone as joyous as if "mercy" were in actual fact in his pocket.

Pavel Vladimirych finally understood that this was not a shadow before him, but the bloodsucker in the flesh. He suddenly seemed to shrink into himself, as though overcome with a fever. Little Judas' eyes had a bright look in them, a brotherly look, but the patient saw full well that a "noose" was lurking in those eyes which was about to leap out and seize him by the throat.

"Goodness me, brother, brother! A fine one you've become!" little Judas continued to jest in brotherly fashion. "Now you just cheer up! Get up and slap your heels! Huppety-huppety—let mama see what a fine fellow you are! Come now, you can do it!"

"Get away from me, bloodsucker!" the patient cried in despair.

"My, my, my! Brother! Brother! Here I am being nice to you and consoling you, and what do you do... the way you talk! My, my, my, what a sin! You are defiling your own mouth talking to your own brother that way! Shameful, dear boy, very shameful! Just let me puff up your pillow for you!"

Little Judas got up and poked the pillow with a single finger.

"There you go!" he continued, "that's just marvellous now! You just lie there nice and quiet—you can wait till tomorrow to get better."

"Go away...you!"

"Goodness, how you've become spoiled by illness! Even your character has become so contrary! Nothing but 'go away' and more 'go away'—now how can I go away! If you feel like having a drink, I'll give you a little water. If the ikon lamp isn't working right, I'll fix the lamp. I'll add a little olive oil to it. You just lie there and I'll sit awhile, nice and calm and quiet—and we'll just see how the time passes!"

"Go away, bloodsucker!"

"There you are cursing me and I'm praying to God for you. But then I know that you're not responsible, it's the sickness that's talking. My brother,

71

I've gotten used to forgiving, I forgive everyone. Just today I was on my way to you and I met a peasant on the road and he said something. My goodness! Well, Christ be with him! He defiled his own tongue! Whereas I... not only did I not lose my temper, but I even made the sign of the cross over him—truly!"

"Did you rob the peasant?"

"Who? Me! No, my friend, I don't rob; it's the thieves on the highways that rob, I act in accordance with the law. I caught his horse in my field, well, let's go to the judge, old chum, I said! If the judge says that it is allowed to graze on other people's fields, then so be it! But if he says that it is not allowed, there's nothing else to be done! You'll have to pay a fine! Yes, sir, I always act in accordance with the law, only with the law!"

"Judas! Betrayer! You kicked your own mother out!"

"And again I say: words of truth are never spoken in a fit of anger! If I weren't a Christian I could also hold this against you!"

"You kicked her out, yes you did, you kicked your own mother out!"

"Now, just stop that, you hear! I'll pray to God, perhaps you'll feel more at rest..."

Despite restraining himself, little Judas was so stung to the quick by the curses of the dying man that even his lips grew twisted and pale. Nonetheless, hypocrisy was such an innate feature of his character that he could not break off the farce once he had started it. With his final words he actually got down on his knees and for fifteen minutes he raised his hands in prayer and whispered. Having completed this, he turned to the dying man's bed, and his face was calm, almost radiant.

"You know, brother, that I have come to have a chat with you," he said, sitting down in the chair, "here you are admonishing me, whereas I'm thinking about your soul. Tell me, please, when was the last time you took the sacrament?"

"Lord! Why all of this...take him away! Ulitka! Agashka! Who's here?" moaned the patient.

"Now, now! Just calm down, old chum! I know that you don't care to talk about this! Yes, brother, you were always a bad Christian and you've stayed the same even now! It wouldn't be a bad idea, no, it wouldn't, to give some thought to your soul in the present moment. After all, our soul...alas, how careful one has to treat it, my brother! What does the church prescribe for us? It says, bring your prayers and thanks... Moreover, a Christian end to our life that is painless and without shame, and peaceful, that's what, my friend! You should send for the priest now, yes, quite frankly, with remorse... Now, now! I won't do it, no, I won't But truly you ought to..."

Pavel Vladimirych lay there all crimson and barely breathing. If he could have smashed his head at that moment, he undoubtedly would have done so.

"Now, about the estate, perhaps you have already made arrangements?"

continued little Judas. "You have a very nice little estate, yes, very nice, there's no denying it. The soil is even better than in Golovlyovo, a nice sandy loam! And your capital...of course, brother I know nothing about that. I only know that you let the peasants purchase their own land, and as far as the details were concerned, I never took any interest. But then today, as I was on my way here, I said to myself: brother Pavel must have some capital, so he probably has made some arrangements for it."

The patient turned away and sighed deeply.

"You didn't? Well, then, so much the better, my friend! According to the law, this is even more in the interests of justice. After all, it should go to one's own people and not to strangers. Here I am already so frail myself, with one foot in the grave! But still I think to myself why should I make arrangements when the law can do so for me. And you know how good that is, old chum! No arrangements, no jealousy, no intrigues...just the law!"

It was terrible. Pavel Vladimirych imagined that he was being buried alive in his coffin, that he was lying there as though chained, in a lethargic sleep, not able to move a single limb of his body and listening to the bloodsucker speaking abuse over his body.

"Go away... for Christ's sake... go away!" he finally began to beseech his tormentor.

"Now, now! Calm yourself! I'm going! I know that you don't love me... shameful, my friend, very shameful not to love your very own brother! And I love you so much! I always say to the children: even if my brother Pavel is guilty before me, nonetheless, I still love him! So, it means that you haven't made any arrangements—that's marvellous, my friend! Incidentally, there are cases when the capital disappears while one is alive, especially if a person has no relatives, if he is alone... but I'll keep an eye out... What's that? Am I boring you? Now, now, so be it, I'm going! Just let me pray to God!"

He stood up, folded his hands and hastily intoned:

"Farewell, friend! Do not be alarmed! Have yourself a nice little nap, may God help you! And mama and I will talk and chat, perhaps we'll think of something! My brother, I have asked for some lenten fare to be prepared for dinner... salt fish, mushrooms and cabbage—so please forgive me! What's that? Am I boring you again? Goodness me, brother, brother!.. Now, now, I'm going, I'm going! The main thing, my friend, is not to excite yourself, to get upset, just have a nice little sleep! Snore away, sno-re-re away..." he teased him by way of conclusion, and decided to leave.

"Bloodsucker!" the piercing cry echoed after him so that even he felt as though he had been scorched.

* * *

While Porfiry Vladimirych was chattering away upstairs, down below grandmother Arina Petrovna had gathered the young people around herself (with the purpose of finding something out) and was talking with them.

"Well, what about you?" she said turning to her oldest grandson, Petenka.

"Alright, grandmother, next year I'll be getting my commission in the army."

"You will? What year are you promising to do that! Are your examinations that difficult—God alone knows what you're doing!"

"Grandmother, he flunked his final examinations on the 'Catechism'. The priest asked him what is God? And he answered that God is a spirit and there is the spirit... and the Holy Spirit..."

"Alas, you poor fellow, you! How could you do that? These two here are orphans and even they know the answer!"

"Moreover, God is a spirit, invisible..." Anninka hastened to shine with her knowledge.

"But no one has ever seen Him at any time or any place." Lyubinka interrupted.

"Omniscient, all-merciful, omnipotent, omnipresent," continued Anninka.

"Whither shall I go from thy spirit? or whither shall I flee from thy presence? If I ascend up into heaven, Thou are there: if I make my bed in hell, behold Thou are there."

"That's the way you should have answered and you'd have your officer's epaulettes now. What about you, Volodya, what have you got in mind for yourself?"

Volodya grew crimson and was silent.

"It looks like the same thing... 'to the Holy Spirit' and so on! Alas, children, children! To look at, you're so bright, but you can't cope with learning. It's not as though your father spoiled you... how does he treat you?"

"The same, grandmother."

"Still whipping you? I heard that he had given up beatings?"

"He does it less often, but still... The main thing is that he pesters us a great deal."

"Now that's something I can't understand. How can he be pestering you?"

"He pesters us a lot. You can't go out without asking his permission, you can't take anything... quite wretched it is!"

"But you ought to ask! I don't imagine your tougue would wither away!"

"Nothing of the sort! You just start talking to him and then he won't stop. Up and down and all around...grandmother, he's so boring when he goes on talking!"

"He eavesdrops on us behind the door, grandmother. Just the other day Petenka found him doing it..."

"Oh, you little tricksters you! And what did he do?"

74

"Nothing. I said to him, 'It's not nice, papa, to eavesdrop behind doors, if you're not careful, you'll get your nose smashed!' But he just poo-pooed and said it was nothing because, he said, 'I'm like a thief in the night!' "

"Grandmother, the other day he picked up an apple in the garden and put it in his desk, but I took it and ate it. So he began to search for it, he demanded everyone be interrogated..."

"What's this! Has he become that miserly?"

"No, it's not that he's miserly, just that he seems to be taken up with triviality all the time. He hides bits of paper and looks for anything he can lay his hands on..."

"Every morning he says his prayers in his study, and then he gives us each a piece of the communion bread... you wouldn't believe how stale it is! But once we played a joke on him. We watched to see where he kept the communion bread, then we cut the bottom out of the bread, removed the soft part and filled it with melted butter and put it back!.."

"But what little thugs you are!"

"No, you just imagine to yourself his amazement the next day! The communion bread with butter inside of it!"

"I expect you caught it then!"

"It was nothing... But the whole day he kept spitting and kept saying to himself: 'The troublemakers!' Naturally we denied everything. But he is afraid of you, grandmother!"

"Why should he be afraid of me... I can't imagine why!"

"He is—that's for certain. He thinks that you'll put a curse on him. He fears curses worse than death itself!"

Arina Petrovna pondered. At first she was struck by the thought: "What if, in fact, I do curse him? I'll just go ahead and curse him... 'I cur-r-rse you!!' " Then another thought replaced this one, a more essential question: "What is little Judas doing? What tricks is he up to upstairs? I suppose he's up to something!" Finally she was struck by a clever thought.

"Volodya," she said, "sweetie, you're light on your feet! Would you go nice and quiet and listen to what they're doing *there?*"

"With pleasure, grandmother."

Volodenka made off towards the doorway on his toes and disappeared through it.

"How was it you picked on today to visit us?" Arina Petrovna started to question Petenka.

"We had been intending to do so for a long time, grandmother, and then today Ulitushka sent an urgent message that the doctor had been and that uncle was sure to die either today or tomorrow at the latest."

"Well, and what about the inheritance... did you talk about that?"

"Grandmother, we've done nothing but talk inheritances all day long. He kept telling us how things had been earlier, even before grandfather... he even recalled the old estate of Goryushkino, grandmother. Now, he said, if Auntie Varvara Mikhailovna had not had any children, Goryushkino would belong to us! And God alone knows whose children they are—but it's not up to us to judge others! We see the mote in the eye of another, but we do not see the beam in our own eyes... that's the way it is, brother!"

"My goodness, a fine one he is! I expect your auntie was married. Even if there had been anything amiss, the husband covered everything up!"

"True, grandmother. And each time we drive past Goryushkino, he recalls this story every time! And grandmother Natalya Vladimirovna, he says, came from Goryushkino—by all rights it should be in the Golovlyov family. But papa, may his soul rest in peace, he gave it away for his sister's dowry! And what melons, he says, grew in Goryushkino! Twenty pounds each they weighed, that's the kind of melons!"

"Really, twenty pounds! I never heard anything of the sort! Well, what plans has he in mind for Dubrovino?"

"Much the same thing. Melons and cantaloupes... all kinds of nonsense! Lately, incidentally, he keeps asking: 'Children, how much capital do you think brother Pavel has?' He's counted it up long ago, grandmother: paying off the loan, so-and-so much, and if the estate is mortgaged, how much of it has been paid off... We saw a paper on which he had been making calculations, only we took it away, grandmother... With that paper we almost drove him crazy! He would put it in his desk and we would take it and put it in the cupboard. Then he would lock the cupboard, but we would get a hold of the key and hide the paper in the communion bread... Once he went to wash in the bathhouse, took one look, and there was the paper on the floor!"

"You have a merry time there!"

Volodenka returned and all eyes were fastened on him.

"I couldn't hear anything," he informed them in a whisper, "the only thing you could hear was father saying: '...a painless, honorable, peaceful death,' and then uncle would say to him: 'go away, bloodsucker!'"

"What about the 'arrangements'...didn't you hear anything?"

"It sounded as though there was some talk, but I couldn't make it out... The door had been shut very firmly, grandmother. Just buzzing sounds and that's all. And then uncle suddenly seemed to cry out: 'Go away-ay-ay!' Well, I willy-nilly took off and came back!"

"If only for the orphans..." Arina Petrovna reflected in despair.

"If father gets everything, he won't give anything to anyone, grandmother," confirmed Petenka, "I even think that he'll deprive us of our inheritance."

"He's not about to take it to the grave with him?"

"No, but he'll think of some way. The other day he was chatting with the priest and with good reason: '...And what would happen, father,' he said to the priest, 'if the Tower of Babel were constructed—and would it take a great deal of money?'"

"Well, he was just asking...probably out of curiosity..."

"No, grandmother, he has some project in mind. If not for a Tower of Babel, then he'll leave his money to the Mt. Athos monastery and not give us anything!"

"Will papa have a large estate, grandmother, when uncle dies?" Volodenka asked out of curiosity.

"God alone knows which of us will die before the others."

"No, grandmother, father is probably making his calculations. This morning we had barely driven as far as the Dubrovino boundary when he even removed his cap, crossed himself: 'Glory be to God,' he said, 'we shall soon be riding on our land once again'!"

"He's already figured everything out, grandmother. He saw a small woods: 'Look at that,' he said, 'if the master owned that, it would be a fine piece of woods!' Then he looked at a meadow: 'Now that's a meadow! just take a look at that, will you, the number of haystacks piled up there! There used to be a stud-farm here before!' "

"Yes, yes...both the woods and the meadow—everything will be yours, my dearies," Arina Petrovna sighed, "heavens, if I'm not mistaken that's the stairs creaking!"

"Quiet, grandmother, quiet! That's him...like a thief in the night... he's eavesdropping by the door."

Silence descended. But it turned out to be a false alarm. Arina Petrovna sighed and whispered to herself: alas, children, children! The young men fastened their eyes on the orphans as though they wanted to devour them. The orphans were silent and envious.

"What about you, cousin, have you seen Mademoiselle Lotare?" Petenka picked up the conversation.

Anninka and Lyubinka exchanged glances as though wondering whether this was a question that concerned history or geography.

"In 'La Belle Hélène'...she plays the role of Hélène in the theatre.

"Ah yes...Hélène...and Paris? 'Being handsome and young, he enflamed the hearts of the goddesses'...Yes, we know it, we do!" Lyubinka rejoiced.

"Yes, that's it all right. And the way she does that 'cas-ca-ader, ca-as-ca-ader'...just marvelous!"

"This morning the doctor kept singing 'Headlong' here."

" 'Headlong'—that was the deceased Lyalova who used to sing it...now, cousin, how marvelous it was! When she died there were about two thousand people accompanying the coffin...people thought there was going to be a revolution!"

"Are you gossiping about the theater or something " Arina Petrovna intruded, "if so, it's not for them to be making the rounds of the theaters, they'll be going to a convent..."

"Grandmother, you're always trying to bury us in some convent!" complained Anninka.

"Instead of the convent, cousin, you should take a spin into Petersburg! We'll show you everything there!"

"They should not have pleasure on their minds, my friend, but only pious thoughts!" continued Arina Petrovna insistently.

"We'll take them for a ride through the fields around St. Sergius in the carriage and that'll be pious enough!"

The orphans' eyes began to sparkle and the ends of their cute little noses turned red on hearing these words.

"How they sing at St. Sergius, people say!" exclaimed Anninka.

"You can be certain of that. Not even father can sing the chorus to 'Holy, holy, holy...' like that. And then we'll drive you up and down all the three main streets."

"We could teach you literally everything, cousin! In Petersburg there are a lot of young ladies like you, you know: they walk about clicking their heels."

"You think you're going to teach them that," intervened Arina Petrovna, "now, you just leave them alone, for Christ's sake...fine teachers! You're about to teach...the sciences and the arts, I can imagine! When Pavel dies they and I will journey to the Khotkov Convent...and we'll spend our lives there!"

"Are you still indulging in vile talk!" suddenly resounded through the doorway.

In the midst of the conversation no one had heard little Judas come stealing up like a thief in the night. He was all in tears, his head downcast, his face pale, hands folded on his chest, his lips atremble. For some time he sought to lay his eyes on the icon, finally he found it and then his spirit was raised.

"Bad! My goodness, how bad he is!" he finally exclaimed as he embraced his sweet friend, mama.

"Is he really that bad?"

"Poorly, very poorly, dearie...and do you remember what a fine fellow he was before!"

"Well, I can't exactly recall when he ever was!"

"Alas, no, mama, don't talk like that! He always was... Just now I recall when he left the military academy: he was so well-built, broad-shouldered, a picture of health... Yes, yes! It's true, mama, my friend! We all walk beneath God! Today we have our health and strength, we might be living and having a good time, sweet idleness, but then tomorrow..."

He waved his hand and felt quite moved.

"Did he at least talk?"

"Very little, dearie; he barely managed: 'Farewell, brother!' And you know, mama, he really does sense, yes he does, he senses that things will go bad for him!"

"You'd feel like that too if your chest were wracked with coughing!"

"No, mama, I'm not talking about that. I'm talking about insight. People say that insight is given to a man, to that man who is dying–he always senses it beforehand. But sinners are denied any such consolation."

"Anyway, did he say anything about making arrangements?"

"No, mama. He wanted to say something, but I stopped him. No, I said, there's nothing to be said about any arrangements! Whatever you leave me, by your good grace, brother, I'll be satisfied with everything, and if you leave me nothing I'll still pray for your soul's peace! And, mama, you can't imagine how badly he wants to live! How badly! Yes he does!"

"Everyone wants to live!"

"No, mama, if I'm to speak for myself. If the Lord God is pleased to call me to Himself, then I'm ready this very moment!"

"What if the devil and not God is pleased to call you?"

The conversation dragged on in this vein until dinner, then all through dinner and even afterwards. Arina Petrovna could not even sit in her chair, so unbearable it all was. The more little Judas babbled on the more often she was drawn to the thought: "And what if I were to say...'I curse you?' " But little Judas did not even suspect that an entire storm had been unleashed in his mother's heart. His gaze was so clear and he just continued to pester his dear friend of a mama so effortlessly with desperate drivel.

"I curse you! I curse you! I curse you!" Arina Petrovna kept repeating to herself more and more resolutely.

* * *

There was the fragrance of incense in the rooms and protracted singing resounded through the house. The doors were wide open and those wishing to pay their respects to the deceased came and went. While he was alive, no one had paid any attention to Pavel Vladimirych, but with his death everyone felt sorry. They recalled that he "had not offended anyone," "had not said a rude word to anyone," "had not looked askance at anyone." All these qualities which had seemed so negative earlier, now represented something positive and from the muffled snatches of the customary funeral eulogizing emerged an example of "a kind master." Many people felt remorse at something. They recognized that at various times they had taken advantage of the deceased man's ingenuousness to his detriment. But then, after all, who was to know that an end would come so quickly to this ingenuousness? They thought it would go on forever, that its time would never come and then suddenly it... Yet if that ingenuousness were still alive they would have fleeced it even now: "...Go ahead, fleece him, fellows! Why spare a fool!" One peasant brought little Judas three silver rubles and said:

"I owed this debt to the deceased Pavel Vladimirych. We never made a promissory note, so here's the money!"

"Little Judas took the money, praised the peasant and said that he

79

would give these three silver rubles to buy oil for an "eternal light."

"And you, my friend, you will see, and everyone else will see, the rejoicing soul of the deceased. Perhaps he will say a prayer for you *there!* You won't be expecting it and then suddenly God will send you happiness!"

It was quite possible that comparison played an indefinite part in this worldly appraisal of the deceased. Little Judas was not loved. It was not that it was impossible to get around him, but merely that he adored all manner of pettiness, he made himself tiresome and pestered people. Peasants were even reluctant to rent any of his land because he would lease a piece of land and if the least extra foot was plowed or mowed, or the repayment of money were the least minute late, he would begin to drag the renting party around to the courts. He did this to a great many people and gained nothing from it for himself (his habit of quibbling was so well known that his claims were turned down practically without any inquiries being initiated), and he just plagued people with red tape and wasted time. "Don't buy yourself a house, buy a neighbor instead," the proverb says, and everyone knew what kind of neighbor they had in the owner of Golovlyovo. There was nothing to be gained if the magistrate vindicated you, he would still torment you with his Satan's law. And since malice (not even malice, but rather a moral ossification), overcast with hypocrisy, always provoked a kind of superstitious fear, then his new "neighbors" (little Judas very politely called them "dearest neighbors") timidly bowed to the waist when passing the bloodsucker who was standing all dressed in black at the grave with his hands clasped in prayer and his eyes turned heavenward.

While the deceased was laid out in the house, the servants walked about on tip-toes, peeked into the dining room (the coffin had been placed there on the dining table) shook their heads and exchanged whispers. Little Judas pretended to be barely alive, shuffling along the corridor, he went in to the "dearly departed," made a scene, straightened the coverlet on the coffin and whispered to the district police officer who was drawing up an inventory and affixing seals. Petenka and Volodenka were fussing around the coffin, placing candles and lighting them, waving the censer and so on. Anninka and Lyubinka were weeping and through their tears their thin voices joined the sextons in the requiems. The servant women, in black cotton dresses, used their aprons to wipe their noses which were red from crying.

Immediately after the death of Pavel Vladimirych, Arina disappeared to her room and locked herself in. She had no time for tears because she realized that she had to make up her mind to do something right now. She could not think of remaining in Dubrovino... "not for anything!" Consequently, there remained but one thing to do: to go to Pogorelka, the orphans' estate, the very same one which at one time had represented the "sop" she had thrown to her disrespectful daughter Anna Vladimirovna. Having made this decision, she felt relieved, as though little Judas suddenly had lost once and for all his power over her. She calmly counted up her five percent bonds (for capital it turned out that she had her own fifteen thousand and the same amount of the orphans' which she had amassed) and she calmly considered how much she would have to spend in order to put the Pogorelka house into shape. Then she immediately sent for the Pogorelka overseer, gave the necessary orders for hiring carpenters and the dispatch to Dubrovino of carts for her effects and those of the orphans. Next she ordered the carriage made ready (in Dubrovino she had her *own* carriage and she possessed *proof of ownership* that it was her very *own*) and then she began to pack. She felt neither hatred nor affection for little Judas: she simply felt repulsed at having anything to do with him. She was even unwilling to eat and ate but little, because from that day forth she had to eat not Pavel's food, but that of little Judas. On several occasions Porfiry Vladimirych glanced into her room to chat with his dear friend, mama, (he understood quite well her preparations for departure, but pretended that he noticed nothing), but Arina Petrovna did not admit him into her room.

"Off you go, my friend, off you go!" she would say, "I don't have any time for that."

At the end of three days Arina Petrovna had everything ready for her departure. Mass was sung, then the requiem and Pavel Vladimirych was buried. At the burial everything transpired precisely the way Arina Petrovna had imagined that morning when little Judas had arrived in Dubrovino. To be exact, little Judas cried: "Farewell, my brother!" when the coffin was lowered into the grave, then he also turned to Ulitushka afterwards and said rapidly:

"Don't forget to take the funeral rice pudding with you! And put it on a nice clean table cloth in the dining room...we'll have to honor my brother's memory in the house as well!"

Three priests (including the archdeacon) and the deacon were invited to the dinner which, according to custom, was then given when people returned from the funeral. The sextons were placed at a separate table in the hallway. Arina Petrovna and the orphans emerged in their travelling clothes, but little Judas pretended that he did not notice. Going up to the hors d'oeuvres, Porfiry requested the archdeacon to bless the food and drink, thereupon he poured himself and the holy fathers a glass of vodka each, grew emotional and pronounced:

"Eternal memory to the newly departed! Alas, brother, brother! You abandoned us! And who should have gone on living if not you. Unkind you are, brother, so unfeeling!"

He spoke, crossed himself and drank. Then he crossed himself again and swallowed a portion of caviar, crossed himself yet again and tasted the smoked fish.

"Eat, father!" he urged the archdeacon "all this is from the kitchen of my deceased brother! The deceased loved to eat! And he ate well himself, but he was even more fond of treating others! Alas, brother, brother!

You have abandoned us! You are so unkind, brother, so unfeeling!"

In short, he went on babbling away so that even he forgot about his mama. He only remembered her when he had scooped up some mushrooms and was about to put the spoon in his mouth.

"Mama, dearie!" he blurted out, "just look at me, what a simpleton, stuffing myself—goodness me, what a sin! Mama! Some hors d'oeuvres! Some mushrooms! Some mushrooms! These are Dubrovino mushrooms, you know! Famous, they are!"

But Arina Petrovna merely nodded her head silently in response and did not move. It appeared that she was listening to something out of curiosity, Some kind of light seemed to be welling up before her eyes, and this entire farce to whose repetition she had become accustomed since childhood and in which she herself had participated, suddenly appeared quite new and unprecedented.

Dinner began with a family argument. Little Judas insisted that mama sit at the head of the table. Arina Petrovna refused.

"No, you are the master here—you sit down wherever you wish!" she murmured drily.

"You are the mistress, you mama, you are always the mistress! Both in Golovlyovo and in Dobrovino, everywhere!" Little Judas attempted to convince her.

"Nothing of the sort! Sit down! Wherever God deems it proper for me to be the mistress, there I'll take my own place as I see fit! But here you are the master, you sit there!"

"Then this is what we'll do!" little Judas softened, "we'll leave the master's place unoccupied! As though my brother were partaking of dinner with us, but unseen... he is the master, and we shall be the guests!"

This arrangement was followed. While the soup was being served, little Judas chose a proper subject and began a conversation with the priests, principally, by the way, addressing the archdeacon.

"Nowadays many people do not believe in the immortality of the soul... but I believe in it!" he said.

"Those must be very desperate people!" replied the archdeacon.

"No, not desperate really, but there is a theory according to which a person lives of his own accord and then suddenly he dies and that's it!"

"There are an awful lot of these ideas springing up nowadays—they ought to be struck down! People believe in these ideas, but not in God. Even the peasants are having pretensions to becoming scholars."

"Yes, father, what you say is the truth. They have such a desire to become learned. The people at Naglovka for example: they have nothing to eat, yet they have all signed a petition because they want to open a school... scholars, they are!"

"Nowadays, science goes against everything. There's a theory against rain, a theory against good weather. Earlier it used to be quite simple: people would come and sing a mass and God would help. If good weather was required, then the Lord sent good weather; if rain was needed, God did not hesitate to send rain. God possessed everything in abundance. But since the time when science came into its own it was as though it all came to an end: everything happened out of season. When it was time to sow—there was a drought, when it was time to mow—rain!"

"What you say is the truth, father, the holy truth. Earlier when people prayed more to God, the earth was more fertile. The harvests were not like they are today, four-fold and five-fold—the earth would return a hundred-fold then. I imagine mama recalls? Do you recall, mama?" little Judas turned to Arina Petrovna with the intention of drawing her into the conversation.

"I never heard it to be so in our region... Maybe you read about the land of Canaan—there, it's said, that was truly the case," Arina Petrovna responded drily.

"Yes, yes," said little Judas as though not hearing his mama's remark, "people don't believe in God, they don't recognize the immortality of the soul... they just want to stuff themselves!"

"Precisely, they just want to stuff themselves and drink!" seconded the archdeacon as he rolled back the sleeves of his cassock to place a piece of the remembrance meat pie on his plate.

Everyone turned to his soup. For a time the only sound was the scraping of spoons against plates and the snorting of the priests as they blew on the hot liquid.

"Just take the Catholics," continued little Judas, pausing from eating, "despite the fact that they do not deny the immortality of the soul, none-theless, they say something to the effect that the soul does not go directly to heaven or hell, but for a while... it enters a kind of in-between place."

"Once again this has no foundation."

"How could one put it, father..." pondered Porfiry Vladimirych, "if one were to speak from the point of view of..."

"There's nothing to be said about such nonsense. How does the holy church sing of this? It sings: 'thou shall walk in a green and cool place, bearing neither sorrow nor sighs...' What 'in-between' place is there any talk about here!"

Little Judas, however, was not in complete accord and wanted to object. But Arina Petrovna, who had begun to wilt from this conversation, stopped him.

"Now, then, eat, eat... you theologian! I imagine the soup has long since grown cold!" she said in order to change the conversation and turned to the archdeacon: "Have you gathered in all your rye, father?"

"Yes, I have, madame. The rye is good right now, but the spring-crops are not very promising! The oats haven't filled out properly yet, and already they've begun to wither away. There's nothing to be hoped for from either the grain or the wheat.

"Everybody is complaining about the oats recently!" sighed Arina Petrovna, watching little Judas as he scooped out the remains of his soup with his spoon.

The next dish was served: ham with peas. Little Judas took advantage of this moment in order to renew the interrupted conversation.

"The Jews don't eat this food," he said.

"The Jews are heathens," responded the archdeacon, "that's why people make fun of them with the ear of a pig."

"However, take the Tatars now... There must be some reason for this..."

"The Tatars are heathens too—that's your reason."

"We don't eat horseflesh, whereas the Tatars disdain pork. In Paris, they say, people ate rats during the blockade."

"Well, that's the French for you!"

The entire dinner proceeded in this fashion. Creamed carp was served—little Judas elaborated:

"Eat, father! These are special carp: my deceased brother was very fond of them!"

Asparagus was then served, —little Judas spoke:

"Now that's real asparagus! In Petersburg you would have to pay a silver ruble for that kind of asparagus. My deceased brother looked after it himself! Just look at how thick it is!"

Arina Petrovna's heart was seething: a whole hour had passed, yet the dinner was only half finished. It was as though little Judas were tarrying on purpose: he would take a bite, then lay his knife and fork down, chatter away, then take another bite and chatter again. How many times in the past Arina Petrovna had shouted at him for this: "Start eating, you devil, God forgive me for saying it!"—yes, apparently, he had forgotten his mama's exhortations. Yet perhaps he had not forgotten and was doing it on purpose, taking his revenge. Perhaps he was not even conscious of taking his revenge, but doing it intuitively, from spiteful nature. Finally, the roast meat was served. At that very moment when everyone had arisen and the archdeacon was just beginning the prayer for the blessed departed, a commotion arose in the hallway, shouts were heard which completely debased the effect of the requiem hymn.

"What's that noise there!" shouted Porfiry Vladimirych, "do people think this is a tavern or something?"

"Don't shout, for heaven's sake! It's me...my trunks are being moved," Arina Petrovna responded and then added with a certain irony: "Do you want to check them, perhaps?"

Everyone suddenly fell silent, even little Judas lost his wits and turned pale. Incidentally he only now realized that he had to smooth over his mother's unpleasant rejoinder, and so, turning to the archdeacon, he began:

"Take grouse, for example... In Russia there is a multitude of them,

84

whereas in other countries..."

"Go ahead and eat, for Christ's sake. We have to travel twenty-five versts; we have to hurry before it gets dark," Arina Petrovna interrupted him, "Petenka! Hurry up there, dearie, and tell them to serve the dessert!"

The silence lingered on for several minutes. Porfiry Vladimirych briskly finished eating his piece of grouse and sat there pale, tapping his foot on the floor and his lips trembling.

"You are offending me, dear friend, mama! You are offending me deeply!" he finally said without looking, incidentally, at his mother.

"Who's offending you! And how did I offend you so deeply?"

"Very, very offending...so offending! so offending! To leave at this moment! Living here all that time...and suddenly... And finally these trunks... talking about checking them...offending!"

"If you wish to know everything, then I can give you an answer. I lived here while my son Pavel was alive; he died and now I'm leaving. As far as the trunks are concerned, Ulitka has been spying on me for a long time on your orders. And as far as I'm concerned, it's better to tell your mother straight out that she is under suspicion than to hiss at her like a snake from behind someone else's back."

"Mama! My friend! But you... But I..." moaned little Judas.

"Enough!" Arina Petrovna would not let him finish, "I have spoken my mind."

"But, my friend, how could I have..."

"I'm telling you, I have spoken and leave it at that. Let me go in peace, for Christ's sake. I hope the carriage is ready."

In fact, the bells and rumbling of the approaching carriage echoed outside. Arina Petrovna was the first to arise from the table and then the others followed suit.

"Now, let us sit down for a minute of silence and then on our way!" she said as she made her way to the living room.

They sat down and were silent for a moment, and meanwhile little Judas was able to regain his wits.

"Wouldn't you like to live here in Dubrovino a little longer, mama...just see how fine it is here!" he said, looking his mother in the eye with all the affection of a wheedling dog.

"No, my friend, enough of that! I don't want to say anything unpleasant to you by way of farewell...but it is impossible for me to remain here! Not for anything! Father! Let us pray!"

Everyone arose and prayed. Thereupon Arina Petrovna exchanged kisses with everyone and blessed everyone...as good relatives do...and walking with difficulty she made her way to the door. Porfiry Vladimirych, at the head of all the house servants, accompanied her to the porch, but when he arrived there and saw the carriage, he was overcome with cupidity. "Surely, that's my brother's carriage!" flashed through his mind.

"So we'll be seeing each other, dear friend, Mama!" he said, seating his mother in the carriage and looking out of the corner of his eye at the carriage.

"If that is God's will...then why shouldn't we see each other!"

"Goodness me, mama, mama! You are a naughty girl, truly you are! Tell them to put the carriage away and return to your old nest with God's blessing...truly!" little Judas coaxed.

Arina Petrovna did not reply: she had already settled into her place and had even made the sign of the cross, but the orphans were hanging back for some reason.

Meanwhile little Judas kept looking and looking at the carriage.

"And what about the carriage, mama? Will you send it back yourself or will you have someone come and get it?" he could not restrain himself any longer.

Arina Petrovna even began to shake all over with indignation.

"The carriage belongs to me!" she shouted in such an excruciating voice that everyone felt awkward and embarrassed. "It's mine! Mine! My carriage! I bought it... I have proof...there are witnesses! And you...well, I'll just wait and see what else you'll try! Children! Are you coming?"

"Mercy, mama! I have no claim to it... Even if it were the Dubrovino carriage..."

"It's my carriage, mine! Not the Dubrovino carriage, but mine! Don't you dare say anything else...do you hear!"

"I hear, mama... Now, dearie, don't you forget us...without fail! We'll visit you and you'll visit us...like good relatives!"

"Are you seated? Let's be off!" shouted Arina Petrovna, barely able to contain herself.

The carriage shuddered and then rolled off at a measured trot along the road. Little Judas stood on the porch waving his handkerchief until the carriage had disappeared completely from view and kept calling out:

"Like good relatives! We'll visit you and you'll visit us...like good relatives."

THE FAMILY WINDUP

It had never occurred to Arina Petrovna that the time would come when she would represent an "extra mouth," and lo, this moment had come stealing up gradually during that very time when for the first time in her life she had become practically convinced that her moral and physical powers had been broken. Such moments always come suddenly. Although a person may perhaps have been long since shattered, nonetheless, he can still summon up enough strength to stand upright—and then suddenly from some unseen direction the final flow is delivered. It is very difficult to beware of this blow, to be conscious of its approach. One is simply and silently compelled to submit to it, for this is that very same blow which can change a man who was formerly cheerful into a wretch in an instant.

Arina Petrovna's situation was a difficult one when, having broken with little Judas, she had settled in Dubrovino, but at that time she had at least known that Pavel Vladimirych, for all his looking askance at her intrusion, nonetheless was a man of means for whom an extra bit of food did not have a great deal of significance. But now the situation had taken a completely different twist: she stood at the head of a household where every "bite" had to be taken into account. And she knew the worth of these "bites," for, having spent all her life in the country, in close quarters with the peasantry, she had completely assimilated herself to the peasant understanding about the detrimental effect which an "extra mouth" could bring to a household which was already overtaxed without it.

Nonetheless, during the initial period of settlement at Pogorelka, she was still cheerful, carefully setting herself up in her new place and displaying her former lucid understanding of running household. But housekeeping in Pogorelka was a fussy and trivial affair, demanding her unrelenting personal supervision, and although in her rashness she had believed it would be possible to arrive at an exact accounting in a place where quarter-kopeks were turned into half-kopeks, half-kopeks into ten-kopek pieces, that it would not require a great deal of wisdom, she soon had to admit that she had been incorrect in her conviction. In fact, there was no wisdom, but there was neither the former desire, nor the former strength. Moreover, all this was going on during the autumn, at the very height of the harvesting, yet at the same time the weather remained foul and placed an involuntary limit on Arina Petrovna's zeal. The feebleness of old age made its appearance and would not allow her to emerge from the house. The long, dreary, autumn evenings set in, condemning one to a fatalistic idleness. The old woman was beset by anxiety and yearning, but she could do nothing.

On the other hand, she could not but notice that something unpleasant was happening with the orphans. They suddenly became bored and hung their heads. Vague plans for the future made them restless—plans wherein ideas about working alternated willy-nilly with ideas of pleasure; naturally of an innocent variety. Accompanying these ideas were recollections about their school in which they had been educated and the odds and ends of ideas they had read about men of labor, and the timid hope that with their school connections they could grasp at some thread and by means of it enter into the radiant realm of life at large. A single gnawing and very well defined idea held sway over all this vagueness: at any cost they must leave hateful Pogorelka. And lo, one fine morning, Anninka and Lyubinka announced to their grandmother that they neither had the will nor the desire to remain in Pogorelka any longer. That it resembled no other place, that they never saw anyone in Pogorelka, other than the priest, who, moreover, when he met them, for some reason always talked about virgins who had extinguished their lamps, and that, in general, "one mustn't do so." The girls spoke sharply, because they were afraid of their grandmother, and so they made a greater show of courage because they expected a fiery outburst and resistance from her quarter. But, to their surprise, Arina Petrovna listened to their complaints not only without anger, but even without manifesting any recourse to a fruitless moralizing to which impotent old age is so prone. Alas! she was no longer that same despotic old woman who at one time had said with such assurance: "I am going to the Khotkov Convent and I'm taking my granddaughters with me." And it was not merely senile feebleness which had played a part in this change, but understanding of something better, more just. The final blows of fate had not simply subdued her, but had in addition illuminated within her mental outlook several corners where her mind had apparently never peeked beforehand. She understood that hidden within a human being were well-know strivings which could slumber for a long while, but once they had awakened, they irresistibly attracted a person to where the ray of life had penetrated, that consoling ray whose manifestation the eye has long sought amid the hopeless gloom of the present. Once understanding the legality of such a striving, she was then powerless to oppose it. True, she attempted to dissuade her granddaughters from their intentions, but did so feebly, without conviction. She was anxious on account of the future which lay in store for them, more so because she herself no longer had any connections in so-called society, but at the same time she felt that it was necessary and inevitable that she part with the granddaughters. "What would happen to them?" This question loomed insistently and constantly before her. But then the person who longs for freedom would not be restrained either by this question or even more terrifying ones. Moreover, the girls were determined solely to break away from Pogorelka. In fact, after some vacillation and postponements made in deference to their grandmother, they did depart.

With the departure of the orphans, the house in Pogorelka was plunged into a kind of desperate silence. However self-centered Arina Petrovna was by nature, the proximity of other human beings produced a soothing effect on her. Once she had seen her granddaughters off, she felt, perhaps for the first time, that something had been torn away from her being and that she had all at once entered a kind of boundless freedom, boundless to the point that she now saw nothing lying before herself other than an empty expanse. In order to conceal this emptiness in her own eyes, she immediately made arrangements to board up the main rooms and the upstairs where the orphans had lived ("moreover, we'll use less firewood"—is what she thought in doing so), and she put aside two rooms in all for herself, in one of which was placed a large icon-stand, and the other encompassed simultaneously a bedroom, study and dining room. For the sake of economy, the house servants were let go and she retained for herself only the old housekeeper Afimyushka who could barely drag her feet along, and the one-eyed soldier's wife, Markovna, who did the cooking and the washing. But all of these precautions did little to help: the sensation of emptiness was not slow in penetrating as well into those two rooms where she thought to protect herself from it. A helpless loneliness and a bleak idleness—those were the two enemies with whom she found herself face to face and with whom from that day forth she was bound to while away her old age. And on their heels, the effect of physical and moral disintegration was not long in coming, an effect which was all the more cruel because a life of idleness offered no resistance to it.

The days gave way to one another with that depressing monotony which was so abundant in country living if such living were not furnished with either comfort or housekeeping chores or material for the mind. Aside from the external reasons which made household work impossible, Arina Petrovna was inwardly repulsed by the penny-pinching which had overtaken her at the end of her life. Perhaps she might have overcome her repulsion if she had had a purpose in mind which would have justified her efforts, but in fact there was no purpose at all. She became disgusting to everyone and tiresome, and everything and everyone disgusted her and proved tiresome. Her former feverish activity suddenly gave way to a drowsy idleness, and the idleness gradually undermined her will and brought with it the kind of inclinations which, of course, Arina Petrovna never would have dreamt of a few months before. From a strong and self-contained woman whom no one would have dared to even call an old woman, there now emerged a wreck for whom neither the past nor the future existed, but only the next moment which had to be lived through.

During the day she dozed for the most part. She would sit in her chair before the table on which grubby playing cards were laid out and she would doze. Then she would give a shudder, awake and look out the window, and then for a long while, without giving it any conscious thought, she would be unable to tear her eyes from the distant horizon which stretched out before her without end. Pogorelka was a miserable estate. It stood, as people said, like a bump on a log, there was no garden, no shade, no sign whatsoever of any comfort. There was not even any fence out in front. The house was single-storied, as though crushed, and all black with time and the elements. In the rear a few outbuildings were situated and these too had fallen into decrepitude. All around stretched fields far and wide, fields without end. Not even a woods was visible on the horizon. But since Arina Petrovna had lived almost exclusively in the country from her childhood, not only did this impoverished nature not seem dreary to her, it even touched her heart and aroused the remnants of any emotions which were still warm within her. The better part of her nature had lived in these barren and endless fields, and her eyes instinctively sought them out at every oppportunity. She would stare at this horizon of fields, stare at these rain-soaked villages, which in the form of black dots were sprinkled here and there on the horizon. She would stare at the white churches of the village churchyards, stare at the colored spots which people, wandering in the rays of the sun, etched on the flat expanse of fields, stare at that unfamiliar peasant who was walking between the furrows in the fields and it seemed to her as though he had become frozen in a single spot. Absorbed in this she would not be thinking about anything, or more accurately, her thoughts were so scattered that she could not fasten on anything for any significant length of time. She merely looked and looked until a senile drowsiness began to hum in her ears once again and enveloped in a mist the fields and the churches and the villages and the peasant wandering along in the distance.

Sometimes she apparently recalled something. But the memory of the past would return all disconnected and in the form of snatches. She could not concentrate her attention on anything and it continuously skipped from one distant recollection to another. At times, however, she was struck by something in particular, not joy—her past had been a cruel miser with happiness,—but some offense or other, bitter and unbearable. Then it seemed as though she was set on fire from within, grief crept into her heart and the tears came to her eyes. She would begin to weep, weep heavily, painfully, she would cry the way pitiful old age cries, when the latter's tears spill forth in the midst of an oppressive nightmare. But while her tears were spilling forth, unconscious thought continued its work and, unnoticed by Arina Petrovna, it would distract her from the source giving rise to her grief-stricken mood, with the result that in a few minutes the old woman would ask herself in amazement what had happened to her.

In general she lived as though she were not personally involved in life, but purely by virtue of the fact that this wreck still harbored some forgotten strands which had to be gathered together, reckoned up and then laid to rest. While these strands were still present, life continued on its way, forcing the wreck to go through all the external motions which were essential to prevent this semi-slumbering being from disintegrating into dust.

But if the days passed in unconscious drowsiness, then the nights were positively excruciating. At night Arina Petrovna *was afraid*; she was afraid of thieves, of ghosts, demons, in short, everything which composed the sum total of her upbringing and life. Her protection against all of this was poor, be-

90

cause, outside of the decrepit servant mentioned above, the night staff at Pogorelka consisted entirely of the single person of the lame husband of Fyodoseyushka, who for two rubles a month would come from the village to be watchman at night for the Pogorelka house and usually dozed in the hallway, going out at pre-set times to bang on his iron sheet a few times. Although several workers and their wives lived by the livestock shed, it was separated from the main house by about a hundred and fifty feet, and it was far from easy to summon anyone from over there.

There is something burdensome and depressing in a sleepless night in the country. From about nine o'clock, or at the most, ten o'clock, it seemed as though everything was cut short, silence descended, bringing fear with it. There was nothing to be done, moreover one begrudged wasting candles and so, like it or not, one had to go to bed. Afimyushka, as soon as the samovar had been cleared away, laid out her felt mat in front of the door leading to her mistress' bedroom—a habit acquired from the earlier days of serfdom, — scratched herself, yawned, and as soon as she tumbled onto the floor, fell fast asleep. Markovna would be up and about in the servants' quarters somewhat longer and would go on muttering something and cursing at someone; but then finally she too would quiet down, and in a minute one could hear her having a proper snore or talking in her sleep. The watchman would bang his iron sheet a few times to announce his presence and then he would fall silent for a long while. Arina Petrovna would sit before the sputtering tallow candle and attempt to chase away sleep by playing solitaire. But she would barely reach for the cards laid out on the table when drowsiness would begin to overcome her. "If I'm not careful, I might fall asleep and cause a fire!" she would say to herself and then decide to go to bed. But she would barely manage to sink into the feather-bed when another misfortune would beset her: sleep, which had beckoned and troubled her all evening long, suddenly disappeared. Moreover, the room was overheated. The heat poured in through the open ventilator and together with the featherbed created a completely unbearable atmosphere. Arina Petrovna tossed from side to side and she felt like calling out to someone, but she knew that no one would come in response to her call. An enigmatic silence reigned all around—a silence in which the straining ear could distinguish a welter of sounds. First, a door would slam somewhere; then suddenly a howling sound; then it seemed as though someone was walking along the corridor; then what seemed to be a draft passed through the room and even blew in her face. The lamp burning in front of the ikon lent a deceptive character to objects with its light, so that the objects themselves did not seem to exist, but only their outlines. In addition to this suspicious light another appeared through the open door of the neighboring room where four or five lamps were lit in front of the ikon-stand. This light lay in a yellow square on the floor as though inscribed in the gloom of the bedroom without merging with it. There were wavering and soundlessly shifting shadows everywhere. A mouse was scratching behind the wallpaper. "Sh-sh, you wretch!" Arina Petrovna shouted at it and then every-thing fell silent once again. Again shadows, again whispering sounds issuing from some unknown source. She would spend the greater part of the night in uneasy and sickly slumber and only towards morning would sleep, properly speaking, overtake her. But at six o'clock Arina Petrovna was already on her feet, wracked by a sleepless night.

To all of these causes, which sufficiently illustrated the pitiful existence led by Arina Petrovna, two more were added: the scarcity of food and the comfortlessness of the dwelling. She ate little and she ate poorly, probably thinking thereby to compensate for the loss incurred in her housekeeping through insufficient supervision. As far as the dwelling was concerned, the Po-gorelka house was ancient and damp, and the room in which Arina Petrovna locked herself was never aired out and went without cleaning for weeks on end. In the midst of this utter helplessness, in the midst of the absence of any comfort at all or care, infirmity drew nigh.

But the more infirm she became, the more powerful became the desire within her to live. Or, more accurately, it was not so much a desire to live as a desire to indulge herself and this was intensified by the complete absence of any idea of dying. Earlier she had feared death, now it was as though she had completely forgotten about it. And since her ideals of life differed but little from those of any peasant, consequently her concept of the "good life," with which she deluded herself, was of a rather lowly nature. Everything she had denied herself during the course of her life—fine fare, rest, conversation with other living people, —all of this became the object of the most insistent de-sires. All the inclinations of an incorrigible hanger-on—idle chatter, toadying for the sake of a hand-out, gluttony—grew with amazing speed. At home she fed herself like the servants: cabbage soup with old salt meat, and at the same time dreamed about the kitchens at Golovlyovo, the carp which were kept in the Dubrovino ponds, the mushrooms which filled the Golovlyovo woods, the fowl which was being fattened in Golovlyovo in the yard. "It'd be nice to have some soup with goose giblets now or mushrooms in cream," flashed through her head, flashed so vividly that even the corners of her mouth fell. At night she tossed from side to side, perishing from fear at each rustle and she thought: "In Golovlyovo there are solid locks and the watchmen are trustworthy, they bang and bang on their sheet without ceasing—go ahead and sleep like you're in the bosom of Christ!" During the day she found her-self unable to exhange a word with anyone and during this involuntary silence the thought came to her mind of itself: "In Golovlyovo there are people, there's folk to amuse oneself with!" In short, she was constantly thinking of Golovlyovo and the more she thought about it, the more it became a kind of bright spot wherein was concentrated the "good life."

The more her imagination became clouded with her representation of Golovlyovo, the more powerfully her will disintegrated and the further away retreated the recent unforgivable offences. By the very nature of her upbringing and life, a Russian woman becomes too easily reconciled to the fate of a hanger-on, and for this reason Arina Petrovna was not spared a similar fate, although, it seemed, her entire past would have prevented it and delivered her from this yoke. If she had not committed errors "at that time," if she had not alienated her sons, if she had not trusted little Judas, she would still have been even now a cantankerous and demanding old woman who would be forcing all the others to eat out of her hand. But since the error had been committed irrevocably, so the transition from the obstreperousness of independence to the submissiveness and toadying of a hanger-on only constituted a matter of time. While her strength had preserved the remnants of her earlier fortitude, the transition had not manifested itself outwardly, but as soon as she admitted herself to be irrevocably condemned to helplessness and loneliness, then immediately all the desires of faintheartedness began to creep into her heart and little by little they totally perverted a will that was already shaken without that. Little Judas, who upon first arriving at Pogorelka had encountered there only the coldest of receptions, suddenly ceased to be hated. The old trespasses were somehow forgotten of themselves and Arina Petrovna was the first to make a move for reconciliation.

It all began with solicitations. At first messengers came to little Judas from Pogorelka rarely, and then more and more frequently. First there was no crop of mushrooms in Pogorelka, then the cucumbers turned out to be spotted from the rain, then the turkeys, "because of the freedom of the times," were dropping dead, "dearest friend, could you have some carp caught in Dobrovino, my deceased son, Pavel, never refused them to his dear old mother." Little Judas would pull a wry face, but he could not bring himself to express his displeasure openly. He begrudged the carp, but above all he feared that his mother would curse him. He remembered how she had once said: I'll come to Golovlyovo, order the church to be opened, summon the priest and shout: "I curse you!" and this recollection had stopped him from all manner of mischief—of which he was a past master. But, having fulfilled the will of "my dear friend, mama," nonetheless, in passing, he hinted to those around him that everyone is elected by God to bear a cross and that this is not done without a purpose, for, if a man does not have a cross to bear, then he will forget himself and fall into sin. However, to his mother he wrote: "Dear friend, mama, I'll send you as many cucumbers as is possibly in my power. As far as the turkeys are concerned, then above those being kept for breeding, there are only the roosters, which on account of their enormous size and the limitations of your table, would be useless to you. But wouldn't you care to allow us to welcome you to Golovlyovo to share with me my humble repast. Then we can take one of these layabouts (that's exactly what they are, layabouts, because my cook, Matvey, is very clever at making them into capons) and have it cooked and then eat to our heart's content, dearest friend, mama."

From that time forth, Arina Petrovna appeared frequently in Golovlyovo. With little Judas she partook of both turkeys and ducks; she slept to her heart's content at night as well, and after dinner she could let herself go in endless trivial conversation for which little Judas himself had a natural inclination, whereas she had become so inclined as a result of old age. The visits were not even interrupted when news reached her that little Judas, after becoming tired with a lengthy widowerhood, had taken for a housekeeper a young priest's daughter by the name of Yevpraksiya. On the contrary, when she learned of this, she immediately went to Golovlyovo and before she had even managed to get down out of the carriage had shouted to little Judas with some senile impatience: "Well, now, you old sinner, you! Come on and show me your beauty!" That whole day she spent in complete satisfaction because Yevprakseyushka herself served the old woman at dinner, laid out the bed for her after dinner, and in the evening Arina Petrovna played cards with little Judas and his beauty. Little Judas was also satisfied with this outcome and, as a sign of filial gratitude, he ordered, among other things, a pound of caviar to be placed in Arina Petrovna's carriage when she departed, a supreme sign of respect, because caviar was not free, but had to be bought. This act moved the old woman so much that she could not restrain herself and said:

"Well, thank you very much for this! And God will love you, dear friend, because you are comforting and treating your mother in her old age. At least when I arrive in Pogorelka I won't be bored now. I always loved caviar and now, because of your kindness, I can give myself a treat!"

* * *

About five years passed from the time of Arina Petrovna's move to Pogorelka. Little Judas, once settled in his native Golovlyovo, did not budge from there. He had grown noticeably older, more sluggish and lifeless, but he cheated, lied and indulged in idle chatter even more than before because now he had almost constantly his kind friend, mama, on his hands, who for the sake of a tasty tidbit in her old age had become the captive audience for his idle chatter.

One should not think that little Judas was a hypocrite in the sense, for example, of a Tartuffe or any other contemporary French bourgeois, who is prepared to warble forth like a nightingale on the topic of social principles. No, if he were, in fact, a hypocrite, then he was a hypocrite of a purely Russian variety, that is, simply a person devoid of any moral judgement and knowing no truth other than that which was indicated in copy-book rules. He was infinitely ignorant, a pettifogger, a liar, an idle chatterer and, to top it all, he feared the devil. All of these are such negative qualities offering no solid material for genuine hypocrisy.

In France hypocrisy is formed through one's upbringing and constitutes, so to speak, the inherent character of "good manners" and almost always possesses a manifestly political or social bias. There are hypocrites for religion, hypocrites for social principles, for property, for the family, for the state, and lately hypocrites have even begun to spring up for "order." If this type of hypocrisy cannot be called conviction, then, in any event, it is a banner around which those people gather who find advantage in being hypocritical for that very reason and no other. They are conscious hypocrites, according to whatever their banner is, and, moreover, they know that this fact is not unknown to others. In the conceptions of the bourgeois Frenchman, the universe is nothing other than an extensive stage where an endless theatrical performance is being presented wherein one hypocrite gives the cue to the next one. Hypocrisy, this is an invitation to propriety, to decorum, to an attractive external arrangement, and what is more important, hypocrisy is a restraint. Not for those, of course, who are practicing hypocrisy, soaring at the heights of the social domain, but rather for those who for want of hypocrisy are crawling about at the bottom of the social cauldron. Hypocrisy restrains society from a licentiousness of the passions and makes of the latter the privilege solely of the most restricted minority. As long as licentiousness of passions does not escape from within the boundaries of a small and solidly organized corporation, not only is it not dangerous, but it even supports and nourishes the traditions of elegance. Elegance would perish if there did not exist a specific number of *cabinets particuliers* in which it was being cultivated during those moments free from the cult of official hypocrisy. But licentiousness becomes positively dangerous as soon as it becomes accessible to society at large and becomes allied to the awarding of freedom to each person to proclaim his needs and substantiate their legality and naturalness. Then there arise new social strata which strive, if not entirely to exclude the older ones, then at least to restrict them to a significant degree. The demand for *cabinets particuliers* would increase to such a point that finally the question would arise: would it not be simpler, for the future, to do without them completely? It is precisely from these undesirable manifestations and questions that the ruling classes of French society are defended by that systematic hypocrisy, and who, not satisfied with having custom as their basis, then proceed to a basis of legality and thus from a simple feature of *mores* arises a law which is binding in nature.

With rare exceptions, the entire contemporary French theatre is based upon this law of respect for hypocrisy. The heroes of the best French dramatic works, that is, those which enjoy the greatest success precisely because of the unusual realism of life's wickedness portrayed in them, always reserve towards the end several free minutes in order to correct this wickedness with loud phrases in which the saintliness and joy of virtue are proclaimed. During the course of four acts, Adéle can defile her conjugal bed in every conceivable fashion, but in the fifth act she inevitably declares publicly that the family hearth is the sole refuge in which a French woman can find happiness. If one were to ask oneself what would have happened to Adéle if the authors had planned to continue their plays for another five such acts, you could reply without fear of error to this question that in the course of the next four acts, Adele would defile her conjugal bed again, but then in the fifth act once again she would turn to the public with the same declaration. One need not make suppositions either, but simply proceed from the *Théâtre Francais* to the *Gymnase,* and from there to the *Vaudeville* or the *Variétés*, in order to confirm that Adéle everywhere is defiling her conjugal bed and everywhere by the end declares that this very bed is the sole altar wherein the honorable French woman can perform a religious ceremony. This has eaten into the *mores* to such a degree that no one even notices the foolish paradox inherent here, that the truth of life appears side by side with the truth of hypocrisy and both go hand in hand, so confused with each other that it becomes difficult to say which of these two truths has more right to recognition.

We Russians do not have strongly biased systems of education. We are not drilled, we are not made into the future champions and propagandists of one or another set of social principles, but simply are left to grow like nettles by a fence. Therefore, there are very few hypocrites among us, and a great number of liars, bigots and idle talkers. We have no need to practice hypocrisy for the sake of some social principles, for we have no knowledge of any such principles and not a single one of them gives us any protection. We exist quite freely, that is we vegetate, we lie and we indulge in idle chatter for their own sake, without any principles at all.

Should one, on this account, rejoice or mourn—it is not up to me to judge. However, I believe that if hypocrisy can prompt indignation and fear, then idle lying is capable of arousing vexation and loathing. And for that reason the best thing would be to set aside the question about the advantages of a conscious versus an unconscious hypocrisy, or vice versa, and disavow both the hypocrites and the liars alike.

Thus, little Judas was not so much a hypocrite as a vile person, a liar and idle chatterer. Closing himself up in the country, he immediately felt himself free, for nowhere, in no other sphere whatsoever, could his proclivities have found such scope for themselves as here in the country. In Golovlyovo not only did he not encounter resistance from any corner whatsoever, but there was not even the slightest, indirect constriction which would have forced him to think: "I would like to pull a dirty trick, but I'm ashamed to do so in front of people." No one's judgement disturbed him, no one's indiscreet glance upset him, consequently, there was no cause for him to exert any control over himself. An unchecked slovenliness became the major feature of his relationship with himself. This complete freedom from moral restrictions had long ago lured him to itself, and if he had not moved to living in the country even earlier, it was simply because he feared idleness. Having spent more than thirty years in the gloomy atmosphere of a government office, he had acquired all the habits and desires of a died-in-the-wool bureaucrat who would not put up with even a single minute of his life remaining free from the senseless emptying of an empty vessel into yet another empty one. But taking a closer look at things, he quickly came to the conviction that the world of busy idleness was so mobile that there was not the slightest difficulty in transferring it wherever one wished, into whatever sphere one desired. And truly, as soon as he had settled in Golovlyovo, he immediately created for himself a mass of trivia and pettiness which he could fiddle with endlessly, without the slightest danger of ever exhausting it. From morning on he would sit down at his desk and begin to work. At first he would check the accounts of the dairymaid, the housekeeper and the bailiff, initially in one fashion, then in another. Secondly, he set up a very complex accounting system, one for the finances, the other for material items: he entered every kopek, every item into twenty ledgers, calculated the sums, at first losing a half-kopek, then gaining an entire kopek extra. Finally he would take up his pen and write out complaints to the justice of the peace and to the legal mediator. All of this not only deprived him of any idle moment, but even possessed all the external signs of an assiduous and unbearably heavy labor. Little Judas did not complain of idleness, but rather that he did not have enough time to re-do everything, although he plodded away for the entire day in his study without changing from his dressing robe. Heaps of assiduously filed, but unchecked, accounts, were constantly stacked up on his desk, including the entire year's account from the dairymaid, Fyokla, whose activity had seemed suspicious to him from the very first moment, but nonetheless, he had never been able to find a free moment to read through the account.

Every connection with the external world was totally severed. He received no books, no newspapers, not even letters. One of his sons, Volodenka, had committed suicide and with the other one, Petenka, he conducted a brief correspondence and only when he sent money. A turgid atmosphere of ignorance, prejudice and the tedious emptying of one empty vessel into another reigned all around him and he did not sense the slightest inclination to become free of it. Even the fact that Napoleon III was no longer on the throne he learned only a year after his death, and from the district police officer, but even at this he did not express any particular emotion, simply crossing himself and whispering: "May he rest in peace!" and then he said:

"How proud he was! My, oh my! That was not very good, and the other was not very nice! Kings used to come to bow down at his feet, princes hung about in the reception rooms! But God just up and overturned all his dreams in a single moment!"

Essentially speaking, he did not even know what was happening on his estate, although from morning till night he did nothing but calculate and draw up accounts. In this regard he possessed all the qualities of a died-in-the-wool bureaucrat. Just imagine the section-head to whom the director on the spur of the moment, would say: "My dear friend! For my purposes I must know how many potatoes Russia produces annually, be good enough to make a detailed calculation!" Would the section-head find himself face to face with a blank wall over such a question? Would he at least give some consideration to the methods which would necessarily be employed in order to fulfill the work requested of him? No, he would proceed in a much simpler fashion: he would trace a map of Russia, divide it up into completely even squares, figure out how many acres there were in each square, then drop into the grocery store, find out how many potatoes are sown per acre and what the average yield would be, then in conclusion, with God's help and the first four rules of arithmetic, he would arrive at the solution that *under favorable conditions* Russia could produce such-and-such a number of potatoes, and *under unfavorable conditions,* such-and-such a number. And not only would this work satisfy his director, but probably would be placed in the one hundred and second volume of some "Transactions" or other.

Even the housekeeper he had chosen for himself was perfectly suitable for the situation he had created. The girl Yevpraksiya was the daughter of a deacon from the church of St. Nikola at Kapelki and represented in all regards a real treasure. She possessed neither a quick mind, nor a resourcefulness, nor even efficiency, but in place of this she was a real worker, submissive and quite undemanding. Even when he had "become intimate" with her, even then she merely asked, "Could she have some cold kvass to drink when she felt like it and not have to ask?"—even little Judas was moved by her submissiveness and immediately gave her to use at her own discretion, over and above the kvass, two barrels of pickled apples, relieving her of having to answer for them. Her appearance did not hold anything particularly attractive for the admirer of beauty, but to the eyes of an undemanding person who knew what he wanted, she was entirely satisfactory. She had a broad white face, her forehead was narrow and encircled by thin, blondish hair, the eyes were enormous and dull, her nose completely straight, an unremarkable mouth that was twisted in that seemingly fleeting and enigmatic smile which one sees in those portraits painted by homegrown artists. In general, there was nothing outstanding other than her back which was so broad and powerful that even the most indifferent person would involuntarily raise his hand in order to, as the saying goes, "give the girl one" between her shoulder blades. She knew this and was not offended so that when for the first time little Judas gave her a gentle tap on her fleshy neck, she merely shrugged her shoulders.

In the midst of this dreary situation, the days trailed after one another, the first just like the second, without any change, without any hope for the intrusion of a fresh breath of air. Only the arrival of Arina Petrovna would enliven this life to a slight degree and to tell the truth, if at first Porfiry Vladimirych had frowned on seeing his mother's carriage off in the distance, then with the passage of time he not only grew accustomed to her visits, but became fond of them as well. They satisfied his passion for idle chatter, for if he had found it possible to indulge in idle chatter with just himself on the subject of diverse accounts and calculations, then it was even more natural for him to do so with his dear friend, mama. Once together they would talk from morning until night without being able to talk their fill. They talked about everything: about how the harvests were earlier and what they were like nowadays; about how the landowners had lived earlier and how they live nowadays; about the fact that salt seemed to be better before, and one could not find a cucumber today that was the equal of the old one.

These conversations possessed that quality of flowing water and were easily forgotten. Consequently, it was possible to renew them without end and with the same interest, as though they were popping up now for the first time. Yevprakseyushka also participated in these conversations and Arina Petrovna was so fond of her that she never let her get out of her sight. Sometimes when they had become bored with talking, all three would sit down to cards and remain there playing until late into the night. They tried to teach Yevprakseyushka how to play dummy-whist, but she did not understand. The huge Golovlyovo house seemed to come alive on those evenings. Lights were burning in all the windows, the shadows flitted past so that a passer-by would think that only God knows what festivity was under way here. Samovars, coffee-pots, snacks did not leave the table the whole day long. And Arina Petrovna's heart rejoiced and frolicked, and instead of visiting for only a single day, she would come for three or four. Even when she departed for Pogorelka, she would already have thought up some pretext whereby she could return more quickly to the temptations of the Golovlyovo "good life."

* * *

November was coming to an end. As far as the eye could see, the whole expanse was covered with a white shroud. Outside it was nighttime and a snowstorm was blowing: a sharp, cold wind whipped up the snow and in a single instant it would pile up snowdrifts and cover everything that fell in its path and the entire region was filled with a wailing. The village, the church, the nearby woods—they all disappeared in the snowy obscurity whirling about in the air. The ancient Golovlyovo orchard produced a powerful hooting sound. But in the master's house it was bright, warm and comfortable. The samovar was set up in the dining room and Arina Petrovna, Porfiry Vladimirych and Yevprakseyushka had gathered there. Off to the side stood the card table on which tattered cards lay. From the dining room the open doors led, on the one hand, into the small chapel, suffused with the light from the burning lamps; on the other hand, into the master's study in which a lamp also burned before the ikon. It was stuffy in the overheated rooms, smelling of wood pitch and the charcoal for the samovar. Yevprakseyushka, seated oppo-

99

site the samovar, was rinsing out the cups and wiping them with a towel. The samovar was bubbling fiercely; first it would vibrate with all its might and then it would apparently begin to puff away and emit a piercing whistle. Clouds of steam spilled out from under the cover and the teapot, which had been sitting on top of the samovar for a quarter of an hour, became enveloped in a haze. The people seated there were chatting.

"Well, now, how much did you lose at cards today?" Arina Petrovna asked Yevprakseyushka.

"I wouldn't have lost if I hadn't lost on purpose. I wanted to make you feel good," replied Yevprakseyushka.

"That's a good one! I saw how good it made you feel when earlier I kept dealing you three and five cards at time. I'm not like Porfiry Vladimirych, you know! He spoils you, just giving you one card at a time, but there's no reason for me to do it, old girl."

"Moreover, you cheated!"

"Now, that's one sin you can't lay at my door!"

"And who was it that I caught earlier? Who wanted to make a pair of the seven of clubs and the eight of hearts? I saw it with my own eyes, I was the one who caught on!"

Saying this, Yevprakseyushka stood up to take the teapot off the samovar and then she turned her back to Arina Petrovna.

"Goodness, what a back you have... God bless it!" Arina Petrovna blurted out despite herself.

"Yes, that's some back..." little Judas responded mechanically.

"A back's a back...you shameless people! And what concern is my back to you!"

Yevprakseyushka looked to the left and right and smiled. Her back was her favorite topic. Earlier even the old man Savelich, the cook, even he had taken one look and said: "God, what a back! As wide as a stove!" She had not even complained about him to Porfiry Vladimirych.

The cups were filled in their turn with tea and the samovar began to simmer down. But the snowstorm was acting up more and more. A whole avalanche of snow was pounding the panes of the windows and then sweeping down the chimney flue with an indescribable wail.

"The snowstorm, it seems, has really set in," noted Arina Petrovna, "listen to it scream and howl!"

"Well, just let it go on howling. While it howls, we'll drink our nice cup of tea here, just so, mama, dear friend!" responded Porfiry Vladimirych.

"Goodness me, it wouldn't be good to be out in the fields now if one were overtaken by this grace of God!"

"It's bad for others, but we have nothing to fear here. It may be nice and dark and cold for someone else, but it's bright and warm here for us. Here we are sitting and having a nice cup of tea. We can have it with sugar and with cream and with lemon. And if we take a fancy to have it with rum, then we'll drink it with rum."

"But what if now..."

"Excuse me, mama, I am saying: right now out in the fields it is bad. There is no road, no path—everything has been swept away. The wolves are out again. But here it's bright and comfy and we have nothing to fear. We'll just sit and sit here, nice and peaceful. If we feel like playing cards—we'll play cards; if we feel like tea—then we'll drink some tea. We're not about to drink more than we need, but as much as we need, we'll drink. And why is this so? Because, dear friend, mama, we have not been abandoned by God's grace. If it weren't for Him, the heavenly Father, we too would be floundering about in the fields and it would be so dark and cold... In an old peasant coat of sorts, a miserable belt and bast shoes..."

"My goodness, bast shoes! I expect you too were born a member of the gentry? However bad they might be, we still have boots to wear!"

"But do you know, mama, why we were born into the gentry? Simply because we were blessed with the grace of God. If it hadn't been so, then we too would be now sitting in a miserable little hut and we wouldn't have a candle to burn, but only a torch, and as far as some nice tea and coffee are concerned—we wouldn't even dare to think about it! We would be sitting there. I would be weaving bast shoes and you would be preparing some kind of watery cabbage soup for supper. Yevprakseyushka would be weaving away... And perhaps to make things worse, the foreman would send me out with the cart..."

"Well, even the foreman wouldn't send you out with the cart in such weather!"

"How do we know, dear friend, mama! What if suddenly troops were on the march! Perhaps a war or an uprising—to make sure the troops got there in time! Just the other day the district police officer was telling me, Napoleon III had died, —probably now the French will be causing mischief! Naturally, our own people will advance—so, come on, you peasant, get your cart! And out into the freezing weather and the snowstorm, and no roads—don't you look around: off with you, peasant, if the authorities so command! But for the time being we'll still be spared, they won't chase us out with a cart!"

"That's telling the truth! God's grace is mighty for us!"

"Isn't that what I was saying? God, mama, is everything. He gives us wood to keep warm and provisions for food—He is everything. We think that we are everything ourselves, that we acquire things with our own money, but if you just stop and look around and give it some consideration—you'll see that God is everything. And if He did not care to, we would have nothing. Right now I would like some oranges and I'd eat them myself and I would treat my dear friend, mama, and I would give everyone an orange, and I have the money to buy oranges, I could just take it out and say—let's have them! But God says: 'Who-a-a!' And so here I sit: with nothing to eat for all my philosophy."

Everyone laughed.

"Tell us another!" Yevprakseyushka responded, "I had an uncle who was the sexton at the Church of the Assumption at Pesochnoye. Now it seems that he was a very God-abiding man, but do you think that God did anything for him! When he was overtaken by a snowstorm in the fields, he froze to death all the same."

"That's exactly what I'm talking about. If God wishes it, a man will freeze to death, if He doesn't wish it, then he'll remain alive. And again it must be said about praying: there is a suitable prayer and an unsuitable prayer. The suitable prayer will achieve its end, whereas the unsuitable one will make no difference whether uttered or unuttered. Perhaps your uncle's prayer was not the suitable one and so it did not achieve its end."

"I recall in 1824 I was travelling to Moscow—I was still carrying Pavel at that time, —and so I was travelling to Moscow in the month of December..."

"Excuse me, mama. I'll just finish about praying. A man prays for everything because he has need of everything. He needs butter, he needs cabbage, he needs cucumbers, in short, everything. Sometimes even things that are not necessary, but, because of his human weakness, he asks for everything. But God sees more clearly from on high. You beg Him for butter, but He'll give you cabbage or onions; you worry about good weather and about warm weather, but He sends you rain, and even hail. But you must understand this and not grumble. Just last September we kept asking God for frosts so that our winter crops wouldn't spoil, but God did not give any frost—so, our winter crops were ruined."

"They certainly were spoiled," sympathized Arina Petrovna, "the peasants at Novinki say the peasants' entire winter crops were a loss. In the spring they'll have to replow the fields and sow summer crops."

"That's precisely the point! Here we are being wise and clever, planning and calculating, then all at once, in a single moment, God turns all our well-made plans into dust. You, mama, wanted to tell us something that happened to you in 1824?"

"What's that! I've already forgotten! It must have been about the same thing, about God's grace. I don't recall, my friend, I don't recall."

"Well, God willing, you'll remember another time. But for the time being it's huffing and puffing outside, and you, dear friend, should eat some of this nice jam. These are Golovlyovo cherries! Yevprakseyushka herself made them."

"I am eating them. I must admit that cherries are a rarity for me now. Earlier I used to treat myself to them rather frequently, but now... You have fine cherries in Golovlyovo, juicy ones, big ones. But in Dubrovino, no matter how we tried to grow them they always came out sour. And you, Yevprakseyushka, did you add some French liqueur to the jams?"

"Of course I did! I did it just the way you taught me. But I wanted to ask you something: when you are pickling cucumbers, do you add cardamon?"

For a while Arina Petrovna pondered and even spread her arms.

"I don't recall, my friend; it seems I used to add cardamon. But now I don't: my pickling isn't anything now! But I added it before... I even remember quite well that I added it! As soon as I get home I'll rummage through my recipes to see whether I can find it. You know, when I had all my energy, I noted everything and wrote it down. If somewhere I had something I liked, I would immediately ask for everything, write it down on a piece of paper and try it out at home. Once I got ahold of such a secret, such a secret that even if a thousand rubles were offered, the person would not have revealed it, and that was that! But I slipped the housekeeper twenty-five kopeks and she told me everything down to the last drop!"

"Yes, mama, in your time you were such a...diplomat!"

"Diplomat or not, I can thank God: I did not squander but increased what I had. Even now I eat the fruits of my labor: after all, I planted the cherries at Golovlyovo!"

"And I thank you for that, mama, many thanks! I give you eternal thanks from both myself and from your descendants—there you have it!"

Little Judas arose, went up to his mama and kissed her hand.

"And I thank you for looking after your mother! Yes, you have very fine provisions, very fine!"

"What provisions do we have! Not like the ones you had, that's so. Just think how many cellars alone there were, and not a single little space left empty!"

"I used to have provisions—I won't lie, I was never a poor housekeeper. As far as having a lot of cellars was concerned, then after all it was all on a larger scale, there were ten times as many mouths compared to today. The number of house servants alone—you had to put aside something for each person and feed each one. A cucumber here, kvass there—little bits and pieces, but just look at how it all amounted to a great deal."

"Yes, it was a marvelous time. There was plenty of everything then. Both bread and fruit were all in abundance!"

"They used more manure, that's why everything grew."

"No, mama, that's not the reason. It was God's blessing, that's what it was. I remember once papa brought a large apple from the garden that amazed everyone: it wouldn't even fit on a plate."

"I don't remember that. In general, I do know there were fine apples, but that some of them were as big as a plate, that I do not remember. A carp weighing twenty pounds was caught in the Dubrovino pond at the time of the coronation, that I know for certain."

"Both the carp and the fruit, they were all enormous then. I remember the melons that Ivan the gardener produced—those were some melons!"

Little Judas first stuck his arms out, then made a circle with them, pretending that he could not make them meet.

"There were melons and melons. Melons, I tell you, my friend, depend on the year. One year there may be a great number of them and they are marvelous, the next year there are few and not very tasty, and then the third year there are absolutely none. And one should add that it depends where you grow what. Over there at Grigory Alexandrych's in Khlebnikovo, nothing would grow, neither berries, nor fruit, nothing. Just cantaloupes. But what cantaloups they were!"

"He must have had such cantaloups by the grace of God!"

"Of course. Without God's grace you won't get by anywhere and there's no escaping it!"

Arina Petrovna had already drunk two cups of tea and had begun to eye the card table. Yevprakseyushka was also burning with impatience to test her strength at cards. But these plans were upset thanks to Arina Petrovna herself, because she suddenly remember something.

"But I have some news," she announced, "I received a letter from the orphans yesterday."

"They've been quiet for so long and then suddenly they make themselves known. Obviously they must be in a fix, asking for money?"

"No, they're not asking for any. Here, take a look."

Arina Petrovna took the letter out of a pocket and gave it to little Judas who read:

Grandmother, don't bother to send us any more turkeys or chickens. Don't send any money either, but put it aside for the interest. We have appeared on the stage in a theatre in Kharkov and not in Moscow, and in the summertime we'll be making the rounds of the country fairs. I made my debut in "Périchole" and Lyubinka in "Pansies." I received several encores, particularly after the scene where Périchole comes out tipsy and sings: 'I am rea-ea-dy, I am re-ea-ea-dy!' Lyubinka was very popular as well. The director is giving me a hundred rubles a month and the receipts from one performance in Kharkov, and Lyubinka is getting seventy-five rubles a month and the receipts from a summer performance at a country fair. In addition to this, there are presents from officers and lawyers. Only sometimes the lawyers give counterfeit money, so one has to be careful. And you, dear grandmother, use whatever you want in Pogorelka, we'll never go back there and we can't even understand how anyone could live there. Yesterday the first snow fell and we went for a ride with some local lawyers in a troika. One of them looks like Plevako—amazing how handsome he is! He placed a glass of champagne on his head and danced the Trepak—it was all so marvelous! Another lawyer, nothing special, reminded us somewhat of Yazykov from Petersburg. Just imagine, he has so upset his imagination by reading "A Collection of the Best Russian Songs and Romances" and has weakened himself to such a degree that he even fainted in court. And so, we spend almost every day either with officers or with lawyers. We go for rides, dine in the best restaurants and pay nothing. And you, grandmother, don't begrudge yourself anything in Pogorelka and any-

thing that grows there: bread, chickens, mushrooms—eat everything. The capital we would gladly... Farewell, our cavaliers have arrived and are calling us to go for a ride in troikas again. Sweetie! You divine lady, you! Farewell!

Anninka
And me too—Lyubinka

"Phew," little Judas spat, returning the letter.

Arina Petrovna sat pondering and did not reply for awhile.

"You haven't answered them yet, have you, mama?"

"Not yet, I only received the letter yesterday and I brought it to show you, but for this and that I almost forgot."

"Don't answer them. It's better."

"How can I not answer? I am responsible for giving them an account. Pogorelka is theirs."

Little Judas also sank into thought; some evil plan had flashed through his head.

"I keep thinking about how they could be leading themselves astray in that den of iniquity!" Arina Petrovna continued in the interim, "after all it's the kind of thing where you only have to slip up once, then a virgin's honor can't be restored: You might as well whistle in the wind as try!"

"A lot of good it will do them!" snapped little Judas.

"Nonetheless...For a girl, one might say, that this is life's most precious treasure... Who would want to marry such a girl afterwards?"

"Nowadays, mama, they live with a husband even without getting married. Nowadays they mock the precepts of religion. They find a bush and get married under it—and that's an end to it. This is what they call a civil marriage."

Little Judas suddenly pulled up short, because after all he was living in sin with a girl from a clerical background.

"Of course, sometimes it has to be done..." he corrected himself, "if a man is still at his prime and a widower as well...sometimes it has to be done and there are exceptions to the law!"

"What's there to say! Under duress a snipe will warble like a nightingale. Even the saints sinned under duress and what can we do, sinners that we are!"

"That's it precisely. Do you know what I would do in your place?"

"Give me some advice, my friend, tell me."

"I would ask them for complete power of attorney over Pogorelka."

Arina Petrovna gave him a frightened look.

"But I do have complete power of attorney for running the estate," she muttered.

"Not just for running the estate. But so that you can sell it or mortgage it, in short, so that you could make whatever arrangments for it according to your own decision..."

Arina Petrovna looked down at the floor and was silent.

"Of course, this is a subject that has to be given some thought. But think about it, mama!" insisted little Judas.

But Arina Petrovna continued her silence. Although as a consequence of old age her power of conception had become significantly dulled, nonetheless, she did not feel right about the insinuations of little Judas. She was afraid of little Judas: she begrudged losing the warmth, and space and the abundance that were the rule at Golovlyovo, and at the same time he would not have initiated the talk about power of attorney without again fashioning a new noose. The situation became so tense that she then began to berate herself inwardly as to why she had been moved to show him the letter. Fortunately, Yevprakseyushka came to her rescue.

"Well! Are we going to play cards or not?" she asked.

"Yes, let's!" Arina Petrovna hastened to reply, and was quick to jump up from her tea. But on the way to the card table a new thought came to her.

"Do you know what day this is?" she turned to Porfiry Vladimirych.

"The twenty-third of November, mama," little Judas replied with surprise.

"The twenty-third, yes the twenty-third, and don't you remember what happened on the twenty-third of November? Have you really forgotten about the requiem?"

Porfiry Vladimirych turned pale and crossed himself.

"Oh, my God! What a misfortune," he exclaimed, "is it really? Are you sure? Just let me take a look at the calendar."

In a few minutes he brought a calendar and found the piece of paper inside it and on which was written: "The twenty-third of November. In memory of the death of my dear son, Vladimir. Rest in peace, sweet remains, until the dawning of the new day! And pray to God for your Papa who on this day will without fail hold a remembrance service."

"How do you like that!" Porfiry Vladimirych exclaimed, "alas, Volodya, Volodya! What an unkind son you are! So ungrateful! Apparently you aren't praying to God for your papa and his memory has been taken away by the Lord! What can we do about this, mama?"

"Even God doesn't know what happened, but tomorrow you can have the service performed. Both the requiem and the mass, we'll set everything right. Old woman that I am, and forgetful, I'm the one to blame. I came here on purpose to remind you and I completely forgot about everything on the way."

"Goodness me, what a sin! It's a good thing that the lamps are still lit in the chapel. You know, it's precisely as though a light fell on me from above. It's not a holiday today or anything, the lamps are still burning from Our Lady's Day. Yevprakseyushka only came to me earlier and asked: 'Should I put out the extra ikon lamps?' But I thought for a moment and said, as though suddenly inspired: don't touch them! Christ be with us, let them burn! And just look!"

"Yes, it's a good thing that the lamps at least were burning! That's one consolation for your soul! Where are you going to sit? Are you going to be dealing to me again or do you intend to indulge your pretty lady?"

"Well, I really don't know, mama, whether I can..."

"What do you mean, you can't! Sit down! God will forgive you! You didn't do it on purpose, consciously, you simply forgot. It can happen even to the saints! Tomorrow, as soon as it's light, we'll have the mass and then we'll do everything the way it should be done. And his soul will rejoice that his parents and other kind folk remembered him and we will be comforted by the fact that we have fulfilled our duty. That's it, my friend. There's no point in grieving over it, that's what I always say. First, you can't bring your son back by grieving, and secondly, it would be a sin in the eyes of God!"

Little Judas reasoned over these words and kissed his mama's hand, saying:

"Goodness me, mama, mama! You have a heart of gold—it's true! If it weren't for you, I don't know what I would have done this very moment! I simply would have been lost! For sure I would have been distraught and lost!"

Porfiry Vladimirych made the arrangements concerning the ceremony for the following day and then everyone sat down to cards. One hand was dealt, then a second, Arina Petrovna became irritated and indignant with little Judas because he kept dealing Yevprakseyushka one card at a time. In the intervals between dealing, little Judas lapsed into recollections about his deceased son.

"How affectionate he was," he said, "he never took anything without asking. If he needed some paper, he would say: 'May I take some paper, papa?' Go ahead, my friend! Or: 'Papa, would you be so kind as to order some carp done in cream for breakfast?' As you like, my friend! Alas, Volodya, Volodya! You were a good boy to everyone, only you weren't a good boy for abandoning your papa!"

A few more hands and once again recollections.

"Whatever happened to him all of a sudden, I can't even imagine! He was getting on just nice and fine, just going along, a joy to me, it seemed it couldn't have been better! Suddenly—bang! Just imagine what a sin it was! Just think about it mama, what a person will sink to! His own life, a gift from the heavenly Father! For what reason? Why? What did he lack? Money, perhaps? It seems I never withheld his allowance; even my enemies cannot hold that against me. And if it did not seem like much, then there was no sense in getting angry, my friend! Your papa doesn't have money lying about! If it's not much money, then find a way of restraining yourself. Everything isn't peaches and creams, you have to take the bad with the good as well! That's the way it is, brother! Take your papa, he too was expecting to get some money the other day, but a messenger came: the peasants from Terpenkovo weren't paying their quit-rents. Well, what can you do! So I wrote a complaint to the justice of the peace! Alas, Volodya! Volodya! No, you aren't a good boy, you abandoned your papa! You left him an orphan!"

The more lively the game went, the more profuse and emotional became the recollections.

"And what a clever fellow he was! I remember one episode. He had the measles—he was no more than seven years old—my deceased wife, Sasha, had just come to him and he said to her: 'Mama! mama! Is it true that only angels have wings?' And she said: 'Yes, only angels.' 'Why then,' he said, 'did papa have wings when he just came in here?' "

Finally the game reached Homeric proportions. Little Judas was caught with all of eight cards in his hands, among which were the ace of spades, and the king and queen. This provoked much laughter and teasing, and little Judas joined in all of this good-naturedly. But in the midst of the cheerful outburst, Arina Petrovna suddenly fell silent and cocked an ear.

"Stop! Don't make any noise! Someone is coming!" she said.

Little Judas and Yevprakseyushka also listened, but without success.

"I tell you, someone is coming! There, hear! I suddenly heard it on the wind... There! They're coming! Now they're close!"

Again everyone began to listen and, truly, they could hear a far-off tinkling of bells, alternately borne on the wind and then receding. About five minutes passed and the bell could now be heard unmistakably, and then after the bell, voices outside.

"The young master, Pyotr Porfirych, has arrived!" echoed from the hallway.

Little Judas arose and froze on the spot, white as a sheet.

* * *

Petenka entered the room somewhat listlessly, kissed his father's hand, then observed the same ceremony in regard to his grandmother, bowed to Yevprakseyushka and sat down. He was a youth of about twenty-five, of rather an attractive appearance, wearing an officer's travelling uniform. That was all that could be said about him, in fact, little Judas himself hardly knew any more of him. The mutual relations between father and son were such that one could not even call them strained; it was as though nothing had ever existed between them. Little Judas knew that this was a person who, according to his documents, bore the name of his son and to whom he was obliged to send a specific, pre-arranged allowance at given intervals, and from whom, in return, he had the right to demand respect and obedience. Petenka, for his part, knew that he had a father who could pester him at any moment. He made trips to Golovlyovo quite willingly, particularly since the time he had become an officer, but not because he found any pleasure in chatting with his father, but simply because any person who has not set himself any specific goals in life seems to be attracted instinctively to *his place*. But now, apparently, he had come for a reason, because he had been forced to, and for this reason he did not express a single one of those signs of joyful confusion by which every prodigal son of the gentry marks his arrival at his place of birth.

Petenka was untalkative. To all his father's exclamations of: "What a surprise! Well, brother, a fine trick you've pulled! Here I am sitting and thinking, who is this, God forgive us, travelling through the night? —and this is who it is!" and so forth, he would respond either with silence or with a forced smile. To the question: "Whatever possessed you to show up so suddenly?" he answered almost angrily: "I just made up my mind and came."

"Well, thank you! Thank you! You remembered your father! You made him happy! I imagine you were thinking of your old grandmother as well?"

"Yes, I was thinking about grandmother too."

"Wait! Perhaps you remembered that today is the anniversary for your brother, Volodenka?"

"Yes, I remembered that as well."

The conversation dragged on for half an hour in this vein, so that it was impossible to comprehend whether Petenka's answers were genuine or whether he was simply avoiding the questions. For this reason, little Judas, who otherwise was indulgent in regard to his children's indifference, nevertheless could not restrain himself any longer and noted:

"Yes, brother, you're not very affectionate! One can't say that you were ever an affectionate son!"

If Petenka had held his tongue this time, if he had accepted his papa's remark unprotestingly, or even better, had kissed his father's hand and said to him: "Forgive me, my dearest papa! I'm just tired from travelling!" then everything would have been circumvented satisfactorily. But Petenka acted with complete ingratitude.

"That's the way I am!" he answered as rudely as though he wanted to say: "Let me alone, for heaven's sake!"

Then Porfiry Vladimirych was so hurt, so hurt that even he found it impossible to remain silent.

"It seems I've taken a lot of trouble over you!" he said bitterly, "I even sit here and keep thinking how best to make things better and smoother, so that everyone would feel good and comfortable, without fuss and bother... But the two of you always avoided me!"

"What do you mean...the *two of you*?"

"Well, you alone...and, incidently, your deceased brother as well, may his soul rest in peace, he was the same..."

"Really! Thank you very much for that!"

"I don't see any gratitude at all from you two! No gratitude, no affection, nothing!"

"An unaffectionate nature, that's all there is to it. Why do you keep re-

109

ferring to the two of us? One is already dead..."

"Yes, he died, God punished him. God punishes disobedient children. But, all the same, I still remember him. He was disobedient, but I still remember him. Tomorrow we'll celebrate mass and have a requiem. He offended me, but all the same I still remember my duty. Lord, my God! What is happening nowadays! A son comes to his father and with the very first word he is snapping at him! Would we have acted so in our day! It used to be that when you were travelling to Golovlyovo, for thirty versts you kept repeating: 'Remember, O Lord, King David and all his meekness!' And here is mama who'll bear me witness—she'll tell you! But nowadays... I don't understand, I just don't understand!"

"Nor do I understand. I came here peacefully, I greeted you, I kissed your hand, now I'm sitting here, not bothering you, drinking tea and if you give me supper, then I'll eat supper. Why have you stirred up all this business?"

Arina Petrovna was sitting in her chair and listening. And it occurred to her that she was hearing that same familiar story which had begun long ago and she knew not when. This story was about to be closed completely, but then, no, no, here it was being taken up again at the very same page. Nonetheless, she realized that a meeting of this sort between father and son promised no good, and for that reason she considered it her duty to interfere in the quarrel and utter a word of reconciliation.

"Now, now, you turkey-cocks!" she said, striving to give her admonishment a jocular note. "You've barely seen each other and already you're fighting! Look at them going for each other, look at them go! Just watch, now the feathers will be flying! Ai-ai-ai! Woe is me! Come now, my fine fellows, sit and have a nice friendly chat with each other, and I, old lady that I am, will listen and admire the two of you! You, Petenka, give in! My friend, one must always give in to one's father, because he is your father! The next time you think your father is being unjust to you, then you just accept it readily and obediently, and with respect, because you are his son! Perhaps something sweet will come of the bitter—and you will be the one to benefit! And you, Porfiry Vladimirych—come down! He is your son, a young man, a little spoiled. He has travelled over seventy-five versts through snow drifts and ruts. He's tired and chilled and he wants to sleep! We've already finished our tea, have them serve supper and then to bed! Come now, my friends! We'll all go off to our places, say a prayer and give our hearts a rest! And whatever evil thoughts we have, they'll all be dispersed by God in our sleep! And tomorrow morning we'll get up nice and early, attend the requiem and then when we come home, then we'll have a talk. And everyone, after he's had a rest, will have a chance to talk about his affairs in the proper order. You, Petenka, about Petersburg, and you, Porfiry, about your life in the country. And now let's have supper—and with God's blessing, to bed!"

This admonishment had its effect not because it contained something that was truly convincing, but because little Judas saw himself that he had gone too far, and that it was better to bring the day to a peaceful conclusion. For this reason he arose from his place, kissed his mama's hand, thanked her for the "lesson" and ordered supper served. Supper passed in gloom and silence.

The dining room emptied as everyone dispersed to his room. The house gradually grew quiet and a deathly silence crept from room to room and finally reached the last refuge where the ritual life persisted longer than in other secluded corners, that is, the study of the master of Golovlyovo. Little Judas finally terminated his genuflections which he counted off for ever so long before the ikons and then he too finally went to bed.

Porfiry Vladimirych lay in bed but he was unable to close his eyes. He sensed that his son's arrival presaged something out of the ordinary and now, prematurely, all manner of idle morals were springing up in his mind. These morals possessed the virtue of being appropriate to any situation at all and did not even represent in themselves any connected chain of thought. They did not require either a grammatical sense or syntactical order: they accumulated in his mind in the form of fragmentary aphorisms and saw the light of day as fast as they could reach his tongue. Nonetheless, as soon as any special pretext occurred in life that departed from the common order, immediately such a confusion arose in his head from the onslaught of aphorisms that not even sleep could pacify it.

Little Judas could not sleep: hordes of trivia crowded around the head of his bed and oppressed him. Essentially speaking, Petenka's enigmatic arrival did not upset him in particular, because, whatever happened, little Judas had already prepared himself *for everything* beforehand. He knew that *nothing* would catch him unawares and *nothing* would force him to depart from that entanglement of empty, thoroughly stale aphorisms wherein he had become thoroughly enmeshed from head to toe. For him neither grief, nor joy existed, as did not hatred or love. In his eyes the entire world was a tomb which was capable of serving solely as a pretext for endless chatter. What could have occasioned more sorrow than when Volodya had committed suicide, yet he had withstood even that. It had been a very sad story which had lasted for all of two years. For all of two years Volodya had struggled. At first he had manifested pride and determination in not relying on his father's help. Then he weakened, began to beg, argued and threatened... But always he encountered, by way of response, a ready-made aphorism which represented a stone given to a hungry man. Whether little Judas realized or not that it was a stone and not bread, is a ticklish question. But in any event, he had nothing else to offer and so he gave his stone as the sole thing that he could give. When Volodya shot himself, little Judas arranged a requiem in his honor, recorded the day of his death in the calendar and promised that in the future he would arrange a requiem on the twenty-third of November together "with a mass." But when at times even he could sense within himself a vague voice murmuring that the resolution of a family conflict by means of suicide was at the very least a rather dubious thing, then he would call forth an entire complex of ready-made aphorisms of the type: "God punishes disobedient children," "the proud are destined to fall," and so on. And he would be consoled.

Even now he did the same. There was no doubt that something untoward had happened to Petenka, but whatever it was, Porfiry Golovlyov had to remain above these fortuitous happenings: "You got yourself into this mess, you can get yourself out...as you sow, so shall you reap...as you make your bed, so shall you lie in it." That was it precisely. He would say precisely that on the morrow to what his son had to inform him. But what if Petenka, like his brother Volodya, refused to accept a stone instead of bread? What if he too... Little Judas spat in disgust at this thought and ascribed it to the temptations of the devil. He tossed from side to side, trying in vain to fall asleep. Sleep would just begin to come to him—and suddenly: "There's no sense in reaching for the sky!" Or: "You must cut your coat according to your cloth...now take me...whereas you...you're in too much of a hurry and do you know the proverb: haste makes waste?" The trivia crowded around, crept, crawled and oppressed. Little Judas could not sleep under the burden of idle chatter with which he hoped to console his own soul the next day.

Nor could Petenka sleep either, although the journey had made a proper wreck of him. He had business which could be resolved only here in Golovlyovo, but this business was such that only God knew how to approach it. Truthfully speaking, Petenka understood quite well that his business was hopeless, that the trip to Golovlyovo would bring only unnecessary unpleasantness, but herein lay the very heart of it, namely, that there is in a person some kind of vague instinct for self-preservation which overpowers all consciousness and which eggs one on to such a degree: let nothing go untried! Thus he had come, and instead of steeling himself to be prepared to put up with everything, almost from the very first step he had begun to quarrel with his father. What would come of this trip? Would that miracle happen which had to transform stone into bread, or would it not?

Would it not be more straightforward to take a pistol and put it to his temple: "Gentlemen! I am unworthy to wear your uniform! I squandered the regiment's money! And therefore I pronounce a just and severe sentence on myself!" Bang—and everything would be finished! The *deceased* Lieutenant Golovlyov is stricken from the lists! Yes, that would have been decisive and... beautiful. His comrades would have said: "You had bad luck, you got carried away, but...you were an *honorable* man!" But instead of acting *in this fashion,* he had let the matter go until his deed became known to all. So they had released him for a specific amount of time in order to make good what he had squandered. And then—out of the regiment. In order to accomplish this purpose, which would have as its conclusion the dishonorable end to a career just begun, he had undertaken the journey to Golovlyovo, he had undertaken the journey with the complete certainty that he would receive a stone instead of bread!

But perhaps something would indeed happen?! After all, such things do... Suddenly the present Golovlyovo disappeared and in its place appeared a new Golovlyovo, under new circumstances, in which he was... Father did not necessarily have to...die—what need was there for that? —but just so that...in general, there would be new "arrangements"... Perhaps, grandmother—after all, she had money! When she found out about the misfortune facing him, she would give it right away! There you are, she would say, on your way quickly, now, before the time is up! And then he would be off, hurrying the drivers, barely making it to the station in time—and he would show up at the regiment precisely two hours before the time expired! Good chap, Golovlyov! —his comrades would say—give us your hand, you honorable fellow, you! And let everything be forgotten from this day forward! Not only would he remain in the regiment as before, but first he would be made into a staff captain, then captain proper, then the regimental adjutant (he had already been treasurer) and, finally, on the day of the regiment's jubilee...

Alas! If only this night would pass more quickly! Tomorrow.... well, tomorrow, whatever will be, will be! But what he would have to listen to the next day...alas, what wouldn't he have to listen to! Tomorrow...but why tomorrow? After all there was still another whole day before him... After all he had given himself two days precisely in order to have time to convince, to move him... To hell with two days! You think you'll convince him, move him! Hardly...

Here his thoughts ultimately became confused and gradually, one after the other, they sank in a sleepy mist. In a quarter of an hour the Golovlyovo house had completely sunk into a profound sleep.

The following day, early in the morning, the entire house was on its feet. Everyone went to the church, with the exception, incidentally, of Petenka, who remained at home on the pretext that he was tired from the journey. Finally the mass and requiem were performed and everyone returned home. Petenka, out of habit, went to kiss his father's hand, but little Judas gave his hand while looking the other way, and everyone noticed that he did not even make the sign of the cross over his son. Tea was poured, the funeral rice pudding was served. Little Judas went about in a gloomy mood, shuffling his feet, avoiding conversation, sighing, continually folding his hands as a sign of mental prayer and not looking at his son. For his part, Petenka sat hunched up and silently smoked one cigarette after the other. The strained situation of the day before had not only not improved overnight, but had taken such sharp overtones that Arina Petrovna was seriously upset and resolved to find out from Yevprakseyushka whether something had happened.

"Whatever happened?" she asked, "that they have been looking at each other like enemies since this morning?"

"How should I know? I don't bother with their affairs!" snapped Yevprakseya.

"Maybe it's because of you? Maybe my grandson has been playing up to you as well?"

"Why should he do that! He was simply on the lookout for me in the hallway earlier and Porfiry Vladimirych saw him!"

"Hm, so that's it!"

To be sure, despite the desperation of his situation, Petenka had not in the least abandoned his customary frivolousness. He too had fastened on Yevprakseyushka's powerful back and had determined to tell her so. With this very purpose in mind he had not gone to church, hoping that Yevprakseya, in her position as housekeeper, would remain at home. And then, when everything had grown quiet in the house, he had thrown his army coat over his shoulders and lain in wait in the hallway. A minute passed, then another, the door slammed which led from the front hall to the maids' quarters and Yevprakseya appeared at the end of the hallway carrying a tray in her hands with a rich, warm tea-roll for tea. But Petenka had hardly had time to give her a proper slap between her shoulder blades, had hardly had time to exclaim: "Now there's a back for you!"—when the door to the dining room opened and his father appeared in it.

"If you've come here to play tricks, you villain, then I'll have you thrown down the front stairs!" little Judas cried in an unmistakably spiteful voice.

Naturally, Petenka disappeared from the spot in an instant.

However, he could not help but understand that the morning's event was not apt to have a positive effect on his fortunes. Therefore he decided to remain silent and delay the confrontation until the next day. But at the same time not only did he not do anything to soothe his father's irritation, but, on the contrary, conducted himself in the most careless and foolish fashion. He did not cease smoking his cigarettes, paying no attention to the fact that his father was violently waving his arms at the clouds of smoke with which he had filled the room. Then he kept making foolish eyes at Yevprakseyushka, who was moved to wry smiles, something that little Judas noticed as well.

The day dragged drearily on. Arina Petrovna tried to play cards with Yevprakseyushka, but nothing came of it. No one played, no one talked, not even the usual trivia seemed to come to mind although everyone had untapped resources of this merchandise in store. After what seemed a long time, dinner arrived, but everyone was silent at dinner as well. After dinner Arina Petrovna prepared to leave for Pogorelka, but little Judas was even stricken at this decision by his dear friend, mama.

"Christ preserve you, dearie," he exclaimed, "do you want to leave me alone, eye to eye, with this...no-good son? No, no, don't even think of it! I won't let you go!"

"What's going on? Did something happen between you? Tell me!" she asked.

"No, for the time being nothing has happened, but you just see... No, don't you leave me! I want you here when it happens... He hasn't come for nothing, no not for nothing... If something does happen—then you'll be a witness!"

Arina Petrovna shook her head and decided to stay.

After dinner Porfiry Vladimirych went off to sleep, sending Yevprakse-yushka, as a precaution, to the priest in the village. Arina Petrovna, having put off her departure for Pogorelka, also went off to her room and, having seated herself in an armchair, was dozing. Petenka figured that this was the most appropriate time to try his luck with grandmother and he made his way to her.

"What do you want? Did you come to play cards with the old lady?" Arina Petrovna greeted him.

"No, grandmother, I'm here on business."

"Well, speak up, what is it."

Petenka collapsed instantly and blurted out suddenly:

"Grandmother, I gambled away the regiment's money."

Everything grew dark before Arina Petrovna's eyes from this unexpected piece of news.

"Was it a lot?" she asked in a frightened voice, looking at him with unblinking eyes.

"Three thousand."

A minute of silence followed. Arina Petrovna looked anxiously from side to side, as though she really expected help to come from some direction.

"Do you realize that you'll go straight to Siberia for this?" she finally uttered.

"I do."

"Alas, you poor soul, you!"

"Grandmother, I want to ask you for a loan... I'll pay good interest."

Arina Petrovna was quite frightened.

"What are you saying! What are you saying!" she floundered about, "but I only have enough money for my burial and funeral expenses! I only have enough to eat because of the good graces of my granddaughters, and whatever my son treats me to! No, no, no! Leave me alone! Have mercy, leave me alone! You know what, you should ask your papa!"

"There's no point in that! You might as well try to get blood out of a stone! Grandmother, you are my only hope!"

"What are you saying! What are you saying! I would gladly do it, but what money have I got! I don't have that kind of money! You should go to your father and be loving and respectful! Here, say to him, papa, this is what happened. Say, 'I'm guilty, it's my youth, I went astray...' Give him a smile, kiss his hand and get down on your knees and cry a bit—he loves that—and papa will loosen his purse-strings for his dear son."

"Just think! Would he really do it? Just a minute, just a minute! Grandmother, what about if you were to say to him: 'If you don't give him the money—I'll curse you!' For a long time he has feared your curse, you know!"

"Now, now, why should I curse him! You just go and ask him. Just ask him, my friend! After all it won't kill you to get down on your knees before him an extra time—he is your father! He'll see how things are from where he stands...go ahead! It's true!"

Petenka paced back and forth with his hands on his hips as though he were giving it some thought. Finally he stopped and said:

"Hardly. All the same he won't give it to me. Whatever I do, even if I get down on my hands and knees and smash my head from bowing—he still won't give it to me. But if you threatened to put a curse on him... So what am I going to do, grandmother?"

"I don't know, I really don't. Try, maybe he'll soften. But how could you have allowed yourself to do such a thing? Is it such an easy thing to gamble away the regiment's money? Did somebody teach you how to do that?"

"I simply took it and gambled it away. But if you don't have any of your own money, then give me some of the orphans' money!"

"What are you saying? Come to your senses! How can I give you the orphans' money? No, have mercy on me, let me be! Don't talk about that with me, for Christ's sake!"

"So you won't do it? A pity. I would have paid a very good interest. Do you want five per cent a month? No? What about 100 per cent interest in a year's time?"

"Don't you try and tempt me, either!" she waved her hands at him, "Get away from me, for Christ's sake! All we need is for your papa to overhear us and then he'll say that I put you up to it! Oh, my Lord! I, an old woman, just wanted to rest, just to doze off completely, and here he comes with this kind of business!"

"All right, fine. I'll go. Do you really mean you won't? Marvelous. Like good relatives. For the sake of three thousand rubles your grandson has to go off to Siberia! Don't forget to say a little prayer to send me on my way!"

Petenka slammed the door and disappeared. One of his frivolous hopes had burst—what would he do now? Only one thing remained: he would confess everything to his father. Just maybe... Maybe something would....

"I'll go now and have done with it once and for all!" he said to himself, "or no! No, why do it today... Maybe something would...yes, what could that something be? No, better tomorrow... All the same, today was the day... Yes, better tomorrow. I'll tell him—and then I'll leave.."

With that he concluded that the next day would be the end to it all...

After his discussion with grandmother, the evening dragged on even more drearily. Even Arina Petrovna was subdued, having learned of the real reason for Petenka's arrival. Little Judas was on the verge of attempting to

116

play cards with mama, but seeing tht she was deep in thought over something, he fell silent. Nor did Petenka do anything, he merely smoked. At supper Porfiry Vladimirych turned to him with the question:

"Will you finally tell us why you have come?"

"I'll tell you tomorrow," Petenka answered sullenly.

* * *

Petenka arose early after an entirely sleepless night. The same two-pronged thought was persecuting him—the thought which began with the hope: maybe he'll give it to me! and invariably ending with the question: why have I come here? Perhaps he did not understand his father, but in any event he did not know of a single emotion or a single weak fiber in him at which he might grasp and by exploiting could achieve something. He felt only that in the presence of his father he found himself face to face with something which he could not grasp or explain. This inability to approach the subject, to initiate a discussion, gave rise to something that was practically terror, or in any event, anxiety. And so it had been from his very childhood. For as long as he could remember, the situation seemed to be that it was better to withdraw any proposal entirely than to have to depend on his father's decision. So it was now. How would he begin? Where would he begin? What would he say?... Why had he bothered to come?

A feeling of dejection took hold of him. Nonetheless, he understood that he had only a few hours left before him and that, as a consequence, he had to do something. Assuming a false determination, buttoning up his jacket and whispering something as he walked, he made his way to his father's study with an utterly firm step.

Little Judas was on his knees praying. He was a religious man and every day he gladly devoted several hours to prayer. But he did not pray because he loved God and hoped by means of prayer to enter into communion with him, but because he feared the devil and hoped that God would deliver him from the evil one. He knew a multitude of prayers and in particular he had studied the technique of praying. That is, he knew when it was necessary to move one's lips and roll one's eyes heavenward, when it was necessary to fold one's hands palm to palm and when to hold them upraised, when one should display a burst of emotion and when one should be decorous, performing graceful signs of the cross. Both his eyes and nose would turn red and grow moist at specific moments which were indicated to him by his experience with prayer. But prayer did not renew him, it did not illuminate his senses, did not bring any ray of light into his dim existence. He could pray and perform all the requisite physical motions—and at the same time glance out the window and notice whether someone were going to the store cellars without asking permission, and so on. It was a totally personal and individualized style of life which was capable of existing and satisfying itself completely independently of any common style of life.

When Petenka entered the study, Porfiry Vladimirych was on his knees with outstretched hands. He did not alter his position, but simply waved one hand in the air to indicate that it was not yet time. Petenka ensconced himself in the dining room where the table was already set for tea and began to wait. The half-hour seemed an eternity to him, the more so because he was certain that his father was making him wait on purpose. The affected determination with which he had armed himself gradually began to give way to a feeling of annoyance. At first he sat there calmly, then he took to pacing back and forth in the room, and finally started whistling something, as a result of which the door to the study opened and the irritated voice of little Judas was heard from inside:

"Whoever feels like whistling, should go and do it in the stables!"

A little later Porfiry Vladimirych came out, dressed all in black, with a clean white shirt as though he were prepared for something solemn. His face was radiant, emotional, exuding humility and joy as though he had only just "made himself worthy." He went up to his son, made the sign of the cross over him and kissed him.

"Greetings, friend!" he said.

"Greetings, father!"

"How did you sleep? Was your bed well made? You didn't feel any bed-bugs or lice, did you?"

"Thank you, no. I slept."

"Well, you slept, praise be to God. It's only possible to sleep nice and soundly at your parents'. I know that myself: however well you may be set up in Petersburg, you'll never sleep as nice and soundly as here in Golovlyovo. It's just as though you were being rocked in a cradle. Well, what should you and I do, drink some tea, maybe, first, or do you wish to say something?"

"No, it would be better for us to have a talk now. I must leave in six hours, so perhaps some time might be needed to think things over."

"Well, all right. Only, brother, I am telling you straight: I never think things over. I always have an answer ready. If you are seeking for something that is justified, then by all means! I never refuse anything that is justified. Even if sometimes it's a rather difficult situation, and not within my power, but if it is justified, I cannot refuse! That's the way my nature is. But if you request something unjustified, just don't get angry now! Even if I feel sorry for you, I'll still refuse! I have no tricks up my sleeve, brother! I'm like an open book. Well, come now, let's go into my study! You'll speak and I'll listen! We'll just listen to what it's all about, yes, we will!"

When both had entered the study, Porfiry Vladimirych left the door slightly ajar and then neither did he sit down, nor did he ask his son to be seated, but began to pace back and forth in the room. It was as though he instinctively sensed that it would be a ticklish business and that it would be much more convenient to discuss such matters while on one's feet. Moreover, it would be easier to hide the expression of his face, and to put an end to the conversation if it took an overly unpleasant turn. And with the door open it would be possible to send for witnesses because mama and Yevprakseyushka would no doubt soon appear for tea in the dining room.

"Papa, I have gambled away the regiment's money," Petenka explained all at once and in a daze.

Little Judas said nothing. The trembling of his lips was the only thing noticeable. And then, as was his custom, he began to whisper.

"I lost three thousand," Petenka went on, "and if I don't return the money by the day after tomorrow, then very unpleasant consequences are in store for me."

"Well then, return it!" Porfiry Vladimirych said in an amiable voice.

The father and son made several rounds of the room in silence. Petenka wanted to explain further, but felt that his throat was constricted.

"But where will I get the money from?" he muttered at last.

"Dear friend, I don't know what your sources are. Whatever sources you were counting on when you gambled away the regiment's money, those are the ones you should use to pay with!"

"You yourself know quite well that under such circumstances people forget completely about sources!"

"I know nothing of the sort, my friend. I never played cards—that is, one plays cards with mama to make the old lady happy. And, if you please, don't drag me into this nasty business, and we had better go and have our tea. We'll drink and sit for awhile, maybe we'll talk about something, only, for Christ's sake, not about this."

Little Judas was about to head for the door to slip quickly into the dining room, but Petenka stopped him.

"Excuse me, but you see," he said, "I must find a way out of this predicament!"

Little Judas grinned and looked Petenka in the eye.

"Yes, you must, dearie!" he agreed.

"So help me then!"

"But that...that is something else again. The fact that you have to get yourself out of this predicament—you've spoken the truth there. But how to do it, that's none of my business!"

"But why don't you want to help?"

"Because in the first place I don't have any money to cover your wretched affairs, and in the second, simply because in general it doesn't concern me. You got yourself into the mess, you can get yourself out. If you want to take chances, you'll have to pay the consequences. That's the way it is, friend. I did say a short while ago that if your request was justified..."

"I know, I know. You always have a ready-made phrase on your lips..."

"Stop, put a rein on your impertinence, let me finish. That these are not simply phrases—I'll prove to you right this moment... Now, I told you a short while ago, if your request is justified, sensible, then, by all means, my friend! I'm always ready to please you! But if you come with a request that is not sensible, then, excuse me, brother! I do not have any money for your wretched affairs, none whatsoever! Nor will there be any—understand that! And don't you dare say that these are only 'phrases,' understand that these phrases coincide very closely with the facts."

"But just think what's going to happen to me!"

"Whatever pleases God, will be," replied little Judas, raising his hands somewhat and glancing sideways at the ikon.

The father and son made several turns around the room again. Little Judas walked unwillingly, as though he regretted the fact that his son was holding him in captivity. Petenka, hands on hips, followed him, biting his mustache and grinning nervously.

"I am your last son," he said, "don't forget that!"

"My friend, God took everything from Job, yet he did not complain, but only said: 'God giveth and God taketh—They will be done, Lord!' That's true, brother!"

"Maybe God taketh, but you yourself take from yourself. Volodya..."

"Now, it seems, you're about to say something vulgar!"

"No, it's nothing vulgar, it's the truth. Everyone knows that Volodya..."

"No, no, no! I don't want to listen to your vulgar words! Moreover, in general that's enough. You said what you had to say. I also gave you my answer. And now let us go and have our tea. We'll sit and talk, then we'll eat, drink a farewell toast, and God go with you. Just see how good God is to you! The weather has settled down, the road is now clear. Nice and easy off you'll go, trippety-trot, and before you know it, you'll be at the station!"

"Listen! For the last time I beg you! If there's at least a drop of feeling in you..."

"No, no, no! We will not talk about this! Let's go into the dining room. Mama must be bored with having to sit and wait for her tea. It's not nice to force an old lady to wait!"

Little Judas made an abrupt about-turn and headed toward the door at almost a run.

"Whether you leave or not, I won't put a stop to our conversation!" Petenka shouted after him, "It'll be worse if we start talking in front of witnesses!"

Little Judas turned around and stood directly in front of his son.

"What do you want from me, you good-for-nothing...speak up!" he asked in an excited voice.

"I want you to replace the money I lost."

"Never!!"

"So that's your final word?"

"Do you see that?" little Judas exclaimed solemnly, pointing with his finger at the ikon hanging in the corner, "do you see that? This is your papa's

blessing on you... Before that ikon I say to you: never!!"
He left the study with a determined step.
"Murderer!" echoed after him.

* * *

Arina Petrovna was already seated at the table and Yevprakseyushka was making all the preparations for tea. The old woman was thoughtful and taciturn and even seemed to be ashamed of Petenka. Little Judas, as was his custom, kissed her hand, and from habit, Arina Petrovna made the sign of the cross over him. Then, as was the custom, questions were exchanged as to whether everyone was well, had they slept well, and the customary monosyllabic answers followed.

She was at a complete loss from the evening before. Ever since Petenka had asked her for the money and had aroused in her memory of the "curse," she had suddenly fallen into a kind of mysterious uneasiness, and the thought began to torment her ruthlessly: what if I really do curse him? Having learned in the morning that the discussion had begun in the study, she turned to Yevprakseyushka with the request:

"Why don't you go, my lady, and listen quietly by the door to what they're saying?"

But even though Yevprakseyushka did try to listen, she was so simple that she could not understand a thing.

"So, they're having a talk between themselves! They're not shouting much!" she explained when she returned.

Then Arina Petrovna could bear it no longer and she herself made for the dining room where in the meantime the samovar had already been set up. But the discussion was already approaching the end. She merely heard Petenka raising his voice while Porfiry seemed to be buzzing in response.

"Buzzing! Yes, he sounds exactly as though he's buzzing!" the thought whirled around in her head, "That's the same way he used to buzz! How is it I didn't realize it then?"

Finally both the father and the son appeared in the dining room. Petenka was red and breathing heavily. His eyes had a wild look, the hair on his head was all dishevelled, his forehead was sprinkled with beads of sweat. On the other hand, little Judas entered pale and spiteful. He wanted to appear indifferent, but despite all his efforts, his lower lip was trembling. Only with great effort could he utter his customary greeting to his dear friend, mama.

Everyone took his place around the table. Petenka sat somewhat further off and leaned against the back of the chair, crossed his legs, lit up a cigarette and gazed ironically at his father.

"There you are, mama, even our weather has subsided," little Judas began, "what a disturbance we had yesterday, but it only took the will of God, and here we have peace and quiet and God's blessing! Isn't that so, my friend?"

"I don't know. I didn't go out of the house today."

"By the way, we'll be saying good-bye to our dear guest," continued little Judas, "I arose even earlier, looked out the window and it was so calm and peaceful outside, just as though the angel of the Lord had flown past and in a single moment had subdued all the uproar with his wing!"

But no one even replied to these amiable words of little Judas. Yevprakseyushka was noisily drinking her tea from the saucer, blowing on it and snorting. Arina Petrovna was gazing into her cup and silent. Petenka, rocking in his chair, continued to stare at his father with an ironic and challenging expression, as though he were doing everything in his power to keep from bursting into laughter.

"Now, even if Petenka doesn't rush," Porfiry Vladimirych began again, "he'll still make it to the railway station easily by evening. We have our own horses, they're well cared for, they'll be rested and fed in Muravyovo for a couple of hours, then they'll be off in a flash. They'll get there in no time flat! Then the engine will come rumbling up! Goodness me, Petka! Petka! You're so unkind! You ought to stay here with us, be our guest for a while, really! It would make all of us happier, and just see if you won't feel better after a week!"

But Petenka still continued to rock back and forth on his chair and gaze at his father.

"Why do you keep looking at me," little Judas finally began to seethe, "have I got three eyes or something?"

"I'm looking and waiting to see what else you'll do!"

"Nothing, brother, don't bother! As I already said, that's the way it'll be. I won't go back on my word!"

A minute of silence ensued during which the whisper clearly resounded: "Little Judas!"

Without a doubt Porfiry Vladimirych heard this utterance (he even turned pale), but he pretended that the exclamation had not reached him.

"Alas, children, children!" he said, "I feel sorry for you and I want to treat you with affection and with love, but apparently there's nothing that can be done—fate is against it! You yourselves run away from your parents, you pick up with your own friends and acquaintances who are dearer to you than your father and mother. Well, there's nothing to be done! One ponders and ponders over it, and finally one gives in. You are young people, and everyone knows that the young want to spend their time with other young people rather than with a grumpy old man! So you just console yourself and don't complain. You merely beg your heavenly Father: Thy will be done, Lord!"

"Murderer!" Petenka whispered again, but now so clearly that Arina Petrovna looked at him in horror. Something suddenly swept before her eyes, something resembling the shadow of Styopka-the-dunce.

"Whom are you saying that about?" little Judas asked, all atremble with agitation.

"I was just talking about an acquaintance."

"So that's it! Is that the way you talk! God knows what's in your mind. Perhaps you were honoring one of the present company in this way!"

Everyone fell silent. The glasses of tea stood untouched. Little Judas leaned against the back of his chair as well and began rocking back and forth nervously. Seeing that all hope was lost, Petenka felt something akin to a pre-death agony and under its influence he was prepared to go to all extremes. Both the father and the son were staring each other in the eye with a kind of inexplicable smile. However well Porfiry Vladimirych had schooled himself, the moment was drawing near when he would no longer be in any condition to restrain himself.

"You had better go while the going's good!" he finally spoke out, "indeed!"

"I'll be going."

"Why wait! I see that you've been heading for an argument, but I don't wish to argue with anyone. We are living here quite calmly and peacefully, with no fuss and no bother—here's our old grandmother sitting there, you could at least show some conscience for her sake! Why did you come to us?"

"I told you why!"

"If that was the only reason, then your labor has been in vain. Leave, brother! Hello, who's there? Order the carriage to be packed up for the young master. And take some roast chicken, and caviar and a few other things, eggs or something...and wrap them up in paper. You can have a snack at the station, brother, while the horses are being fed. God go with you!"

"No! I'm not going yet. I want to go to the church yet and request a requiem sung in honor of God's murdered servant, Vladimir."

"You mean for the suicide..."

"No, for my murdered brother."

Father and son looked directly into each other's faces. It seemed as though both were about to leap to their feet. But little Judas made a superhuman effort and turned his chair to face the table.

"Amazing!" he said in a strained voice. "A-ma-zing!"

"Yes, for my murdered brother!" Petenka said with rude insistence.

"Just who killed him, then?" little Judas inquired with curiosity, apparenly hoping all the same that his son would come to his senses.

But Petenka was not embarrassed in the least and thundered like a cannon:

"You!!"

"Me?"

Porfiry Vladimirych could not recover himself from the surprise. He rose hastily from his chair, turned to face the ikon and began to pray.

"You! You! You!" Petenka repeated.

"There we are! Well, praise be to God! Now I feel better after praying!" said little Judas, once again seating himself at the table, "now, just stop, wait a moment! Despite the fact that as your father I do not have to enter into any explanations with you, well, so be it! According to you, I killed Volodenka?"

"Yes, you!"

"In my opinion, that's not so. In my opinion he shot himself. At that time I was here, in Golovlyovo, and he was in Petersburg. Where else could I have been but here? How could I have killed him from a distance of seven hundred versts?"

"Can't you really understand?"

"I do not understand, God is my witness, I do not understand!"

"Who was it who left Volodya without a kopek? Who cut off his allowance? Who?"

"Now, now, now! So why did he marry against his father's will?"

"Would you really have given him your permission?"

"Who? Me? God forfend! I never would have allowed it! Ne-ver-r!"

"Of course, that is, in this situation you would have acted in your usual fashion. Every word of yours has ten different meanings: just try and figure it out!"

"I never would have allowed it! He wrote me at that time: 'Papa, I want to marry Lidochka.' Understand, he said 'I want' and not 'I beg your permission.' Well, I said to him: 'If you *want* to get married, then get married, I can't stand in your way!' That's all there was to it."

"That's all there was to it," Petenka mimicked him, "But isn't that, in fact, permission?"

"That's the point, no it isn't. What did I say? I said: 'I can't stand in your way'—that's all there was to it. Whether I gave my permission or not, that's another question. He did not ask for my permission, he just wrote: 'I *want* to marry Lidochka, papa.' As far as permission was concerned, I simply kept quiet. If you *want* to get married, then, Christ be with you, my friend! Marry Lidochka, or any other girl you like, my friend, I can't stand in your way!"

"All you could do was leave him without a piece of bread. You could have at least written: 'I don't like your intention,' you could have said, 'and therefore, although I can't stand in your way, nonetheless, I am warning you that you can no longer count on any financial assistance from me.' At least it would have been clear then."

"No, I never would have allowed myself to do that! Using threats on some account with a son who is fully grown—never!! I have a rule that I do not stand in anyone's way! He wanted to get married—so get married! But as far as any inheritance is concerned, —just don't get angry! He himself should have given it some previous consideration. God has given you brains for that. But I, brother, do not interfere in the affairs of others. And not only do I not interfere, but I do ask that others not interfere in mine. Yes, not only do I ask, do you hear, in fact...I forbid it! Do you hear that, you no-good, disrespectful son, I for-bid it!"

"Go ahead and forbid it, if you want! You won't stop everyone from talking!"

"If only he had repented! If only he had understood that he had insulted his father! He did something rude, now go ahead and repent! Ask forgiveness! Forgive me, dearest heart, papa, he could have said, for offending you! Now, that would have done it!"

"But he did write you. He explained that he had nothing to live on, that he no longer had the strength to go on..."

"You don't explain things to your father, sir. You ask your father for forgiveness, that's all there is to it."

"But he did that too. He was in such torment that he even asked your forgiveness. He did everything, everything!"

"Even if he did, still he was not in the right. He asked only once for forgiveness and when he saw that his papa did not forgive him, he should have asked another time!"

"Oh, you!"

Saying this, Petenka suddenly ceased rocking on his chair, turned to the table and leaned both his elbows on it.

"And now I too..." he muttered in a barely audible voice.

His face was gradually becoming distorted.

"And now I too..." he repeated, shaking from hysterical sobbing.

"And who is to blame..."

But little Judas did not succeed in finishing his moral, for at that very instant something completely unexpected happened. During the exchange of fire just described, it was as though Arina Petrovna had been forgotten. But she had not in any sense remained the indifferent witness to this family drama. On the contrary, from the very first glance one might have suspected that something not entirely ordinary was taking place within her and that, perhaps, the moment had come when the reckoning for her own life arose before her inner eye in all its fullness and nakedness. Her face came to life, her eyes flashed and grew dilated, her lips were moving as though they were trying to form some words and could not. And suddenly, at that very moment when Petenka filled the dining room with his sobbing, she rose heavily from her chair, stretched her hand forth and a shriek burst from her breast:

"I cur-r-rse you!"

THE NIECE

All the same, little Judas did not give Petenka any money, although, as a kind father, he ordered placed in the sled at the moment of departure some chicken, veal, and meat-pies for his son. Then, despite the cold and the wind, he personally went out on the porch to see his son off, made sure that he was comfortably seated, saw that he had wrapped up his feet properly, and then, returning to the house, made signs of the cross through the window in the dining room, sending off his unseen farewell to the sled carrying Petenka. In short, he fulfilled all of the rituals as demanded, like a good relative.

"Alas, Petka, Petka," he said, "a bad son you are! No good! Just look at how you've gotten yourself into trouble...ai-ai-ai! Just to live, it seems, nice and quietly, all calm and peaceful, with your papa and your old grandmother—it's not to be! Fie on you! My head will tell me what to do, you say! I can follow my own mind! Well, there's your mind for you! Alas, what misery has come of it!"

But meanwhile not a single muscle trembled in his wooden face, not a single note in his voice had the ring of anything resembling a summons to his prodigal son. Incidentally, no one even heard his words because only Arina Petrovna was in the room and she was still under the effects of the shock she had just experienced and had somehow lost her vital force all at once and was sitting behind the samovar, her mouth wide open, hearing nothing and staring numbly directly before herself.

Then life flowed on as before, filled with the idle bustle and endless idle chatter...

Contrary to the expectations of Petenka, Porfiry Vladimirych bore his mother's curse rather calmly and did not retreat a whit from the decisions which, so to speak, were already prepared ahead of time in his mind. True, he had turned somewhat pale and had rushed to his mother with the cry:

"Mama! Dearest heart! Christ preserve you! Calm yourself, dearie! God is merciful! He'll fix everything!"

But these words were more an expression of alarm for his mother's sake than for himself. Arina Petrovna's attack had been so sudden that little Judas could not even collect himself enough to pretend to be shocked. Just the evening before, mama had been very amiable with him, she had joked, played cards with Yevprakseyushka. Apparently, she must have, on the spur of the moment, taken it into her head, but there had been nothing premeditated or "genuine" in it. In fact, he very much feared his mama's curse, but he had imagined it in completely different terms. An entire scene had been composed in his idle mind for this event: ikons, illuminated candles, mama standing in the middle of the room, awesome, her face darkened...and cursing him! Then: lightning, the candles being extinguished, the curtains rent asunder, darkness covering the earth, and up above, in the midst of the clouds, the wrath-filled face of Jehovah, illuminated with lightning, growing visible. But

126

since nothing of the sort took place, it meant that mama was simply acting up, she was fantasizing, and nothing more. Moreover, there was no "proper" reason for her to curse him, because lately they had not even had any pretexts for a confrontation. Since the time he had expressed his doubt over mama's ownership of the carriage (little Judas agreed inwardly that *then* he had been guilty and had deserved her curse), much water had flowed under the bridge. Arina Petrovna had become reconciled, whereas Porfiry Vladimirych only thought of how to comfort his kind friend, mama.

"The old girl is in a bad way, my, what a bad way she's in! At times she even forgets what she's started!" he consoled himself. "She sits down, the old dear, to play cards, and before you know it, she's dozed off!"

In all justice it should be said that Arina Petrovna's feebleness even worried him. He had not yet prepared himself for this loss, he had not thought things over, he had not managed to make any of the proper calculations: how much capital mama had when she left Dubrovino, how much interest this capital could gain in a year, how much she was apt to spend of this income and how much she would lay away. In short, he had not created that entire mass of trivia without which he always felt himself caught unawares.

"The old girl is tight-fisted!" he would muse at times, "she won't spend *everything*—how could she! When she divided up the estate among us, she had a fair amount of capital! Surely she couldn't have made it all over to the orphans—of course not, she won't give the orphans much! The old girl has money, she does!"

But these musings did not, for the time being, represent anything serious and flitted off without remaining in his brain. The mass of everyday trivia was great enough without having to increase it with any new trivia for which as yet there was no essential necessity. Porfiry Vladimirych kept putting it off over and over again, and only after the sudden scene in which he had been cursed did he pull up short and realize it was time to begin.

The catastrophe had set in earlier, incidentally, than he had supposed. The day after Petenka's departure, Arina Petrovna left for Pogorelka and then no longer returned to Golovlyovo. She spent an entire month in complete isolation, not emerging from her room and ever so rarely allowing herself to exchange a word with her servant. Arising in the morning, she sat down at her desk, as was her custom, and began to lay out the playing cards, again as was her custom, but she hardly ever finished and seemed to freeze on the spot with her eyes staring out the window. What she was thinking, and whether she was even thinking about something—the most astute connoisseur of the human heart's most precious secrets could not have surmised. It seemed as though she wanted to recollect something, even, for example, how she had come to be there, within those walls and—could not. Upset over her silence, Afimyushka would peek into the room, straighten the chair cushions which were wedged in all around her, attempt to begin a conversation about something, but merely received monosyllabic and abrupt responses. During this time Porfiry Vladimirych made several trips to Pogorelka, invited his mama to Golovlyovo, attempted to stir her imagination with pictures of mushrooms, carp and other Golovlyovo temptations, but she merely smiled enigmatically at his suggestions.

One morning, as was her custom, she was about to rise from her bed and could not. She felt no particular pain at all, complained of nothing, but simply could not rise. This circumstance did not even particularly upset her, as though it were in the proper order of things. The day before she had been still sitting at the table, she was strong enough to walk about, and now today she was lying in her bed, "unwell." She even felt more at peace. But Afimyushka grew alarmed and, without letting the mistress know, sent a messenger to Porfiry Vladimirych.

Little Judas came early the next morning. Arina Petrovna was already significantly worse. He questioned the servant in detail as to what mama had eaten, whether or not she had allowed herself too much to eat, but was given the response that Arina Petrovna had been eating almost nothing for a month now, and the day before had refused food entirely. Little Judas demonstrated his grief, he waved his arms and like a good son, before going in to his mother, he warmed himself by the stove in the maids' quarters so that he would not bring cold air in to the invalid. And by way of precaution (where the dead were concerned he had the nose of the devil), he immediately began to make arrangements. He made inquiries concerning the priest, whether he was at home so that in the case of an emergency he could be sent for immediately. He learned where mama's chest of papers were kept, whether it was locked and then, having put his mind at rest as far as the essentials were concerned, he called the cook and ordered dinner for himself.

"I don't need much!" he said, "do you have any chicken? —Well, make some soup out of the chicken! Perhaps you have some salted meat, prepare a piece of salted meat as well! Some sort of roast meat...and that will do me!"

Arina Petrovna was lying stretched out on her back in the bed, her mouth open and breathing laboriously. Her eyes were dilated; one hand had gotten out from under the hairskin blanket and had grown cold in the air. Apparently she had been listening to the noise which her son's arrival had provoked, perhaps even the orders given by little Judas had reached her as well. Thanks to the lowered blinds in the room, darkness reigned. The wicks had burned low in the lamps and one could hear them sputtering from being in contact with the water. The air was heavy and foul. The closeness of the air from the stoked-up ovens, from the odor of pitch spread by the lamps and from the stench had become unbearable. Porfiry Vladimirych, in his felt boots, like a snake, slid up to his mother's bed. His elongated and shrivelled figure swayed mysteriously in the grip of the shadows. From beneath the cover Arina Petrovna watched him with eyes that seemed filled with both fear and surprise.

"It's me, mama," he said, "what's this that you're feeling under the weather today! My, my, my! For some reason I didn't sleep well last night. All night I was troubled by something: I kept thinking to myself, I should go and see how our old friends at Pogorelka are doing! I got up this morning, immediately took the carriage and a pair of nice horses—and lo and behold, here I am!

Porfiry Vladimirych giggled amiably, but Arina Petrovna did not answer and shrank more and more under the blanket.

"Now, God is merciful, mama!" little Judas continued, "the main thing is not to lose heart! Just turn up your nose at this little infirmity, get up from your bed and skip about your room like a fine fellow! Like this!"

"Now, hang on a minute, just let me raise the blind here and take a look at you! My! Don't you just look fine, now, dearie! All you have to do is cheer up a little and pray to God and kick up your heels—just as though you were at a ball! Here now, I've brought you some nice holy water, have some of this!"

Porfiry Vladimirych took a vial out of his pocket, found a glass on the table, poured it out and took it to the invalid. Arina Petrovna made a motion to raise her head but could not.

"I want the orphans..." she moaned.

"Just look at you now, already asking for the orphans! Goodness, me, mama, mama! How could you so suddenly...now, now! Just a teensy bit sick and already you're losing heart! Everything will be taken care of! We'll send a message to the orphans, and we'll write Petka to come from Petersburg. Everything will be done in proper order! There's no need to rush. You and I still have some living to do! And just watch how we'll do it! The summer is coming, we'll go to the woods for mushrooms, for strawberries, raspberries, black currants! And that's not all, we'll go and catch carp at Dubrovino! We'll hitch up the old piebald to the tandem cart, and off we go nice and easy, trippety-trip, we'll just sit down and away we go!"

"I want the orphans..." Arina Petrovna repeated mournfully.

"The orphans will come too. Give us time, we'll get everyone together, everyone will come. We'll all come and seat ourselves around you. You'll be the mother hen and we'll be the little chicks...peep-peep-peep! Everything will be done if you're a good girl. But you know you're not a good girl for taking it into your head to go and get sick. What have you gone and done now, you mischief-maker, you, my, oh my! You should be setting an example to others, but just look at you! That's not right, dearie! My, that's not good!"

But despite all of Porfiry Vladimirych's attempts to cheer up his sweet friend, mama, with jests and quips, her strength fell with each passing hour. An express messenger was sent to town for the doctor, and because the invalid continued to mourn and call out for the orphans, little Judas wrote a letter in his own hand to Anninka and Lyubinka in which he compared their behavior with his own, calling himself a Christian and them ungrateful. The doctor arrived in the night, but it was already too late. As they say, Arina Petrovna "was done for" in one day. Towards four o'clock in the morning the death agony began and at six o'clock in the morning Porfiry Vladimirych was on his knees at his mother's bed and wailing:

"Mama, my friend, give me your blessing!"

But Arina Petrovna did not hear him. Her open eyes gazed mistily into the distance as though trying to comprehend and yet unable to do so.

Little Judas did not comprehend either. He did not comprehend that the grave opening up before his eyes was bearing away his final tie with the world of the living, the final being with whom he could share the dust which had filled him to full. And that from this day forth this dust, having no other outlet, would accumulate within him until the point where it would ultimately suffocate him.

With his customary fussiness he plunged into the abyss of trivia which accompany the burial rites. He had requiems sung, ordered masses for the mourning period, discussed things with the priest, dragged his feet, going from room to room he peeked into the dining room where the deceased lay, crossed himself, raised his eyes to heaven, arose at night, soundlessly approached the door, listened to the monotonous recitation by the psalmist and so on. Moreover, he was pleasantly surprised that the occasion did not present him with any particular expenses, because Arina Petrovna, while still alive, had put aside a sum of money for her burial, having specified in writing with great detail how much was to be spent and where to spend it.

After burying his mother, Porfiry Vladimirych immediately set about informing himself of his mother's affairs. Sorting through the papers, he found ten different wills (in one of them she had called him "disrespectful"). However, they had all been written at the time when Arina Petrovna was the despotic mistress and had not been legalized, but were still in draft form. For this reason little Judas was quite satisfied that he would not have to act contrary to his conscience in proclaiming himself the sole legal heir to his mother's remaining possessions. These possessions consisted of fifteen thousand rubles capital and some paltry personal belongings, including the well-known carriage which had almost served as the apple of discord between mother and son. Arina Petrovna had assiduously separated her own accounts from the accounts she held in trusteeship for the orphans, so that it was immediately possible to see what belonged to her and what to the orphans. Little Judas immediately pronounced himself the heir wherever necessary, sealed the papers relating to the trusteeship, distributed his mother's paltry wardrobe to the servants. The carriage and two cows which, according to Arina Petrovna's list, were entered under the title "mine," were sent off to Golovlyovo and then, after the final requiem, little Judas departed to his own home.

"Wait for the owners," he said to the people who had gathered on the porch to see him off, "they will come—may God be merciful! Or they may not come—however they see fit! For my part, I have done everything. The trustee accounts I have put in order, I hid nothing, I concealed nothing, I did everything in the open. The capital which remained after mama's death belongs to me, according to the law. The carriage and the two cows, which I sent to Golovlyovo, are mine as well, according to the law. Perhaps there's even something of mine left *here*—well, so be it! God wishes it to go to the orphans! I feel sorry for mama! She was a kind old lady! Thoughtful! Just look how she was concerned for you, the servants, she left you her wardrobe! Alas, mama, mama! It was not a good thing you did, dearie, abandoning us like orphans! But if that is the will of God, then we must submit to his holy will! We only hope that your soul will be at rest and as far as we're concerned that you'll think about us."

A second grave followed quickly after the first.

Porfiry Vladimirych reacted to the case of his son rather mysteriously. He did not subscribe to newspapers, nor did he carry on any correspondence with anyone and therefore he did not have any sources to receive information from about the trial in which Petenka figured. But he hardly wished to know anything about the subject. In general he was a man who, above all, avoided anxiety, who was buried up to his ears in the mire of trivia with the vilest self-centeredness and whose existence, in consequence of this, never left behind itself any traces on anything at all. There are quite a few such people in the world and they all live estranged, having no idea or desire of how to accommodate themselves to anything, not knowing what awaits them the next minute and finally bursting like rain bubbles burst. They have no ties with friends, because common interests must exist for friendship; nor do they have any business connections, because even in the moribund business of bureaucracy they display a kind of completely unbearable deathly pallor. For thirty years in a row Porfiry Vladimirych had knocked and flitted about the department. Then one fine morning he disappeared—no one noticed. Thus, he was the last to learn about the fate which had overtaken his son, —when the news of this had already spread among the gentry. But even then he pretended to know nothing, so that when Yevprakseyushka attempted to broach the subject of Petenka, little Judas waved his arms at her and said:

"No, no no! I don't want to know, I didn't hear and I don't want to hear! I don't want to know about his filthy affairs!"

But finally he was forced to learn about it all the same. A letter came from Petenka in which he informed him about his forthcoming departure to one of the distant provinces and asked whether papa would send him his allowance in his new circumstances. After receiving this, Porfiry Vladimirych found himself at an apparent loss for the entire day. He poked from one room to the next, peeked into the chapel, crossed himself and sighed. Towards evening, however, he gathered himself together and wrote:

My guilty son, Pyotr!

As a faithful subject, bound to respect the laws, I should not even reply to your letter. But as your father, as one who shares in human weaknesses, I cannot, out of a feeling of sympathy, refuse good advice to a child who has, by virtue of his own sin, plunged into the depths of iniquity. And so, here in brief is my opinion on this subject. The punishment to which you have been subjected is heavy, but completely deserved by you—such is the first and most important thought which from this day forward must always accompany you in your new life. You must abandon all other whims and even ideas about anything else, for in your situation all of these can only cause irritation and provoke you to complaint. You have already tasted of the bitter fruits of arrogance, try now to taste as well of the fruits of humility, all the more so because nothing else awaits you in the future. Do not complain of your punishment, for the authorities are not even punishing you, but are simply teaching you the means for correction. Being thankful for this and attempting to make amends for what you have done—this is what you should be thinking about constantly, and not about passing the time in luxury, something, by the way, I myself, even without having been convicted, do not do. Follow this wise advice and be reborn for the new life, be reborn completely, satisfied with what the authorities, in their mercy, consider warranted for you. And I, for my part, will pray ceaselessly to the Provider of all blessings to give you firmness of will and humility, and even on this very day as I am writing these lines, I was in church and raised fervent prayers on high. Finally, I bless you on your new path and remain,

your indignant but ever-loving father,
Porfiry Golovlyov

No one knows whether Petenka received this letter. But no later than a month after its dispatch, Porfiry Vladimirych received an official communication stating that his son, prior to arriving at his place of exile, had entered a hospital in one of the towns along the way and had died.

Little Judas found himself alone, but in the heat of the moment he did not yet understand that with this loss he was now totally cast into the wilderness, face to face with his own idle chatter. This had happened shortly after Arina Petrovna's death when he had become all immersed in drawing up accounts and making calculations. He reread the papers of the deceased, counted up every half-kopek, searched for the connection between that half-kopek with those of the orphans' trusteeship fund, not wishing, as he had said, either to take what belonged to others, or to give up what belonged to him. Amid this confusion he did not even conceive of the question of why he was doing all of this and who would reap the benefits of his fussing. He slaved from dawn to dusk at his desk, finding fault with the arrangements made by the deceased and even phantasizing, with the result that gradually he came to ignore the accounts for his own estate.

Everything now grew still in the house. The servants, who even before had preferred to huddle in the servants' quarters, walked about on their tiptoes and spoke in a whisper. A sense of forfeiture made itself evident in this house, and in this man there was something that inspired an involuntary and superstitious fear. The shades of darkness which had in any event enveloped little Judas, were to thicken more and more with each day.

During Lent, when performances were halted, Anninka arrived in Golovlyovo and announced that Lyubinka could not come with her because she had earlier made a contract for all of Lent, and, as a consequence, had departed for Romny, Izyum, Kremenchug and so on, where she was to give some concerts and perform the entire vaudeville repertoire.

During the course of her brief artistic career, Anninka had matured significantly. She was no longer the former naive, anemic and somewhat wan girl who, while at both Dubrovino and Pogorelka, had walked from room to room, awkwardly swaying and softly humming, as though not knowing where to find herself a place. No, this was a young girl who was completely formed, with confident manners, and who, one could see unmistakably at first glance, would not be at a loss for words. Her external appearance had changed as well and Porfiry Vladimirych was rather pleasantly struck. Before him appeared a fully grown and shapely woman with a beautiful and rosy-cheeked face, a high, well-developed bust, with large gray eyes and the most marvelous ash-blonde braid which hung heavily on her neck, —a woman who apparently was fully conscious of the fact that she was none other than La Belle Hélène herself, over whom the gentlemen officers were fated to sigh. She arrived in Golovlyovo early in the morning and immediately locked herself in her own room, whence she appeared in the dining room for tea wearing a magnificent silk dress with a rustling train which she maneuvered very adroitly among the chairs. Although little Judas loved his God more than all else, it did not prevent him from having a taste for beautiful women, particularly for large-busted women. Thus, he first made the sign of the cross over Anninka, then with particular precision he kissed her on both cheeks, meanwhile letting his eyes slip down to her bust so queerly that Anninka smiled almost imperceptibly.

They sat down to tea; Anninka raised both arms upward and stretched.

"My-y-y, uncle, how boring it is here!" she began, yawning slightly.

"Just look at that! She's barely had time to turn about and already she feels bored! Just live with us awhile, then we'll see; perhaps you'll feel cheerful then!" Porfiry Vladimirych replied, his eyes suddenly becoming covered with an oily gleam.

"No, it wouldn't be interesting! What do you have here? Snow everywhere, no neighbors... Is there a regiment stationed here?"

"There is a regiment, and we do have neighbors, but to tell the truth, I'm not interested in that. By the way, if..."

Porfiry Vladimirych looked at her, but did not finish, he simply snorted. Perhaps he had stopped on purpose, wanting to arouse her feminine curiosity. In any event, the earlier, barely perceptible smile slipped across her face once again. She leaned on the table and stared rather fixedly at Yevprakseyushka, who, blushing deeply, was wiping the glasses and peering at her sideways with her large, murky eyes.

"This is my new housekeeper...a hard worker!" Porfiry Vladimirych spoke up.

Anninka barely nodded her head and softly purred: "Ah! ah! que j'aime...que j'aime...les mili-mili-mili-taires!" —all the while her hips seemed to sway by themselves. During the ensuing silence, little Judas, his eyes modestly lowered, gradually sipped his tea from the glass.

"Boredom!" Anninka yawned once again.

"Nothing but boredom and more boredom! That's the only tune she knows! Just you wait, live here awhile... We could have the sleigh hitched up and away you go, as much as your heart could desire."

"Uncle! Why didn't you join the hussars?"

"For the reason, my friend, that God circumscribes each man's life. The one serves in the hussars, the next in government service, the third in commerce, the fourth..."

"Alas, yes, the fourth, the fifth, the sixth... I did forget! And all this is determined by God...is that so?"

"Of course, who else but God! My friend, there's nothing to laugh about in this! Do you know that in the Scriptures it's written: without the will of God..."

"You mean about the hair? Yes, I know that one! But that's very unfortunate: nowadays everyone wears chignons, and it seems that no one foresaw that! By the way, just take a look, uncle, at what a marvelous braid I have... It is nice, isn't it?"

Porfiry Vladimirych came close (for some reason on his tiptoes) and held the braid in his hand. Yevprakseyushka also reached forward without putting down her saucer of tea and murmured through the lump of sugar held between her teeth:

"I expect it's a 'chillion' or something?"

"No, it's not a chignon, but my very own hair. Sometime I'll let it down for you to see, uncle!"

"Yes, it's a fine braid," said little Judas admiringly and seemed to puff his lips out lewdly all the while. But then he caught himself, realizing that he should scorn such temptations and added: "Goodness, you flighty thing, you! All you have on your mind are braids and dresses, yet you do not even think of asking about the real thing, the main thing!"

"Yes, you mean about grandmother... But she died, didn't she?"

"She passed away, my friend! And the way she went! Peacefully, quietly, no one even heard a word! She achieved an honorable end to her life! She remembered everyone, blessed everyone, summoned the priest and took communion... And all at once she grew so peaceful, so peaceful! Even she, the dear, said that. 'How wonderful,' she said, 'I suddenly feel!' And just imagine, no sooner had she said this than she started to sigh! She sighed once, twice, thrice—and when we looked, she was no longer there!"

Little Judas stood up, turned to the ikon, pressed his palms together and prayed. Even tears came to his eyes, so wonderfully did he lie! But apparently Anninka was not one of those sentimentalists. True, she fell into thought for a minute, but for a completely different reason.

"Do you remember, uncle," she said, "the way she fed me and my sister sour milk when we were little? Not later...later she was marvelous...but when she was still rich?"

"Now, now what's the point in recalling the past! You may have been fed sour milk, but just look what a fine girl it made of you, God preserve! Are you planning on visiting her grave?"

"Of course I am!"

"Only you know what! You should first purify yourself!"

"What do you mean...purify myself?"

"Well, all the same...an actress...you think that grandmother found that easy to accept? So, before you go to the grave, you ought to attend mass and purify yourself! Now tomorrow morning early I'll have mass served and then God go with you!"

However absurd little Judas' suggestion seemed, Anninka still was taken aback for a moment. But then she frowned angrily and replied sharply:

"No, I'll still... I'll go right now!"

"I don't know, but as you wish! But my advice would be: attend mass tomorrow, have tea, order a pair of horses hitched to the sleigh and go together. And that way you would have purified yourself and grandmother's soul would..."

"Goodness, uncle, you really are so silly! God knows what nonsense you carry on and even insist on it!"

"What? You don't care for that? Well, just don't be offended, I, brother, am a forthright person! I don't like falsehood, and I'll speak the truth to others and I'll listen to it myself! Even if at times the truth goes against the grain, even when it's the bitter truth—one should still listen to it! And one should listen to it because it is the truth. That's the way it is, my friend! You just live here awhile with us, the way we do, and you'll see for yourself that it's better than making the rounds of the fairs with a guitar."

"God knows the way you speak, uncle! Really, with a guitar!"

"Well, maybe not with a guitar, but something like that. With a mandolin, or something. Anyway, you insulted me first, calling me silly, and an old man, like me, has all the more right to tell you the truth."

"Fine, let that be the truth then. We won't talk about that. Tell me, please, did grandmother leave any inheritance?"

"Of course she did! Only the legal heir was there in person!"

"You mean yourself... So much the better. Is she buried in Golvlyovo with you?"

"No, in her own parish, near Pogorelka, by the Church of St. Nikola on the Voplya. She wanted it that way herself."

"So then, I'm going. Can I hire horses here, Uncle?"

"Why hire them? We have our own horses! I don't imagine you're a stranger! My niece...you are related to me!" Porfiry Vladimirych gesticulated, smirking *like a member of the family,* "The sleigh, a pair of horses, praise be to the Lord! I don't live like a pauper! And why shouldn't I go with you! We could visit the grave and then drop in at Pogorelka! We could take a peek there and look around and have a chat and think over what and how... You have a fine little estate, there are some nice and handy spots there!"

"No, I had better go alone...why should you go? By the way, did Petenka really die too?"

"He did, my friend, Petenka died as well. And I feel sorry for him, on the one hand, so sorry I could cry, yet on the other hand, he himself is to blame! He never was respectful to his father. God punished him for that very reason! And if God so arranged something in His wisdom, then it's not up to us to change it!"

"Naturally, we won't change anything. The only thing I was thinking about was: aren't you terrified living here?"

"And what should I be terrified of? You see how many blessings surround me?"Little Judas made a sweeping gesture with his arm, pointing to the ikons,"There's a blessing here, and there's a blessing in the study, and in the chapel there's a veritable paradise! Just look at all the intercessors I have!"

"All the same... You're always alone...it's frightening!"

"And if it's frightening, then I get down on my knees, I pray awhile, and it's as though you've brushed it all away with your hand! What's there to be afraid of? During the day it's bright, and at night I have lamps burning everywhere, in all of the rooms! When it gets dark outside it looks as though there's a ball going on! And what a ball I have here! God's intercessors and saints—that's my entire ball!"

"Did you know that before he died Petenka wrote to us?"

"What of it! As a relative... I'm grateful for the fact that he did not at least lose his sentiments for his relatives!"

"Yes, he wrote. It was already after the trial, when the decision had been handed down. He wrote that he had lost three thousand and that you would not give them to him. But, uncle, you must be rich?"

"It's easy, my friend, to count the money in other people's pockets. Sometimes we think that a person has piles of gold, but if we just take a closer peek, we'll see that he has only enough for ikon-lamp oil and a candle—and even that doesn't belong to him, but to God!"

"Well, then, we must be richer than you. By forcing our cavaliers to subscribe as well, we ourselves put together six hundred rubles and sent it to him."

"What kind of 'cavaliers' are these?"

"Goodness, uncle! After all we are actresses! You yourself just suggested that I should 'purify myself!'"

"I don't like the way you talk that way!"

"What good is it! Like it or not, what is done cannot be undone. After all, according to you, that's the way God works!"

"Don't commit sacrilege, at least. You can say whatever you wish, but I shall not allow sacrilege! Where did you send the money to?"

"I don't recall. To some town or other... He himself told us which one."

"I don't know. If there were any money, I should have received it after his death! Surely he couldn't have spent it all at once! I don't know, I didn't receive anything. The warders and escort guards, I expect, must have made good use of it!"

"We're not demanding it back—I was just mentioning it. But all the same, uncle it is frightening the way a person was lost for the sake of three thousand rubles!"

"Now, now, it's not because of the three thousand. It only seems to us that it was because of the three thousand—that's what we keep saying: three thousand! three thousand! But God..."

Little Judas was now about to soar off, he wanted to explain in the greatest detail the way God...about Providence...working in unseen ways...and all manner of such things... But Anninka yawned unceremoniously and said:

"Goodness, uncle! How boring it is here!"

This time Porfiry Vladimirych was seriously offended and fell silent. For a long while they walked side by side back and forth through the dining room. Anninka was yawning, Porfiry Vladimirych crossed himself in each corner. Finally news was brought that the horses were ready and the usual comedy of family send-offs began. Golovlyov donned his fur coat, went on the porch, kissed Anninka goodbye, shouted at the servants: "Her feet! Wrap them more warmly!" Or: "The funeral pudding! Did you take the funeral pudding! Goodness, don't forget it!" And all the while he was making the sign of the cross in the air.

Anninka made it to her grandmother's grave, asked the priest to serve a requiem and when the sextons began the mournful "eternal memory," she started to weep. The picture in the midst of which the ceremony took place was a sad one. The church where Arina Petrovna had been buried belonged to the category of poor churches. The plaster had fallen away in spots and had bared large patches in the brick foundation. The bell had a hollow and weak ring to it. The priest's robes were old and tattered. A deep snow covered the graveyard so that it was necessary to dig out the path with spades in order to reach the grave. There was still no headstone, only a simple white cross stood there on which there was not even an inscription. The churchyard lay in isolation off to the side from any settlement. Not far from the church huddled the blackened huts of the priest and the sextons, and in every direction all around stretched a deserted snowy plain on whose surface here and there loomed some bare branches. The strong March wind swept over the graveyard, cease-lessly whipping up the robes on the priest and carrying the singing of the sex-tons off to the side.

"And who would have thought, mistress, that beneath this modest cross, by our poor church, a landowner who was once the richest one in this region would have found her rest!" the priest said at the conclusion of the litany.

At these words Anninka cried even more. She recalled the lines: "Where once the banquet table stood—there now stands a coffin," and her tears start-ed to pour. Then she went to the priest's hut, drank some tea, chatted with the priest's wife, and again recalled the lines: "And pale death gazes upon all" —and once more she wept long and profusely.

Nobody was informed in Pogorelka about the young mistress' arrival and for that reason the rooms had not been heated up. Without taking off her fur coat, Anninka made the rounds of all the rooms and stopped for a moment only in her grandmother's bedroom and in the chapel. In grandmoth-er's bedroom stood her bed on which several grimy feather quilts and cover-less pillows were piled up. The desk was strewn with various scraps of paper. The floor had not been swept and a thick layer of dust covered all objects. Anninka sat down and pondered. At first there appeared recollections of the past, then they gave way to the pictures of the present. The former appeared in the form of fragments, fleeting and passing; the latter settled in more solid-ly. Had it been so long ago that Pogorelka had seemed so hateful to her—and now suddenly her heart was overfilled with some kind of contagious desire to live awhile in this hateful place. It was quiet here, uncomfortable, unattrac-tive, but quiet, so quiet that it seemed as though everything had died all around. There was plenty of fresh air and space: just look at that field—how she longed to go running across it. To run without purpose, without a back-ward glance, so that her breast would ache from the effort. But *there,* in that semi-nomadic realm, from which she had only just torn herself away and whence she *must* once again return, what awaited here there? And what would she bring back with her? The recollection of hotels saturated with foul odors, of the eternal racket coming from the general dining room and from the billiard room, of the unkempt and unwashed waiters, of the rehearsals in the middle of darkened stages, in the midst of painted canvas backdrops which were revolting to the touch, in the piercing wind, in the damp... If that were only all! But then there were the officers, the lawyers, the shameless talk, the empty bottles, tablecloths soaking with wine, the clouds of smoke and the racket, the racket, the racket! And the things they said to her! The shameless way they touched her!... Particularly that one with the mustache, his voice hoarse from drink, eyes inflamed, the ever-present smell of the stab-le... God, the things he said! At this recollection Anninka even shuddered and closed her eyes. But then she came to herself, sighed and went into the chap-el. There were only a few ikons left now in the ikon-stand, only the ones which *without a doubt* belonged to her mother, but the rest, grandmother's, had been removed and carried off to Golovlyovo by little Judas, the rightful heir. The empty spots, which appeared as a consequence, looked just like eyes that had been plucked out. Nor were there any ikon-lamps. Little Judas had taken everything. Only a single yellow wax candle end cringed in abandonment, forgotten in its tiny tin candle holder.

"They wanted to take the ikon-stand as well, they kept inquiring whether it really did belong to the young mistress," Afimyushka reported.

"What of it? They should have taken that too. What about it Afimyushka, did grandmother suffer for a long while before she died?"

"Not especially, barely two days. It was as though she just ate her heart out. She didn't suffer any real pain, nothing like that! She didn't really say anything, she only mentioned you and your sister a few times."

"Porfiry Vladimirych must have taken the ikons away?"

"He did. He said they were his own mother's ikons. And he took the carriage and two cows for himself. He took all of the mistress' papers, the ones which didn't belong to you, but to your grandmother. He wanted to drag off a horse as well, but Fedulych wouldn't give it up. The horse is ours, he said, it's been here at Pogorelka for as long as he could remember. Well, he left it, he was afraid to take it."

Anninka walked around outside, peeked into the sheds, at the threshing yard, and the barnyard. There, in the midst of the manure pile stood her "working capital": about twenty emaciated cows and three horses. She had some bread brought, saying: I'll pay for it! And gave each cow a piece. Then the dairy maid invited the young mistress into her hut where a jug of milk was placed on the table, and in the corner by the stove, behind a low partition of boards, huddled a new-born calf. Anninka drank some milk, ran up to the little calf and kissed it passionately on the muzzle, but immediately wiped her lips hurriedly, saying that the calf's muzzle was disgusting, all slimy. Finally she took three yellowish bills out of her purse, gave them to the old servants and began to collect her things.

"But what will you do?" seating herself in the sleigh she asked old Fedulych who, as the village elder, had been following after the young mistress with his arms crossed on his chest.

"What can we do! We'll go on living!" Fedulych answered simply.

Once again Anninka felt sad: it seemed to her that Fedulych's words had an ironic ring to them. She stood and stood on the same spot, sighed and said:

"Well, farewell!"

"But we were thinking that you might return to us! That you'd live with us!" Fedulych uttered.

"What's the use! All the same, you just carry on."

Again the tears began to flow from her eyes and everyone else also began to weep at this point. The whole thing had come out strangely, somehow. It seemed as though she had no regrets, there was nothing to mention, yet she was crying. And they as well. Nothing had been said which departed from the usual series of questions and answers, but everyone felt miserable, "sorry." She was seated in the sleigh, wrapped up and everyone sighed deeply.

"Good luck!" the cry rang out after her when the sleigh moved forward.

Driving past the churchyard, she again gave the order to stop and alone, without any priest or deacons, she walked along the road which had been cleared to the grave. By now it had grown quite dark and in the homes of the churchfolk the lights were lit. She stood there, holding onto the graveside cross with one hand, but not crying, simply swaying to and fro. She was not thinking about anything in particular, she could not have formulated any specific thought, yet she felt grieved, grieved with all of her being. Not over her grandmother, but over herself she felt grieved. She swayed back and forth unconsciously and, bowed over, she stood there for a quarter of an hour and suddenly she imagined Lyubinka who, perhaps at that very moment was singing like a nightingale in some Kremenchug or other, in the midst of a joyful company:

> Ah! ah! que j'aime, que j'aime!
> Que j'aime les mili-mili-mili-taires!

She almost fell down. She rushed towards the sleigh at a run, seated herself and gave the order to drive to Gololyovo as fast as possible.

* * *

Anninka returned to her uncle all bored and subdued. In any event, it did not prevent her from feeling somewhat hungry (her uncle, in the scurrying back and forth, had not even sent some chicken with her), and she was very happy that the table had already been set for tea. Naturally, Porfiry Vladimirych did not tarry in striking up a conversation.

"Well, were you there?"

"I was."

"Did you pray at the grave? Did you have a requiem?"

"Yes, a requiem as well."

"The priest must have been at home, then?"

"Of course he was, who else could have performed the requiem!"

"Yes, yes... Were both sextons there? Did they sing 'in eternal memory?' "

"They did."

"Yes. Eternal memory! Eternal memory to the deceased! She was a thoughtful old lady, a good relative!"

Little Judas arose from the table, turned to the ikons and prayed.

"Well, how did you find Pogorelka? Everything all right?"

"To tell the truth, I don't know. It seems that everything was in order."

"Well, now, 'seems!' It always 'seems' to us, but you just take a peek here and there, and you'll find that something's not right here, and something is rotten there... That's the way we make up our minds about the conditions of other people: 'seems!' it always 'seems!' By the way, you have a very fine little estate there. My deceased mother organized things there most admirably, she used more than a little of her own means on the estate... But then there's no sin in helping out orphans!"

Listening to these praises, Anninka could not restrain herself from teasing her tender-hearted uncle.

"But, uncle, why did you take the two cows away from Pogorelka?" she asked.

"Cows? What cows? You mean Chernavka and Prevedenka? But, my friend, they were mother's, you know!"

"And you were her legal heir? Well, what of it! Keep them! Do you want me to have the little calf sent over as well?"

"Now, now, now! You're losing your temper! Be sensible now. Whom do you think the cows belonged to?"

"How should I know! They were in Pogorelka!"

"But I do know, I have proof that the cows were mother's. I found the register she kept in her own hand and there it was written: 'mine'."

"Well, let it be. It's not worth talking about."

"There's a horse in Pogorelka, a patchy one—well, I can't say about this one for sure. It seems that it was mama's horse, but in any event I don't know! And what I don't know about, I can't talk about!"

"Let's leave it, uncle."

"No, why leave it! I, brother, am a straightforward person, I like to have everything out in the open! Why not talk about it! Everyone begrudges what is his. I begrudge it and you do too, so let's talk about it! And if we're going to talk about it, then I'll tell you straight off, I have no need of what belongs to others, nor will I surrender what is mine. Because even though you are not a stranger to me, that's the way it is."

"You even took the ikons!" Anninka could not restrain herself again.

"I took the ikons as well, and I took everything that belongs to me as legal heir."

"Now the ikon-stand seems all full of holes..."

"What's to be done! Pray before what's left! God does not need your ikon-stand, it's your prayer he wants! If you go about it in a sincere fashion, then your prayers before poor ikons will still reach Him! But if you merely go mumble-mumble, keep glancing all around and just make nice little curtsies—not even fine ikons will save you!"

Nonetheless, little Judas arose and thanked God for the fact that he had "fine" ikons.

"If you don't care for the old ikon-stand, then have a new one built.

Or put some other ikons in place of the ones that were removed. My deceased mama purchased and installed the earlier ones, so you yourself can purchase some new ones!"

Profiry Vladimirych even giggled. This reasoning seemed so sensible and simple to him.

"Tell me, please, what must I do now?" asked Anninka.

"Now, just wait awhile. First rest, make yourself comfortable and have a sleep. We'll chat and consider and take a look and figure things out—perhaps we can come up with something together!"

"My sister and I are of age, so it seems?"

"Yes, that you are, madam. You can run your own affairs and your estate yourselves!"

"Thank God for that at least!"

"We have the honor of congratulating you, madam!"

Porfiry Vladimirych rose and crept up to exchange kisses.

"Goodness, uncle, what a strange person you are! You're always kissing!"

"And why not kiss! You're no stranger to me—you're my niece! I'm just doing it, friend, like a good relative! I'm always ready to do things for relatives! Even if it's a third or fourth cousin, I'm always..."

"It would be better if you were to tell me what to do. Do I have to go to town, or something? To look after things?"

"We'll go to town and we'll look after things—everything in good time. But first of all, rest and take it easy! Praise be to God! You're not in some tavern but in your very own uncle's house! There's food to eat and tea to drink and one can treat oneself to some nice jam. There is plenty of everything! If some dish doesn't please you, ask for something different! Ask, tell us! If you don't care for cabbage soup, have them give you some nice soup! A fine little cutlet, some nice duckie, or juicy suckling pig!... Just take Yevprakseyushka aside!... By the way, Yevprakseyushka! Here I am boasting about some nice juicy suckling pig and I really don't know for sure whether we have any?"

Yevprakseyushka, meanwhile, holding a saucer full of hot tea before her mouth, snorted in the affirmative.

"Well, there you see! We even have some nice suckling pig! In other words, anything your little heart desires, just ask for it! Really!"

Little Judas again reached for Anninka, patted her on the knee with his hand and of course, purely by chance, lingered there awhile, so that the orphan girl moved instinctively away.

"But really I do have to go," she said.

"That's just what I'm talking about. We'll cast about and have a chat and then we'll go. We'll just take our good old time, we don't have to break our necks by hurrying! Haste makes waste! Some people go rushing off to a fire, but praise be to God, there's no fire here! Look at Lyubinka—that one has to rush off to the fair, but why should you! And there's something more I want to ask you: are you going to be living in Pogorelka?"

"No, what's there for me to do in Pogorelka?"

"I wanted to say something else to you. Come and settle here with me. We'll sit here and take it easy—we'll have a fine time!"

Saying this, little Judas gave Anninka such an oily look that she felt awkward.

"No, uncle, I won't settle here with you. It's boring."

"Goodness me, silly, silly girl! Why do you keep saying that it's boring! Boring, and more boring, but why it's boring, you yourself couldn't say, I expect! Whoever has something to do, my friend, that person knows how to direct himself, that person never knows any boredom. Take me, for example: I don't even notice the way time flies! During the week I'm busy with the estate: you take a look here and a look there, drop in there, have a chat, think things over, and before you know it the day is done! And on holidays—to church! You could do the same! Live with us and you'll find something to do, and if there isn't anything, you can play cards with Yevprakseyushka or have the sleigh hitched up and off you go for a ride! When summer comes, we'll go for mushrooms in the woods! We'll have a picnic on the grass!"

"No, uncle, there's no use in what you're suggesting!"

"Really, come live with us."

"No. But I'll tell you what: I'm tired from travelling, couldn't I lie down for a sleep?"

"You can go sleepy-bye, too. I have a bed ready for you and everything you need. If you want to go sleepy-bye, then just go and have a sleep. Christ go with you! But think about it all the same: where could it be better than staying here with us in Golovlyovo?"

* * *

Anninka spent a restless night. The nervous fancy which had overcome her in Pogorelka continued. There are moments when a person, who up until that point had only been *existing*, suddenly begins to understand that he is not truly *living*, but that there is some kind of canker in his life. Where this canker has come from, precisely how and when it was formed, this person cannot properly explain to himself in the greater number of instances and more often than not ascribes the canker's origin not at all to the causes which in actual fact had given rise to it. But he does not even find it necessary to consider these facts: it is sufficient alone that the canker does exist. The effect of such a sudden revelation, likewise excruciating for everyone, undergoes a metamorphosis in the subsequent practical results, depending on individual temperaments. Awareness of the canker regenerates some people, inspires them with a determination to begin a new life on new principles. In others it is simply reflected in a transitory pain which does not produce a

143

break for the better in the future, making itself felt in the present even more painfully than in a situation when there are at least several rays of hope in the future coming as the result of resolutions embarked upon by virtue of a stricken conscience.

Anninka did not belong to the category of the kind of individuals who in recognizing their cankers discover a pretext for regenerating their lives. As a fairly bright girl she understood quite well that there existed a wide gulf between those vague dreams of a life of earning one's own bread—which had served as the point of departure for abandoning Pogorelka once and for all—and the position of a provincial actress in which she found herself. Instead of a quiet life of labor she had come upon a stormy existence replete with endless carousing, coarse shamelessness, disorderly and pointless bustle. Instead of the deprivations and harsh external circumstances to which she had once reconciled herself, she had encountered relative plenty and luxury which she now, however, could not recall without blushing. Moreover, this entire transformation had somehow come about without her noticing it herself. She had been on her way to some good place, but instead of finding the one door she had ended up at another. Her desires were, in actual fact, very modest. How many times while sitting in her attic in Pogorelka had she envisioned herself in her dreams as a serious girl striving and thirsting to educate herself, bearing dire need and deprivation with determination, for the sake of an ideal of the good (it is true that the word "good" hardly had any specific meaning). But barely had she entered the broad road of independence, when practical experience arose of itself and turned her entire dream into dust. Serious work did not come by itself, but only through persistent effort and a kind of preparation which even though incomplete could still aid that effort. But neither Anninka's temperament nor her upbringing answered these demands. Her temperament was not at all outstanding for its passion, but simply was easily excited. The material afforded her by her education, and with which she prepared to enter into a life of work, was so insubstantial that it could not have served as the basis for any serious profession at all. This upbringing was, so to speak, a combination of girl's school and vaudeville in which vaudeville practically had the edge. Mixed up in this chaotic jumble was the typical problem of the flock of geese on the wing, the *pas de châle*, the teaching of Pierre Picardy and the escapades of la belle Hélène and the "Ode to Felitsa" and a sense of thankfulness for one's superiors and the patrons of well-born maidens. In this disorderly potpourri (with the exception of which she could, with good reason, call herself a *tabula rasa*) it was difficult even to make any sense, never mind find any point of departure. This kind of preparation did not arouse any love for work, only a love for fashionable society, a desire to be surrounded, to listen to the charming compliments of cavaliers and in general to plunge into the noise, glitter and whirlwind of so-called society life.

If she had kept a closer eye on herself, then even in Pogorelka, in those moments when her plans for a life of work were just beginning to be born, when she was seeing in them something in the form of a liberation from the Egyptian Captivity, even then she might have caught herself in dreams where rather than working she was surrounded by the company of like-minded people and whiling away the time in intellectual conversation. Of course, even the people in these dreams were intellectual and their conversations were honorable and serious, but all the same the idle aspect of life still assumed the primary place on the stage. Poverty was tidy, deprivation only bore witness to the absence of luxury. Therefore, when in actual fact the dreams about earning one's own bread were resolved by her being offered a career in vaudeville on the boards of one of the provinicial theatres, then, despite the contrast, she did not waver for long. She quickly refreshed her school knowledge about the relationship of Helene to Menelaeus, expanded it with a few biographical details from the life of the magnificent Prince Tavrida and considered that this was entirely sufficient to produce "La belle Hélène" and "Excerpts from the Life of the Duchess of Gerolstein" in provincial towns and fairs. Meanwhile, to cleanse her own conscience, she would remember that one student with whom she had become acquainted in Moscow, had exclaimed at every step: "Sacred art!" —and she made these words the motto for her life all the more willingly because they gave decency to her freedom and afforded at least some manner of external decorum to her embarking on a path for which she had yearned instinctively with all her being.

The life of an actress disturbed her equilibrium. On her own, without any preparation to guide her, without any conscious purpose, armed only with a temperament that longed for noise, glitter and praise, she quickly found herself whirling about in a kind of chaos wherein thronged an endless multitude of faces giving way to one another without any coherence. These were the faces of the most diverse characters and convictions, so that the very motives for finding any common interests with one or the other could not be at all similar. Nonetheless both the one person and the other, as well as any other, indiscriminately made up her circle, and from this one might conclude that here, essentially speaking, there could not be any discussion of motives. It must have been clear that her life had become something in the fashion of a road-side inn at whose gates everyone could knock who showed himself to be cheerful, young and possessing the usual material means. It was clear that here no consideration was given to *selecting* company that appealed to one, but rather to accommodating oneself to whatever company happened along, if only not to languish in loneliness. In essence, "sacred art" had led her into a cesspool, but her head had begun to whirl so quickly that she was unable to recognize it for herself. Neither the unwashed mugs of the floor-waiters, nor the miserable stage-sets covered with grime, nor the noise, stench and racket of the hotels and inns, nor the cynical advances of her admirers—nothing sobered her up. She did not even notice that she constantly found herself in the company of men alone and that between her and other women who possessed a *respectable position* there lay a kind of unassailable wall...

145

Her arrival in Golovlyovo sobered her up for the moment.

From that morning, almost from the very moment of her arrival, something disturbed her. As an impressionable girl, she very rapidly became involved in new sensations and no less rapidly adapted herself to all kinds of situations. Thus, with her arrival in Golovlyovo, she suddenly felt like a "young lady." She became reminded of the fact that she owned something that was hers: her own house, her graves, and she wanted once again to see the old circumstances, to breathe once again that air from which she had fled without a backward glance not so long ago. But this impression was bound to shatter immediately when she came face-to-face with reality in Golovlyovo. In this regard she could be likened to the person who with a friendly expression on his face enters the society of people whom he had not seen for a long while and suddenly notices that everyone is reacting somehow strangely to his friendliness. The shameless sidelong glances of little Judas at her bust immediately reminded her she possessed in her background the kind of baggage which could not easily be ignored. And when, after the edifying sighs of the priest and his wife and after the fresh moralizings of little Judas, she found herself by herself, when at her leisure she had re-examined the day's impressions, then it seemed unmistakable to her that the former "young lady" had died once and for all, that from now on she was simply an actress in a miserable provincial theatre and that the position of the Russian actress was not very far removed from that of a harlot.

Up until now she had been living in a kind of dream. She had bared herself in "La belle Hélène," she had appeared drunk in "Périchole," sung all manner of shameless things in "Excerpts from the Life of the Duchess of Gerolstein" and even regretted the fact that it was not accepted to present "la chose" and "l'amour" on stage, imagining to herself how she would wiggle her hips seductively and twist the train of her dress so adroitly. But it never occurred to her to give any thought to what she was doing. She simply strove so that she could do everything "attractively" and "with chic" and at the same time please the officers from the regiment quartered in the town. But what it meant and what sort of sentiments were produced in the officers by her wigglings—she had never even asked herself. The officers represented the decisive public in the town and she knew that her success depended on them. They forced their way behind the stage, unceremoniously pounded at the door to her change-room when she was still half-dressed, called her by cute nicknames and she looked on all of this as though on a simple formality, a kind of unavoidable circumstance of the trade, and asked herself only whether she had been "attractive" in her role or "unattractive" in the situation. But she did not as yet acknowledge her body or her soul to be public property. And now, when she had once again sensed herself to be a "young lady," she suddenly felt unbearably vile. As though all the veils, down to the very last one, had been removed and she had been displayed publically in her nakedness. As though the vile breath of all these people, saturated with the smell of alcohol and the stable, had engulfed her simultaneously. As though she could

146

feel on her body the touch of sweaty hands, slavering lips and the wandering of glazed eyes filled with a cannibalistic brutishness, slipping senselessly along the curved outline of her naked body, seeming to demand an answer from her: what is "la chose"?

Where could she go? Where could she abandon this baggage which was crushing down on her shoulders? This question spun hopelessly about in her head, but without finding or even seeking for an answer. This too was a kind of dream. A young girl turns indignant, becomes emotional—and that is all there is to it. It will pass. There are good moments, but there are also bitter ones, this is all in the order of things. But both the good and the bitter merely slip by without in the least altering the direction taken by life as it unravels. In order to change the direction of life, a great deal of effort is required, there is not only a moral demand to be made, but a physical courage as well. It is almost the same thing as suicide. Although before committing suicide a person curses his life, although he knows positively that death represents freedom for him, nonetheless, the instrument of death still trembles in his hands, the knife slips from his throat, the pistol instead of being aimed at the forehead fires somewhat lower and merely disfigures him. The same is true here, only it is even more difficult. Here too one's former life must be killed, but at the same time as one kills it, one remains alive. The "destruction" which is achieved by the instant release of the trigger is a genuine suicide. But in that particular type of suicide which is called "regeneration," achievement comes through an entire series of stern, almost ascetic efforts of will. And all the same it is a kind of "destruction" that is being achieved, because it is impossible to call normal the existence whose content consists only of efforts of will over oneself, of deprivation and restraint. Whoever's will is spoiled, whoever has been weakened by the habit of an easy life, that person's head will begin to spin from the prospect alone of such a "regeneration." Instinctively, even as he turns his head away, frowns, feels shame and accuses himself of cowardice, nonetheless he will once again proceed along the well-trod path.

A life of work is a magnificent thing! But only strong people can accommodate themselves to it, and those who have been condemned to it by some inborn and accursed misfortune. Those people alone are not frightened. The former because once they recognize the meaning and resources of labor, they are able to discover pleasure in it; the latter because for them labor is above all an inborn requirement, and for that reason a habit as well.

It did not even occur to Anninka to establish herself in Pogorelka or in Golovlyovo, and in this regard she found support in the business position dictated by circumstances and which she instinctively did not abandon. She had been given leave and beforehand she had parcelled out her leave, even designating the day of departure from Golovlyovo. For people of a weak character, those external boundaries which encompass life significantly reduce its burden. In difficult situations weak people instinctively embrace these boundaries and find for themselves a justification in them. This is precisely the way Anninka proceeded as well: she decided to leave Golovlyovo as quickly as possible and if her uncle insisted, then she would protect herself from his insistence by claiming the necessity of appearing at the pre-arranged time.

When she awoke the following morning, she made her way through all the rooms of the enormous Golovlyovo house. It was deserted and uninviting everywhere, there was the smell of estrangement, of forfeiture. The thought of settling in this house without ever leaving ultimately frightened her. "Not for anything" she affirmed in a kind of unaccountable agitation, "not for anything!"

* * *

The following day Porfiry Vladimirych greeted her once again with his customary deference in which it was totally impossible to distinguish whether he wanted to embrace a person or whether he was intent on sucking the blood out of him.

"Well, now, my flutter-bug, did you sleep well? Where will you rush off to now?" he joked.

"In fact, uncle, I am in a hurry. After all I've only taken a leave and must make it back on time."

"You're going to do that side-show stuff, again? I won't let you!"

"Whether you do or not, I'll still leave by myself!"

Little Judas shook his head sadly.

"But what would your deceased grandmother say?" he asked in a voice of gentle reproach.

"Grandmother knew about it when she was alive. And what kind of a way is this, uncle, that you have of speaking? Yesterday you were packing me off to the fairs with my guitar and now today you've turned the conversation to side-show amusements? Listen to me! I don't want you to talk that way!"

"Aha! Obviously, the truth hurts! And I do love the truth. As far as I'm concerned, if the truth..."

"No, now! I don't want to hear it! I don't! I don't need your truth or your untruth! Listen! I don't want you to use those kind of expressions!"

"Now, now! Have you lost your temper? Come now, my little dragon-fly, while there's still time, and have some tea! I expect the samovar is already huffing and puffing and steaming away, on the table."

Porfiry Vladimirych wanted to smooth over the impression aroused by the words "side-show amusements" with jokes and jests, and as a sign of conciliation he even reached for his niece to embrace her around the waist, but Anninka still found all of this so disgusting that she abruptly turned away from the hug that awaited her.

"Uncle, I repeat to you in all seriousness that I must hurry!" she said.

"Then we'll go in a moment, first we'll have tea and then we'll have a chat!"

"And why does it have to be after tea? Why can't we talk before tea?"

"Just because. Because everything must be done in the proper order. First one thing, then the next, first we'll have tea and chat, then we'll discuss business. We'll have time for everything."

In the face of such irresistible and idle chatter one could only submit. They began to drink their tea and here little Judas tarried in the most malicious fashion, sipping a little bit out of the glass, crossing himself, slapping his thighs, babbling on about his deceased mother and so on.

"Well, now we'll have a talk," he said finally, "are you intending to be my guest for long?"

"I can't stay longer than a week. I still have to go to Moscow."

"A week, my friend, is a good length of time. One can accomplish a great deal in a week, or one can accomplish very little—depending on how one approaches it.

"We had better do a great deal, uncle."

"That's just what I'm saying. One can accomplish a great deal, or very little. Sometimes you want to accomplish a lot, but you only achieve a little, and sometimes it seems that very little is being done, but before you know it, with God's help, you have finished everything without noticing it. Here you are rushing about, you have to go to Moscow, you see, but if someone were to ask you why, you yourself could not give a proper answer. In my opinion, instead of Moscow you would be better off spending this time on business."

"I must go to Moscow because I want to see whether we can't appear on the stage there. As far as business is concerned, then you yourself say that one can take care of a great deal of business in a week."

"Depending on how you go about it, my friend. If you go about it the right way, everything will go swimmingly for you. But if you do it the wrong way, well, the thing will elude you, escape your grasp."

"Then you direct me, uncle!"

"Now, there you go. When you need me, then you say 'you direct me, uncle!' and when you don't need me, then you find it boring here with your uncle and you want to leave him as quickly as possible! Isn't it the truth what I'm saying?"

"Just tell me what I have to do."

"Just wait! Now this is just what I'm saying: when your uncle is needed, he's a sweetie and a dear and a honey; but when he's not needed, then you turn your back on him! You never think of asking your uncle: what do you think, uncle dear, you should say, can I go to Moscow?"

"What a strange person you are, uncle! After all, I do have to be in Moscow and suddenly you want to say that I mustn't?"

"That's exactly what I will say, you mustn't, and just sit down! It's not a stranger talking, but your uncle, you could at least listen to your uncle. Goodness me, my friend, my friend! It's a good thing you do have an uncle, someone who can take pity on you and stop you! Now just take other people, they don't have anyone! No one to take pity on them, or to stop them. They fend for themselves! And to them...well, all kinds of things happen to them in life, my friend!"

Anninka was about to object, but she understood that this would only pour fat on the fire and she kept silent. She sat and looked in despair at Porfiry Vladimirych who was getting a full head of steam up.

"Now, I've been wanting to say to you for a long while," little Judas continued in the meantime, "I don't care for, no I don't, for the way that you travel around these...around these fairs! Even if it displeases you that I talk about guitars, nonetheless..."

"It's easy enough to say that you don't care for it! You should indicate some way out!"

"Live with me—there's a way out for you!"

"Certainly not...not for anything!"

"Why not?"

"For the reason that there is nothing for me to do here. What's there to do here! In the morning you get up, go and have tea, over your tea you are thinking: they'll soon be serving breakfast! Over breakfast: they'll soon set the table for dinner! Over dinner: will it be tea-time again soon? And then supper and bed... A person would perish here!"

"Everybody, my friend, does likewise. First they have their tea, then whoever is accustomed to having breakfast, he has breakfast, but I am not accustomed to eating breakfast, and so I don't eat breakfast. They they have dinner, then they have late tea and finally go to bed. What's wrong with that! To my mind there's nothing ridiculous or reprehensible in this! Now, if I were to..."

"There's nothing reprehensible in it, it's simply not to my liking."

"If I had offended anyone or censured them or spoke badly about anyone, well, then, that would certainly be such! One could even censure oneself for this! But having tea, eating breakfast, dinner, supper... Christ preserve you: and however nimble you are, you won't last long without food!"

"Of course, all that is fine, only it's just not to my liking!"

"Don't you go measuring everything according to your yardstick, think about the older folk as well! All you can say is 'not to my liking,' 'not to my liking'—is that really any way to talk! You should be saying 'to God's liking' or 'not to God's liking'—now that would be more to the point, it certainly would! If things here in Golovlyovo are not to God's liking, if we act contrary to God, if we sin, if we complain or become envious, or commit any other bad deeds, well, then we truly are guilty and we deserve to be censured. Only here too it must be proven that we have not acted in truth according to God's liking. And there you have it! Really, 'not to my liking'! And now I'll say at least something about myself. So you think everything is to my liking! Well, it's not to my liking that here you are talking to me this way and finding fault with my hospitality, yet here I sit and remain silent! Here I am

150

thinking: I'll just quietly nudge her in the right direction, perhaps she herself will come to her senses! Perhaps while I'm responding to your pranks with a joke and a jest, your guardian angel will put you on the road of truth! After all I'm not offended for myself, but rather for you! Goodness me, my friend, how unkind of you! Even if I had said something nasty to you or acted in a nasty fashion against you, or you felt that I had offended you, well, then, God preserve you! Even though God commands that one listen to the teachings of one's elders, well, then, if I've offended you, God preserve you! Go ahead and be angry with me! I'll just sit here nice and quietly, just sit here, saying nothing, merely thinking what the best and proper way would be for everyone to enjoy happiness and comfort. But you! Well, goodness me! Just look at the response you give to my affections! Don't you go saying everything right off, my friend, but first think and pray to God and beg him to give you wisdom! And then if..."

Porfiry Vladimirych spouted forth for a long while without stopping. The words dragged on one after the other in a turgid slavering. Anninka looked at him in incalculable horror and thought: how is it that he doesn't choke himself? Be that as it may, her uncle still did not say what she had to do concerning the death of Arina Petrovna. Again at dinner she posed this question, and again at evening tea, but each time little Judas got sidetracked with his dawdling so that Anninka grew unhappy that she had provoked the conversation and could think only of one thing: when would all of this end?

After dinner, when Porfiry Vladimirych went off to sleep, Anninka remained alone with just Yevprakseyushka and she suddenly had a whim to chat with her uncle's housekeeper. She wanted to know why Yevprakseyushka was not frightened of being in Golovlyovo and what gave her the strength to withstand the floods of frivolous words spewed forth by her uncle's lips from dawn till dusk.

"Yevprakseyushka, are you bored in Golovlyovo?"

"What's there to be bored with? We're not aristocrats!"

"Still...you're always alone...you have no amusements, no pleasures— nothing!"

"What pleasures do we need! If it's boring, then I look out the window. I was living with my papa at St. Nikola's church in Kapelki, I certainly didn't see any good times there!"

"All the same, I suppose it would be better for you at home. You had your friends, you could go visiting, play..."

"That we could!"

"But with uncle... He's always saying something boring and he does seem to go on. Is he always like that?"

"Always, he talks like that the whole day long."

"And you don't find it boring?"

"What do I care! I just don't listen!"

"It's impossible to stop listening completely. He might notice it and be

151

offended."

"How would he know! You see, I look at him. He talks and I look at him but all this time I'm thinking about my own business."

"But what are you thinking about?"

"I think about everything. The cucumbers have to be pickled, so I think about the cucumbers; something has to be fetched from town, so I think about that. Something has to be done around the house, so I think about everything."

"Even though you're living here together, you must in fact be all alone?"

"Yes, I'm pretty much on my own. Sometimes in the evening he'll take it into his head to play cards, so we play. But then right in the very middle of the game he'll stop, put his cards down and begin talking. And I just look at him. When the deceased Arina Petrovna was here, things were more cheerful. When she was present he was afraid of talking too much nonsense. Hold on there, the old girl would stop him. But nowadays I've never seen the like of the way he allows himself to carry on!"

"There, don't you see! After all, Yevprakseyushka, it is terrible! It's terrible when a person is talking and doesn't know why he's talking and what he's saying and whether he will ever finish. It is terrible, isn't it? You do feel uncomfortable, don't you?"

Yevprakseyushka glanced at her as though for the first time her mind had been illuminated by a striking thought.

"You're not the only one," she said, "many of our people can't stand him for that very reason."

"There, you see!"

"Yes. Even the valets. There has not been one of them who could live in peace here. We change valets practically every month. The same with bailiffs. And it's all because of this."

"Does everyone get fed up with him?"

"He plays the tyrant. Now drunkards, those can manage because a drunkard doesn't hear. You might as well shout up a drain-pipe, it makes no difference to a drunkard because it's the same as though he had a pot over his head. But we run into another misfortune here: he doesn't like drunkards."

"Goodness, Yevprakseyushka, Yevprakseyushka! And he's still trying to convince me to live in Golovlyovo!"

"My goodness, mistress! Would you really live with us! Maybe he would mind his step in your company!"

"Certainly not! A submissive servant! I can hardly bear to look him in the eye even now!"

"What's there to say! You are a lady! You are independent! However, I imagine that before you knew it, you'd have to be dancing to someone else's tune as well!"

"More often than not!"

152

"That's just what I was thinking! But there's something else I've been wanting to ask you: do you like working as an actress?"

"I earn my own living, and that's one good thing."

"But is it true what Porfiry Vladimirych told me? It seems that strange men are always putting their arms around the waists of actresses!"

Anninka flared up instantly.

"Porfiry Vladimirych does not understand," she answered irritably, "that's why he's always talking nonsense. He cannot even distinguish between play-acting and reality."

"But still! The way he, Porfiry Vladimirych... When he saw you, he even smacked his lips! He kept saying 'niece' this and 'niece' that! —like a decent fellow! But all the while his shameless eyes were roving about!"

"Yevprakseyushka! Why are you talking so silly!"

"Who, me? What do I care! You live here awhile and you'll see for yourself! But what do I care! If I'm let go, then I'll just return to my father the priest again. And it is boring here. You were speaking the truth there."

"You are just wasting your time suggesting that I should stay here. And as far as it being boring here in Golovlyovo, that's a fact. The longer you live here the more boring it'll be."

Yevprakseyushka pondered a short while, then she yawned and said:

"When I was living with my priest father, you wouldn't believe how thin I was. But now, just look at me! As big as a stove! It must be the boredom that doesn't agree with me!"

"All the same, you won't hold out for long. Just remember my words, you won't hold out."

With this the conversation came to an end. Fortunately, Porfiry Vladimirych did not hear it, otherwise he would have had a new and thankful topic which no doubt would have renewed the endless string of his moralizing conversations.

For two more entire days Porfiry Vladimirych tormented Anninka. He kept saying over and over again: "Just hold your horses! Take it nice and easy! Praise the Lord and say your prayers!" And so on. He had completely exhausted her. Finally, on the fifth day, he made ready to go to town, although even then he found a way of torturing his niece. She was already standing in the entry-way in her fur-coat, while he, almost maliciously, fiddled around for an entire hour. He got dressed, washed, slapped himself on the thighs, made the sign of the cross, walked about, sat down, gave commands of the type: "Well, this and that, brother!" or "Well, you just look after, brother, whatever it was!" In general he acted as though he were leaving Golovlyovo not for several hours, but forever. Having exhausted everyone, both the folk and the horses, who had been standing in the driveway for an hour and a half, he finally became convinced that even his own throat had dried up from the trivia he was saying and he decided to leave.

In town all the business was concluded while the horses were eating their oats at a road-side inn. Porfiry Vladimirych presented an account according to which it turned out that the orphan's capital, on the day of Arina Petrovna's death, amounted to almost twenty thousand rubles in five-percent bonds. Then a request to dissolve the trusteeship, together with the papers bearing proof of the orphans' coming of age, was taken care of and hereupon followed the arrangements for the awarding of the trusteeship title and the transferal of the estate and capital to the owners. The evening of that very same day, Anninka signed all the papers and inventories prepared by Porfiry Vladimirych and could finally breathe a sigh of relief.

The remainder of the days Anninka spent in the greatest agitation. She wanted to leave Glovlyovo immediately, that very moment, but to all her impulses her uncle responded with jokes, which, despite their kindhearted tone, concealed within themselves the kind of foolish stubbornness that no human power was capable of breaking.

"You said yourself that you would stay a week, well, then, stay!" he would say. "Come now! You don't have to pay for a flat, we are begging you to stay even without paying! You can drink tea and eat, anything you care to, you will have it all!"

"But, uncle, I really do have to go!" Anninka would implore.

"You can't sit still, and I won't give you any horses!" little Judas joked, "I won't give you any horses, and you'll be my prisoner! When a week has passed, then I won't say a single word! We'll attend mass, have a farewell dinner, drink tea and have a chat... We'll take a good look at each other, and then Godspeed to you! Now here's something! Wouldn't you like to visit the grave in Voplino again? You still ought to say farewell to grandmother. Maybe your deceased grandmother will have a good word of advice to give you!"

"If you wish!" Anninka agreed.

"Then this is what we'll do. Early on Wednesday we'll attend mass here and then have a farewell dinner, and then my horses will take you as far as Pogorelka, and from there to Dvoriki you can go with your own horses, the Pogorelka horses. You're a landowner yourself! You have your own horses!"

Anninka was forced to submit. Utter triviality possesses an enormous strength. It always catches an untainted person unawares and all the while he is being amazed and casting about, it quickly enmeshes him and grasps him in its clutches. Probably everyone has had the experience of walking past a cesspool and not only holding one's nose, but even trying not to breathe. The person who enters a realm saturated with idle chatter and utter triviality must exert precisely the same effort of will. He must dull within himself the senses of sight, hearing, smell and taste. He must overcome every sense of perception, turn himself into wood. Only then will the foul odors of utter triviality not suffocate him. Anninka understood this, even though it was too late. In any event, she decided to leave the business of her liberation from Golovlyovo to the natural course of events. Little Judas had so defeated her with the unassailability of his idle chatter that she did not even dare resist when he ambraced her and patted her back like a good relative, repeating: "Now, there's a good girl!" Each time she shuddered involuntarily when she felt the bony and slightly trembling hand of his creeping along her back. But she was restrained from any further expressions of disgust by the thought: "Lord! At least he'll let me go in a week's time!" Fortunately for her, little Judas was not a squeamish fellow and even if he did perhaps notice her impatient gestures, he kept his silence. Apparently he held to that theory of the mutual relations between sexes which was expressed in the saying: "Like it or not, you must put up with it!"

At last the impatiently awaited day of departure arrived. Anninka arose at almost six o'clock in the morning, but little Judas had forewarned her all the same. He had completed his usual period of prayer and, in expectation of the first chime of the church bell, he was slouching about the rooms in his dressing gown, peeking and listening here and there, and so on. Apparently he was agitated and when he met Anninka he seemed to look askance at her. Outside it was already quite light, but the weather had turned ugly. The entire sky was covered everywhere with dark clouds from which a spring sleet came showering down. It was neither rain nor snow. On the blackened road to the village one could see puddles which foretold of fields of soaking snow. A strong wind was blowing from the south, promising a sudden thaw. The trees were stripped of their snow and their soaked and denuded crowns were swaying haphazardly from side to side. The master's outbuildings had turned black and seemed to grow slimy. Porfiry Vladimirych led Anninka to the window and pointed to the picture of spring regeneration.

"Haven't you had enough of going, now," he asked, "wouldn't you rather stay?"

"No, no!" she screamed in fear, "It...it...will pass!"

"Hardly. If you leave at one o'clock, then you'll hardly reach Pogorelka before seven. And you can hardly travel at night with these impassable roads. All the same you'll have to spend the night at Pogorelka."

"No! I'll go even at night, I am leaving right now...after all, uncle, I am a brave girl! And why should I wait until one o'clock? Uncle! Sweetie! Let me go now!"

"And what would granny say? She would say: 'Just look at my granddaughter! She came, popped off and did not even want my blessing!' "

Porfiry Vladimirych stopped and fell silent. For a while he stood with his feet planted in one place, first looking at Anninka and then lowering his eyes. Apparently he was trying to make up his mind to say something.

"Just wait a moment, I want to show you something!" he finally decided and he removed a folded sheet of letter paper from his pocket, gave it to Anninka and said, "Go ahead, read it!"

Anninka read:

"Today I have prayed to and begged my dearest God that He would leave me my Anninka. And dearest God said to me: 'Take Anninka by her

155

plump waist and press her to your heart.' "

"Well, what do you think?" he asked, turning slightly pale.

"Phew, uncle! How disgusting!" she replied, looking at him distractedly.

Porfiry Vladimirych grew even paler and uttered through his teeth:

"Obviously, we prefer our hussars!" He crossed himself and, shuffling his slippers, left the room.

In a quarter of an hour, however, he returned as though nothing had happened and even began to joke with Anninka.

"Well, what about it," he said, "will you drop in at Voplino on your way from here? Do you want to say goodbye to the old girl, granny? Say goodbye, my friend, do say goodbye! You did a good deed remembering your granny! One must never forget one's relatives, particularly those relatives who, one might say, have laid down their soul for us!"

They attended mass and a requiem, ate some of the funeral rice pudding in church, then came home, again ate some pudding and then sat down to tea. Porfiry Vladimirych, as though maliciously, sipped his tea even more slowly than usual from his glass and excruciatingly dragged his words out, spouting forth in the intervals between mouthfuls. Towards ten o'clock, however, tea was finished and Anninka spoke up:

"Uncle! May I go now?"

"What about eating? You must have your farewell dinner! You didn't really think that your uncle would let you go like that! No, no no! Don't you even think of it! We're not used to doing that here in Golovlyovo! My dearly departed mama wouldn't let me lay eyes on her if she knew that I had sent my own flesh-and-blood niece out without the proper hospitality! Don't even think of it! Don't even take it into your head!"

Once again she was forced to submit. An hour and a half passed, however, and still no thought had been given to laying out the table. Everyone had disappeared. Yevprakseyushka, rattling her keys, flashed by outside between the storehouse and the cellar. Porfiry Vladimirych was talking things over with the bailiff, wearing him out with his incoherent orders, slapping himself on the thighs and generally plotting on stretching out the time somehow. Anninka was pacing back and forth in the dining room alone, glancing at the clock, counting her steps and then the seconds: one, two, three... At times she would look outside and confirm the fact that the puddles were becoming larger and larger.

Finally there was the clatter of spoons, knives and plates. The valet Stepan entered the dining room and threw a tablecloth over the table. But it seemed that a particle of that same dust which filled little Judas had infected him as well. He barely moved the plates, blew on the glasses, looked at the light through them. Precisely at one o'clock they sat down at the table.

"Now, here you are on your way!" Porfiry Vladimirych began a conversation suitable for send-offs.

A plate of soup was before him, but he did not touch it and he was looking at Anninka so sweetly that even the tip of his nose turned red. Anninka quickly gulped down one spoonful after the other. He too took up his spoon and was about to plunge it into the soup but immediately laid it back down on the table.

"Now God forgive me, old man that I am!" he buzzed, "Here you've eaten your soup post-haste and I'm taking so long. I don't like to deal so carelessly with God's gift. Bread has been given for our daily sustenance, but we squander it without thinking. Just look at how much you've crumbled! In general, I like to do everything thoroughly and carefully, then it comes out more solidly. Perhaps it makes you angry that here at the table I'm not jumping through hoops or whatever you call it there. Well, what's to be done! Go ahead and get angry if you feel like it! Angry, angry you'll be, but then you'll forgive me! And you won't always be young, you won't always be leaping through hoops and some day when you'll have gained a little experience, then you'll say: 'But uncle, if you please, was right!' That's so, my friend. Now, perhaps, you're listening to me and thinking: 'Nasty old uncle! The old grouchy uncle!' But when you reach my age, you'll sing a different tune, you'll be saying: 'Nice uncle! He taught me well!' "

Profiry Vladimirych crossed himself and swallowed two spoonfuls of soup. With that he again placed his spoon on the plate and leaned back against the back of his chair serving notice of an ensuing conversation.

"The bloodsucker!" This is what hovered on Anninka's tongue. But she restrained herself, quickly poured herself a glass of water and drank it down in a single draught. Little Judas seemed to sense by smell what was happening inside her.

"What! You don't like it! Well now, even if you don't like it, you must listen to your uncle all the same! I've been wanting to talk to you for a long while concerning this haste of yours, but there was never any time. I don't care for this haste in you. One can see frivolity in it, thoughtlessness. Just look at that time you went away from grandmother without thinking, you were unconscionable in upsetting the old girl! And what for?"

"Oh, uncle! Why do you want to remember this! After all, it's all done with! It's not very nice on your part!"

"Stop! I'm not talking about whether it's good or bad, but about whether if something has been done, can it be undone. Not only are we sinners, but God too changes His acts: today He might send a little rain, but tomorrow He'll give us some fine weather! God only knows that the theatre is no treasure! Really! Now, make up your mind!"

"No, uncle! Stop it! I beg you!"

"And I'll say something more to you: your frivolity is not very becoming in you, but I am even more displeased with the fact that you treat the opinions of those older than you so lightly. Your uncle wishes you only well, but you say: 'Stop it!' Your uncle treats you with affection and hospitality, but you just snap at him! Incidentally, do you know who gave you your

157

uncle?"

Anninka looked at him in perplexity.

"God has given you your uncle—that's who! If it weren't for God, you would be alone now, you wouldn't know how to act, where to submit your petition and what kind of petition to submit and what to expect in reply to it. You might as well be in the woods. One person would have insulted you, another would have deceived you and the third would simply have made a laughing-stock of you! But since you do have an uncle, then we, with God's help, wrapped up the entire business in a single day. We made a trip to town, visited the trustee office, handed in our petition and received a statement! Now, my friend, that's what it means to have an uncle!"

"But I am grateful to you, uncle!"

"If you're grateful to your uncle, then don't snap at him, but listen well. Your uncle wishes you well, even though sometimes it seems to you that..."

Anninka could barely control herself. There remained but one means of escaping her uncle's moralizings: to pretend that she, in principle at least, was accepting his suggestion of staying in Golovlyovo.

"Fine, uncle," she said, "I'll give it some thought. I understand myself that to live alone, far from one's relatives, is not very satisfactory... But, in any event, I cannot decide on anything at the moment. I must give it some thought."

"Now, just see, here you've understood. What's there to think about! We'll order the horses to be unhitched, have your suitcases removed from the sleigh—that's all there is to think about!"

"No, uncle, you're forgetting that I do have a sister!"

It would be difficult to say whether this argument convinced Porfiry Vladimirych, or whether this entire scene had been performed by him simply for appearance's sake, and he himself did not know for certain whether he wanted Anninka to stay in Golovlyovo, or had simply taken a momentary fancy. But in any event dinner proceeded in a more lively fashion afterwards. Anninka agreed with everything, she responded to everything with the kind of answers which would not offer any pretext for idle chatter. Nonetheless, the clock showed half past two when dinner was concluded. Anninka leapt up from the table as though she had been sitting all the while in a steam bath and ran up to her uncle to say goodbye to him.

In ten minutes little Judas, in a fur coat and bearskin boots, was already seeing her off on the porch and personally supervising how the young lady was being seated in the sleigh.

"Take it easy going down the mountain, do you hear! And in Senkino mind you don't overturn on the slope!" he ordered the coachman.

At last Anninka was seated and bundled up, and the windbreak over the cab was fastened in place.

"But won't you stay!" little Judas cried to her once more, in his desire to make a good impression on the assembled household, to act like a good relative. "You will at least come visit us, won't you? Speak up now!"

But Anninka felt liberated now and she felt like being mischievous. She leaned out of the sleigh, pronounced very clearly each word, and said:

"No, uncle, I won't come visit you! It's frightening with you!"

Little Judas pretended that he did not hear her, but his lips turned pale.

* * *

Anninka was so overjoyed by her liberation from the Golovlyovo imprisonment that she did not even once consider that behind, in eternal captivity, there remained a person for whom every connection with the world of the living was broken by her departure. She was only thinking of herself: the fact that she had broken away and that she felt good. The influence of this sensation of freedom was so strong that when she visited the Voplino graveyard again, she no longer noticed any trace of that nervous sentimentality which she had displayed during her first visit to her grandmother's grave. She calmly attended the requiem, she kneeled over the grave without tears and quite willingly accepted the priest's invitation to have some tea in his hut.

The circumstances in which the Voplino priest lived were very wretched. In the single clean room of the house, which served as the reception room, reigned a kind of bleak poverty. Along the walls about a dozen painted chairs were arranged and upholstered with a hairlike material which in places was noticeably torn, and there was also the same kind of couch with a puffed-out back, just like an old-fashioned general's chest. Between two windows one could see a simple table covered with a soiled cloth on which lay the parish's church registers and from behind them an ink-well, with a pen stuck in it, peeked out. In the east corner hung an ikon-frame and a burning lamp that had been inherited from their parents. Beneath the ikon-frame stood two chests with the trousseau of the priest's wife and covered with a gray, faded cloth. There was no wallpaper on the walls. In the middle of one wall hung several discolored daguerrotypes with portraits of the saints. There was a strange odor in the room, as though it had long served as a graveyard for cockroaches and flies. Although still a young man, the priest himself had noticeably faded in these circumstances. Wispy blond hair hung from his head in straight strands, like the branches of a weeping willow. His eyes, once blue, had a lifeless look to them. His voice trembled, his beard was scanty. A cloth cassock did not fasten properly in front and hung limply as though on a hanger. The priest's wife, a young woman as well, seemed even more exhausted than her husband from her annual bout of child-bearing.

Nonetheless, Anninka could not help but notice that even these crushed, exhausted and poor people treated her not as a genuine member of the parish, but rather with pity, as though she were a lost sheep.

"Were you at your uncle's?" the priest began, carefully taking a cup of tea from the tray held by his wife.

"Yes, I spent almost a week there."

"Now Porfiry Vladimirych has become the principal landowner in our entire region. There's none more powerful than he. Only success appears to elude him in life. First the one son died, then the other, and finally his mother. It's amazing that they did not beg you to settle in Golovlyovo."

"Uncle offered, but I myself did not want to stay."

"Why not?"

"It's better to have one's freedom."

"Freedom, my lady, is of course not a bad thing, but even it is not spared certain dangers. And if you were at the same time to bear in mind that you are Porfiry Vladimirych's closest relative, and, consequently, the direct heir of all his lands, then perhaps one might think that as far as freedom was concerned, you might endure a little constraint."

"No father, one's own bread is better. Somehow it's easier to get by when you feel that you are not responsible to anyone."

The priest gave her a dull look as though he wanted to ask: "Do you really know the meaning of 'one's own bread?' " but thought better of it and merely drew the edges of his cassock tighter about himself.

"Do you receive very much pay for being an actress?" the priest's wife joined in the conversation.

The priest really grew alarmed and even winked in the direction of his wife. He was quite expecting that Anninka would be offended. But Anninka was not offended and replied without frowning in the least:

"Now I receive a hundred and fifty rubles a month, and my sister receives a hundred. In addition we receive the proceeds from a single performance. In a year the two of us earn about six thousand rubles."

"Why does your sister receive less? Is she not as good, or something?" the wife continued out of curiosity.

"No, my sister performs in a different genre. I have a good voice and I sing. The public likes that more, but my sister's voice is weaker and so she performs in vaudevilles."

"It must be the same thing there as well: some are meant to be priests, some deacons, others sextons?"

"Anyway, we share our money equally. Right at the beginning we made a condition that we share the money in equal parts."

"Like good relatives? What could be better than to do it like good relatives? How much would that be, father? Six thousand rubles, if it were divided into months, how much would that come to?"

"Five hundred rubles a month divided by two—two hundred and fifty each."

"Now that's some money! We couldn't spend it all in a year. Something else I wanted to ask you is whether it's true that actresses are not treated as though they were real women?"

The priest was thoroughly alarmed and even let the skirts of his cassock fall. But, seeing that Anninka accepted the question quite differently, he thought: "Aha! It looks as though in fact you can't catch her off balance!" and he relaxed.

"What do mean by saying real women?" asked Anninka.

"Well, it seems as though people kiss them, embrace them, or something like that... Even, it seems, when they don't want to, even then they have to do it..."

"They don't kiss, but merely pretend that they are kissing. As to whether they want to or not, it doesn't even enter the question under these circumstances because everything is done according to the play. Whatever is written in the play, that's the way it must be done."

"Even if it's in the play, still... Someone comes crawling up with a slavering snout so that it would make you sick to look at him, and you have to offer your lips to him!"

Anninka turned crimson despite herself. Through her mind suddenly flitted the slavering face of the brave cavalry captain Papkov, who had in fact "come crawling up" and alas, he had done so even though it was not "according to the play!"

"You do not have the proper idea of how it takes place on the stage!" she said rather drily.

"Of course, we've never been in theatres, but still, I expect, there's all kinds of things go on there. The father and I often talk about you, young lady. We feel sorry for you, even very sorry."

Anninka was silent. The priest sat and plucked at his beard as though trying to bring himself to speak his own mind.

"Incidentally, young lady, there are pleasant and unpleasant things in every calling," he finally spoke, "but a person, because of his weakness, rejoices over the pleasant ones and tries to forget about the unpleasant ones. Why does he forget? Precisely because, young lady, he won't have to be reminded of his duty and a virtuous life wherever possible."

And then, sighing, he added:

"But the main thing, young lady, is for you to protect your treasure!"

The priest glanced at Anninka instructively. His wife shook her head dejectedly as though to say: too late for that!

"And one might think that to protect this here treasure in the actor's calling would be a rather dubious affair," continued the priest.

Anninka did not know what to say to these words. Little by little it had begun to appear to her that the conversation of these simple-hearted folk about the "treasure" was altogether of the same value as that of the gentlemen officers of the "regiment quartered in the local town" about "la chose." In general, she had become convinced that here too, as at her uncle's, people saw in her a quite peculiar phenomenon which might be treated condescendingly, but certainly at a given distance, so as not to "dirty oneself."

"Why is your church so poor, father?" she asked in order to change the conversation.

"There's nothing for it to be rich with—that's why it's poor. The landowners have all gone off to work in the government service and the peasants have nothing to give. Besides, there are barely two hundred of them in the parish!"

"Our church bell is really badly off!" sighed the wife.

"The bell and everything else as well. Our bell, young lady, only weighs about five hundred pounds and even at that, to make things worse, it's cracked. It doesn't ring, just makes a strange noise—just to spite us. The deceased Arina Petrovna promised to have a new one set up, and if she were alive then we would probably have a bell now."

"You should have told uncle that grandmother promised!"

"I did, young lady, and he, to tell the truth, listened to my complaint quite graciously. Only he could not give me any satisfactory answer. You see, he did not hear anything from his mama! The deceased had never talked about it to him! And if, as he said, he had heard, then he would have executed her will at once!"

"When could he not have heard," said the priest's wife, "the entire region knows, but he didn't hear!"

"So this is the way we live. Earlier we at least had some hope, but now we find ourselves without any. Sometimes there's nothing to hold mass with, neither wafers nor red wine. Not to mention anything about ourselves."

Anninka wanted to arise and take her leave, but a new tray appeared on the table with two plates, one with mushrooms, the other with some bits of caviar, and a bottle of madeira.

"Do sit down! Forgive us! Have something to eat!"

Anninka obeyed, quickly gulped down two mushrooms, but refused any madeira.

"There's something I wanted to ask you about," the wife said in the meanwhile, "in our parish there is a certain girl, the daughter of a house servant by the name of Lyshchevsky. She was in the service of an actress in St. Petersburg. Life is fine with actresses, she says, only every month she has to renew her ticket*...is that true?"

Anninka looked wide-eyed and did not understand.

"That's for the sake of more freedom," explained the priest, "but anyway, we think that she's not telling the truth. On the contrary I heard that many actresses even receive pensions from the state treasury for services ren-

---

*The "ticket" referred to is the document issued by the police to prostitutes; it must be renewed periodically.

dered."

Anninka was convinced that the further she went into the woods, the harder it would be to make out the trees and she began finally to take her leave.

"We were thinking that you might now leave your work as an actress?" the priest's wife said insistently.

"Whatever for?"

"All the same, you are a young lady. You've now come of age, you have your own estate—what could be better!"

"And after your uncle you're the direct heir," added the priest.

"No, I won't be living here."

"But we were hoping somehow! We kept saying to one another: our young ladies will be living in Pogorelka for sure! And it's very nice here in the summer. You can go picking mushrooms in the woods!" the wife tempted her.

"We have mushrooms even when it's not a wet summer, an awful lot of them!" the priest seconded her.

Finally Anninka left. On arriving in Pogorelka her first words were: "Horses! Please, horses as quickly as possible!" But Fedulych merely shrugged his shoulders in response to this request.

"What do you mean 'horses!' We still haven't fed them!" he grumbled.

"But why haven't they been fed! Oh, my God! It's as though you've all conspired against me!"

"We did conspire. How could we do otherwise when everyone can see that it's impossible to travel at night when the roads are all impassable. Even if you went across the fields you'd bog down in the wet snow—so we figure it's better to be at home!"

Granny's rooms were heated up. In the bedroom stood a completely made-up bed and on the desk a samovar was steaming away. Afimyushka scraped up the remainder of the tea preserved after Arina Petrovna's death from the bottom of granny's ancient tea jar. While the tea was brewing, Fedulych, with his arms crossed and facing the young lady, hung about the door and on either side stood the dairy-maid and Markovna in such expectant poses as though they were prepared to jump at the drop of a hat.

"The tea is your granny's," Fedulych was the first to begin talking, "it was left at the very bottom by the deceased. Porfiry Vladimirych was about to carry off the tea jar as well, but I wouldn't let him. 'Maybe,' I said, 'the young ladies will come and they'll want some tea to drink until they can get their own.' 'Well, it doesn't matter,' he said and then made a joke: 'You old rogue, you,' he said, 'you'll drink it yourself! Make sure,' he said, 'that you deliver the jar to Golovlyovo afterwards!' Just watch, tomorrow he'll be sending for it!"

"You should have given it to him then."

"Why give it to him—he has enough of his own tea! But now at least we'll be able to drink some after you're gone. What about it, young lady, are you going to hand us over to Porfiry Vladimirych?"

"I wasn't thinking of it."

"So. We were about to rise up in arms earlier. If, so we were thinking, they give us over right away to the master of Golovlyovo, then we would all ask to retire."

"Really? But is uncle so horrible?"

"Not too horrible, but he does tyrannize you, and he's not afraid of talking. He can cause a person to rot with his words."

Anninka smiled despite herself. It was indeed rot of a sort that was being exuded through little Judas' twaddle! It was not simply idle chatter, but a foul canker which constantly oozed putrefaction.

"Well, what have you decided to do with yourself, young lady?" Fedulych continued to question her.

"You mean what must I 'decide' to do with myself?" Anninka became slightly embarrassed, having a presentiment that here too she would be forced to withstand the same twaddle about her "treasure."

"Won't you now retire from acting?"

"No...that is, I still haven't thought about it... But what's bad about the fact that I earn my own living the way I can?"

"What's good about it! Travelling around country fairs with your mandolin! Making drunkards feel good! You are a lady!"

Anninka said nothing in response, she simply knitted her brows. A question was pounding painfully in her head: "Lord, when will I ever get away from here!"

"Naturally, you know better how to act for yourself, but we were simply thinking that you would return to us. We have a warm and spacious house —you could play catch in it if you wanted, it's so big! Your deceased granny fixed it up nicely! If you get bored, you can hitch up the sleigh, and in the summer you can go picking mushrooms in the woods!"

"We have all kinds of mushrooms here: so many different ones you couldn't imagine!" Afimyushka whispered alluringly.

Anninka leaned both arms on the table and tried not to listen.

"One of our girls here was telling us," Fedulych insisted mercilessly, "she was in service to someone in Petersburg, so she said, it seems all the actresses are ticket-holders. Every month they have to present their tickets at the police station!"

Anninka felt as if she had been scorched: for a whole day she had been hearing nothing but *these* words!

"Fedulych," a scream tore out of her, "what have I done to you? Do you really find any pleasure in insulting me?"

She had had enough. She felt that she was being suffocated, that just one word more—and she would not be able to stand it.

FORBIDDEN FAMILY JOYS

Once, not too long before the catastrophe with Petenka, Arina Petrovna noticed during a visit to Golovlyovo that Yevprakseyushka seemed to be puffed up. Raised during the time of the practices of serfdom, when the pregnancy of household servant girls served as a pretext for detailed and not unentertaining investigations and when the same pregnancy was practically considered as a capital gain, Arina Petrovna possessed a sharp and unerring eye on this account. Consequently, all she had to do was to lay her eyes on Yevprakseyushka's midriff for the latter to turn away her flaming face from Arina Petrovna without saying a word and in full recognition of her guilt.

"Well, well, well! Mistress! Look at me! Pregnant?" the old lady interrogated her guilty little darling. But her voice held no reproach, on the contrary, there was a jesting, almost cheerful tone to it, just as though she had caught a whiff of the good old days.

Yevprakseyushka remained silent in a mixture of shame and self-satisfaction, only her cheeks grew more and more flaming under the examining eye of Arina Petrovna.

"So that's it! Only yesterday I was watching the way you were trying to hold your waist in! You were walking about wagging your tail—just like a good little girl! But, brother, you won't fool me with all that tail-wagging! I can see your little girl's tricks from five versts off! Did the wind puff you up like that? When did it happen? Own up! Tell me about it!"

A detailed examination ensued together with a no-less-detailed explanation. When had the first signs been noticed? Did Porfiry Vladimirych know about the joy awaiting him? Was Yevprakseyushka looking after herself, was she lifting anything heavy? And so forth. It turned out that Yevprakseyushka was already in her fifth month of pregnancy. A midwife had not yet been consulted. Porfiry Vladimirych had said nothing, although he had been informed, but had merely folded his palms together, whispered through his lips and looked at the ikon, all of which indicated that all things came from God and that He, the Heavenly King, would take care of everything. Finally, Yevprakseyushka had not been careful once, had lifted the samovar and that very moment felt as though something had ripped loose inside her.

"But you are crazy as I do lay eyes on you!" Arina Petrovna said concernedly when she listened to these admissions, "I can see that I'll have to take charge of this business myself! Just look at her, five months pregnant and she hasn't even consulted a midwife yet! You silly girl, you ought to have shown yourself to Ulitka at least!"

"I was going to, but the master doesn't care for Ulitka very much..."

"Nonsense, mistress, utter nonsense! Whether Ulitka has wronged the master or not—that's not our concern! In this kind of situation he can just forget about it! We don't have to go make up to her, do we? No, a serious business like this means I'll have to take over!"

Using the situation as a pretext, Arina Petrovna felt like indulging in some self-pity: even now, in her old age, she would have to bear hardships. But the subject of the conversation was so attractive that she merely smacked her lips and continued:

"Well, mistress, just try having a good time of it now! You didn't mind being taken for a ride, but now you try pulling the load yourself! Just try! Go ahead! I raised three sons and a daughter and I buried another five in their infancy—I know! These no-good men are nothing but a millstone around our necks!" she added.

Then suddenly it seemed as though a light dawned in her.

"Heavens! It must have been on a fast day! Stop, just a minute, let me count!"

They began to count on their fingers, they counted once, twice, thrice—and it came out precisely on a fast day.

"Well, now! This is supposed to be a pious man! Just you wait, I'll certainly tease him! Our fine monk! The mess he's gotten into! I'll tease him some! I'll be, if I won't let him have it!" the old woman joked.

In fact, that very same day, at evening tea, Arina Petrovna made fun of little Judas in Yevprakseyushka's presence.

"Our fine pious man of God! Look at the trick you've pulled! Now I suppose you'll say that it was the wind that puffed up your little beauty? Well, brother, you're amazed!"

At first little Judas cringed squeamishly at his mama's jokes, but when he was convinced that Arina Petrovna was talking "like a good relative," "from her heart," he too gradually cheered up.

"You're a naughty girl, mama! It's true, you're a naughty girl!" he too began to joke in his turn. But in any event, as was his custom, he reacted evasively to the subject of a family discussion.

"What do you mean, 'naughty girl!' One has to talk this over seriously! This is important business, you know! This is 'God's mystery,' I'll have you know! Even if it's not quite right, still... No, this entire business has to be thought out in great detail, and I do mean in great detail! What do you think? Should she have the baby here or do you want her taken to the town?"

"I don't know, mama, I don't know a thing, honestly!" Profiry Vladimirych avoided the question, "You're a naughty girl, mama! It's true, you are!"

"Well, just stop right there, mistress! Looks like you and I will have to deal with this business properly! The ins and the outs—we'll figure out everything in detail! These menfolk here, all they want to do is satisfy their whim and then we have to go and fend for ourselves afterwards as best we can!"

Having made her discovery, Arina Petrovna felt like a fish in water. The whole evening she spent talking with Yevprakseyushka and she couldn't say enough. Even her cheeks were flushed and her eyes had a youthful sparkle to them.

"Have you really given any thought, mistress, to what all this is about? After all, it's...divine!" she insisted, "because even though it's not quite in order, it's still the real thing. But you take care now! If it really was on a fast day—God forbid—I'll make you a laughing-stock! And I'll plague you to the ends of the earth!"

Ulitushka was also called into the consultations. At first they talked about practical matters, what and how, whether she should be administered an enema, whether her belly should be rubbed with ointment, then once again they turned to their favorite topic and began to count on their fingers—and it kept coming out precisely on a fast day! Yevprakseyushka turned the flaming color of poppies, but she did not deny it, simply pointing out her subordinate position.

"What can I do," she said, "it's not up to me what 'he' wants! If the master gives the orders, can I go against those orders?"

"No, now, my little innocent! Don't go wagging your tail!" Arina Petrovna joked, "I expect, you yourself..."

In short, the women became involved in this business to their heart's content. Arina Petrovna recalled an entire series of incidents out of her past, and of course she did not hesitate to relate them. At first she told about her own pregnancies. The way she had suffered with Styopka-the-dunce, how, when she was pregnant with Pavel Vladimirych, she had travelled by post-chaise to Moscow so she would not miss the Dubrovino auction, and then because of this almost was despatched to the next world, etc. etc. All births were remarkable in their individual fashion. Only one came off easily—that was the birth of little Judas.

"I simply did not feel even the least bit of discomfort," she said, "there I was sitting and thinking: Lord! Am I really pregnant! And when the time came, I just lay down on the bed for a moment and I don't know how it happened myself—suddenly it was all over! That was the easiest son for me! The very, very easiest!"

Then began the stories about the servant girls: how many she herself had "caught," how many she had tracked down with the help of trusted people, for the most part with that of Ulitushka. Her decrepit memory had preserved these recollections with amazing clarity. In all of her past, so gray and totally engulfed with petty and major avarice, this tracking down of her lustful servant girls was the sole romantic element which touched a living chord within her.

It was the belles-lettres of the sort to be found in a thick journal where the reader expects to meet up with studies into fog formation and the place of Ovid's burial—and suddenly, instead of this, he finds: *Lo, a distant troika rushes on...* The denouements of these naive girls' romances were usually very severe and even inhuman (the guilty girl was married off invariably to some

167

peasant widower with a large family in a distant village; the guilty man would be demoted to cattle herder or packed off to the army). But the recollections of these denouements seemed to have been wiped away (the memory of cultured people is generally deferential in regard to their own past), and the very process of this tracking down of an "amorous intrigue" flashed before her eyes as though still vivid even to this day. And it's no wonder! At one time this process of tracking down was taken up with the same consuming interest with which people nowadays read a serialized novel where the author, instead of immediately consummating the mutual desire of the hero and heroine, places a period in the most pathetic place and writes: "to be continued."

"They caused me more than a little torment!" Arina Petrovna related. "One of them thought she could get away with it until the very last minute, she kept fawning, hoping to deceive me! But you won't outwit me, my darling! I myself cut my teeth on these affairs!" she added almost sternly, as though threatening someone.

Finally there followed stories from the realm of pregnancies that were, so to speak, political, and where Arina Petrovna figured not as the avenger, but as the protectress and intriguer.

So it was, for instance, with her own papa, Pyotr Ivanych, a decrepit old man of seventy, who also had a "mistress" and she too suddenly proved to have made a capital gain, but it was necessary for higher considerations to conceal this capital gain from the old man. To make matters worse, Arina Petrovna was in the midst of a quarrel with her brother, Pyotr Petrovich, who also for the sake of some political considerations had tracked down this pregnancy and wanted to open the old man's eyes about the "mistress."

"And just imagine! We took care of the mechanics of the whole thing almost under the eyes of papa! He was sleeping, the darling, in his bedroom and there we were in full swing right next door! Whispering and on our tip-toes! I myself, with my own hands, was holding her mouth so she wouldn't cry out, and I cleared away the dirty linen with my own hands, then her son—she had given birth to such a fine, healthy little fellow—I took him and got into the coach and went with him to the foundling hospital! When my brother found out a week later, he could only gasp: 'My goodness, sister!' "

"There was yet another political pregnancy: my sister Varvara Mikhaylovna had something happen to her. Her husband had gone off to fight the Turks and she up and made a slip! She came leaping over to Golovlyovo like one scalded—save me, sister!"

"Well, even though we were at odds with each other at that time, I still didn't hold it against her: I received her graciously, consoled her and calmed her, and under the pretext of going on a visit, the whole business was so roundly taken care of that her husband went to his grave without knowing a thing!"

Arina Petrovna told her stories in this fashion, and, the truth must be told, it's a rare story-teller that would have found for himself such attentive listeners. Yevprakseyushka strove not to miss a word as though before her very eyes were passing the adventures of some marvellous and amazing fairy-tale. As far as Ulitushka was concerned, as a co-participant in the greater part of this narrative, she merely smacked her lips.

Ulitushka also blossomed and relaxed. Her life had been troubled. From an early age she had been consumed with servile ambitions, and both waking and asleep she fantasized on how she might serve her masters and rise above her equals—and it all came to naught. She would just be raising her foot a step higher when it seemed as though some invisible force would knock her off and plunge her into the nethermost regions. She possessed to perfection all the qualities required of a servant to the gentry: she was spiteful, had a malicious tongue and was always prepared for any treachery whatsoever. Yet, at the same time, she suffered from an unrestrained desire to please which turned all her spite to naught. In the past Arina Petrovna had willingly employed her as a servant when she had to make some secret investigation in the servant girls' quarters or generally perform some dubious business, but she never esteemed her service and did not allow her to achieve any solid position. Consequently Ulitka complained and spoke venomously. But no attention was paid to her complaints because everyone knew that Ulitka was a spiteful girl who would at one moment be cursing you to the depths of the earth, and then a moment later you had but to beckon with a finger and she would come running again to serve like a dog fawning on its hind legs. Thus she had struggled on, always beating her way forward and never managing to achieve anything until the disappearance of serfdom ultimately put an end to her servile ambitions.

When she had been young there had even been an incident which afforded her very serious expectations. During one of her sojourns at Golovlyovo Porfiry Vladimirych became involved with her and even, as rumor at Golovlyovo ran, had a child by her, for which he had to endure his mother's wrath for a long while. It is unknown whether this involvement persisted subsequently during little Judas' further visits to his paternal home. In any event, when Porfiry Vladimirych was about to take up his final residence in Golovlyovo, Ulitushka's dreams were forced to collapse in the most shameful fashion. Immediately upon little Judas' arrival she rushed to him with a multitude of slander in which Arina Petrovna was practically accused of swindling. But the "master" merely gave his benevolent attention to the slander, was cold to her and did not remember her previous "service." Deceived in her calculations and now insulted, Ulitushka ran off to Dubrovino where the brother Pavel Vladimirych willingly took her on out of hatred for his brother and even made her his housekeeper. Here it seemed as thought her abilities were appreciated. Pavel Vladimirych would sit upstairs and down one glass after another, while from dawn to dusk she would be boisterously running around the store-rooms and the cellars, rattling her keys, lashing out noisily with her tongue and even intriguing against Arina Petrovna.

But Ulitushka was so enamored of every form of perfidy that she found it impossible to enjoy in peace the good fortune that had come her way. All of this was taking place precisely at that very time when Pavel Vladimirych had been drinking so heavily that one could entertain certain expectations as to the outcome of this incessant alcoholism. Porfiry Vladimirych understood that under such circumstances Ulitushka represented a treasure of inestimable worth—and once again beckoned her with his finger. She was given a direction from Golovlyovo: not to so much as let the beloved victim out of her sight, not to contradict him in any way, even in his hatred for his brother Porfiry, but simply to prevent with all possible means Arina Petrovna's interference. This was one of those family crimes which little Judas resolved upon not out of some mature deliberation, but rather that he performed somehow unconsciously as though it were the most ordinary undertaking. It would be superfluous to say that Ulitushka fulfilled her assignment to perfection. Pavel Vladimirych had not ceased to despise his brother, but the more he despised him the more he drank and the less capable he bacame of listening to any of Arina Petrovna's comments on the subject of "arrangements." Every move the dying man made, every word he spoke, was immediately known in Golovlyovo, so that little Judas could with complete knowledge of the state of affairs determine the moment when he should emerge from behind the scenes and make his appearance on the stage as the true master of the situation which he had created. He took full advantage of this arrangement: he suddenly showed up unannounced in Dubrovino precisely at the time when, so to speak, the estate was falling into his hands.

Porfiry Vladimirych gave Ulitushka a dress-length of wool for her service, but all the same he kept her at arm's distance. Once again Ulitushka had come tumbling down from the heights of greatness into the nethermost depths, and this time it appeared that no one on earth would ever beckon to her again.

As a form of special benevolence for the fact that she had "cared for his dear brother during his last moments," little Judas gave her a corner in the hut where those deserving servants remained sheltered after the abolition of serfdom. There Ulitushka finally became reconciled so that when Porfiry Vladimirych bestowed his favor on Yevprakseyushka, not only did Ulitushka not manifest the least disobedience, but was even the first to bow to and kiss the "master's mistress" on the shoulder.

But suddenly at that moment when she recognized herself as being forgotten and abandoned, once again fortune shone on her: Yevprakseyushka became pregnant. People remembered that somewhere in the servant's hut a "person of gold" was huddled and beckoned to her with their finger. True, it was not the "master" himself who beckoned, but it was quite sufficient that he did not stand in the way. Ulitushka signalled her entry into the master's house by taking the samovar out of Yevprakseyushka's hands and, leaning somewhat to the side, carried it ostentatiously into the dining room where Porfiry Vladimirych happened to be sitting at the time. And the "master" did not say a word. It seemed to her that he even smiled when, on another occasion, carrying the same samovar in her hands, she met him in the corridor and cried out while still at some distance:

"Master! Step aside or you'll get scalded!"

Summoned by Arina Petrovna to a family consultation, Ulitushka acted up for a while and would not sit down. But when Arina Petrovna cried out affectionately to her:

"Do sit down now! Sit down! There's no sense in putting on airs! The Tsar has made us all equals—sit down!" Then she did sit down. At first she kept her peace, but then her tongue became loosened.

This woman had memories as well. Her memory had stored up a great deal of all manner of sordidness from the earlier practices of serfdom. Aside from fulfilling delicate assignments in the area of tracking down the servant girls' wantonness, Ulitushka had occupied the position of pharmacist and physician in the Golovlyovo house. How many plasters, poultices and, in particular, enemas, had she administered in her life! She had administered enemas to both the old master, Vladimir Mikhailych, and the old mistress, Arina Petrovna, and to every single one of the young masters—and she had preserved the most grateful memories from this. And now an unlimited horizon had presented itself for these memories...

In some mysterious fashion the Golovlyovo house came to life. Arina Petrovna now began to come from Pogorelka to visit her "dear son" in earnest, and under her supervision the as-yet-unnamed preparations proceeded apace. After evening tea all three women would betake themselves to Yevprakseyushka's room, treat themselves to homemade jam, play cards and indulge themselves until all hours in memories which at times would make the "mistress" turn a deep crimson. Every detail of the most insignificant order would serve as a pretext for more and more tales. Yevprakseyushka would serve some raspberry jam—and Arina Petrovna would relate how when she was pregnant with her daughter Sonka, she could not even bear the smell of raspberries.

"No sooner was it brought into the house than I would smell it! I would curse to the heavens and shout: 'Out! Take the damned stuff out!' But after I gave birth, it was all right again! And I took a fancy to it again!"

Yevprakseyushka would bring a snack of caviar—Arina Petrovna would recall some incident on account of the caviar.

"Something happened to me once because of caviar, something really amazing! At that time I had been married for only a month or two and suddenly I had such a desire for this caviar, out it comes and on a plate! So I steal off quietly into the storeroom and keep eating and eating! I said to my truest one: 'What, I say, does it mean, Vladimir Mikhailych, that I keep eating caviar?' And he just smiled and said: 'Well, you see, my friend, you're pregnant!' And sure enough, exactly nine months after that I gave birth to Styop-ka-the-dunce!"

Meanwhile Porfiry Vladimirych continued to react to Yevprakseyush-ka's pregnancy with his former inscrutability and did not express anything specific even once about his implication in the business. Quite naturally this put a constraint on the women and interfered with their gushings, and for this reason they abandoned little Judas almost entirely and would chase him away unceremoniously whenever he dropped in on the comfortable little gathering in Yevprakseyushka's room in the evening.

"Away with you, away young fellow!" Arina Petrovna would say cheer-fully, "You've done your part and not it's time for us women to do ours! This is our own party!"

Little Judas would depart submissively and although he did not miss the opportunity of reproaching his kind friend, mama, for treating him in an unkind fashion, at the bottom of his heart he was very pleased that they did not upset him and that Arina Petrovna had taken an impassioned part in a si-tuation that was so complicated for him. If it were not for her participation, God only knows what he would have been forced to undertake in order to clear up this nasty business, the very recollection of which caused him to shrink and curse. But now, thanks to Arina Petrovna's experience and Uli-tushka's adroitness, he hoped that the "misfortune" would pass without giv-ing rise to rumor and that perhaps he himself would learn of the outcome when everything was already resolved.

* * *

However, Porfiry Vladimirych's calculations were not borne out. First there was the catastrophe over Petenka, then, shortly after, followed the death of Arina Petrovna. He was forced to settle accounts personally, and what is more, without any hope of making some nasty little deal. It was im-possible to pack Yevprakseyushka off to her family for being immoral be-cause, thanks to Arina Petrovna's intrusion, the business had already ad-vanced too far and had become common knowledge. He could not have much confidence in Ulitushka's zeal either, because although she was a clever girl, one would hardly be safe from the public prosecutor if one were to trust her. For the first time in his life, little Judas lamented his loneliness in all serious-ness and sincerity, for the first time he vaguely understood that the people around him were not simply pawns suitable only for manipulating.

"It would hardly have cost her a whit to hang on a while longer," he complained of his mother many times in silence, "she would have organized everything properly, nice and quietly and cleverly—and then may Christ let her soul rest in peace! But when the time to die has come, what can one do! You feel sorry for the old girl, but if that is God's will, then our tears and the

172

doctors and all our medicines and all of us—it's all powerless in the face of God's will! The old girl lived her life, she made good use of it! She lived like a member of the gentry for her entire life and she made her children masters! She lived her life and that's all there is to it!"

As was its custom, his fidgety mind, which did not care to linger on a subject presenting any practical difficulties, immediately became side-tracked on an easier subject which offered an opportunity to indulge in endless and unrestrained idle chatter.

"Just look at the way she passed away, only saints are graced with such an end!" he lied to himself, without, incidentally, understanding whether he was lying or telling the truth, "without any illness, without any fuss...so it was! She gave a sigh, we looked, and she was no longer there! Alas, mama, mama! A smile on her face, her cheeks rosy...her hand held as though she wanted to bestow a blessing and then she closed her eyes...adieu!"

Suddenly, at the very height of these compassionate words, something seemed to prick at him again. Again this nasty business...curses! It would hardly have cost mama much to linger awhile! Maybe a month in all or even less was all that was needed—and just look at what she did!

For a while he attempted to avoid Ulitushka's questions the way he had avoided them in front of his dear friend, mama: I don't know! I know nothing! But it was not as easy to use the same techniques with Ulitushka, who was a rude peasant girl and who, moreover, sensed her own power.

"How am I supposed to know! I didn't get myself in that condition, did I!" she cut him off at first in such a fashion that he understood that from now on any calculations for a happy union of the role of fornicator with that of the independent observer of the results of that fornication itself had completely crumbled for him.

Misfortune loomed ever closer and closer, a misfortune that was inexorable and almost tangible! It haunted him at every minute, and to make things worse, paralysed his frivolous thinking. He employed every possible effort to remove all thought of it, to drown it in a flood of idle words, but he was only partially successful. He attempted somehow to seek refuge in the unassailability of the laws of a higher will, and as was his custom, he made an utter tangle of this theme which he then endlessly unwound, bringing in the proverb about the hairs of one's head being numbered and the legend about the house constructed on sand. But at that very moment when his idle thoughts were tumbling unchecked, one after the other, into a mysterious abyss, when the endless unwinding of the tangle seemed to be entirely secure, suddenly, as though stealing up out of some corner, a single word would intrude and break off the thread. Woe! This word was "fornication," and designated the kind of activity in which little Judas did not wish to acknowledge his own participation.

And lo, when after these vain attempts to forget and suppress it finally became clear that he was trapped, he was seized with melancholy. He took to pacing around the room, thinking about nothing and merely sensing a gnawing and trembling sensation within himself.

This was a completely new restrain which his frivolous mind had come to know for the first time in his life. Until now, regardless of what direction his petty imagination had taken, it had encountered an unbounded horizon whose expanse left room for every conceivable scheme. Even the destruction of Volodka and Petka, even the death of Arina Petrovna did not impede his trivial thought. These were facts of everyday life, recognized by one and all, and a generally recognized format, long since ritualized, existed for coping with them. Requiems, mourning periods, funeral dinners and so on—all of this he performed, according to custom, in the proper fashion and in so doing he vindicated himself, so to speak, before people and before Providence. But fornication...what was that? That was, after all, the unmasking of an entire life, that was the manifestation of the inner falsehood of that life! Even though before people had known him to be a pettifogger, let us say even a "bloodsucker," there was very little legal proof in all of this popular gossip, so that he could with complete justification object: prove it! But suddenly now...a fornicator! A convicted and indubitable fornicator (thanks to Arina Petrovna he had not even had time to make up his lies), and moreover "on a fast day..." Curses!

In these inner monologues, regardless of how intricate the content matter, something resembling the first pangs of conscience was to be noted. But the question presented itself: would little Judas continue farther along this path, or would his trivial mind perform its usual service and present a new loophole thanks to which he would manage, as always, to come away unscathed?

While little Judas was languishing in this fashion under the burden of this spiritual emptiness, a completely unexpected inner transformation was taking place gradually in Yevprakseyushka. The expectation of motherhood had apparently loosened the mental bonds which had kept her tied up. Until now she had reacted indifferently to everything, and she had looked upon Porfiry Vladimirych as the "master" to whom she had a subservient position. Now for the first time she came to a kind of understanding that she was involved in something of her own, in something in which she was important and where she could no longer be mistreated with impunity. As a result even the expression on her face, which was usually dull and impassive, seemed to take on intelligence and grow radiant.

Arina Petrovna's death was the first fact in her semi-conscious life which had had a sobering effect on her. However peculiar the old mistress' reactions might have been to Yevprakseyushka's impending motherhood, they radiated nonetheless an unmistakable sympathy and not merely the vile and despicable evasiveness that was to be encountered in little Judas. Thus, Yevprakseyushka began to see in Arina Petrovna something of a protectress, as though suspecting that some future onslaught was being prepared against her. The premonition of this onslaught haunted her all the more persistently because it was not clearly conscious, but merely filled her entire being with a constant melancholy agitation. The thought was strong enough to indicate unwaveringly the direction from which the attack would come and what it would consist of. But her instincts were already so aroused that at the sight of little Judas she felt an incalculable terror. "Yes, the attack will come from that direction," reverberated in the innermost depths of her heart, "from that direction, from that coffin filled with ashes, for which until now she had been merely the simple hireling and which in some wondrous fashion had become the father and master of *her* child!" The feeling which this latter thought aroused in her resembled hatred and would have directly become hatred if it had not been distracted by the participation of Arina Petrovna, who with her good-natured chatter did not give her the time to think things over.

But then Arina Petrovna had first disappeared to Pogorelka and finally had faded entirely. Yevprakseyushka felt quite eerie. The silence into which the Golovlyovo house was plunged was broken only by the rustling which announced that little Judas, stealthily and holding the skirts of his housecoat, was wandering along the corridor and listening in at the doors. On rare occasions one of the menials would come running in from outside, bang the door to the servant girls' quarters and once again silence would come creeping out of all the corners. It was a deadly silence filled with a superstitious atmosphere and aching with depression. But since at that time Yevprakseyushka was in confinement, she did not even have the outlet of domestic cares which formerly had so tired her physically that she would be walking around by evening as though in her sleep. She attempted to be affectionate with Porfiry Vladimirych, but each time these attempts occasioned brief but spiteful scenes which had a painful effect even on her unschooled nature. Thus, she was forced to sit with idle hands and think, that is, to worry. The causes for worry grew with each day, because Arina Petrovna's death had untied Ulitushka's hands and had introduced into the Golovlyovo house the new element of slander which from now on became the sole and active occupation offering food for little Judas' mind.

Ulitushka understood that Porfiry Vladimirych was a coward and that in his spiritually empty and deceitful nature cowardice closely verged on hatred. Moreover, she understood perfectly that Porfiry Vladimirych was not only incapable of attachment, but of simple pity as well; that he kept Yevprakseyushka simply because she prevented the domestic routine from ever deviating from the designated track. Armed with these simple facts, Ulitushka found it fully possible to nurture and feed constantly the feeling of hatred which began to seethe every time when something reminded him of the impending "misfortune."

In short time an entire web of slander had enveloped Yevprakseyushka from every direction. Ulitushka would make "reports" to the master. One time she would complain of the mindless disposition of household supplies.

"My goodness, master, what a lot of goods you use up here! Earlier I went to the cellar for some salt meat, I was thinking that it was not long since another barrel had been started—and I look and there are only two or three pieces lying there on the bottom!"

"Really?" little Judas would fasten his eyes on her.

"If I hadn't seen it with my own eyes I wouldn't have believed it!"

"It's amazing where all the stuff goes! Butter, cereals, pickles—everything! Other masters give their servants porridge with goose-fat drippings—that'll do them! But here everything is with butter, and with fresh butter at that!"

"Really!" Porfiry Vladimirych was almost frightened.

Another time she came and casually reported on the master's linen:

"You ought to stop Yevprakseyushka, master dear. The trouble is, she's a girl, inexperienced, and just take a look at the linen now... She's used up whole piles of linen for sheets and diapers, and it's all fine linen." Only Porfiry Vladimirych's eyes flashed in response, but his inner emptiness, too, took a turn at these words.

"Naturally, she's thinking about her child!" Ulitushka continued in her honeyed voice, "the Lord knows she must be thinking it's going to be a little prince! In any case the child could just as well sleep on hempen sheets...considering his position in life!"

Sometimes she would simply tease little Judas.

"I've been wanting to ask you, master dear," she began, "what arrangements will you make for the child? Will you make him your legal son or will you send him off to the foundling hospital like the others?"

But Porfiry Vladimirych would interrupt the question right at the beginning with such an ominous look that Ulitushka would hold her tongue.

And so, in the midst of the hatred welling up on all sides, the moment drew ever closer when the appearance into the world of a wee crying "servant of God" was supposed to resolve in some fashion the moral confusion reigning in the Golovlyovo house and at the same time increase the number of other weeping "servants of God" inhabiting the universe.

* * *

It was approaching seven o'clock in the evening. Porfiry Vladimirych already managed to have a sleep after dinner and was sitting in his study covering sheets of paper with numerical calculations. This time he was engrossed in the question: how much money would he have had now if his mama, Arina Petrovna, had not taken for herself the hundred paper rubles presented to him as a christening present by his uncle Pyotr Ivanych, but had invested it at the bank in the name of the minor Porfiry? However, it did not amount to much: in all, eight hundred paper rubles.

"Let us suppose that it's not a great deal of capital," fantasized little Judas, "but all the same it's a good thing when you know that there's something put aside for a rainy day. If you require it, you just go ahead and take it. There is no one to ask, no one to bow to—you just take it yourself, it's your very own sweat and blood, given by your uncle! Alas, mama! Mama! How could you, my friend, go and act so rashly?"

Alas, Porfiry Vladimirych had already recovered from the anxiety which only a short time before had paralyzed his frivolous thinking. Those peculiar flashes of conscience which had been aroused by the difficulties assailing him by virtue of Yevprakseyushka's pregnancy and the unexpected death of Arina Petrovna had gradually subsided. His frivolous mind performed its usual service here as well and ultimately little Judas succeeded, with the help of incredible effort, to submerge the idea of "misfortune" in an abyss of idle words. It could not be said that he had made a conscious decision in any direction, rather the old beloved formula was suddenly recalled as though by itself: "I know nothing! I authorize nothing and I permit nothing!"—to which he always sought recourse in difficult circumstances and which soon put an end to the inner confusion which had temporarily upset him. Now he could view the forthcoming birth as an affair which had nothing to do with him and therefore attempted to impart a dispassionate and inscrutable expression to his own face. He practically ignored Yevprakseyushka and did not even call her by name, but would express himself in the following fashion whenever he had occasion to inquire about her: "What about *that one*... still sick?" In short, he proved to be so resolute that even Ulitushka, who had received sufficient training, in the school of serfdom, in the science of human nature, understood that it was completely impossible to resist this kind of person who was prepared to do anything and who would agree to anything.

The Golovlyovo house was plunged into darkness. Only in the master's study and in Yevprakseyushka's room in the distant wing was a light still burning. In little Judas' half of the house reigned a silence broken only by the clatter of the abacus and the scratching of a pencil which Porfiry Vladimirych was using to make numerical calculations on paper. When suddenly, in the midst of the general silence, a distant but rending moan penetrated the study, little Judas shuddered, his lips began to twitch in an instant and his pencil made an inadvertant stroke.

"One hundred and twenty-one rubles plus twelve rubles and ten kopeks..." whispered Porfiry Vladimirych attempting to drown out the unpleasant impression caused by the moan.

But the moans were repeated more and more frequently and finally became quite unsettling. Work grew so uncomfortable that little Judas left his desk. At first he paced about the room, trying not to listen. But curiosity finally gained the upper hand over his faintheartedness. He softly opened the door of the study part way, stuck his head out into the darkness of the neighboring room and cocked an ear in an expectant pose.

"Goodness! Just look, they've forgotten to light the lamp in front of the ikon 'Console my sorrows!'" —flashed through his mind.

177

But then someone's rapid and anxious footsteps were heard in the corridor. Porfiry Vladimirych quickly pulled his head back into the study again, carefully closed the door and ran on tip-toe to the ikon. In a second's time he was already "in the proper position," so that when the door was flung open and Ulitushka ran into the room, she caught him kneeling with clasped hands in prayer.

"It looks as though Yevprakseyushka might give up the ghost!" Ulitushka said, not fearing to disturb the prayerful stance of little Judas.

But Porfiry Vladimirych did not even turn around to her but simply moved his lips more rapidly than usual and instead of a reply he waved one hand in the air as though chasing away a bothersome fly.

"What are you poking about with your hand for! Yevprakseyushka's in a bad way, I said, it looks as though she'll die!" Ulitushka insisted rudely.

This time little Judas turned around, but his face was so calm, so pious, just as though he had but put aside all his earthly cares in the contemplation of the divine and could not even comprehend on what pretext he could be disturbed.

"Even though it's a sin to speak abuse when someone is praying, still, as a person I cannot complain. How many times have I requested not to be disturbed when I am praying," he said in a voice befitting his prayerful mood, yet allowing himself to shake his head as a sign of Christian reproach, "now what is going on over there?"

"What do you expect? Yevprakseyushka is suffering birth pains, she can't give birth! As though it's the first time you've heard of it...ah, you! You ought to at least take a look!"

"What's there to look at! Am I a doctor or something? Can I give advice? And I know nothing, I know nothing about your affairs! I know that there's a sick person in the house, but why she's sick and what her sickness is —I must confess that I was not curious enough to find out! Send for the priest if a sick person is having a difficult time of it—that I can advise! Send for the priest, pray together, light the ikon lamps...and afterwards the priest and I will have some tea!"

Porfiry Vladimirych was very pleased that he had expressed himself so categorically in this decisive moment. He looked at Ulitushka brightly and self-assuredly as though to say: now then, just try and refute me! Even Ulitushka could not gain her wits in the face of this complacency.

"You ought to come! You should take a look!" she repeated once again.

"I will not come because there's no reason for me to come. If it were on business, I would go without you summoning me. If I had to go five versts on business, then I would go five versts. If I had to go ten versts, then I would go ten versts! Even if it were freezing outside and a snowstorm, I would still go on and on! Because I know: there's business, I must go!"

"Ulitushka felt as though she were asleep and that it was Satan himself

178

standing before her in a dream and he was holding forth.

"Now send for the priest, that's one thing. That will be business-like. And prayer—do you know what is said in the Scriptures about prayer? Prayer is a *great healer of the ailing*—that's what it says! So you go and make your arrangements accordingly! Send for the priest, pray together with him...and at the same time I'll be praying! You'll pray over there in the chapel and I'll be here in my study begging for God's mercy... With our combined efforts, you over there and me here, just see if our prayer doesn't reach God!"

The priest was sent for, but before he managed to arrive, Yevprakse-yushka, in torment and suffering, had already given birth. Porfiry Vladimi-rych was able to guess from the running to and fro and the slamming of doors which suddenly arose in the servant girls' quarters, that something decisive had taken place. And, in fact, after a few minutes once again hasty steps were heard in the corridor and immediately thereupon Ulitushka came flying full tilt into the study, holding in her arms a tiny creature all wrapped up in linen.

"There we are! Just take a look here!" she exclaimed in a triumphant voice, holding the child up to Porfiry Vladimirych's very face.

It seemed as though little Judas was almost wavering, even his body lurched forward and a kind of spark flashed momentarily in his eyes. But it was only for a single moment, because immediately thereupon he squeamish-ly averted his face from the baby and waved his hands in its direction.

"No, no! I'm afraid of them... I don't like them! Away...away with it!" he babbled, his face registering infinite disgust.

"You should at least ask whether it's a boy or a girl!" Ulitushka admonished him.

"No, no...not for anything...and it isn't any of my business! It's your business and I know nothing, nothing, and there's nothing for me to know... Go away from me, for Christ's sake, go away!"

Again a dreamlike vision and again Satan... Ulitushka exploded.

"Here I'll take it and throw it on your couch...you nurse it yourself!" she threatened.

But little Judas was not a person who was easily stung to the quick. While Ulitushka was pronouncing her threat, he had already turned his face to the ikons and modestly raised his hands to the ikons. Apparently he was asking God to have forgiveness on everyone: both those "who sin knowingly and unknowingly," and those "who do so in word and deed and thought," and he gave thanks on behalf of himself that he was not a thief and not a bribe-taker and not an adulterer, and that God, in his mercy, had given him strength to proceed on the road of the righteous. Even his nose began to tremble from an excess of emotion, so that at the sight of him Ulitushka spat and left.

"Behold, God has taken Volodka away—and now He has given us another Volodka!" This thought, which had somehow surfaced independent-ly, he immediately brushed aside and inwardly spat in disgust.

The priest arrived, sang mass and waved the censer. Little Judas listened to the deacon intone, "Oh, Mother of God, protect us!" and he himself was taken with the spirit and sang in accompaniment to the deacon. Ulitushka came running again and shouted through the door:

"They've named him Volodimir!"

The strange coincidence of this circumstance with his recent mental aberration recalling his deceased son Volodka moved little Judas greatly. In this he saw the divine will and now he did not spit in disgust as he said to himself:

"Glory be to the Lord! The Lord took one Volodka away and now he has given us another! That is surely the work of the Lord! You lose something in one place and believe you won't find it again—but then God up and rewards you a hundredfold elsewhere!"

Finally it was announced that the samovar was ready and that the priest was waiting in the dining room. Porfiry Vladimirych was totally at peace with himself and deeply moved. Father Alexander, in fact, had already taken his seat in the dining room as he waited for Porfiry Vladimirych. The priest of Golovlyovo was a diplomatic person who made an effort to restrict himself to mundane topics in his relations with little Judas. But he understood full well that evening vigils were performed weekly and on important holidays in the master's house, and in addition, a general service was held on the first day of each month and that all of this brought the clergy no less than one hundred rubles a year income. Moreover, it was not unknown to him that the church land had not been marked out in the proper fashion and that little Judas more than once on driving past the priest's meadow, had said, "My what a fine meadow!" Consequently, in the priest's behavior was incorporated more than a small portion of "the fear of the Jews" which found expression in the fact that whenever the priest met with Porfiry Vladimirych, he attempted to put himself in a bright and cheerful mood, although he had no reason to feel that way. Moreover, when Porfiry Vladimirych allowed himself in conversation to develop various heretical thoughts in regard to the ways of Providence, life after death and so forth, then, without directly countenancing them, he nonetheless did not see any sacrilege or profanation in them, but merely that audacity of thought so typical of the gentry class.

When little Judas entered, the priest hastily blessed him and withdrew his hand even more hastily as though he feared that the bloodsucker might bite it. He wanted to congratulate his spiritual son on the birth of Vladimir, but he thought he would see how little Judas himself reacted to this situation and so remained cautious.

"It's foggy outside today," the priest began, "according to popular belief, in which incidentally superstition has a notable part, this kind of weather forecasts a thaw."

"But perhaps a frost as well. We make predictions about a thaw—and then God goes and sends us a nice little frost!" Little Judas objected, as almost cheerfully he made a fuss of sitting down at the tea table which for this time was being waited on by the lackey Prokhor.

"It's true that a person frequently, in his imagination, strives to attain the unattainable and reach the unreachable. As a consequence, he gains for himself only a cause for remorse or affliction itself."

"And for this reason we should restrain ourselves from telling fortunes and taking glimpses into the future, and be satisfied with what God sends us. If God sends a nice little frost—we will be grateful for the frost! We order the stoves to be stoked up more warmly and those who must make a journey will wrap themselves up more snugly in their fur coats—and lo, we'll be nice and warm!"

"Truly said!"

"There are many people nowadays who love to go around complaining that one thing is not right and another doesn't suit them and yet something else should be done in such a fashion, but I don't care for any of this. I myself do not make any predictions and I don't find it praiseworthy in others. This is intellectual pretention and that's my view of such ventures!"

"That's truly said!"

"All of us here are pilgrims. That's the way I see myself! Go ahead and drink some tea, have a bite to eat, not too much...that we are allowed! This is why God has given us our body and other parts... Not even the government forbids us this: if you want to eat, go right ahead, but mind you hold your tongue!"

"And again, truly spoken!" the priest grunted and tapped the bottom of his empty glass against the saucer from inner rejoicing.

"I consider that a person has been given his reason not in order to examine the unknown, but to restrain himself from committing any sins. Now if I, for example, experience an infirmity of the flesh or some discomfort and summon my reason to my aid: show me, I say, the ways to overcome this infirmity—then I am acting in the correct fashion! Because in these instances, reason can really prove to be of use."

"But all the same, belief is greater," the priest gently corrected him.

"Faith is one thing, reason is another. Faith shows us the purpose, whereas reason seeks out the ways. Reason tries one place, knocks at another...wanders about and meanwhile searches for something useful. Take the various medicines, herbal remedies, poultices, decoctions—reason gathers all this and discovers something. But it's fitting that everything should agree with faith—for the good and not for the bad!"

"There's nothing I can say to contradict that!"

"Father, I read one little book where it was in fact stated that one should not ignore the services rendered by reason by proceeding on faith alone, for a person without reason will in a short time become a plaything of the passions. I even believe that man's original sin was caused by the fact that the devil, in the shape of a serpent, clouded human reason."

The priest did not object to this, but restrained himself from any praise

181

because he could not yet comprehend in which direction little Judas' words were leading.

"Often we see that people not only fall into conscious sin, but commit transgressions as well—and all because of the lack of reason. A person is tempted by the flesh and is devoid of reason—lo, he flies headlong into the abyss. And he has a desire for something nice and sweet and cheerful and pleasant, and in particular if it's the feminine sex...how might one beware here without reason! But if indeed I do have reason, I would take some camphor or oil, rub it there, sprinkle it elsewhere, and before you know it, the temptation has been completely removed!"

Little Judas fell silent as though waiting to see what the priest would say to this, but the priest still was at a loss to see where the words of little Judas were leading and consequently merely grunted and said, totally off the subject:

"I have these chickens of mine outside... They fuss about whenever there's a solstice: they run about hither and yon and can't seem to settle down anywhere."

"And it's all because neither the birds nor the animals, nor the reptiles have any reason. What is a bird? It knows neither sorrow nor cares, it just flies around! Just this morning I was looking out the window: they were all rummaging about with their noses in the manure pile—what else can you expect of them! But a person hardly needs that!"

"However, in other situations even the Scriptures make reference to the birds of heaven!"

"In other situations that's true. In those instances when faith without reason can save, then birds should be imitated. That is when we pray to God and compose verses..."

Porfiry Vladimirych was silent. He was talkative by nature, and in fact, the day's event was hovering constantly on his tongue. But apparently he had not yet found the mode of giving respectable utterance to this subject.

"Birds have no need of reason," he said at last, "because they have no temptations. Or, it would be better to say that there are temptations but no one makes the birds answer for them. Everything is natural to them: they have no property which must be looked after, there are no legal marriages, consequently there is no widowhood. They do not have to answer to either God or to the authorities. They have only one authority—the cock!"

"The cock! The cock! That's it precisely! For them he's something like a Turkish sultan!"

"But man has organized everything for himself so that there's nothing natural left for him, and therefore he has need of much reason. Moreover, so that he doesn't fall into sin and lead others into temptation. Isn't that so, father?"

"That's the genuine truth. Even the Scriptures advise us to pluck out the offending eye."

"If one were to understand that literally, perhaps the eye need not be plucked out if we could arrange things so that the eye does not offend us. By turning to prayer more frequently and by subduing our physical wickedness. Take me, for example: I'm not at an age where one can say that I'm already decrepit... Well, and I happen to have female servants...as though I didn't have enough sorrow! I know that I can't get by without female servants and so I keep them on! I keep male servants as well as female—I keep all kinds of servants! One needs a female servant to run the house as well. To fetch things from the cellar, to pour tea, to make arrangements for eating...well, Christ be with her. She goes about her business and I about mine...and that's the way we live!"

Saying this, little Judas tried to look the priest in the eye; for his part the priest also tried to look little Judas in the eye. But fortunately there was a candle standing between them so that they could stare at each other as much as they wanted and all they saw was the candle-flame.

"Moreover, this is what I figure in addition: if one were to get intimate with a servant, she would quickly begin to give the orders in the house. There would be all manner of nonsense and chaos, fights and vulgar scenes. For every word you said, she would have two... But I avoid this sort of thing."

Everything began to swim before the priest's eyes, so fixedly was he staring at little Judas. As a result, feeling that social decorum demanded of a person that at least from time to time he add a word to the general conversation, he nodded his head and uttered:

"Hm..."

"But if in addition one were to act in this situation the way others do... like my neighbor, Mister Anpetov, for example, or another neighbor Mr. Utrobin...then sin is not far off. Take Mr. Utrobin there: from that sort of vileness he has some six children rooting about in the yard... But I don't care for that. This is what I say: if God has taken my protecting angel from me—it must be in accordance with his holy will that I be a widower. But if I am, according to God's grace, a widower, then it must be meant that I should be so with honor and maintain my bed undefiled. Isn't that so, father?"

"It's difficult, sir!"

"I know myself that it's difficult, but all the same I do fulfill my duty. One person will say it's difficult! But I say that the more difficult it is, the better, and may God give me the strength! Things are not nice and easy for all of us—someone has to labor on behalf of the Lord! The person who denies himself *in this world,* will receive his reward *in that world! Here* it is called hardship, but *there* it is called virtue! Am I not speaking the truth?"

"What could be more truthful than that!"

"Something should be said about virtues as well. They too are frequently unequal. One virtue is great, while another virtue is small! What do you think about that?"

"How could it be otherwise? Virtue is either great or small!"

183

"That's just what I'm saying. If a person conducts himself properly, if he doesn't slander, if he doesn't speak idly or condemn others, if, moreover, he doesn't offend anyone and takes nothing from anyone...well, and as far as these temptations are concerned, acts with caution—then that person's conscience will be forever at peace. And nothing can be held against him, no filth whatsoever! And if someone condemns him behind his back, then in my opinion such condemnations should not even be taken into consideration. Simply spit on them and waste no further time over them!"

"In these instances Christian rules recommend forgiveness all the more!"

"Well, they can be forgiven as well! I always proceed in the following fashion: if someone condemns me, I forgive him and in addition pray to God for his sake! And he feels good because my prayer has reached God, and I feel good as well: I prayed and then I forgot!"

"That is quite correct: nothing lightens the soul like prayer. Including afflictions and wrath and even illness—everything flees before prayer like the darkness of night before the sun!"

"Well, and God be praised for it! And we should always conduct ourselves so that our lives are like a candle in a lantern that can be seen from all directions... And people will not turn to condemnation as much, because there will be no reason to do so! People should take a look at us here: we sit awhile, chat a bit, talk—who could condemn us for that? And now we'll go and pray to God and then sleepy-bye. Then tomorrow we'll arise again...isn't that so, father?"

Little Judas arose and noisily pushed his chair back as a sign that the conversation was at an end. For his part, the priest also rose and was about to raise his hand in blessing. But Porfiry Vladimirych, in view of the special circumstances this time, caught his hand and pressed it in both of his.

"So, father, they called him Vladimir?" he said, nodding his head sadly in the direction of Yevprakseyushka's room.

"In honor of the holy and apostolic Prince Vladimir, sir."

"Well, praise be to the Lord! She is a zealous servant, and faithful, but as far as reason is concerned—you won't find much! That's why people like her fall into a-dul-ter-y!"

* * *

All the following day Porfiry Vladimirych did not leave his study; he prayed, asking God for guidance. The third day he emerged for morning tea wearing not his housecoat, as was his custom, but festively attired in his suit-jacket, the way he always did when he was intending to take some decisive action. His face was pale, but exuded an inner radiance. A blissful smile played on his lips. His eyes had a tender look, seemingly all-forgiving. The tip of his nose had become somewhat red as a consequence of his prayerful excess. He silently drank his three glasses of tea and in the intervals between mouthfuls he moved his lips, folded his hands in prayer and gazed at the ikon as though despite all his prayerful labors of the day before he still expected some immediate aid and intercession from it. Finally, taking a last swallow, he summoned Ulitushka and stood before the ikon so as to reinforce himself once more through spiritual discussion with God, and at the same time to give Ulitka visible proof that what was to follow was not his doing but that of God. Incidentally, from the very first glance at the face of little Judas, Ulitushka understood that he had resolved upon some perfidy within the depths of his soul.

"I have just been praying to God!" Porfiry Vladimirych began, and as a sign of submission to His holy will he lowered his head and spread his arms to the sides.

"And a marvellous thing it is!" replied Ulitushka, but her voice had such an unmistakable biting quality to it that little Judas could not help but raise his eyes to her.

She was standing in front of him in her usual pose, one arm across her chest and the other supporting her chin; but flashes of mockery hovered about her face. Porfiry Vladimirych nodded his head gently as a sign of Christian reproach.

"I suppose God has sent you grace?" Ulitushka continued, unabashed by the warning motion of little Judas.

"You still go on committing sacrilege," little Judas could not restrain himself, "how many times have I tried to guard you from that with affection and good humor, but you still insist! You have a wicked tongue...a vile tongue!"

"It seems to me I meant nothing... Usually, whenever you pray to God, it means that God has sent you grace!"

"There it is again, 'it seems!' Don't you go babbling everything that 'seems.' The next time you should learn how to keep your tongue! I'm talking about business and she goes on about 'it seems!' "

Ulitushka merely kept shifting her weight from one foot to the other instead of replying, as though expressing with this motion that she had foreseen for a long while and all too well everything that Porfiry Vladimirych had to say to her.

"Well, then, listen to me," little Judas began, "I was praying to God, I prayed to God yesterday and today, and everything turns out that one way or another we have to find a home for Volodka!"

"Everyone knows that we have to find one for him! He's not a pup— you can't throw him into the swamp!"

"Stop, wait a moment! Let me say my piece...you plague, you! Well! Now this is what I'm saying: one way or another a home must be found for Volodka. The first business is to have pity on Yevprakseyushka, the second is to make a real person out of him."

Porfiry Vladimirych glanced at Ulitushka, probably expecting that any moment now she would have a good long chat with him, but she reacted to the business with utter simplicity and even cynicism.

"What do you want me to do, take him to the foundling home?" she asked, staring directly at him.

"My, my," little Judas broke her off, "you've already made up your mind...you have all the answers! Goodness, Ulitka, Ulitka! Your mind is always jumping to conclusions! You love to fidget about and babble everything! And how do you know, maybe I'm not thinking about the foundling home! Maybe I've got...well, something else in mind for Volodka."

"Of course, if there is something, there's nothing wrong in that!"

"That's what I'm saying: even though on the one hand I feel sorry for Volodka, on the other hand, no matter how you wrack your brains, it still emerges that we must not keep him at home!"

"Everyone knows that! What would people say? They would say: 'Where did that strange little boy in the Golovlyovo house come from?' "

"Yes, and that too. There's no advantage in it for him at home. The mother is young—she would spoil him. Me, I'm an old man, even though I'm just a bystander, but I might spoil him too because of the mother's faithful service! No, no, one would he too easy with him. Whenever he should have a whipping for doing wrong, for one reason and another...you wouldn't bear the woman's tears and cries—well, you'd just let it pass! Isn't that so?"

"That's true. You would get fed up with it."

"But I want everything to be nice and fine for all of us. So that with time a real man would be made out of Volodka. A servant of God and a subject of the Tsar. So that if God blesses him to be a member of the peasantry, he'll know how to work the earth... Some mowing here, some plowing there, woodchopping—at least a little of all that. But if fate has another calling in store for him, so that he would know a craft or science... You know that some of them from the foundling home even become teachers!"

"Really, from the foundling home? Sure they make them straight off into generals!"

"Generals or not, all the same... Perhaps some important kind of person will come of Volodka! And the way they educate them there, —just first-rate! That I know for myself! The little beds are nice and clean, the nurses are nice and healthy, the pretty little shirts on the tiny children are all nice and white, the feeding-bottles, the pacifiers, the diapers...in short, everything is wonderful!"

"What could be better...for illegitimate children!"

"And if he should end up in a village among foster children, what of it, Christ be with him! He'll be accustomed to hard work from an early age and hard work is the same thing as prayer! Look at us—we pray in the proper fashion! We kneel before the ikon, make the sign of the cross and if our prayer is pleasing to God, then He will answer it! But a peasant—he does hard work! He would be happy to be able to pray properly, but he hardly has the

186

time even on a holiday. Nonetheless the same God sees his hard work and rewards him for that work the way he does us for our prayers. It's not given to everyone to live in palaces or to skip about at balls—someone has to live in a smoky little hut, look after mother-earth and tend her lovingly! But good fortune—grandmother herself put it paradoxically before—where is it then? One person lives in a palace and in complete comfort, yet he weeps tears of gold, while another burrows into a straw hut, eats his miserable piece of bread with kvass, and he knows paradise in his heart! Is that not so, what I'm saying?"

"What could be better than to have paradise in one's heart!"

"So this is what you and I are going to do, my dear. You take that mischievous little Volodka, wrap him up nice and warm and comfortably, and take him on the double to Moscow. I'll make the arrangements to fix you up with a covered sled and have them hitch up a nice pair of horses and you'll find the road smooth and even—no bumps, no pot-holes—you go for a nice little drive! Only mind you listen to me and make sure that everything is done well and honorably. The way I would want it done, in the Golovlyovo fashion...the way *I* prefer it! Make sure the pacifier is nice and clean, and the feeding-bottle, too...nice clean shirts, sheets, blankets, diapers, coverlets, make sure everything is satisfactory! Take whatever is necessary! Give them their orders! And if they won't give it to you, then you take me, the old man, aside and you complain to me! And when you get to Moscow, you stay in a roadside inn. Some hearty soup, a samovar, tea, you just ask for it! Ah me, Volodka, Volodka! Just look what a sad thing has come to pass! Such a pity to part with you, but there's nothing, brother, to be done about it! You yourself will see the good of it later, you'll thank me for it yourself!"

Little Judas slightly raised his hands and his lips trembled in a sign of mental prayer. But this did not prevent him from glancing at Ulitushka from under his brows and noting the poisonous flashes which made her face twitch.

"What's the matter with you? Did you want to say something?" he asked.

"I have nothing to say. Of course, like you say, he'll thank you if he'll be able to find his benefactors."

"Goodness, you are so nasty, so nasty! Do you think we would really give him away there without a receipt! And you get a receipt, now! We'll be able to find him right away ourselves with the receipt! Someone will take him, feed him, teach him some sense and then we'll show up on the spot with the receipt and say, 'Thank you very much, let's have our mischievous little Volodka back!' With that receipt we'll be able to fetch him back even from the bottom of the ocean... What I'm saying is true, isn't it?"

But Ulitushka said nothing in response to this question. Only the poisonous flashes on her face showed up even more sharply than before. Porfiry Vladimirych could not restrain himself.

"You're a plague, you are, nothing but a plague," he said, "you've got a devil inside of you, a demon...curses! Well, enough of that! Tomorrow, as soon as it's light, you'll take little Volodka and be quick about it so that Yevprakseyushka doesn't hear, Godspeed to Moscow. Do you know the foundling hospital?"

"I've taken them there before," Ulitushka replied as though hinting at something in the past.

"You have—so there's nothing more for you to learn. It must be you know all the ins and outs. Take care, find a good place for him and ask the authorities there nicely and politely—that's the way to do it!"

Porfiry Vladimirych stood up and bowed, touching the ground with his hand.

"Make sure that he's comfortable there! Not just maybe, but properly! And make sure you check the receipt! Don't forget now! Afterwards we'll be able to find him anywhere! And I'm giving you two twenty-five ruble notes for expenses. I know all about it, you see, I know everything! You'll have to slip somebody something there, line someone's pocket elsewhere... Dear me, what sins we do commit! We are all people, we are all human, we want everything to be nice and sweet and fine! Just take our Volodka here! It seems he's no bigger than a thumbnail and just look at how much money he's costing us already!"

Having said this, little Judas crossed himself and bowed low before Ulitushka, silently begging her to take good care of the mischievous little Volodka. The future of his illegitimate seed was thus arranged in the most simple fashion.

* * *

The following morning after this conversation, while the young mother was tossing and turning with fever and delirium, Porfiry Vladimirych stood in front of the window in the dining room, moving his lips and making the sign of the cross out the window. A covered sleigh was emerging out of the main courtyard, carrying Volodka away. Then the sleigh climbed up the hill, drew even with the church, made a turn to the left and disappeared in the village. Little Judas made a final sign of the cross and sighed.

"Just yesterday the priest was talking about a thaw," he said to himself, "but God sent us a frost instead of the thaw! Sent us a frost and a good one at that! God is always with us! We indulge in dreams, build our castles in the sky, make plans and think that we can outwit even God, but God just goes and turns all our pretentious thought to nil in a single minute!"

FORSAKEN

The agony of little Judas began at the point at which his resource of idle chatter, which he had up until then misused so willingly, began visibly to dry up. Everything had been depleted around him: some had died off, others had left. Even Anninka, despite the miserable future of an itinerant actress, was not seduced by the luxuries of Golovlyovo. Yevprakseyushka alone remained, but aside from the fact that this was a very limited resource, a deterioration took place in her which was not slow in coming to the surface and which once and for all convinced little Judas that the good old days were now beyond recall for him.

Up until now Yevprakseyushka had been defenceless to such a degree that Porfiry Vladimirych was able to oppress her without the least qualm. Thanks to the extreme immaturity of mind and an inborn flaccidness of character, she had not even been aware of this oppression. Whenever little Judas abused her, she would look him in the eye impassively and be thinking about something completely different. But now she suddenly grasped something and the most immediate result of this nascent ability to understand was manifested in a sudden, as yet unconscious, but malicious and unconquerable disgust. Apparently the sojourn in Golovlyovo of the young mistress from Pogorelka had not been without effect on Yevprakseyushka. Although the latter could not have accounted for the kind of pain which her chance conversations with Anninka had summoned forth, still, inwardly she felt herself completely aroused. Earlier it would never have entered her head to ask herself why Porfiry Vladimirych, as soon as he met a real person, would immediately begin to entangle him in an entire web of verbal trivia wherein it was impossible to make head or tails of what was being said, and which made a person feel unbearably depressed; now she saw clearly that little Judas, in the strict sense, did not make conversation, but "tyrannized" and that, as a consequence, it was not unfitting to "harrass" him, to make him feel that it was time for him "to halt this abuse." And so she began to listen carefully to his endless verbal outpourings and in fact only understood a single thing in them: namely, that little Judas was boring, that he pestered people and droned on.

"The young mistress was saying that it seems as though he doesn't know himself why he goes on talking," she reasoned, "but no, it's malice at work in him! He knows which person is defenseless against him, and he just twists him around his finger any way he likes!"

Incidentally, this was only of secondary consideration. For the most part, Anninka's arrival at Golovlyovo had had the effect of arousing Yevprakseyushka's awareness of her youth. Up until now this awareness had somehow simply languished dimly within her, but now it flared up aggressively and passionately. She understood a great deal of what she had treated quite indifferently earlier. Thus, for instance: why wouldn't Anninka agree to remain in Golovlyovo? She had come right out and said so: it's horrible! Why was it so? Simply because she was young and she "felt like living." Now Yevprakse-yushka, she too was young... Yes, young! It only seemed as though her youth had disappeared under fat—but no, there were times when this youth made itself felt most poignantly! It summoned and beckoned to her. First it would subside, but then it would flare up again. She had thought that she would be able to manage with little Judas, now just look... "Ah, you old rotter, you! Look at the way you've gotten around me!" How nice it would be to live with a lover now, with a real one, nice and young! They would embrace, tumble about and her sweet lover would kiss and cuddle her, whisper tender words in her ear: "Just look at you," he would say, "so white and tasty!" "Ah, the cursed old bogeyman! How did he ever manage to attract me with those old bones of his! I bet the young Pogerelka mistress has a young lover! That's for certain! That's why she picked up her skirts and made off so quickly. And just look at me stuck here inside these four walls, waiting until the old man takes it into his head!..."

Naturally, Yevprakseyushka did not give notice of her rebellion immediately, but once embarked on this path she was not to be held back. She looked for faults, recalled the past and in the meantime, while little Judas did not yet even suspect that some kind of nasty work was brewing inside her, she silently but constantly was stoking up her hatred. The first manifestations were general complaints of the type: "someone else has wasted my life away," then a series of comparisons would ensue. "Look at Palageyushka who lives with the master there in Mazulino as his housekeeper. She sits around on her hands all day and goes about in silk dresses. She doesn't have to go to the cattle-shed or down into the cellar, no, she just sits in her own room and embroiders with beads!" All these insults and protests usually ended with a single general cry:

"Oh, the way my heart is burning with spite for you, you hateful old man! Yes, it's burning now, it is!"

To this general pretext yet another was added which was particularly treasured in that it served as the most perfect provocation for starting a quarrel. Specifically, this was the recollection of her son Volodya's birth and disappearance.

While this disappearance was taking place, Yevprakseyushka reacted to it in a kind of daze. Porfiry Vladimirych restricted himself to announcing to her that the newly-born had been delivered into good hands and in order to console her had made her a present of a new shawl. Thereupon, everything was once again smoothed over and proceeded in the old fashion. Yevprakse-yushka plunged into a multitude of housekeeping details even more zealously than before, as though she sought to console her unsuccessful motherhood with them. But whether it was a secret maternal instinct in Yevprakseyushka or some fancy which she had taken into her head, in any event the recollection of Volodka was resurrected. Moreover, it was resurrected at the very moment when Yevprakseyushka felt the wind of something new, free and liberated, when she sensed that there was a different kind of life taking a form other than that within the walls of the Golovlyovo house. Understandably, the opportunity to find fault was too good to be missed.

"Just look at what he's done," she incited herself, "he's taken my child away! Just as though he were drowning a pup in the swamp!"

Gradually this thought took possession of her entirely. She herself turned to a passionate desire to be reunited once again with her child and the more insistently this desire waxed, the more her spite for Porfiry Vladimirych gained in strength.

"At least I would have had some amusement now! Volodya! My little Volodya! My baby! Where are you! I expect they got rid of you to some rough peasant woman in a village! God, hell is too good for you, you damned master! You go and make children and then you discard them like pups in a ditch: no one, you say, can touch us! It would have been better if I had slit my own throat than to let that beast dishonor me!"

The hatred began to manifest itself, along with a desire to plague Porfiry Vladimirych, to make his life miserable and to wear him down. The most unbearable of all wars began—the war of fault-finding, of aggravation, of tiny pin-pricks. But it was precisely only that kind of war which could break Porfiry Vladimirych.

* * *

One morning at tea, Porfiry Vladimirych was very unpleasantly surprised. Usually at this time he would spew forth endless amounts of verbal rot, while Yevprakseyushka, holding a saucer of tea in her hand, would silently listen to him, a lump of sugar clamped between her teeth and occasionally making snorting sounds. But on this particular morning, he had only begun to develop the thought (some warm, freshly-baked bread had been served at morning tea that day) that there were various kinds of bread: the visible bread which we *eat* and thereby nourish our bodies, and an invisible bread, a spiritual bread which we *partake of* and thereby nurture our souls, when suddenly Yevprakseyushka interrupted his idle prattle in the most unceremonious fashion.

"They say that Pelageyushka lives quite well at Mazulino!" she began, turning her entire body to the window and swinging her crossed legs in the most uninhibited fashion.

Little Judas trembled slightly from surprise, but at first did not see any particular significance in the incident.

"And if for a long while we do not eat the visible bread," he continued, "then we feel a physical hunger; but if over a long period of time we do not partake of the spiritual bread..."

"Did you hear what I said? Pelageyushka lives quite well in Mazulino!" Yevprakseyushka interrupted him once again and this time, apparently, quite intentionally.

"If Pelageyushka is living quite well, then Christ be with her!" he uttered curtly in response.

"Her master," Yevprakseyushka continued mischievously, "doesn't cause her any unpleasantness, doesn't force her to work, and by the way, always gives her silk dresses to wear!"

Porfiry Vladimirych's amazement grew. Yevprakseyushka's words were nonsensical to such a degree that he could not even gather his wits as to what he should do under the circumstances.

"And she has a different dress for each day," Yevprakseyushka seemed to be going on in some delirium, "she has one for today, another for tomorrow and a special one for holidays. And when they go to church in their four-horse carriage, she sits in the front and then comes the master. And as soon as the priest sees the carriage, he sets the bells ringing. And then she can sit in her own room. If the master wishes to pass the time with her, she receives the master in her own quarters, and if not, then she spends it with a servant girl or with the chambermaid, chatting or doing embroidery with beads!"

"Well, and what of it?" Porfiry Vladimirych finally came to his senses.

"What I'm saying is that Pelageyushka's life is very good!"

"And I suppose your life is bad? My, my, my, what a...greedy one you are!"

If Yevprakseyushka had kept silent this time, Porfiry Vladimirych, of course, would have burst forth in an entire flood of idle words in which all of her foolish hints, disturbing the proper flow of his idle chatter, would have been inundated without a trace. But apparently Yevprakseyushka had no intention of remaining silent.

"What can I say," she snapped, "my life isn't bad! I don't go about in rags, thanks be to the Lord for that! This past year you paid out five rubles each for two cotton dresses...you really strained yourself that time!"

"And have you forgotten the woolen dress? And for whom did I only recently buy the shawl? My, my, my!"

Instead of replying, Yevprakseyushka leaned the arm holding the saucer on the table and cast a sideways glance in little Judas' direction that was filled with such profound contempt that he felt uncustomarily frightened.

"And do you know how the Lord punishes ingratitude?" he babbled somehow without conviction, hoping that at least a reminder about the Lord would to some degree put sense into this wench who had been aroused for some unaccountable reason. Not only was Yevprakseyushka not moved by this reminder, but she interrupted him at the very first words.

"No, you don't! You're not getting away with anything. Stop talking about God!" she said, "I'm not a child! Enough of that! You've played the master, tyrannized me long enough!"

192

Porfiry Vladimirych fell silent. The glass full of tea stood practically cold before him, but he did not even reach for it. His face turned pale, his lips were trembling slightly as though trying to form a grin, but without success.

"This must be Anninka's tricks! It was she, the viper, who poisoned you!" he finally pronounced, without himself being clearly aware of what he was saying.

"What tricks are you talking about?"

"Just what you've started to talk about with me... She did it! She taught you that! It couldn't be anyone else but her!" Porfiry Vladimirych was growing excited. "Just look at how all of a sudden you've taken a shine for silk dresses! And did you know, you shameless hussy, who goes about in silk dresses from your calling?"

"Why don't you tell me so I'll know!"

"Quite simply the most...well, the most wanton, those are the only ones!"

But Yevprakseyushka's conscience was not moved by this; on the contrary, she responded with an insolent logic.

"I don't know why they're the wanton ones... Everyone knows it's the masters who demand it... When a master draws one of our kind into a love-affair with him...well, all she can do is live with him! You and I don't spend all our time praying either, do we now, but carry on the same way as the Mazulino master does."

"Oh, you...curses on you!"

Porfiry Vladimirych even grew numb from amazement. He was staring wide-eyed at his rebellious companion and an entire mass of idle words began to seethe in his breast. But for the first time in his life he had a vague suspicion that there were situations in which a person could not be eliminated with idle talk.

"Well, my dearest, I can see that there's no getting along with you today," he said as he rose from the table.

"You won't be getting on with me today and you won't be getting on with me tomorrow either...never! I've had enough! You've been lording it over me for some time! I listened to you enough; now you just listen to what I'll have to say!"

Porfiry Vladimirych was about to hurl himself on her with clenched fists, but she puffed her chest out so defiantly that he was suddenly dumbfounded. He turned to the ikon, raised his hands in prayer, moved his lips and quietly strolled into his study.

He was not himself all that day. He still did not have any definite apprehensions over the future, but already he was upset by something that did not at all enter into the customary schedule of his day and that something had passed by unpunished. He did not even emerge for dinner, but feigned illness and in a timid and affectedly weak voice asked to have his dinner brought to his study.

In the evening after tea, which for the first time in his life passed entirely in silence, he proceeded, as was his custom, to pray. But it was in vain that his lips whispered the customary sequence of bed-time prayers. His excited mind refused to concentrate on the prayers even in a superficial fashion. Some nasty but incessant agitation had taken possession of his entire being and his ear hearkened involuntarily to the dying echoes of the daytime which still sounded here and there in the various corners of the Golovlyovo house. Finally, when the last desperate yawn faded somewhere behind the wall and thereupon everything suddenly fell silent, as though having plunged deeply to the bottom, he could restrain himself no more. Stealing noiselessly down the corridor, he approached Yevprakseyushka's room and pressed his ear to the door to listen. Yevprakseyushka was alone and all that could be heard was her yawning and the exclamation: "Lord! Dearest Savior! Mother of God!" —And at the very same time she was giving her stomach a good scratch. Porfiry Vladimirych tried to turn the door-handle, but the door was locked.

"Yevprakseyushka! Are you there?" he called.

"I am, but not for you!" she snapped back so insolently that all little Judas could do was to retreat to his study.

The following day ensued another conversation. Yevprakseyushka, as though on purpose, chose the time of morning tea to cast her barbs at Porfiry Vladimirych. It was as though she instinctively sensed that all of his frivolity was calculated so finely that a spoiled morning would provoke agitation and pain for the entire day.

"I'd just like to take even a little peek to see how some people live!" she began in an enigmatic way.

Porfiry Vladimirych gave a start. "It's beginning!" he thought, but kept silent and waited to see what would happen.

"Really, I would! With a lover, nice and sweet and young! They would go walking around the rooms in a pair and admiring each other! He wouldn't say a single reproachful word to her, nor she to him. 'My darling' this and 'my dearest' that, that's the only conversation they would make! How sweet! How noble!"

Porfiry Vladimirych found this subject matter particularly despicable. Although he allowed adultery within the bounds of severe necessity, nonetheless he considered amorous indulgence a fiendish temptation. However, even this time he cringed, all the more since he wanted some tea which had been steeping for several minutes already on top of the samovar, while Yevprakseyushka had not even given any thought to pouring it.

"Of course, there are many of us girls who are stupid," she continued, rocking back and forth impudently on her chair and drumming on the table with her hand, "one may be so foolish as to be prepared to do anything for the sake of a cotton dress, while another will simply sell herself for nothing!... Someone will say to her to go ahead and eat and drink all the kvass and pickles she wants! They all have some way of tempting us!"

"Well, if it's really only for the sake of self-interest..." Porfiry Vladimirych ventured to note timidly, keeping his eyes on the tea-pot from which steam had begun to well forth.

"Who said that it was only for the sake of self-interest? I suppose that means I'm doing it only for self-interest!" Yevprakseyushka suddenly remarked on the side. "It seems he's counting every piece now! Are you starting to begrudge me my portion?"

"I'm not begrudging it, but merely saying that people shouldn't do it just for self-interest, that's what I'm saying..."

"Now it's 'I'm saying!' You do go on saying, but don't try any of your nonsense! A fine one you are! Now I'm working just for self-interest! But allow me to ask what interest have I gained working for you? Besides kvass and pickles..."

"Well, it's not just the kvass and the pickles..." Porfiry Vladimirych could not restrain himself and became involved in his turn.

"Well, speak up! Speak up, what else?"

"And who sends four bags of flour each month to your parents in Nikola?"

"Sure, four bags! Isn't there something more?"

"Meal, fresh butter...in general, all kinds of things..."

"Sure, meal, fresh butter...so now you begrudge it to my people! Oh, you!"

"I'm not saying that I begrudge it, but here you are..."

"Now I'm the guilty one! He won't let me eat my portion without begrudging it to me and now I'm made out to be the guilty party!"

Yevprakseyushka bore it no longer and burst into tears. Meanwhile the tea continued to steep and steep on top of the samovar, so that Porfiry Vladimirych, in all seriousness, grew very agitated. Consequently, he overcame himself, sat down quietly beside Yevprakseyushka and patted her on the back.

"Enough of this, now, please pour the tea... What's there to get all worked up over!"

But Yevprakseyushka gave two or three more sobs, pouted with her lips and stared with turbid eyes off into space.

"You were just talking about young people," he continued, trying to lend his voice an affectionate tone, "well now, I don't imagine that we're exactly old folk as well!"

"What next! Leave me alone!"

"Really, it's true! Did you know that when I worked in the ministry the director wanted me to marry his daughter?"

"Obviously she must have been overripe...some cripple or other!"

"No, she was a real girl...and the way she could sing 'Oh, matushka, don't sew me that dress!' The way she sang it! Ah, the way she sang it!"

"She may have sung it well, but no doubt the person joining in was bad!"

"No, I thought I was..."

Porfiry Vladimirych lost his wits. He was not against making up, showing that he too could be a lady's man. With this in mind he began to sway awkwardly with his entire body and even tried to embrace Yevprakseyushka about the waist, but she rudely refused his outstretched arms and shouted angrily:

"I honestly mean it: get away from me, you imp! Or I'll scald you with boiling water! And I don't need your tea either! I don't need anything! Just look at what he's taken into his head—he's begun to begrudge me my portion! I will leave this place! By Christ, I will!"

In fact, she did leave, slamming the door and leaving Porfiry Vladimirych alone in the dining room.

Little Judas was completely at a loss. He was about to pour himself some tea, but his hands were shaking so badly that the lackey's help was required.

"No, it cannot go on like this! I must fix things somehow...I have to deliberate!" he whispered, walking back and forth agitatedly in the dining room.

But he was in no condition either to "fix things" or to "deliberate." His mind had become so used to skipping from one fantastic subject to another without encountering any obstacles anywhere that the simplest fact of day-to-day reality had caught him unawares. He had barely begun "to deliberate" when an entire mass of trivia assailed him from all sides and obscured for his mind every insight into real life. He fell into the grip of a kind of indolence, a general intellectual and moral anemia. Thus he was drawn away from real life to the soft couch of specters which he could move about from one place to another, ignoring certain ones and advancing others to the fore—in a word, arranging things the way he wished.

Once again he spent the entire day in complete isolation because this time Yevprakseyushka did not appear either for dinner or for evening tea, but had gone off for the entire day to visit the priest in the village and returned only late in the evening. There was nothing to occupy himself with since even trivia had seemed to desert him for a time. A single desperate thought oppressed him: he had to fix things somehow, he just had to! He could neither do his frivolous calculations nor could he pass the time in prayer. He felt that he was being threatened by some malady which he was still unable to define. Stopping before the window more than once, he attempted to come up with something to concentrate his vacillating mind on, something to distract himself with, and it was all in vain. Outside spring had begun, but the trees stood naked, even the new grass had not yet appeared. In the distance could be seen the black fields which were mottled here and there with white patches of snow lingering on in the depressions and hollows. The road was nothing but black mud and glistening puddles. But all of this appeared before him as though seen through a film. An utter desolation reigned in the vicinity of the outbuildings, although the doors were wide open everywhere. In the house, as well, it was impossible to summon anyone although various sounds resembling the distant slamming of doors reached his ears incessantly. Now if he could only have made himself invisible and overhear what this godless spawn were saying about him! Did the villains appreciate his generosity, or, perhaps they were slandering him for his very kindness? You could stuff their traps from morning till night and it would still be just like water off a duck's back! Had it been that long ago that a new barrel of pickles had been started and yet... But no sooner did he begin to lose himself in this thought than he would begin to deliberate on how many pickles there might be in a barrel and how many, according to the most generaous calculation, should be figured on for each person, when once again a ray of reality flashed through his mind and instantly turned all his calculations topsy-turvy.

"Just look at you! You did not even ask permission—you just left!" he thought, while his eyes roamed in the distance trying to distinguish the priest's house where, in all probability, Yevprakseyushka was singing forth like a nightingale at this very moment.

But then dinner was served. Porfiry Vladimirych sat at the table alone, sipped the watery soup without enthusiasm (he could not stand soup with nothing in it, but *she* had ordered precisely that kind of soup for today on purpose).

"I expect the priest is sick to death of her intruding on him," he thought, "it's still an extra serving of food that's required! And cabbage soup and porridge...and for the guest, if you please, some fried meat or other..."

Again his fantasy was set loose, again he began to forget himself, just as though a dream had come over him. How many extra spoonfuls of cabbage soup would do? How much porridge? And what would the priest and his wife say about Yevprakseyushka's arrival? How would they curse her between the two of them?... All of this, both the eating and talking, passed before his eyes as though in the flesh.

"I expect they are all eating out of the same bowl! She just went off! She knew where to find a treat for herself! The slush and the mire outside—as though we needed that! She'll come home, her skirts all soiled...oh, you viper, you! That's just what you are, a viper! I must, I just have to somehow or other..."

In the midst of this sentence his thought broke off irretrievably. After dinner he lay down to sleep, as was his custom, but he merely agonized, tossing from side to side. Yevprakseyushka arrived home only after it had grown dark and she managed to steal off to her corner without his even noticing it. He had given his servants orders to alert him without fail when she returned, but as though conspiring, they all kept their silence. Again he attempted to gain entry to her room, but this time as well he found the door locked.

On the morning of the third day, Yevprakseyushka, even though she appeared for tea, began talking even more threateningly and pointedly.

"Where is my little Volodya now?" she began, pretending to lend her

197

voice a tearful note.

Porfiry Vladimirych almost expired on hearing this question.

"I'd so like to take even a little peek at him to see how my little baby is getting on! What about if he's already dead...really!"

Little Judas moved his lips tremblingly as he whispered his prayers.

"Things aren't done here the way other people do them! That Mazulino mistress Palageyushka gave birth to a little girl and now they've done her all up in fine linen, made a pink little bed for her... Just the number of sarafans and head-dresses they've made presents of even to the wet-nurse! But here...a fine one you are!"

Yevprakseyushka abruptly turned her head to the window and sighed loudly.

"People tell the truth when they say all masters are cursed! They beget children and then they throw them in the swamp just like pups! And what do they know of the suffering! They don't have to answer to anyone, just as though there was no God over them! Not even a wolf would do anything like that!"

All of Porfiry Vladimirych's insides took a turn. He struggled for a long while to overcome himself, but finally he could not restrain himself and hissed through his teeth:

"Just look at the new fashions you've taken up! Here it's the third day in a row that I have to listen to your talk!"

"What do you mean, fashions! Fashions or not! You're not the only one who is supposed to talk! I expect others can get a word in as well! Really, now! You beget a child and what do you go and do with it? I expect you've left it to rot off in some village with a peasant woman in some hut! With no care, no food, no clothing... I bet it's lying there in the filth and sucking on a sour old pacifier!"

She dissolved into tears and wiped her eyes with the end of her kerchief.

"The Pogorelka mistress was telling the truth when she said that it was terrible here with you. It is terrible. There's no pleasure, no joy, nothing but your tricks... Prisoners live better in jail. At least if I had my child now there would be something to amuse myself with. But just look! I had a child and it was taken away!"

Porfiry Vladimirych sat in his place and shook his head in agony just as though he were being driven against the wall. From time to time moaning sounds even escaped from his chest.

"Alas, it's hard!" he pronounced at last.

"None of your 'it's hard!' As you sow, so shall you reap! Really, I'm going off to Moscow to at least have a little peek at Volodka! Volodka! My dear little Volodka! Sweetheart! Master! Should I go off to Moscow?"

"By no means!" Porfiry Vladimirych responded hollowly.

"But I will go! And I won't have to ask anyone's permission, and no one can forbid me! Because I'm his mother!"

"What kind of a mother are you? You're just a whore—that's what you are," Porfiry Vladimirych finally exploded, "tell me what you want from me!"

Apparently Yevprakseyushka had not been prepared for this question. She fixed her eyes on little Judas and was silent as though pondering what she in fact wanted.

"So that's it! Now you're starting to call me a whore!" she cried, dissolving into tears.

"Yes! A whore, that's what you are! Curses on you!"

Porfiry Vladimirych had completely lost control of himself. He jumped from his place and rushed out of the dining room practically at a run.

That was the final burst of energy which he allowed himself. Thereafter he quickly seemed to grow emaciated, phlegmatic and faint-hearted when there was no apparent end to Yevprakseyushka's harrassment. She had at her disposal an enormous force: this obstinacy of dull-wittedness. And since this force hammered incessantly at a single point, namely, harrassing and befouling his life, then there were times when it seemed something frightening. Little by little the arena of the dining room no longer sufficed for her. She would burst into his study and overtake little Judas there as well (earlier she would not even have dared consider entering there when the master was "busy"). She would come and sit by the window, staring with her tear-stained eyes off into the distance, scratching her back against the window-jamb and begin to act up. In particular she had latched onto a single favorite theme for her conversations—a theme whose content consisted of her threat to leave Golovlyovo. Essentially speaking, she never thought seriously about it and would even have been very surprised if it had been suggested to her that she return to her parents' home. But she surmised that Porfiry Vladimirych feared more than anything else that she would leave. She would always return to this subject gradually and in a round-about fashion. She would be silent for a while, scratch her ear and then suddenly, as though recalling something:

"I bet they're making pancakes at home in Nikola today!"

At this intrusion Porfiry Vladimirych would turn green with malice. Just prior to this he had begun a very complicated calculation—how much could he annually sell his milk for if all the cows in the region were to die, and only his own, with God's help, not only remained unharmed but moreover were to produce twice as much milk as before. However, in view of Yevprakseyushka's entrance and the question she posed about the pancakes, he left his work and even forced himself to smile.

"But why would they be making pancakes at your house," he asked, a grin all over his face, "Oh, my Lord! In fact it's remembrance day for the deceased today and here I am with my mouth wide open and couldn't remember! What a sin! And there's nothing to pay our respects with to poor deceased mama's memory!"

"I wouldn't mind some pancakes...some of my parents'!"

"And why not order them! Go ahead and make the arrangements! Take the cook Maryushka aside! Or what about Ulitushka! Yes, Ulitka can certainly make pancakes well!"

"Maybe she's been able to please you in some other way!" Yevprakseyushka said venomously.

"No, may I be forgiven, Ulitka knows well how to make pancakes very well indeed! They're light and soft—ah, a pleasure to eat!"

Porfiry Vladimirych wanted to distract Yevprakseyushka with jokes and merriment.

"I'd like some pancakes, not the Golovlyovo ones, but my own parents'!" she said stubbornly.

"That's no reason to hold us back! Get hold of Arkhipushka the coachman! Tell him to harness up a pair of nice horses and off you go for a nice ride!"

"Too late now! That's it! The bird has been trapped...she was stupid enough herself! Who wants me the way I am now? You yourself called me a whore not long ago... What can I do now?"

"My, my, my! Aren't you ashamed of yourself, making false accusations against me! Don't you know how God punishes people for making false accusations?"

"You did, you called me a whore outright! Right in front of the ikon there, before the Lord himself! How I detest this Golovlyovo! I'm running away from here! Really, I'm running away!"

Saying this, Yevprakseyushka acted without constraint: she rocked back and forth on her chair, picked her nose, scratched herself. Obviously she was performing a little comedy and teasing him.

"Porfiry Vladimirych, there's something I wanted to say to you," she continued, acting up, "I have to go home, really."

"Do you intend to pay a visit to your mother and father?"

"No, for good. I mean I want to stay in Nikola."

"Why then? Are you hurt over something?"

"No, not hurt, it's just that... I have to sooner or later... Besides, it's boring here with you...even terrible! In the house it's as though everything has died off! The servants are like a gang, they're always hiding out in the kitchens and in the servants' quarters, and here I am sitting alone in the house and before I know it they could slit my throat! When you go to bed at night you hear whispers come creeping out of all the corners!"

However, the days succeeded one another and Yevprakseyushka gave no thought to carrying out her threat. He suddenly seemed to understand that despite the fact that he slaved from morning till night over his so-called work, essentially speaking he was doing the equivalent of nothing and he could go without dinner, not have any clean linen or proper dress if there were not someone's eye to insure that his domestic routine was not interrupt-

200

ed. Up until now it had seemed as though he did not have any feeling for life, did not comprehend that it possessed a kind of organization that did not come into being of its own accord. Formerly his entire day had proceeded in the prescribed fashion. Everything in the house had been arranged personally to suit him and for his sake. Everything had been carried out on time. Everything had been in its place. Such an immutable exactness had reigned everywhere that he had not even given it any significance. Thanks to this order of things he could devote himself to his own whims, together with his idle chatter and idle contemplation, without fearing that the pricks of everyday life might bring him at some time face to face with himself. It was true that all of this artificial scheme hung by a slender thread. But it could never occur to a person who was constantly self-centered that this thread was something very slight and easily broken. It had seemed to him that life had been organized firmly once and for all. Then suddenly all of this had to be destroyed, destroyed in a single moment, at the mention of a few foolish words: "Too late, what can I do, I'm going!" Little Judas completely lost his wits. What if in actual fact she did go? Mentally he began to construct all possible nasty intrigues with the purpose of somehow keeping her back; he even resolved on the kind of concessions in favor of Yevprakseyushka's rebellious youth which never would have occurred to him previously.

"Curses! Curses!" he spat in disgust when he imagined the possibility of a clash with the coachman Arkhipushka or the bookkeeper Ignat in all of its offensive nakedness.

Soon, however, he became convinced that his fear over Yevprakseyushka's departure had at least been without any basis and after this his existence seemed abruptly to enter a phase which was completely unexpected for him. Not only did Yevprakseyushka not leave, but she even allowed her harrassment to subside noticeably. Instead, she completely abandoned Porfiry Vladimirych. May came and with it marvelous days, and she almost never showed herself inside the house. Only by the constant slamming of doors could little Judas surmise that she had run to her room for something again and then again she would disappear. Rising in the morning he no longer found his clothing in the customary place and he was forced to carry on lengthy negotiations in order to get clean linen. His tea and dinner were served either ahead of time or too late and, moreover, served by the half-drunken lackey Prokhor who would appear at the table in his stained jacket and who smelled eternally of a disgusting combination of fish and vodka.

Nonetheless, Porfiry Vladimirych was at least happy that Yevprakseyushka left him in peace. He even became reconciled with the disorder, knowing that at least there was someone in the house who kept control of the disorder in her hands. He was terrified not so much by the confusion as by the thought that he would have to personally take a hand in the organization of life. It was with horror that he imagined to himself that the moment could arrive when he himself would be forced to make arrangements, give orders, su-

201

pervise. In the premonition of this moment he attempted to suppress every inner protest, he closed his eyes to the anarchy which was mounting in the house, kept to the background and maintained his silence. But out in the main courtyards, meanwhile, a daily, unrestrained revelry was going on. With the arrival of warm weather the previously staid and even sullen Golovlyovo estate came to life. In the evening the entire population of servants, both the retired and active workers, both young and old—all flowed out onto the street. They sang songs, played on the accordion, laughed, screeched, played catch. On Ignat, the bookkeeper, appeared a brilliant red shirt and an incredibly narrow vest whose lapels did not even cover a chest that was youthfully puffed out. Arkhip, the coachman, had on his own taken over the ceremonial silk shirt and velveteen sleeveless vest and apparently was vying with Ignat for Yevprakseyushka's affections. Yevprakseyushka ran between the two of them and like a madwoman rushed first to the one and then to the other. Porfiry Vladimirych was afraid to look out the window so as not to become a witness to this amorous display. Yet he could not help but hear. From time to time the sound of a weighty slap resounded in his ears: that was the coachman Arkhipushka giving Yevprakseyushka one with his full hand as he chased her in a game of catch (and she was not angry, but merely hunched over a bit). From time to time the conversation would reach his ears:

"Yevprakseya Nikitishna! Hey, Yevprakseya Nikitishna!" a tipsy Prokhor would call from the porch of the main house.

"What do you want?"

"The key to the tea cabinet, the master is asking for tea!"

"Let him wait...the old bogeyman!"

* * *

Before long Porfiry Vladimirych became completely estranged. The entire routine of his life was upset and turned inside out, but somehow he ceased to pay any attention to that any more. He demanded nothing from life other than that he not be disturbed in his final refuge—in his study. To the same degree that he had previously nagged and pestered those around him, he now had become fearful and sullenly resigned. It seemed as though all intercourse with real life had been cut off for him. To see no one and to hear nothing—that was what he wished. Yevprakseyushka would not show up for entire days on end in the house, the servants could indulge themselves and lounge about outside as much as they wanted—he reacted indifferently to it all as though it did not exist. Earlier, if the bookkeeper had allowed himself even the least inaccuracy in the presentation of his reports on the condition of the various branches of the estate management, he would probably have oppressed him with his lectures. But now, he was forced to sit for entire weeks without any reports and he became only rarely depressed over this, namely when he had need of some figure to support his imaginary calculations. On the other hand, in his study, all by himself, he felt himself the unchallenged master who possessed the possibility of indulging in idle thought as much as his heart desired. In the same way that both of his brothers had died as victims of intoxication, he too suffered from precisely the same disease. Only this was an intoxication of a different sort—the intoxication of idle thought. Locking himself in his study and sitting at his writing desk, he would slave away from morning until night over his fantastic work: he constructed all possible, but improbable, propositions, he audited himself, he chatted with imaginary partners and created entire scenes in which the first individual who happened to flash across his mind appeared as a major participant.

In the midst of this turmoil of fantastic scenes and images the major role was performed by a sickly thirst for money-grubbing. Although Porfiry Vladimirych had in general always been a trivial person and inclined to pettifoggery, nonetheless, thanks to his practical awkwardness, no direct benefits were achieved for him out of these inclinations. He bored, tormented, oppressed (principally the most defenseless people who, so to speak, were begging to be taken advantage of), but he himself, more often than not, was the loser as a result of his trouble-making. Now these qualities were totally transferred to an abstract and fantastic footing where there was no room either for any rebuff or for apologies, where there were neither the weak nor the strong, where there existed neither the police nor justices of the peace (or more accurately, they did exist, but solely for the sake of protecting little Judas' interests) and where, consequently, he could freely enmesh the entire world in a network of chicanery, harrassment and affrontery.

He loved to mentally torment, to spoil, to wrong others and suck their blood. He carefully sorted through all the branches of his estate one after the other: the forest, the livestock, grain, the meadows and so on, and in each one he created a decorative building of fantastic harrassments accompanied by the most complicated calculations into which also entered fines and usury and general afflictions and the accumulation of valuable papers—in short, an entire complicated world of frivolous gentry ideals. Since everything here depended on willfully conjectured overpayments or underpayments, then every kopek, whether paid in excess or deficient, served as a cause for the remaking of the entire building, which underwent infinite alterations in this fashion. Afterwards, when his exhausted mind could no longer find the strength to pay proper attention to all the details of the confused calculations involved in the operations of his money-grubbing, he would transfer the arena of his fantasy to broader inventions. He would recollect all the confrontations and clashes which he had experienced with people not only in recent time, but even in his most distant youth, and he would rework them so calculatedly that he would always emerge the victor. He mentally revenged himself on his former colleagues in the government ministry who had outstripped him in the government service and had so poisoned his pride that he had been forced to reject a government career. He took revenge on his classmates who used to

203

take advantage of his physical weakness in order to tease and harrass him. He took revenge on neighboring members of the gentry who resisted his claims and protected their own rights. He took revenge on any of the servants who had ever spoken back to him or who had simply not shown sufficient respect. He took revenge on his mama, Arina Petrovna, for the fact that she had used up a great deal of money on the rebuilding of Pogorelka, money which "by all rights" belonged to him. He took revenge on his brother Styopka-the-dunce for the fact that he had given him the nickname of little Judas. He took revenge on his aunt Varvara because at a time when no one even expected it, she suddenly and indiscriminately bore children "left and right," as a consequence of which the village of Goryushkino had slipped out of the Golovlyov family for good. He took revenge on the living and he took revenge on the dead.

Fantasizing in this fashion, he imperceptibly drew near intoxication; the earth disappeared from beneath his feet, it was as if wings had suddenly sprouted on his back. His eyes sparkled, his lips trembled and became covered with foam, his face grew pale and assumed a threatening expression. And in ratio with the growth of his fantasy, the air around him became populated with specters whom he engaged in imaginary combat.

His existence achieved such fullness and independence that there remained nothing for him to desire. The entire world was at his feet, of course—that simple-minded world which was accessible to his miserly world-view. He could produce endless variations of the most simple motif and he could take up each one afresh a number of times, reworking it each time in a new fashion. This represented a kind of ecstasy, a clairvoyance, something resembling what happens in mediumistic seances. Uninhibited by anything, his imagination created an ephemeral reality which, as a consequence of the continual incitement of his mental powers, was transformed into a concrete, almost tangible reality. This was not a faith or a conviction, but a mental debauchery, an ecstasy. People became dehumanized; their faces were distorted, their eyes burned, their tongues pronounced involuntary speeches, their bodies produced involuntary motions.

Porfiry Vladimirych was joyful. He would firmly lock the doors and windows so as to hear nothing, lower the shades so as to see nothing. All normal functions of life which did not directly coincide with the world of his fantasy he quickly discarded, almost with disgust. When the drunken Prokhor would knock at the door of his room, announcing that food had been served, he would impatiently run into the dining room, and contrary to all his previous habits, would rapidly eat his three courses and again disappear into his study. Even in the manners he displayed when he confronted living people there appeared something that was partially timid, partially stupidly derisive, as though at one and the same time he was afraid and yet challenging. In the morning he would hurry to rise as early as possible in order to get down to work immediately. His prayer time was curtailed. He pronounced the words of the prayer indifferently, without penetrating into their meaning; he performed the signs of the cross and raised his hands in prayer in a mechanical fashion and carelessly. Even the thought of hell and its agonizing retributions (for each sin there was a particular form of retribution) apparently had abandoned him.

But meanwhile, Yevprakseyushka had abandoned herself to carnal desire. Prancing indecisively between the bookkeeper Ignat and the coachman Arkhipushka, and at the same time casting glances at the red-faced carpenter Ilyusha, who with an entire artel had been contracted to repair the master's cellar, she noticed nothing of what was going on in the master's house. She thought that the master was enacting "a new comedy" and more than a few words of jest were uttered on this account in the friendly company of servants who feared no reprisals. But once, as though by chance, she passed the dining room at the very time when little Judas was hastily finishing off a piece of roast goose and suddenly she felt awe-struck.

Porfiry Vladimirych was sitting in a soiled housecoat with the cotton batten sticking out in various places. He was pale, unkempt and had sprouted a kind of stubble instead of a beard.

But Porfiry Vladimirych merely gave a stupidly poisonous smile in response to her outcry as though meaning to say: "Well now, just try and hurt me with anything!"

"Master! But what is it? Speak! What's happened?" she repeated.

He rose, fixed a hate-filled look on her and uttered deliberately:

"If you, you whore, ever try again...to come into my study...I'll kill you!"

* * *

Thanks to this occurrence, Porfiry Vladimirych's existence changed for the better externally. Feeling no material wants at all, he voluntarily surrendered to his solitude so that he did not even see the summer passing. August had already advanced into the second half. The days shortened. Outside a fine rain was drizzling incessantly. The earth grew sodden. The trees stood drearily, dropping their yellowed leaves onto the ground. Outside, near the servants' quarters, an undisturbed silence reigned as well. The servants were huddled up in their corners, partially because of the gloomy weather, partially because they surmised that something untoward was happening with the master. Yevprakseyushka had ultimately come to her senses. She forgot about silk dresses, about her sweet lovers, and she would sit for hours on end on a chest in the maids' quarters, not knowing what to do or think. The drunken Prokhor teased her, saying that she had worn the master out, gotten him intoxicated and that she would not escape taking a trip along the Vladimirka Highway* for that.

*i.e., to Siberia.

But meanwhile little Judas was sitting locked up in his study and dreaming. He felt even better now that it had become fresher outside. The rain, ceaselessly pattering against the windows of his study, induced a drowsiness in him in which his fantasy could expand more freely and widely. He imagined himself to be invisible and in this form he mentally inspected all his holdings in the company of old Ilya, who had served as elder even earlier during his papa's time and now was long since buried in the graveyard.

"A clever peasant, that Ilya! A servant from the old days! You can't find them like that nowadays. Nowadays all they do is ingratiate themselves and gossip, but as soon as work is mentioned—there's no one in sight!" Porfiry Vladimirych reasoned with himself, very pleased that Ilya had risen from the dead.

Taking their good old time, invisible to everyone, across fields and ravines, through valleys and meadows, they picked their way to the waste plot of land at Ukhovshchina and for a long while they could not believe their eyes. Before them stood a woodlot like a wall and only the tops of the trees murmured high above. The trees were all alike, handsome pines; some were twice the circumference of a man's embrace, others three times so. Their trunks were straight, clear of branches and the tops were mighty and bushy: that woodlot would go on standing for a long while yet!

"Take a look brother, what a woods!" little Judas exclaimed in raptures.

"It was set aside," old Ilya explained, "during the time of your deceased grandfather, Mikhail Vasilych, it was blessed with ikons—just see how it's grown!"

"And how many, do you think, *desyatinas** would there be?"

"At that time they measured out exactly seventy *desyatinas*, well, nowadays...at that time a country *desyatina* was half again as big as today."

"Well, what do you think, how many trees are there on each *desyatina*?"

"Who can tell! Only God has them counted!"

"Well, I think there must be at least six hundred to seven hundred per *desyatina*. Not the old *desyatina*, but the one we use now. Wait a minute! Hang on! If there are six hundred each...well, let's say six hundred and fifty... how many trees would there be on one hundred and five *desyatinas?*"

Porfiry Vladimirych took a sheet of paper and multiplied one hundred and five by six hundred and fifty: the answer came out to 68,250 trees.

"Now, if we were to sell this forest...piecemeal...do you think we could get ten rubles a tree?"

Old Ilya shook his head.

"Too little," he said, "after all this is some forest! From every tree you could get two saw-mill shafts and in addition a heavy beam that would do for any structure, as well as two smaller beams, and then there's still the branches... What do you think a mill-shaft is worth?"

*1 *desyatina* = 2.7 acres.

Porfiry Vladimirych pretended he did not know, although he had long since determined and fixed everything down to the last kopek.

"According to local prices a mill-shaft is worth about ten rubles, but if it were in Moscow, then you could set any price you wanted, so it seems! After all, this is some shaft! You could barely drag it away with a troika of horses! And then there is still another shaft, smaller, and two more beams and the lumber and the branches... At the absolute worst a tree would go for about twenty rubles."

Porfiry Vladimirych listened to Ilya's words and could not get his fill of them! This Ilya was a clever and faithul peasant! And God had smiled upon him by giving him such an unusually successful staff for his estate! Among Ilya's assistants there was old Vavilo (also long since at rest in the graveyard)— now, brother, there's a solid fellow! For a bookkeeper he had his mama's accountant, Philip (some sixty years before he had been transferred from the Vologda estates); the forest wardens were experienced and tireless; the dogs by the barns were fierce! Both the dogs and the servants were ready to take even the devil by the throat for their master's good!

"Well, brother, let's figure out: how much would it come to if we sold the entire woodlot piecemeal?"

Once again Porfiry Vladimirych made some mental calculations as to how much a large mill shaft cost, then one smaller, how much two beams would be, then the lumber and the branches. Then he added it up, multiplied, in one place he would remove the fractions and then add them on elsewhere. The sheet of paper filled up with columns of figures.

"There you go, brother, just take a look at what it's come to!" little Judas showed the imaginary Ilya an entirely incredible figure, so incredible that even Ilya, who for his part was not averse to increasing his master's wealth, it seemed that even he was taken aback.

"Seems like rather a lot!" he said, shrugging his shoulders thoughtfully.

But Porfiry Vladimirych had already discarded all doubts and could merely giggle delightedly.

"A strange fellow you are, brother! It's not me, but the figures that speak for themselves... There's a science, brother, it's called arithmetic...and it's not about to lie, brother! Well fine, we're finished with the Ukhovshchino woodlot now. Let's go over to Fox Hollow, brother, I haven't been there for a long while! Seems to me that the peasants there are up to no good, yes, that they are! And there's Garanka the foreman... I know! I know! Garanka is a fine fellow, a zealous foreman, trustworthy—what more can you say? But all the same...it looks as though he's been starting to act up a little!"

They walked along soundlessly and invisibly through a birch grove, barely able to pick their way through, before they came to a sudden halt, in order to catch their breath. A peasant cart was lying on its side right on the road and the peasant was standing there fretting as he looked at the broken axle. He fretted and fretted, he cursed the axle and cursed himself as well, gave the horse one on the back with his whip ("you old nag, you"), but something had to be done—he could not stay in the same spot until tomorrow! The thieving peasant looked all about himself, cocked his ear to listen whether anyone was coming, then he selected a suitable birch, fetched his axe... But little Judas just stood his ground without moving a muscle... The birch shuddered, began to waver and then suddenly tumbled to the ground as though mowed over. The peasant was about to cut a piece off the thicker end that would have been suitable for an axle, but little Judas had already decided that the decisive moment had come. He crept stealthily up on the peasant and in a flash he seized the axe out of his hands.

"What!" was all the thief could utter, as he was caught unawares.

"What," Porfiry Vladimirych mimicked him, "so it's permitted to rob other people's woods? What! And whose birch do you think you've cut down, your own?"

"Forgive me, sir!"

"Brother, I have long since grown accustomed to forgiving others! I myself am guilty before the Lord and I dare not judge others! It's not I, but the law which judges. Bring the tree you've cut down for an axle to my estate and in addition you'd better grab a ruble to pay a fine as well. For the time being I'll hang onto the axe! It'll be safe with me!"

Satisfied that he had managed in fact to prove to Ilya that his opinion of Garanka had been justified, Porfiry Vladimirych proceeded from the scene of the crime to drop in mentally at the forest-warden's hut and deliver a proper lecture. Then he made for home and along the way he caught three of the peasants' chickens in his own oats. Having returned to his study he again took up his work and a whole novel economic system was suddenly born in his head. Everything that grew or vegetated on his land, both what was sown and what was wild, was converted into money according to a schedule of prices, and in addition, of fines. Everyone suddenly became wood-stealers and despoilers, yet not only did little Judas not experience any grief over this, but on the contrary, he even rubbed his hands with pleasure.

"Go ahead and spoil things, gentlemen, chop it down! All the better for me," he repeated, entirely pleased.

Here he took a new sheet of paper and set about his calculations and computations.

How many oats grew on a *desyatina* and how much money would these oats bring if the peasants' chickens trampled it down and a fine had to be paid for everything that was trampled?

"But even if the oats were trampled down, after a little rain they would straighten up again!" little Judas added mentally.

How many birches are there growing in Fox Hollow and how much money could be gotten for them if the peasants were to chop them down like thieves and paid a fine for everything they chopped down?

"But even though the birch is chopped down, it will come to my house

208

to be used for firewood and then I certainly won't need to have any wood sawed myself!" little Judas added again mentally.

Enormous columns of figures adorned the paper: at first rubles, then tens of rubles, hundreds of rubles and thousands... Little Judas grew so exhausted over his labor and, more importantly, grew so excited over it that he arose from the table all in a sweat and lay down to rest on the couch. But his fired-up imagination did not curtail its activity even here, but merely selected a different and less demanding theme.

"Mama was a clever woman, that Arina Petrovna was," Porfiry Vladimirych fantasized, "she knew how to ask for things and how to cosy up to people—that's why everyone served her with pleasure! But even she committed a few sins! Yes, indeed, the deceased had a lot of shortcomings!"

Little Judas barely had time to think about Arina Petrovna and there she was all of a sudden. It was as if in her heart she sensed that she would have to give an account of herself and so she herself appeared out of the grave before her son.

"I don't know, my friend, I just don't know why I'm guilty before you," she said somewhat dejectedly, "it seems to me that I..."

"No, now, now dearest! You'd better not sin," little Judas accused her unceremoniously, "if it's come to that, then I'll lay it all out before you this very moment! Why, for example, didn't you stop auntie Varvara Mikhailovna at that time?"

"How could I stop her? She herself was a grown woman, she had the right to organize her own life!"

"That's not true, forgive me now! What kind of a husband did she have? An old drunkard, and absolutely...well, absolutely...ineffectual! Yet at the same time four children suddenly appeared around her... Now I ask, where did these children come from?"

"What's the meaning of this, my friend, the way you're talking so queerly! As though I were the cause of it!"

"Whether or not you were the cause, all the same you could have tried to exert some influence on her! By being nice and pleasant with her and calling her 'dearest' and 'sweetie'—just see if she wouldn't have felt some conscience! But you did just the opposite! Always on your high horse with her or treating her indifferently! Calling her nasty names, saying she was shameless and despicable! You practically paired her off with everyone around! And so, she up and got on her high horse too! A pity! Goryushkino would have been ours now!"

"You're always carrying on about that Goryushkino!" Arina Petrovna said, apparently at a dead loss over her son's accusation.

"What do I care about Goryushkino! I need nothing, if you please! As long as there's enough for a candle and some ikon-oil, then I'm quite satisfied! But in general, by all rights... Yes, mama, I'd be happy to remain silent, but I can't help but say that you have a great sin on your soul, a very great sin indeed!"

Arina Petrovna no longer even attempted to reply, but merely raised her hands in a sign of something bordering on both resignation and incomprehension.

"Or there is, for example, something else," little Judas continued meanwhile, enjoying his mama's dismay, "why did you buy a house for brother Stepan in Moscow at that time?"

"I had to, my friend; I had to throw him some kind of sop, too," Arina Petrovna justified herself.

"But he up and squandered it! As if you didn't know him any better: he was a rowdy and foul-tongued and disrespectful. And, in addition, you wanted to give him papa's Vologda estate! And what a nice little estate it is! All in one piece, no neighbors, not broken up by strangers' properties, a fine little forest, a nice lake... As clean as a peeled egg, Christ be praised! It was a good thing that I happened to be there at the time and opposed it... Goodness, mama, mama isn't that sinful of you!"

"After all, he is my son...do you understand, he is my son!"

"I know, and I even understand that quite well! Yet all the same there was no need to do that, it wasn't called for! Twelve thousand in silver was paid out for the house and where are they now? Now you can kiss that twelve thousand goodby, and auntie Varvara Mikhailovna's Goryushkino, at the worst, must have a value of fifteen thousand... What an awful lot of money that all comes out to!"

"Well, enough! Just stop now! Don't get angry, for Christ's sake!"

"Mama, I'm not angry, I'm just saying by all rights...what is true is true—I cannot bear falsehood! I was born with the truth, I've lived with the truth and I'll die with the truth! Even God loves the truth, and has commanded us to love it as well. I just wanted to mention Pogorelka. I've always said that you spent a lot, my goodness, a lot of money on rebuilding it."

"After all I had to live there myself..."

Little Judas could read the words on his mama's face full well: "You absurd bloodsucker, you!" But he pretended that he did not notice them.

"There was no helping the fact that you had to live there, but all the same... The ikon-stand is still at Pogorelka to this very day, and whose is it? The little horse as well; and the tea jar... I myself saw it with my own eyes at Golovlyovo when papa was alive! And a fine little thing it is, too!"

"Well, I never!"

"No, mama, don't say it! Naturally, it isn't immediately plain that when you have a ruble here, fifty kopeks there and twenty-five kopeks elsewhere... And then before you know it, it all adds up... By the way, if you'll just allow me, I'll put everything down in figures! Figures are a sacred business. They don't lie!"

Porfiry Vladimirych again made for the table to produce clearly once and for all the losses which his good friend, mama, had caused him. He worked the abacus, produced columns of figures on the paper—in short, he prepared everything to convict Arina Petrovna. But, fortunately for the latter, his vacillating mind could not concentrate for long on one and the same subject. Imperceptibly even for him, a new object of money-grubbing came stealing up and as though by some magical means directed his thought onto a completely new track. Arina Petrovna's face, which only a moment before had been hovering so vividly before his eyes, suddenly became submerged in the murkiness of oblivion. The figures grew confused...

Porfiry Vladimirych had been meaning for some time to calculate what income farming might afford him, and now the most suitable moment had arrived. He knew that the peasant was always in need, that he was always seeking to borrow and always paid his debts without default and with interest. The peasant was particularly generous with his labor which "cost him nothing" and for this reason, when settling accounts, it was never taken into consideration and was a labor of love. How many needy people there were in Russia, goodness, how many! There were a great many people who were incapable of determining today what awaited them on the morrow, a great many who, wherever they might turn their longing eyes, saw everywhere nothing but a desperate emptiness, everywhere heard but a single phrase: "Pay back! Pay back!" And lo, it was around this desperate folk, around this vacillating poor folk that little Judas cast his unending web as he fell from time to time into a kind of frenzied and fantastic orgy.

Outside it was April and the peasant, as was customary, had nothing to eat. "They've stuffed themselves, the dears! Made a holiday of the winter and by spring they have to tuck in their belts!" Porfiry Vladimirych reasoned with himself, but as though on purpose, he had only just straightened out all the accounts from the preceding year's farming. In February the final stocks of wheat had been threshed, in March the seed had been poured into the bins and only a few days before all the cash amounts had been entered into the books in the corresponding columns. Little Judas was sitting by the window and waiting. There in the distance, on the bridge, appeared the peasant Foka in his cart. At the turning to Golovlyovo he tugged hastily at the reins and for want of a whip, he shook his hand threateningly at the horse which could barely drag its feet.

"He's coming here," little Judas whispered, "just look at that horse of his! Barely alive! But if you were to feed it for a month or two—it wouldn't be a bad beast at that! You could get twenty-five, or maybe thirty rubles for it."

Meanwhile Foka had driven up to the servants' hut, tied the horse to the fence, tossed it an armful of spoiled hay and in a minute was already shifting from foot to foot in the maids' quarters where Porfiry Vladimirych was accustomed to receive such supplicants as these.

"Well, my friend! What good have you got to say for yourself?" Porfiry

211

Vladimirych began.

"Well, sir, a bit of rye perhaps..."

"What's that! It seems you've already eaten up your own? Goodness me, what a pity! Now if you had drunk a little less vodka and worked a little more and prayed to God, well then, the earth might have responded to that better! Where today you had only a single crop, before you know it, you'd have two or three in the same time! Then you wouldn't have to borrow!"

Foka smiled uncertainly instead of replying.

"Do you think that God is so far away that he doesn't see?" Porfiry Vladimirych continued to moralize. "But God is right here. He's here and there and right with us now while we're talking! He's everywhere! And He sees everything, hears everything, only He pretends that He doesn't notice. 'Go ahead,' He says, 'let people follow their own mind; I'll just see whether they remember me or not!' And we go and take advantage of this and instead of putting something aside from what we have for a candle in God's name, we go off to the tavern again and again! For this reason, for this very one, God does not give us any rye—isn't that so, friend?"

"What can I say! That's the truth!"

"Well, so there you see, don't you, and you understand now. But why have you understood? Because God has withheld His grace from you. But if your rye were to be plentiful, you'd go back to your old tricks and then as soon as God went and..."

"That's right...and if now we might..."

"Just a minute! Let me speak! And it's always that way, my friend, that God makes the forgetful remember Him. And we mustn't complain of this, but understand that this is being done for our very own good. If we remember God, He too wouldn't forget about us. He would give us plenty of everything: rye and oats and potatoes—there you are, eat your fill! And He would watch out for your animals—just look at that horse of yours! It's barely got the spirit in it! And any fowl that you might have, He would have given it a helping hand!"

"It's all true, what you're saying, Porfiry Vladimirych."

"Respect God, that's the first rule, and then your elders who have received their distinction from the tsars themselves, like the gentry, for instance."

"We do, Porfiry Vladimirych, and it seems..."

"There's that 'it seems' of yours, but if you just stop and ponder and judge for yourself, then maybe it just won't be borne out the way you think. Now, the way you've come to me for some rye, it's a real sin! You are very respectful to me and polite too. But just the year before last, do you recall when I needed some harvesters and I came begging to you peasants? 'Help me out,' I said, 'brothers, if you'd be so good!' What did you say to my request? 'We have our own harvesting to do,' you said! 'It's not like the old days now,' you said, 'that we have to work for the masters, nowadays we have our freedom!' Freedom indeed, but no rye!"

Porfiry Vladimirych looked at Foka instructively. The latter did not move a muscle, but seemed to have frozen.

"You are very proud and that's why you're so unlucky. Take me, for instance: it seems as though God has blessed me and the tsar has rewarded me, but I—I'm not proud! What have I got to be proud of? What am I, then? A worm! An insect! Pfui! But God has gone and blessed me for my humility! And He Himself has, in His mercy, sought out the tsar and inspired him with the thought of rewarding me."

"I figure, Porfiry Vladimirych, that in the old days, under the gentry, things were better!" Foka tried to flatter him.

"Yes, brother, those were your good times! You kicked up your heels and had a good life! You had plenty of everything, of rye and hay and potatoes! But why recall the old days? I'm not a spiteful person. I, brother, have long since forgotten about the harvesters, it only occurred to me at the mention of it! So you're saying that you need some rye?"

"Yes, some rye, perhaps..."

"Are you about to pay for it?"

"How can I pay for it? I meant to borrow it until the new harvest!"

"Goodness me, now! Nowadays, my friend, rye is awfully expensive! I don't know quite what to say to you..."

Profiry Vladimirych fell into a momentary thoughtfulness, as though in actual fact he did not know how to proceed: "I do want to help the fellow, but then the rye is expensive..."

"That I can, my friend, I can lend you some rye," he said finally, "I must admit that I don't have any rye to sell: I can't bear to deal in one of God's gifts! So I'll loan it to you, I'll do that with pleasure. But I just wanted to remind you, brother: today I'm lending something to you, but tomorrow you'll have to lend something to me! Today I have some surplus and so I say, take it and owe it to me! If you wish to take a quarter measure, then take a quarter measure! If you need an eighth, then pour yourself out an eighth! And tomorrow, it may be that things will take such a turn that I'll have to come knocking at your window: 'Lend,' I'll say, 'Fokushka, an eighth of rye I've nothing to eat!' "

"Come now! You wouldn't come now, would you, sir?"

"I won't come, that's just as an example... And don't think that such turnabouts don't happen in the world! The other while they were saying in the papers what a pillar Napoleon was and now he's lost out, didn't seem to please anyone. That's the way it is, brother. How much rye are you asking for?"

"A quarter measure if you would be so kind."

"You can take a quarter. Only I'm telling you beforehand, my friend, rye is awfully expensive nowadays! So this is what you and I are going to do: I'll have my people measure out three quarters of what you're asking for and

213

then at the end of eight months you'll make up the difference so that it'll come out to a quarter measure exactly! I won't charge you any interest, I'll just take it from your surplus rye..."

Foka's heart practically stopped at little Judas' proposition. For some time he said nothing, only shrugged his shoulders.

"Wouldn't that be rather a lot, sir?" he finally uttered, obviously embarrassed.

"If it's too much, then go to someone else! I, my friend, am not forcing you, but rather offering it from my heart. I didn't send for you, you yourself came to me. You're the one with the request, I'm the one with the response. That's the way it is, my friend!"

"That's true, but the levy does seem a bit much."

"My oh my! And here I was thinking that you were a just peasant, upright! But you go ahead and tell me then how I'm supposed to live? How am I supposed to take care of my expenses? Do you have any idea of how many expenses I have? There's no end in sight to my expenses, dearest, I have to give something to the one, satisfy a second and put out for a third! When everyone needs something, everyone pesters Porfiry Vladimirych, and Porfiry Vladimirych has to answer for everyone! What's more, if I sold the rye to a merchant, then I would have the money here on the table right now. Money, brother, is a sacred business. With money I could buy myself bonds and put them away in a safe place and use the interest! No fuss, no bother, I cut off a coupon—hand over the money, if you please! But with the rye I still have to fuss about and worry over it and put myself out! How much will spoil, how much will be blown away, how much will the mice eat? No, brother, money is the best thing possible! I should have come to my senses long ago! I should have turned everything into money long ago and leave you all!"

"Do stay with us, Porfiry Vladimirych."

"I would be happy to, dearest, but I don't have the strength. If I had my former strength, of course, I could still go on, I could still take charge. No! It's time for a rest, it is! I shall leave here for the Monastery of the Holy Trinity of St. Sergius, I'll find shelter for myself under the wing of the saint— no one will hear of me. And how good I'll feel: peaceful, honorable, quiet, no uproar, no arguments, no fuss—just like in heaven!"

In short, no matter how Foka twisted, the business followed the course desired by Porfiry Vladimirych. But that was not all there was to it. At the very moment when Foka had already agreed to the terms of the loan, there suddenly appeared a new condition in the shape of a place called Shelepikha. Well, if you wouldn't mind, a waste meadow plot, only about a *desyatina* to mow and it would hardly be too much...

"I'm making a loan to you—and you owe it to me," Porfiry Vladimirych said, "this has nothing to do with any interest, but just for the sake of the loan! God helps us all and we help each other! If you take a moment to mow that *desyatina* I'll remember you in the future! I'm quite straightforward, brother! You'll be doing me a mere ruble's worth of work, but for you I'm doing..."

Porfiry Vladimirych arose and signalled the end of the business by praying in the direction of the church. Following his example, Foka also crossed himself.

Foka disappeared. Porfiry Vladimirych took a sheet of paper, armed himself with the abacus and the counters began to leap under his nimble hands... Little by little began an entire orgy of figures. The whole world seemed to cloud over in little Judas' eyes. With feverish haste he went from the abacus to the paper, from the paper to the abacus. The figures multiplied and multiplied...

THE RECKONING

Outside it was the middle of December. The surrounding area, in the grip of a snowy shroud as far as the eye could see, silently grew numb. During the night so many drifts had piled up on the road that the peasants' horses floundered heavily in the snow as they tried to drag the empty sleighs out. There was practically no track left leading to the Golovlyovo estate. Porfiry Vladimirych had grown so disused to visits that the main gates leading to the house and the main porch had been solidly nailed up with the onslaught of fall, forcing the servants to communicate with the outside world by way of the maids' entrance and the side gates.

It was morning. Eleven o'clock was chiming. Dressed in his housecoat, little Judas was standing by the window and aimlessly peering before him. Beforehand he had been wandering back and forth in his study and had been thinking the whole while about something and calculating some imaginary income so that finally he had become confused with the figures and grown tired. Both the orchard stretching out opposite the main facade of the manor, as well as the village huddling to the rear of the orchard, had disappeared in the snowy drifts. A frosty day had come on the heels of the storm of the previous day and the snowy shroud was all agleam with a million sparks in the sun, so that Porfiry Vladimirych involuntarily squinted. Outside it was quiet and deserted. There was not the slightest movement near the servants' quarters or in the vicinity of the stables. Even the peasant village had grown so peaceful that one might have thought it had died. Only over the priest's house did a gray puff of smoke curl and attract the attention of little Judas.

"Eleven o'clock has struck and the priest's wife still hasn't finished cooking," he thought to himself, "these priests are always stuffing themselves!"

Extrapolating from this point he becan to ponder the following: was it a holiday today or an ordinary day, a fast or meatless day and what was the priest's wife cooking, —when suddenly his attention was distracted off to the side. On top of the hill, right at the road out of the village of Naglovka, appeared a black spot which gradually advanced and grew. Porfiry Vladimirych became absorbed in it and, naturally, above all began to ask an entire mass of frivolous questions. Who was coming? A peasant or someone else? In any event it could not be anyone other than a peasant...yes, it was a peasant! Why was he on the road? If he was going for firewood, then the Naglovka forest lay on the other side of the village...no doubt the rascal was getting ready to rob the master's forest! If he was headed for the mill, then coming from Naglovka he would have had to turn to the right... Perhaps he was going for the priest? Was someone dying or had they already died? Or perhaps someone had been born? What peasant woman was it that gave birth? Nenila was pregnant in the fall, but it seemed rather early for her... If it was a boy who was born, then he would still make it into the census—how many souls would that make it now in Naglovka according to the last census? If it was a girl, then she would not be counted in the census and in any case... But all the same it was impossible to get on without the female sex...curses!

Little Judas spat and looked at the ikon as though seeking protection against the evil one.

In all probability he would have continued on his mental wandering in this fashion for a long time yet if the black spot which had appeared near Naglovka had flashed by and disappeared in the usual manner. But it kept growing and growing and finally turned onto the bridge leading to the church. Then little Judas could see quite clearly that it was a small covered sled hitched up to a pair of horses in tandem. When it made the top of the incline and drew level with the church ("I wonder if it's the archdeacon?" flashed through his mind. "So that's why they haven't finished cooking even at this hour at the priest's!"), and then turned to the right and made directly for the estate: "It's true, it's coming here!" Porfiry Vladimirych instinctively pulled his housecoat tight and leapt back from the window as though he feared that the passerby might notice him.

He had guessed right: the sled drove up to the estate and stopped by the side gates. A young woman jumped hastily out of it. She was not seasonally dressed, wearing a padded city coat that was more for the looks than for the warmth and trimmed with fleece and she was obviously numb with cold. This personage, whom no one came out to meet, skipped across to the maids' entrance and inside of a few seconds one could hear a door slamming in the maids' quarters and then a running to and fro, a banging of doors and a bustling followed in all the rooms in the vicinity of the back door.

Porfiry Vladimirych stood by the door of his study and listened. It had been so long since he had seen an outsider and he had generally become so unaccustomed to the company of people that he was taken unawares. About a quarter of an hour passed. The running to and fro, the banging of doors did not subside, but still no one came to report to him. This upset him all the more. It was clear that the newcomer belonged to the category of "family folk" who have no reason to doubt their rights to hospitality. But what "family folk" did he have? He began to try and remember but his memory seemed to respond only sluggishly. He had had a son Volodka and another son Petka, there was his mama, Arina Petrovna...goodness how long ago that was! Nadka Galkina, the daughter of his deceased auntie Varvara Mikhailovna, had settled here in Goryushkino the past autumn—could it be her? Not likely, she had earlier tried to force her way into the Golovlyovo nest, but she had disappeared in a flash! —"She doesn't dare! She wouldn't!" —little Judas assured himself, growing indignant at the very thought of the possibility of Galkina's arrival. But who else could it be?

While he was thus trying to recall, Yevprakseyushka cautiously approached the door and reported:

217

"The Pogorelka mistress has come, Anna Semyonovna."

In fact, it was Anninka. But she had changed to such a degree that it was almost impossible to recognize her. It was not the same beautiful, lively girl who had appeared earlier in Golovlyovo, bubbling with youth, with rosy face, large protruding gray eyes, a well-shaped bosom and a thick ash-blond braid on her head, but some weak, puny creature with a flat chest, sunken cheeks, an unhealthy flush, languid physical movements, stooped, almost hunched over. Even her magnificent braid of hair seemed to have grown somehow miserable and only her eyes, as a result of the general gauntness of her face, seemed even larger than before and burned with a feverish glitter. Yevprakseyushka peered at her for a long time as though she were a stranger, but then she finally recognized her.

"Mistress! Is it you?" she cried, throwing her hands up.

"It is. Well?"

Having said that, Anninka laughed softly as though wanting to add: "Well, there you have it! That's all that's left of me!"

"Is uncle healthy?" she asked.

"What can I say about uncle? Yes and no... The Lord be praised that he's alive at least, but to tell the truth we never see him!"

"What's the matter with him?"

"It seems he's got that way from boredom..."

"Has he really stopped talking all that nonsense?"

"Nowadays, mistress, he keeps silent. He used to talk and then suddenly he would shut up. Sometimes we hear him talking to himself about something in his study and he even seems to laugh, but when he comes out into the other rooms, he shuts up again. People say the same thing happened with his deceased brother, Stepan Vladimirych... He was always cheerful—and then suddenly he just shut up. What about you, mistress, are you still well?"

Anninka merely waved her hand in response.

"Is your little sister still well?"

"It's been a whole month since she's been laid in her grave in Krechetovo along the main highway."

"What are you saying, God preserve us? By the main highway as well?"

"Everyone knows that's where the suicides are buried."

"Heavens! She was a young lady and suddenly she went and laid hands on herself... How could that happen?"

"Yes, at first we were young ladies, but then we ruined ourselves—that's all there is to it. But I lost my courage, I wanted to live! So I've come to you! Not for long, don't fear... I'm going to die!"

Yevprakseyushka looked at her wide-eyed as though not understanding.

"What are you looking at me like that for? Do I look that good? Well, I'm afraid this is how I am... Incidentally, we'll talk about that later...later... But now tell the coachdriver to tally up and inform uncle."

Saying this, she took an ancient purse out of her pocket and removed two yellowed bills.

"This is all I own!" she added, pointing to a flimsy suitcase. "It's all here, everything that I inherited and acquired! I'm freezing, Yevprakseyushka, I'm really freezing! I am all sick, there isn't a healthy bone in me, and to make things worse, there's this cold spell... While I was travelling here I could think of only one thing: I must get to Golovlyovo so that I can die where it's warm! Give me a little vodka...do you have any?"

"But some tea might be better for you, mistress. The samovar will be ready in a moment."

"No, the tea later, but now a little vodka... By the way, don't say anything to uncle about the vodka just yet... Everything will be taken care of later."

While the table was being set in the dining room for tea, Porfiry Vladimirych made an appearance. It was Anninka's turn to greet him with amazement: he had grown so thin, so wan and strange-looking. He acted queerly with Anninka: not exactly cold, but as though she had nothing to do with him. What little he said was forced, just like an actor recalling with difficulty lines from distant roles. Generally, he was distracted, as though his mind were occupied with some entirely different and very important work from which he had, to his annoyance, been torn away on account of some trivialities.

"Well, here you are, you've come," he said, "What would you like? Some tea? Coffee? Ask for what you will!"

At an earlier time, whenever family reunions took place, it was usually little Judas who performed the emotional role, but this time it was Anninka who was deeply moved and genuinely so. She must have been suffering badly inside, because she threw herself into Porfiry Vladimirych's arms and hugged him tightly.

"Uncle! I've come to you!" she cried, and suddenly dissolved into tears.

"My goodness, heaven preserve us! I have plenty of room—by all means!"

"I'm sick, uncle dear! Very, very sick!"

"If you're sick, then you should pray to God! Whenever I'm sick that's what I do myself, I cure myself with prayer!"

Porfiry Vladimirych turned an examining eye on her and a barely perceptible smirk flitted over his lips.

"Have you played yourself out?" he muttered in a barely audible voice, almost to himself.

"Yes I have. Lyubinka—she's 'played herself out,' as well and is dead, and here I am alive!"

At the news of Lyubinka's death, little Judas piously crossed himself and murmured prayerfully. Meanwhile, Anninka sat down at the table, leaned on her elbows and continued to weep bitter tears as she gazed in the direction of the church.

"Crying and growing depressed—that's a sin!" Porfiry Vladimirych remarked in a lecturing voice, "You know what you should do like a good Christian? Don't weep, be humble and have faith—that's what a good Christian should do!"

But Anninka threw herself back against her chair and, letting her hands hang down despondently, repeated:

"Alas, I just don't know what to do! I don't, I don't, I don't!"

"If you're going to torment yourself so over your sister, that is a sin!" little Judas in the meanwhile continued to lecture her, "Because although it's praiseworthy to love one's sisters and brothers, nonetheless, if God sees fit to call one, or even several, of them to Himself..."

"No, no! Uncle, are you good? Are you good? Tell me!"

Anninka rushed to him again and embraced him.

"Well, good, yes, I am good! Now, speak! Is there something you want? A bite to eat! Some tea, coffee? Go ahead! Ask for it yourself!"

Anninka suddenly recalled how during her first visit to Golovlyovo her uncle had asked: "Would you like some nice veal? Some suckling pig? Nice potatoes?" —and she understood that there was no other consolation for her to be found here.

"I thank you, uncle," she said, again sitting down to the table, "I don't need anything in particular. I know beforehand that I'll be satisfied with everything."

"If you'll be satisfied, then praise be to the Lord! Are you intending to go on to Pogorelka?"

"No, uncle, for the time being I'll stay here with you. You don't have anything against that, do you?"

"Christ preserve you! Do stay! If I was asking about Pogorelka, it was merely because if you were intending to go, then arrangements would have to be made: a sleigh, horses..."

"No, later! Later!"

"That's fine. You can go there sometime later, but for now you stay with us. You can help around the house—I'm alone, you know! This beauty here," little Judas pointed almost with hatred at Yevprakseyushka who was pouring the tea, "is always hanging about the servants' quarters, so that I can never summon anyone, the whole house is empty! But farewell for the moment. I'm going to my room. I want to pray and I have business to do and then I must pray again...so there, my friend! Was it long ago that Lyubinka passed away?"

"About a month, uncle."

"Then tomorrow we'll go to mass nice and early and in addition have a requiem sung in memory of Lyuba, this servant newly presented to the Lord... So farewell for now! Go ahead and have your tea, and if you feel like a bite to eat after travelling, then order them to serve you a snack. We'll see each other at dinner again. We'll talk, and chat. If anything is required, we'll make the arrangements, if not, then we'll just sit awhile!"

And so transpired this first family reunion. At its conclusion Anninka embarked on a new life in that very hateful Golovlyovo from which she could not escape fast enough twice before in the course of her brief life.

* * *

Anninka had gone downhill very rapidly. The awareness of the fact that she was a "lady"—a feeling that had been aroused by her Golovlyovo visit after the death of her grandmother Arina Petrovna,—that she had her own nest and her own graves, that not everything in her life was consumed in the stench and racket of hotels and roadside inns, that there was, ultimately, a refuge where she would not be reached by foul breath reeking of the smell of alcohol and the stable, where that "mustachioed"man with a voice hoarse from excess drink and inflamed eyes could burst in (God, the things he had said to her! The gestures he had made in her presence!), this awareness had taken wing almost immediately after she had lost sight of Golovlyovo.

At that time Anninka had made her way from Golovlyovo directly to Moscow and had begun to take pains to have her sister taken on for the imperial stage. With this purpose in mind she had turned not only to *maman*, the directress of the institute where she had been educated, but to several of her comrades from the institute as well. But everywhere she went, she received a strange reception. *Maman,* who at first had greeted her joyfully enough, suddenly altered the gracious expression on her face to one that was severe and condescending when she learned that Anninka was performing in provincial theatres. Anninka's comrades, who for the most part were married women, looked at her with such outspoken amazement that she simply lost her nerve. Only one of them, more kind-hearted than the others, wanting to show sympathy, asked:

"Do tell me, darling, is it true that when you actresses are getting dressed in your studios, officers do up your corsets for you?"

In short, her attempts to establish herself in Moscow remained nothing more than attempts. Incidentally, it should be said, that she did not have the proper qualities to be a success on the stage in the capital. Both she and Lyubinka belonged to that category of lively but not particularly talented actresses who play one and the same role all their lives. Anninka was successful in "Périchole," Lyubinka in "Pansies" and "The Old-Fashioned Colonel." Moreover, whatever they might attempt, it always came out as "Périchole" and "Pansies," or in a majority of cases, with all respect, it did not succeed at all. Anninka had to play "La Belle Hélène" as well (according to the terms of her contract, even quite frequently). She would put quite a fiery wig over her own ash-blonde hair, make a slit in her tunic right up to her waist, but for all that it still came out quite mediocre, drab and not even very daring. From "La Belle Hélène" she went on to "Excerpts from the Life of the Duchess of Gerolstein," and since a perfectly ridiculous production was added to a lacklustre performance, the result was something quite inane. Finally, she took up the role of Clairette in "Daughter of the Market," but here, in striving to electrify the public, she overacted to such a degree that even to her undemanding provincial audience it seemed as though it were not an actress throwing herself about on the stage, trying to "please," but simply some kind of indecent strumpet. Generally speaking, Anninka gained a reputation for being an adroit actress who possessed a pleasant enough voice, and since in addition to this she was very attractive to look at, consequently in the provinces she could, with all due respect, attract an audience. But there it ended. She could not force people to remember her and there was nothing outstanding about her. Even in the circles of her provincial audiences her following was made up exclusively of every conceivable army officer whose main ambition consisted of gaining ready access behind the cutrains. But in the capital she would have gained consideration only if she acquired very powerful patronage, but even for all that, she probably would have merely earned the unenviable title of "hack artist" from the public.

She was forced to return to the provinces. In Moscow Anninka had received a letter from Lyubinka from which she learned that the company had transfered from Krechetovo to the provincial town of Samovarnov, for which Lyubinka was very pleased because she had become friendly with a certain Samovarnov official from the Land Council who was so taken with her that he was "prepared, so it seemed, to steal funds from the Council," if only to fulfill any of her wishes. And in fact, once she arrived in Samovarov Anninka found her sister in the midst of relative luxury and having frivolously made up her mind to give up the stage. When she arrived, Lyubinka's "friend" was already there, the official from the Land Council, Gavrilo Stepanych Lyulkin. He was a retired cavalry captain still retaining much of his good looks but already somewhat on the heavy side. His face was noble, his manners noble, his way of thinking noble, but at the same time, all in all, he inspired a certainty that this was a person who would not in the least be loathe to seek recourse to the Council funds. Lyubinka received her sister with outstretched arms and announced that a room had been made ready in her flat.

But under the influence of her recent trip to "her own place," Anninka grew angry. A heated conversation arose between the sisters and then followed disagreement. Despite herself Anninka recalled at this time how the Voplino priest had said that it was difficult for persons in the acting profession to preserve their "treasure."

Anninka settled in a hotel and broke off all relations with her sister. Easter had passed and shortly thereafter the performances began and Anninka learned that a girl from Kazan by the name of Nalimova, an indifferent actress but completely uninhibited from the point of view of physical movements, had been hired in place of her sister. As usual, Anninka appeared

222

before the public in "Périchole" and drove the inhabitants of Samovarnov to ecstacy. On returning to the hotel she found a package in her room which proved to contain a hundred-ruble bill and a very brief note which read: "In case you're interested, there's as much to follow. Kukishev, Merchant Specializing in the Latest Fashions." Anninka grew angry and went to complain to the owner of the hotel, but the owner announced that Kukishev was known to have this "custom" of greeting all of the actresses on their arrival, and, in any event, he was a mild person and it was not worth feeling insulted with him. Following this advice, Anninka sealed the letter and the money in the envelope and, after having returned it to where it belonged the following day, felt reassured.

But Kukishev proved to be more obstinate than the owner of the hotel had reputed him to be. Kukishev counted himself among Lyulkin's circle of friends and enjoyed friendly relations with Lyubinka. He was a man of means and, moreover, like Lyulkin, as a member of the city administration he found himself in favorable circumstances as regarded the city treasury. And at the same time, like Lyulkin again, he was fearless. He had, from the point-of-view of less sophisticated circles, a captivating appearance. To be precise, he recalled the beetle which, as the words of the song go, Masha found in the field instead of berries:

> A beetle black I found
> With whiskers and with curly hair,
> With brows of darkest brown—
> Handsome and oh so fair!

Consequently, possessed of such an appearance, he felt all the more justified in his bold designs so that Lyubinka promised outright to aid him. In general it appeared as though Lyubinka had irrevocably burned all her ships and rumours circulated about her which were most offensive to her sister's pride. People said that every evening a riotous company would gather in her flat and dine from midnight until morning. Further, that Lyubinka would preside over this company, playing the part of a "gypsy" and only half-dressed (at which Lyulkin, turning to his drunken friends, would exclaim: "Just take a look! Now those are real breasts!"), her hair let down and a guitar in her hands, singing:

> Ah, what joy I discovered
> With my moustachioed lover!

Anninka listened to these stories and was upset. And what amazed her above all was the fact that Lyubinka was singing the ballad about the moustachioed lover in the gypsy fashion: exactly like Matryosha in Moscow! Anninka had always given Lyubinka her full due, but if she had been told that, for instance, Lyubinka sang the lines from "The Old-Fashioned Colonel" "inimitably," she naturally would have found that perfectly natural and would have readily believed it. And it would have been impossible not to believe it insofar as the audiences of Kursk, Tambov and Penza recalled even up until then with what inimitable naivete Lyubinka, with her thin little voice, had announced her desire to serve *under* the colonel... But that Lyubinka could sing in gypsy, in the style of Matryosha, that, forgive it being said, was an outright lie! Now, Anninka, she *could* sing that way and there was no doubt about that. That was her genre, that was her forte, and all of Kursk, when they saw her in the play "Dramatizations of Russian Ballads," would willingly bear witness to the fact that she *could* do it.

Anninka would take the guitar into her hands, throw the striped shoulder strap over her shoulder, sit down on a chair, cross her legs and begin to sing those "ta-ra-ri's" and "ta-ra-da's"! And really, it would come out precisely, exactly like the gypsy woman Matryosha.

However that may have been, Lyubinka was still living in luxury, and Lyulkin, so as not to cloud the picture of drunken bliss by not cooperating, apparently had already sought recourse to borrowing from the Council funds. Leaving aside the mass of champagne which overflowed and overflowed unto the floor every night in Lyubinka's flat, she herself was becoming more capricious and demanding with each day. At first dresses ordered from Mme. Minangois in Moscow appeared on the scene, then diamonds from Foulde's. Lyubinka was a calculating person and did not disdain valuables. A drunken life was one thing, but gold and stones, and in particular, lottery tickets, were another thing. In any event, if the life she was living was not exactly cheerful, it was wild and desperate, going from one revelry to another. One thing was unpleasant: it became necessary to curry favor with the chief of police who, although he belonged to Lyulkin's circle of friends, at times still loved to make his authority felt. Lyubinka always guessed when the chief of police was disatisfied with her entertaining, because in such circumstances the following morning a police inspector would appear at her place and demand her passport. And she would submit: in the morning she would serve the inspector a snack and vodka, and in the evening she would personally prepare for the chief of police a "Swedish" punch much beloved by him.

Kukishev looked on this expansive way of life and was consumed with envy. He wanted at any cost to have exactly the same kind of open house and precisely the same kind of "beauty." Then it would be possible to spend one's time in a more interesting fashion: tonight at Lyulkin's "beauty," and the next night at his own "beauty's." This was his sacred dream, the dream of a stupid man, who, the more stupid he was, became all the more obstinate in achieving his goals. The most suitable person for realizing his dream was to be found in Anninka.

However, Anninka would not submit. Up until now her passions had not been aroused, although she had had many admireres and had not been shy in her treatment of them. There had been a moment when it seemed to her that she was ready to fall in love with the local tragedian, Miloslavsky X, who apparently for his part was consumed with passion for her. But Miloslavsky X was so stupid and, moreover, so inveterately drunk that he never once declared himself to her, but merely rolled his eyes and hiccuped so absurdly whenever she passed by. Thus, this love was squelched at the outset. Anninka regarded all the remaining admirers simply as the unavoidable circumstances to which any provincial actress was condemned by the very conditions of her craft. She submitted to these conditions, took advantage of these minor favors (applause, bouquets, troika rides, picnics, etc.) which were offered her, but beyond this, so to speak, external wantonness, she did not go.

She acted in this fashion even now. In the course of an entire year she had remained unswervingly on the path of virtue, jealously guarding her "treasure" and wishing, apparently, to prove to the Voplino priest from afar that even in the world of actresses there were those to whom heroism was not alien. Once she even made up her mind to complain of Kukishev to the governor of the district who listened to her graciously and praised her for her heroism, recommending that she abide by it in the future. But at the same time, seeing in her complaint only a pretext for an indirect attack on his own person as the district governor, he allowed himself to add that since he had spent his energy in struggling with internal enemies, he had no firm basis for believing that he could be of any help in the required sense. Hearing this, Anninka blushed and left.

Meanwhile, Kukishev was working so cleverly that he managed to interest the public in his solicitations as well. The public seemed suddenly to feel that Kukishev was right and that the Number One Miss from Pogorelka (that was the way she appeared in the posters) was not, God knows, so much of a "grande dame" to play the part of an untouchable. An entire party was formed which set itself the task of bridling this obstinate upstart. It all began with the backstage regulars avoiding her dressing room and nesting themselves in the neighboring dressing room of Nalimova. Then—without displaying, incidentally, any outright actions of animosity—they began to greet the Miss from Pogorelka with deadly indifference when she appeared on the stage, as though it was not the star who was appearing on stage, but only some supernumerary. Finally, they insisted that the entrepreneur deprive Anninka of several roles and give them to Nalimova. What was even more curious was that Lyubinka was taking an active part in all of this underground subterfuge and Nalimova had become a real confidant to her.

Towards autumn Anninka learned with amazement that she was being forced to play the part of Orestes in "La Belle Hélène" and that only Périchole remained of her former roles, and that was only because the girl Nalimova herself had decided not to compete with her in that play. Moreover, the entrepreneur announced to her that in view of the public's growing coolness

225

towards her, her salary would be curtailed to seventy-five rubles a month plus only half the proceeds from a benefit performance once a year.

Anninka lost heart because in view of such a salary she would be forced to move from the hotel to a roadside inn. She wrote letters to two or three entrepreneurs, offering her services, but from everyone she received the reply that there was no shortage of Péricholes at that time and since, in addition, her uncooperativeness had become known from a number of reliable sources, therefore no prospects seemed to be in the offing.

Anninka was down to the last of her savings. Another week and she would not escape moving to an inn, on the same level with the girl Khoroshavina who played Parthenes and who enjoyed the patronage of a police officer. She began to feel the first onslaught of something akin to despair, all the more so because every day a note was thrown into her room under the door by a mysterious hand and bearing one and the same content: "Périchole! Surrender! Your Kukishev." And precisely at this desperate moment Lyubinka came bursting in on her quite unexpectedly.

"Tell me, for mercy's sake, what prince you're guarding your treasure for?" she asked curtly.

Anninka was struck dumb. Above all she was struck by the fact that both the Voplino priest and Lyubinka had used the word "treasure" in the same sense. Only the priest saw a "principle" in the treasure, whereas Lyubinka looked upon it as some insignificant thing which, incidentally, would drive those "villainous men" to distraction.

Then she involuntarily asked herself: what in fact was this treasure? Was it actually a treasure and was it worthwhile preserving it? —And alas! She could not find a satisfactory answer to this question. On the one hand, it seemed to bother her conscience to lose this treasure, yet on the other hand... to hell with it! Could it really be that all the meaning and worth of life had to find their sole expression in conducting a constant battle for one's treasure?

"In half a year I've managed to save up thirty lottery tickets," Lyubinka continued in the meanwhile, "and all the things I have... Just take a look at my dress!"

Lyubinka turned around, showed her dress off first from the front and then from the back and then from all angles. The dress was really very expensive and marvelously tailored: straight from Mme. Minangois in Moscow.

"Kukishev is a good man," Anninka began again, "he could dress you up like a doll and give you money. You could put the theater aside... enough of that!"

"Never!" Anninka cried hotly, still not having forgotten her slogan: sacred art!

"You could stay on if you want. You'd get your old salary again, be a star instead of Nalimova."

Anninka was silent.

"Well, farewell. They're waiting for me downstairs. Kukishev is there as well. Shall we go?"

But Anninka continued her silence.

"Well, think about it, if there's anything to think about... And when you've made up your mind—come over! Farewell!

The seventeenth of September, Lyubinka's nameday, the poster from the Samovarnov theater announced a special performance. Anninka was to appear again in the role of "La Belle Hélène" and that very same evening, "for this one performance only," the Number Two Miss from Pogorelka, that is, Lyubinka, would play the role of Orestes. To top off the festivity and again "for this performance only," Miss Nalimova would be attired in tights and a short jacket, her face lightly touched with soot, armed with a sheet of iron and cast in the role of the blacksmith Cleon. In view of this, the public was also in an enthusiastic mood. Anninka barely appeared from behind the wings when she was met with such an uproar that she, quite unaccustomed for some time to any ovations, felt the sobs mounting in her throat. When in the third act, in the scene where she is awakened at night, she arose from her couch almost naked, a moan, in the genuine sense of the word, arose in the hall. This had the result that one overly electrified viewer shouted at Menelaeus as he appeared at the door: "Go away, you hateful man!" Anninka understood that the public had forgiven her. For his part, Kukishev, in evening dress, with a white tie and white gloves, gave notice of his triumph with dignity and during the intermission feted friends and strangers alike with champagne in the buffet. Finally, even the entrepreneur of the theater, overwhelmed with jubilation, appeared in Anninka's dressing room and falling to his knees he said:

"There you go, my lady, now you're a good girl! And therefore, from this very evening, you will be raised to the highest salary you received formerly and with the appropriate number of benefit performances!"

In short, everyone praised her, everyone congratulated her, and expressed their warmest feelings, so that she herself, once so uncertain of herself and knowing no rest from a gnawing anguish, suddenly became unexpectedly but thoroughly convinced that she... had fulfilled her mission!

After the performance, everyone made his way to Lyubinka's flat for the nameday celebration and there the congratulations mounted higher. In Lyubinka's flat such a crowd was gathered and the air was filled so quickly with tobacco smoke that it was difficult to breathe. They immediately sat down to supper and the champagne was poured. Kukishev was never a step away from Anninka's side and she apparently was somewhat embarrassed, but at the same time not really bothered, by these attentions. It seemed slightly humorous to her, yet flattering as well, that she had acquired so easily this mature and powerful merchant who could effortlessly bend and unbend a horseshoe and whom she could order to do anything, and with whom she could do anything she wanted. At dinner, there began a general celebration that kind of drunken and disorderly celebration in which neither the head nor the heart plays any part and which causes headaches the following day and brings on fits of nausea. Only one of those present, the tragedian Miloslavsky X, looked sullen, refused to drink champagne and downed glass after glass of straight vodka. As for Anninka she restrained herself for a while from the general "intoxication" but Kukishev was so insistent and begged her so pitifully on his knees: "Anna Semyonova! You owe it to us! Allow me to beg you! For our happiness! For our help and love! Repay your debts!" that even though she was annoyed to see his silly face and listen to his silly speeches, nonetheless, she could not refuse and before she could come to her senses her head was already spinning. Lyubinka, for her part, was so magnanimous that she herself suggested that Anninka sing "Ah what joy I discovered with my mustachioed lover," which she did perform to such perfection that everyone exclaimed: "That's exactly the way Matryosha does it!" In exchange Lyubinka gave a masterly rendition of some lines about how pleasant it was "to serve *under* the colonel," and immediately convinced everyone that this was her true genre in which she had no other rivals, just as Anninka had done in songs performed in the gypsy manner. In conclusion Miloslavsky X and Miss Nalimova presented a "masquerade scene" in which the tragedian declaimed excerpts from "Ugolino" ("Ugolino" was a five-act tragedy from the works of N. Polevoi), while Nalimova responded with lines from an unpublished tragedy by Barkov. The result was something so extraordinary that Miss Nalimova almost eclipsed the Pogorelka girls and nearly became the heroine of the evening.

It was almost light when Kukishev seated Anninka in a carriage after leaving the nameday celebrations of dear Lyubinka. Devout townsfolk were returning from early morning mass and looking at the gaudily dressed and slightly tipsy Number One Girl from Pogorelka, sullenly grumbled:

"People are going to church and they're filling themselves with wine... hell's too good for you!"

From her sister's, Anninka now made her way not to the hotel but to her *own* flat, small but comfortable and very sweetly decorated. Kukishev followed her into the flat as well.

The entire winter passed in a kind of extraordinary daze. Anninka had been totally entrapped and if from time to time she remembered about her "treasure," then it was simply for the purpose of now adding mentally: "What a fool I certainly was!" Kukishev, under the influence of a prideful awareness that his idea about having a "beauty" equal in stature to Lyubinka had been realized, not only did not begrudge the money, but, aroused by a sense of competition, would unfailingly order two gowns when Lyulkin ordered only one and set out two dozen bottles of champagne when Lyulkin put out only a dozen. Even Lyubinka began to envy her sister because the latter had managed to save up forty lottery tickets over the winter in addition to a decent quantity of gold baubles with and without stones. Incidentally, they became friends again and decided to make a common savings of everything they amassed. In doing so Anninka was still dreaming about something and in an intimate conversation with her sister she said:

"When *all of this* is over, then we'll go to Pogorelka. We'll have money and we'll run the estate ourselves."

To this Lyubinka made a cynical response:

"Do you really think that *this* will ever come to an end... you fool!"

To Anninka's misfortune, Kukishev came up with a new "idea" which he began to pursue with his customary obstinence. Being an immature and, moreover, indubitably unintelligent man, he thought that he would truly find himself in heaven if his "beauty" would "play along with him," that is, start to drink vodka together with him.

"Let's toss one off! Together! At the same time!" he pestered her relentlessly (he always addressed Anninka in a formal way, first of all appreciating her gentry background and, secondly, wishing to show that it had not been for nothing that he had "studied as an apprentice" in a Moscow store).

For some time Anninka resisted, pointing out that not even Lyulkin forced Lyubinka to drink vodka.

"But she does all the same drink it, out of love for Mr. Lyulkin," Kukishev objected, "and allow me to inform you, my beauty, are the Lyulkins -any kind of model for us? They are the Lyulkins and you and I are the Kukishevs! So we'll toss one back, our own way, in the Kukishev fashion!"

In short, Kukishev won out. Once Anninka took from her beloved's hands a glass filled with a green liquid and downed it at a single go. Naturally her eyes blurred, she choked, coughed and her head began to swim and thus she caused Kukishev wild delight.

"Allow me to inform you, my beauty! You are not drinking it properly! You are doing it too quickly," he instructed her when she had somewhat regained her composure, "you should hold your little goblet (this is what he called the glass) like this! Then raise it to your lips slowly: one, two, three... God bless us!"

And he calmly and seriously downed the glass as though he were pouring the contents into a bucket. He did not even wince but merely took a tiny piece of black bread from the plate, dipped it in the salt and chewed it.

In this way Kukishev managed to realize his second "idea" as well and now already began to consider what new "idea" he could think up in order to outdo the Lyulkins. Naturally, he thought one up.

"You know what," he suddenly announced, "now that summer's coming, what do you say we take a trip with the Lyulkins for company to my mill, take a *sac-voyage* with us (this is what he called a basket with wine and snacks) and go bathing in the river all together, with everyone's consent!"

"Not if I have anything to do with it!" Anninka protested indignantly.

"Why not! At first we could go swimming together, then toss a little one down, and then when we cool off a bit go for another swim? It will be simply marvelous!"

No one knows whether this new "idea" of Kukishev's was ever realized, but it is known that this drunken revelry went on for an entire year and during this time neither the city administration, nor the Land Council, as such, uncovered the least bit of disquieting information about Messieurs Kukishev and Lyulkin. Lyulkin, incidentally, made a trip, for appearances' sake, to Moscow and on his return said that he had sold a forest for lumber, but when he was reminded that he had already sold that forest four years before when he was living with the gypsy girl, Domashka, he objected that he had gotten rid of the Drygalovsky woodlot at that time, whereas now it was the woodlot known as Dasha's Shame. To give his story more credibility he added that the woodlot just sold had been called that because during serfdom the girl Dasha had been "caught" in these woods and had been whipped on the spot with switches for what she had done. As far as Kukishev was concerned, he set a rumor afoot, to avert attention, that he had brought in some lace duty-free from abroad in a shipment of pencils and had made a good profit with that operation.

Nonetheless, in September of the following year, the chief of police asked Kukishev for a thousand rubles, by way of a loan, but Kukishev had the poor sense to refuse. Then the chief of police began to exchange whispers with his friend the prosecutor ("Both of them used to lap up the champagne at my place every evening!" Kukishev testified subsequently at the trial). And lo, on the seventeenth of September, on the anniversary of Kukishev's "loves," when together with others he was once again celebrating Lyubinka's name-day, a town councilor from the city administration came running in and announced to Kukishev that a meeting had been called at the city administration and a protocol was being drawn up.

"They must have discovered the 'deficit!' " Kukishev exclaimed rather unperturbed and without any further conversation he followed the messenger to the city administration and from there to the jail.

The following day the alarm was sounded by the Land Council as well. The members gathered, sent to the treasury for the cash box, counted it up and recounted it, but no matter how they pounded on the abacus, ultimately a "deficit" proved to be here as well. Lyulkin was present at the inquiry, pale, sullen, but... noble! When the "deficit" was uncovered beyond any doubt and each member was mulling over in his own mind which Drygalovsky woodlot he would have to sell in order to make good the deficit, Lyulkin went up to the window, pulled a revolver out of his pocket and planted a bullet in his temple right there on the spot.

A great deal of talk in the town was spent on this incident. Judgments were passed and comparisons made. Lyulkin was pitied and people said: "At least he ended his life in a noble fashion!" The opinions of Kukishev were: "He had been born a lowly shopkeeper and a lowly shopkeeper he would die!" As far as Anninka and Lyubinka were concerned, people said outright that they were the "ones," that is was all "because of them" and it would not hurt to put them in jail as well so as to serve as a lesson for other such villains in the future.

The prosecutor, however, did not put them in jail, but frightened them so badly that they were utterly at their wits' end. People were found, of course, who in a friendly fashion advised them to hide their most valuable possessions, but they listened without understanding anything. Taking advantage of this the lawyer for the plaintiffs (both the city administration and the Land Council hired one and the same lawyer), a fine and fearless chap, by way of securing any claims, appeared together with a policeman of the court at the sisters' and made an inventory and sealed up everything that he found, leaving at their disposal only their dresses and those gold and silver articles which, judging from the engraved inscriptions, turned out to be presents from an ecstatic public. Lyubinka managed, however, during all of this to seize a packet of bills which had been given her the evening before and hide them under her corset. There turned out to be a thousand rubles in the packet—all that the sisters had to live on for an indefinite time.

They were detained in Samovarnov for about four months waiting for the trial. Then began the trial at which Anninka in particular was subjected to utter torture. Kukishev was revoltingly cynical. There was no need to disclose the details which he exposed, but apparently wanting to cut a dashing figure before the ladies of Samovarnov he described absolutely everything. The prosecutor and the counsel for the plaintiffs, people who were young and also wanting to entertain the ladies of Samovarnov, took advantage of this in order to lend the trial a frivolous atmosphere and, of course, succeeded. Anninka fainted several times, but the counsel for the plaintiffs, concerned only with securing the plaintiffs' claims, studiously paid no attention and asked one question after another. Finally the inquest came to an end and the different sides presented their summations. It was already late at night when the jury delivered the verdict of guilty against Kukishev, but with extenuating circumstances, as a consequence of which he was immediately condemned to banishment to any nearby place in Western Siberia.

With the conclusion of this business the sisters were given permission to leave Samovarnov. And it was high time because the thousand rubles which had been concealed was just about finished. Moreover, the entrepreneur from the Krechetov theater, with whom they had made an agreement beforehand, now demanded that they show up in Krechetov immediately, threatening that if they did not, he would break off any negotiations. Not a word was breathed about the money, articles and papers which had been sealed at the demand of the counselor for the plaintiffs...

Such were the consequences of treating one's "treasure" without caution. Tormented, tortured, crushed by the general scorn, the sisters had lost all faith in their own strength and all hope for a brighter future. They grew thin, depressed and timid. And to top everything off, Anninka, having studied in Kukishev's school, had learned how to drink.

Things became even worse. The sisters had barely managed to climb out of the train in Krechetov when they were immediately parceled out. Lyubinka went to a Captain Papkov, Anninka to the merchant, Zabvenny. But there was nothing left of the earlier luxuries. Both Papkov and Zabvenny were coarse and aggressive people, but modest in their spending (as Zabvenny put it: "it depended on the merchandise"), and in three or four months they grew noticeably cool. On top of everything, side by side with their mediocre success in love went extremely mediocre successes on the stage. The entrepreneur who had hired the sisters, counting on the scandal they had caused in Samovarnov, had completely miscalculated. At the very first performance, when both the Misses from Pogorelka were on stage, someone from the gallery shouted: "Hey you, jailbirds!" and this nickname stuck with the sisters, deciding once and for all their dramatic fate.

A life that was vitiated of all interest, dreary and monotonous, dragged on. The public was cold, the entrepreneur sulked, their patrons did not intercede. Zabvenny, who like Kukishev dreamt about how he would "coerce" his beauty into learning gradually how to toss them back with him, was quite put out when he saw that she had had her schooling and his only consolation was to gather his friends and watch Anyutka "swill vodka." For his part, Papkov was not satisfied either and found that Lyubinka had grown thin, or as he expressed it, "had grown scruffy."

"You used to have some meat on you before," he questioned her, "tell me, what did you do with it?"

And as a consequence of this not only did he not stand on ceremony with her, but more than once he would beat her in a drunken fit.

By the end of winter the sisters had no "genuine" patrons, nor any "permanent position." They still hung on around the theater, but roles such as "Périchole" and "The Old-Fashioned Colonel" were already out of the question. Incidentally, Lyubinka appeared somewhat more cheerful, whereas Anninka, being more nervous, became quite depressed and seemingly had lost all recollection of the past and was not even conscious of the present. Moreover, she began to cough suspiciously: some mysterious malady was apparently headed her way...

The following summer was terrible. Little by little the sisters began to be dragged around the hotels to traveling gentlemen and a fixed but moderate price was put on them. Scandal followed scandal, beating followed upon beating, but the sisters were like cats with nine lives and kept hanging on and kept wishing to live. They reminded one of those miserable mongrels who, despite being scalded, wounded and with broken legs, still crawl off to their favorite spot, howl and still manage to crawl on. Retaining such personages at the theater proved to be awkward.

In that gloomy year only once did a ray of light penetrate into Anninka's existence. It concerned the tragedian Miloslavsky X who sent a letter from Samovarnov in which he insistently offered her his hand and his heart.

232

Anninka read the letter through and wept. The whole night long she tossed and turned. She was, as people say, not herself, but the next morning she sent a short reply: "What for? So that we can drink vodka together?" Then the gloom thickened worse than before and again began the endless vile debauchery.

Lyubinka was the first to come to her senses, or better, did not come to them, and felt instinctively that she had had enough of life. No work could be foreseen now: youth and beauty and those scraps of talent, it was as though they had all disappeared. The fact that they had a shelter in Pogorelka did not even occur to her. It was something far-off, vague, and completely forgotten. If Pogorelka had not held any attraction earlier for them, then now it was a bit late. Yes, precisely at this time when they were practically being forced to perish from hunger, now, above all, it held even less attraction. What face would she show up with? With a face on which all imaginable drunken breathing had branded its mark: vile creature! This accursed breath lay everywhere, it could be felt everywhere, in every spot. And what was all the more horrible was that she and Anninka had become so accustomed to this foul breath that it had imperceptibly become an inextricable part of their existence. They found disgusting neither the stench of taverns nor the uproar of inns nor the brazenness of drunken words, so that even if they had gone off to Pogorelka, they probably would have missed it all. But in addition, one had to have something to live on, even in Pogorelka. How many years they had knocked about the wide world and had not heard a single thing about any income from the Pogorelka estate. Was it not a myth? Had everyone died off there? All these witnesses of a distant and eternally memorable childhood, when Arina Petrovna, their granny, had raised them on sour milk and spoiled salt meat... God, what a childhood that had been! What kind of a life that had been...all of it together... Their whole life long, every last bit of it! It was clear that death was the only way. Once this idea had illuminated the conscience, it became relentless. Both sisters would frequently rouse themselves from riotous life, but for Anninka these awakenings were accompanied by fits of hysterics, sobbing and tears; thus they passed more quickly. Lyubinka was colder by nature and for that reason she did not weep, did not curse, but merely recalled obstinately that she was "vile." Moreover, Lyubinka was a logical person and seemed to realize perfectly clearly that there was nothing to be gained in going on with life. Nothing loomed on the horizon other than shame, poverty and the street. Shame was a matter of habit, it could be tolerated, but poverty—never! Better to put an end to everything once and for all.

"There's nothing else but to die," she said once to Anninka in that very same coldly logical voice with which two years before she had asked her what she was guarding her treasure for.

"Why?" Anninka asked with fright.

"I'm telling you seriously: there's nothing else but to die!" Lyubinka repeated, "Do understand! Wake up! Just try!"

"Well then, we shall die!" Anninka agreed, barely conscious, however, of the stern significance contained in this decision.

On that same day Lyubinka broke off the heads of phosphorus matches and prepared two glasses of a mixture. One of them she drank herself and the other she gave to her sister. But Anninka instantly lost her courage and did not want to drink it.

"Drink it...you vile creature," Lyubinka screamed at her, "Sister, dear! Sweet! Drink it!"

Almost out of her mind from terror, Anninka screamed and flailed about the room. And at the same time she instinctively clutched with her hands at her throat as though trying to choke herself.

"Drink it, drink it! You vile creature!"

The artistic career of the Misses from Pogorelka was at an end. That same evening Lyubinka's body was taken out into a field and buried. Anninka remained alive.

* * *

With her arrival in Golovlyovo, Anninka very quickly introduced an atmosphere of the most desperate disorder into little Judas' nest. She rose late; then, undressed and unkempt, with heavy head, she slouched about from corner to corner, right up until dinner, and coughed so agonizingly that Porfiry Vladimirych, sitting in his study, took fright each time and shuddered. Her room was never cleaned: the bed was messed up; articles of her toilette and linen were scattered about in heaps on chairs and on the floor. At first she would see her uncle only during dinner and at evening tea. The Golovlyovo lord would emerge from his study all dressed in black, he would speak little and the only reminder of the past was the unbearably slow manner in which he ate. Apparently he was scrutinizing her, and Anninka, judging from the furtive glances in her direction, guessed that he was in fact scrutinizing her.

On the heels of dinner came the early shades of December and the melancholy pacing up and down the long series of reception rooms. Anninka loved to follow the gradual fading of the gray winter day's last light and the surrounding area growing dark and the rooms filling with shadows and then the entire house plunging into impenetrable gloom. She felt easier in the midst of this gloom and for this reason she almost never lit any candles. Only at the end of the long hall an inexpensive palm-oil candle sputtered and flickered, forming a small gleaming aureole with its flame. For a short while arose that customary after-dinner movement in the house: the clatter of dishes being washed, the banging of drawers being opened and closed, but in a short time the sound of receding footsteps reached her and then a deathly silence ensued. Porfiry Vladimirych would lie down for his after-dinner rest, Yevprakseyushka would bury herself in the featherbed in her room, Prokhor would disappear into the servants' quarters and Anninka would be left completely on her own. She paced back and forth, humming under her breath and trying to tire herself out and, principally, trying not to think about anything. Going in the direction of the hall, she would peer into the gleaming aureole formed by the flame of the candle. Coming back she would attempt to distinguish some point in the thickening gloom. But despite her efforts, reminiscences came trailing in her direction. There was the dressing room papered with cheap wallpaper along the wooden partitions, with the inevitable full mirror and the equally inevitable bouquet from some Lieutenant Papkov; and there was the stage with the sooty, grimy decorations slimy from the dampness; and there she was herself, pirouetting on the stage, that's exactly what she was doing, pirouetting, imagining that she was acting: and then there was the theatre hall, which seemed from the stage to be so luxurious, almost brilliant, when in actual fact it was wretched, dark with mismatched furniture and boxes upholstered in frayed crimson velveteen. And then finally officers, officers and more officers without end. Then the hotel with the stinking corridor, weakly lit with a smoking kerosene lamp; the room to which she scurried at the conclusion of the performance in order to change her dress for the subsequent festivities, a room where the bed had not been made since morning, the sink filled with filthy water, sheets heaped on the floor and forgotten underwear hung on the back of the chair. Then the main dining room filled with kitchen smells and a table set in the middle; supper, cutlets with peas, tobacco smoke, a racket, shoving, drunkenness, debauchery... And again those officers, officers and more officers without end...

Such were the reminiscences which belonged to that time which she at one period had called the time of her successes, her triumphs, her well-being...

A series of other reminiscences would follow these. Here the main role was played by the roadside inn which was now quite foul-smelling, with walls frozen through in the winter, sagging floors, the shiny bodies of bedbugs peeking out of the cracks of wooden partitions. Drunken and rowdy nights; travelling landowners, hastily extracting a green three-ruble note from their thick wallets; dashing merchants forcing the "actresses" to have a good time practically with a whip in their hands. Then the following morning, a headache, nausea and depression, depression without end. In conclusion—Golovlyovo...

Golovlyovo—that was death itself, malicious, spiritually empty; that was death eternally lying in wait for a new victim. Two uncles had died here. The two brothers, her cousins, had received here "particularly serious" wounds of which death was the consequence. Finally, there Lyubinka as well... Although it seemed as though she had died somewhere in Krechetov "on her own," nonetheless the beginning of those "particularly serious" wounds of which death was the consequence. Finally, there was Lyubinka as poison, all the sores—everything originated here. It had been here that they had been fed with putrid salt meat, here the words had echoed for the first time in the orphans' ears: you hateful miserable parasites, you greedy guts,

235

and so on. Here nothing had been taken for granted as far as they were concerned, nothing had been concealed from the penetrating gaze of that hardhearted and ill-tempered old woman: no extra piece of food, no broken penny-doll, no torn rag, no worn-out shoe. Every transgression met unfailingly with a scolding or a slap. And then, they had gotten the chance to fend for themselves and they had understood that they could run away from this misery, and they did run away...to *there!* No one had prevented them from running off, and it would have been impossible because nothing more hateful than Golovolyovo could have been imagined.

God, if only she could forget all of this! If only she could create something different in her fantasy, some magical world which would erase both the past and the present. But alas, the reality she had experienced had been imbued with such an implacable tenacity that beneath its oppression all flashes of imagination were extinguished of their own accord. Fantasy strove in vain to create angels with pretty silver wings—but peeking out relentlessly from among all these angels were the Kukishevs, Lyulkins, Zabvennys and Papkovs... God! Was everything really lost? Had even the ability to lie, to deceive oneself—had that drowned in the nocturnal revelries, in alcohol and debauchery? Still, somehow or other this past had to be destroyed so that it would not poison the blood, would not tear the heart to shreds! A way had to be found to place something heavy on it which would crush it, destroy it once and for all.

How strangely and cruelly all this had come about! It was impossible even to imagine that any kind of future might be possible, that there existed a door whereby one could leave for somewhere else, that anything at all could happen. Nothing could happen. And what was all the more unbearable was the fact that in essence she had already died and at the same time all the external signs of life were there to see. She should have ended it *then,* together with Lyubinka, but for some reason she was left behind. How could it be that she had not been crushed by the weight of that shame which had converged on her from all directions at that time? And what kind of miserable worm did one have to be in order to come crawling out from under such a heap of rocks all cast at her at the same time?

These questions forced her to moan. She ran and spun about the hall, striving to pacify her excited recollections. But they still came rolling towards her: the Duchess of Gerolstein flaunting her hussar's cape, Clairette Angot in her wedding dress with a plunging neckline that reached right down to her waist, and La Belle Hélène, with slits in the front, the rear and all sides... Nothing but shamelessness and nakedness...that was what her entire life had been spent in! Had all of that really taken place?

Around seven o'clock the house began to awaken once again. The preparations for upcoming tea could be heard and finally even Porfiry Vladimirych's voice rang out. The uncle and his niece seated themselves at the tea table, exchanged remarks on the events of that day, but since the content of that day had been miserly, then the conversation turned out to be just as miserly. Having drunk his tea and fulfilled the ritual of the family bed-time kiss, little Judas crawled off to his lair for good, while Anninka went off to Yevprakseyushka and played cards with her.

From eleven o'clock began the drinking bout. Making certain beforehand that Porfiry Vladimirych had settled down, Yevprakseyushka would place various country preserves on the table and a carafe of vodka. Senseless and shameless songs were recalled, the sounds of the guitar rang out and in the pauses between songs and lewd talk, Anninka would drink. She drank at first "in the Kukishev fashion," coldbloodedly, "God bless us!" But then gradually she would give way to a gloomy mood and begin to moan and curse...

Yevprakseyushka looked at her and "felt sorry."

"I look at you, mistress," she said, "and I feel so sorry for you, so sorry!"

"Come and drink with me, then you won't feel sorry!" Anninka objected.

"Goodness no, how could I! I've practically been disowned because of your uncle, and if on top of that I..."

"Well, there's no sense talking about it! How about I sing the song about the 'Mustachioed Lover' for you."

Again the guitar strumming rang out, again the gypsy cries resounded: "hai-ta-ri, ta-ri-tum!" It was long after midnight when sleep smothered Anninka like a stone. This longed-for stone destroyed her past for a few short hours and even pacified her malady. But the following day, shattered, half out of her mind, she again would crawl out from beneath it and again begin to live.

And lo, on one of these miserable nights when Anninka was frenziedly performing for Yevprakseyushka her repertoire of lewd songs, suddenly the emaciated, deadly pale figure of little Judas appeared at the door of the room. His lips were trembling; his eyes were sunken and in the murky gleam of the palm-oil candle, they seemed to be like unseeing cavities; his hands folded with the palms turned inward. He stood for several seconds in front of the stunned women and then, slowly turning, left.

* * *

There are families over whom an inescapable fatalism seems to weigh heavily. This is particularly noticeable in the midst of the small folk of the petty, insignificant gentry, who, having nothing to do, without any connection with life in general and without any administrative importance, at first found themselves sheltered beneath the shield of serfdom, scattered across the face of the Russian land, but nowadays living out their final days defenselessly in their crumbling estates. The lives of these miserable families experienced both success and misfortune—everything seemed to be somehow blind, unforeseen and unpremeditated.

Sometimes it was as though a ray of joy suddenly spilled over a family of this type. With some impoverished lieutenant and his wife, peacefully wasting away in the backwoods of the country, there suddenly appeared an entire brood of young people who were strong, pure, clever and extremely quick at taking in the real essence of life. In short, "clever folk." Every last one of them was clever, including both the lads and the girls. The lads completed their studies at "institutes" with excellent grades and while still on their school benches set up connections and patronage for themselves. At the opportune time they knew how to act modestly *("j'aime cette modestie!"* – their superiors said of them) and at another opportune time how to act independently *("j'aime cette indépendance!"*); they keenly divined the direction of all the winds of fortune and they did not ignore any of them without first leaving behind some reliable loop-hole. Thanks to this, they ensured for their entire lives the possibility of abandoning the old skin and arraying themselves in a new one at any time at all without causing any scandals; but if the occasion demanded it, again they could slip on the old skin. In short, these were the genuine activists of this era who always commenced by soliciting favor and *almost always* ended up by resorting to some perfidy. As far as the girls were concerned, in keeping with their specialty, they furthered the rebirth of the family, that is to say, they made successful marriages and thereupon manifested so much tact in the manipulation of their charms that they were able to gain conspicuous positions in so-called society without difficulty.

Thanks to these circumstances, which had evolved quite fortuitously, success greeted the impoverished family. The first to succeed, after having cheerfully endured through the struggle, in their turn raised a new and tidy generation who now found life somewhat easier because the principal roads had been not only cleared, but well-trodden as well. After this generation there sprang up new generations until ultimately you had the family who quite naturally assumed that, without any preparatory struggle, it belonged to the category of those having a pre-ordained right to a life of exultation.

Lately, with the increase in demand for so-called "fresh people," a demand which has been conditioned by the gradual extinction of people who are "not fresh," the examples of similar successful families have begun to force their way to the fore quite often. Earlier it had been the case that from time to time a "new star" would appear on the horizon. Yet this happened but rarely, first because the wall encircling that carefree realm, and whose gates bore the inscription: "Here stuffed meat pies are eaten at any time," presented practically no cracks; and second, because in order to penetrate into this realm, escorted by this "new star," one truly had to show one's mettle. But nowadays the cracks have multiplied and the very process of penetration has become simplified so that the newcomer is not required to display his mettle. The only thing that is required is "freshness," and nothing more.

But side by side with the successful families existed a great multitude of other families whose representatives, apparently from the very cradle on, received nothing other than unmitigated misfortune from the household gods. Suddenly, almost like vermin, a family was attacked either by some adversity or some vice and it commenced to devour the family from all sides. It crept throughout the entire organism, stole into the very marrow and spoiled one generation after another. Groups of frail and miserable folk make their appearance, drunkards, petty dissolutes, senseless idlers and misfits in general. The further the process continued, the more petty, miserable folk would emerge, until finally on the scene appeared the emaciated living dead, similar to the Golovlyovs which I have described, the living dead who at the very first onslaught of life cannot endure, and so perish.

It was precisely this manner of ill-starred fate that hung over the Golovlyov family. In the course of several generations three characteristic features penetrated the history of this family: idleness, unsuitability for any business whatsoever, and hard drinking. The first two had brought with them frivolous speech, frivolous thought and an inner shallowness, the latter appeared as the requisite conclusion to a general disorder in life. Before his very eyes, Porfiry Vladimirych had witnessed how several victims of this fate had been consumed, and in addition, the same legend was voiced about his grandparents and great-grandparents. They had all been mischievous, idle-minded and good-for-nothing drunkards, so that the Golovlyov family probably would have wasted away ultimately if Arina Petrovna, like a chance meteor, had not flashed through in the midst of this drunken chaos. Thanks to her personal energy, this woman raised the level of the family's well-being to a higher degree, but after all of that, her labor went in vain because not only did she not pass on her qualities to any of the children, but on the contrary she herself died entangled in triviality, idle chatter and spiritual emptiness.

Up until now, however, Porfiry Vladimirych had remained strong. Perhaps he consciously avoided drunkenness in view of the previous examples, but perhaps he had still been satisfied for the time being with the intoxication of idle thought. However, with good reason, local rumor doomed little Judas to a proper "alcoholic" drunkenness. Even he himself seemed to feel at times that there was something missing in his existence; that although idle thought offered a great deal, it was not everything. Specifically he was lacking something stupefying, penetrating, which ultimately would abolish all awareness of life and once and for all cast him out into the void.

Then the longed-for moment had turned up by itself. For a long while, from the very moment of Anninka's arrival, Porfiry Vladimirych, locked away in his study, had listened to the vague noise which reached him from the other end of the house. For a long while he had tried to gues at its origin but had been stumped... And finally he had come to suspect what it was.

The following day, Anninka was expecting moral lectures, but nothing of the sort ensued. As was his habit, Porfiry Vladimirych spent the entire morning locked in his study, but when he emerged for dinner, instead of a single glass of vodka (for himself) he poured two and silently, with a silly smile, pointed with his hand to one of them for Anninka. This was, so to speak, a silent invitation which Anninka accepted.

"So you say that Lyubinka is dead?" little Judas blurted out in the midst of the meal.

"She is, uncle."

"Well, may she rest in peace! It's a sin to complain, we should drink to her memory instead. Shall we?"

"Yes, let's, uncle."

They drank one more each and then little Judas fell silent; apparently he had not yet completely recovered after his extended estrangement. Only after dinner when Anninka went up to thank her dear uncle with a kiss on the cheek, fulfilling the usual family ritual, did he for his part pat her on the cheek and mutter:

"So that's what you're like!"

In the evening, on that very same day, during tea-time, which this time went on longer than usual, Porfiry Vladimirych gazed at Anninka for some time with that same enigmatic smile, but then he finally suggested:

"Shall I ask them to put out a snack for us?"

"Why not...go ahead!"

"There we are, better before your uncle's eyes than secretly... At least, your uncle..."

Little Judas did not finish. Probably he had wanted to say that her uncle, at least, could "restrain" her, but the word could not seem to come out.

From that time every evening a snack appeared in the dining room. The window shutters were closed, the servants went off to bed and the niece and her uncle remained eye-to-eye. At first little Judas could not keep up, but a brief practice was sufficient for him to be able to match Anninka fully. They both sat there, without hurrying, drinking, and in between the glasses, remembering and chatting. At first the conversation was indifferent and dreary, but the more their heads began to whirl the more lively it became, until finally it would invariably end up in a messy quarrel at the basis of which were recollections over the Golovlyovo deaths and injuries.

Anninka was always the instigator of these quarrels. With a merciless persistence she dug into the Golovlyov archives and in particular loved to tease little Judas, proving that he had played, together with the deceased grandmother, the major role in all of these injuries. In doing so, every word of hers breathed such a cynical hatred that it was difficult to imagine how so much of life's flame could still be harbored in this tormented and half-extinguished organism. These instances of harrassment stung little Judas beyond all bounds. But he could only protest feebly and become even more angry, and then when Anninka in her mischievous baiting went too far, then he would let forth a scream and curse her.

Such were the scenes which were repeated day in and day out, without alteration. Although all the details of this mournful family book of remembrance were exhausted very rapidly, nonetheless this book remained so persistently before the eyes of these crushed beings that all their mental capacities seemed to be chained to it. Every episode, every recollection of the past irritated some sore or other, and every sore recalled a fresh bundle of Golovlyov injuries. Some kind of a bitter, spiteful enjoyment made itself felt in the unearthing of these irritations, in their enumeration and exaggeration. Nowhere, either in the past or in the present did there prove to be a single moral principle that one could cling to. Nothing other than avarice on the one hand and a senseless spiritual emptiness on the other. Instead of bread, a stone had been offered, instead of instruction a blow would be dealt. And by way of a variation, there was the vile reminder of being a parasite, eating other people's bread, beggary, and furtive meals... This was the response which a youthful heart thirsting for sympathy, warmth and love had received. And that was only the beginning! By what bitter mockery of fate had this cruel school produced not an austere view of life, but rather a passionate desire to enjoy its poisons instead? Youth had performed the miracle of forgetfulness. It had not allowed the heart to turn to stone, had not allowed the first seeds of hatred to develop in it, but, on the contrary, had intoxicated that heart with a thirst for life. This explained the reckless backstage revelry which in the course of several years had kept her from coming to her senses and deeply suppressed everything associated with Golovlyovo. Only now, when the end could be sensed, did a gnawing pain flare up in her heart, only now did Anninka genuinely comprehend her past and begin to loathe it with a genuine hatred.

These intoxicated conversations continued long past midnight and if they had not been mollified by the intoxicated jumble of thoughts and speeches, then they might have resulted in something terrible at the very outset. But, fortunately, if alcohol had vented the inexhaustible sources of pain in these tormented hearts, then it also appeased them. The deeper the night descended over the participants, the more disconnected their speech became and the more impotent became the hatred which had incited them. By the end not only could no pain be felt, but everything in their daily life had disappeared from before their eyes and had been replaced with a gleaming void. Their tongues became twisted, their eyes closed, their bodily motions grew sluggish. Both the uncle and his niece would arise from their places with difficulty and stumble off to their lairs.

It goes without saying that these nocturnal adventures could not remain a secret in the house. On the contrary, their nature became so immediately clear that no one found it strange when one of the house servants, as a result of these adventures, pronounced that "there's murder in the air." The Golovlyovo mansion finally fell into a stupor. Even in the mornings there was no sign of any movement. The masters awoke late and then, from one end of the house to the other right up until dinner, Anninka's heart-rending cough resounded, accompanied by uninterrupted curses. Little Judas listened in terror to these rending sounds and guessed that some misfortune was staring him in the face as well and it would ultimately crush him.

From every direction, from every corner of this hateful house, the dead victims seemed to come creeping out. Wherever one turned, wherever one went, the gray specters were rustling. There was papa, Vladimir Mikhailovich, in a white bed cap, sticking his tongue out at everyone and quoting from Barkov. There was brother Styopka-the-Dunce and beside him brother Pashka-the-Silent and there was Lyubinka, and there was the final offspring of the Golovyov family, Volodka and Petka... All of this drunkenness, lechery, torment, oozed blood... And over all of these specters hovered a living specter, and this living specter was none other than Porfiry Vladimirich Golovyov himself, the final representative of this family which had forfeited itself.

* * *

Ultimately, the constant reminders of the old victims had to take its toll. The past had become so apparent that even the least reference to it produced pain. The natural consequence was something that was not entirely fear or even an awakening of conscience, or more of the latter than the former in any event. Amazingly, it turned out that conscience was not entirely lacking, but had merely been suppressed and seemingly forgotten. And as a result of this it had lost that active responsiveness which unfailingly reminds a person of its existence.

Such pangs of a conscience that had become estranged were particularly torturous. Deprived of any intellectual care, envisioning no ray of hope ahead, conscience offered no reconciliation, indicated no possibility of a new life, but merely tortured relentlessy and futilely. A person found himself in a stone cell, mercilessly delivered up as a victim to the agonies of remorse, a single agony, to be exact, without any hope for a return to life. And no other means existed for pacifying this futile, gnawing pain other than the chance to utilize a moment of gloomy decisiveness in order to smash one's head against the stone cell...

In the course of a long, spiritually empty life, little Judas never once, even in his thoughts, imagined that right here, face to face with his own existence, that this process of decay would take place. He had lived nice and quietly, taking his good old time, and did not suppose in the least that this would result in a more or less serious injury. As a result, he was all the less capable of allowing that he himself had been responsible for the injuries.

Then suddenly, the terrifying truth had illuminated his conscience, but had done so too late, to no avail, only when the irreversible and incorrigible fact was staring him in the face. He had now grown old, estranged, with one foot in the grave, and there was no being in the world who might have come close to him, "felt sorry" for him. Why was he alone? Why did he see around himself not only indifference but hatred as well? Why had everything perished that he had touched? Right here, in this Golovlyovo, there had been a whole nest of humanity at one time—how had it happened that not a single feather had remained from this nest? Out of all the fledglings who had been nursed in it, only one niece had survived, but even she had turned up in order to curse him and finish him off. Even Yevprakseyushka—as simple as she was— even she hated him. She was living in Golovlyovo because her father, the sexton, received monthly supplies for the household from here, but she was living there and doubtless hating it all the while. He, Judas, had dealt her the heaviest of injuries as well, he had known how to take away from her the light of her life when he took her son away and cast him into some nameless pit. What had his entire life come to? Why had he lied, indulged in idle chatter, pestered people and played the miser? Even from the material point of view, from the point of view of "inheritance"—who would gain advantage of the results of this life? Who?

I repeat: conscience awoke, but to no avail. Little Judas moaned, grew vexed, flailed about and with a feverish malice he waited for the evenings not only in order to drink himself brutishly drunk, but in order to drown his conscience in alcohol. He hated this "dissolute Miss" who with such cold impudence opened those sores, and at the same time he was irresistibly drawn to her, as though everything between them had not yet been put into words, and there were yet more sores which also had to be aggravated without fail. Every evening he forced Anninka to repeat the story about Lyubinka's death and every evening the idea of self-destruction ripened within his mind more and more. At first this thought had flashed through his head quite by chance, but as the process of victimization became clearer, it crept deeper and deeper and finally became the one gleaming point in the gloom of the future.

Moreover, his physical health had been dealt a blow. Now he was coughing seriously and from time to time felt unbearable attacks of breathlessness which, aside from the moral torments, were capable of filling life with nothing but agony. All the external signs of that special Golovlyov poisoning were evident, and already the moans of his brother, Pavlushka-the-Silent, gasping for air upstairs in the Dubrovino house, were echoing in his ears. However, this sunken, emaciated chest which seemingly was prepared to burst at any minute, proved to be amazingly tenacious. With each day it found room for greater and greater amounts of physical suffering, yet it hung on and did not fade. It was as though even his organism, with its unexpected resilience, were taking revenge for the previous victims. "Isn't this really the end?" little Judas said hopefully each time as he sensed the approach of an attack. But the end still would not come. Apparently, a special effort was demanded to hasten it.

In short, from whichever way one looked at it, all accounts with life were closed. It was torturous to go on living and it was uncalled for. What was called for would be to die. But misfortune lay in the fact that death would

243

not come. There was something perfidiously vile in this mischievous retardation of death's process when, in fact, death was being summoned with all the heart's power and death merely beguiled and teased...

. . . .

Things reached the end of March and Easter Week was drawing to a close. However depressed Porfiry Vladimirych had grown during the last years, his attitude towards the holiness of these days, an attitude which had been formed even when he was a child, still had an effect on him. His thoughts became attuned to a serious mood all by themselves. His heart experienced no desire other than a longing for utter silence. In keeping with this mood, the evenings lost their chaotically drunken nature and were spent silently in melancholy restraint.

Little Judas and Anninka were sitting together in the dining room. Not more than an hour before, the evening service, together with the readings from the twelve gospels, had come to an end and the strong smell of incense was still evident in the room. The clock had struck ten, the servants had dispersed to their corners, a profound, concentrated silence reigned in the house. Leaning with her elbows on the table and her head between her hands, Anninka was deep in thought. Porfiry Vladimirych was sitting opposite her, silent and mournful.

This service had always had a deeply unsettling effect on Anninka. While still a child she had wept bitter tears when the priest had pronounced: "And when they had platted a crown of thorns, they put it upon his head, and a reed in his right hand," —and in her whimpering descant she had sung the response to the sexton: "Glory be to your long suffering, Lord, Glory be to Thee!" And after the evening service, all excited, she would run into the maids' quarters and there, in the midst of thickening shadows (Arina Petrovna did not pass out candles in the maids' quarters when there was no work to be done), she would relate to the serfs "the Passion of Our Lord." Silent tears would stream from the serfs' eyes and their deep sighs resounded. The serfs sensed their Lord and Redeemer in their hearts, they believed that He would arise, that He would truly arise. Anninka sensed it as well and believed. Beyond the deep night of torments, of vile mockery and nodding-off, all of these who were the poor in spirit could envision the kingdom of light and freedom. Even the old mistress herself, Arina Petrovna, usually so threatening, became quiet during those days, did not snap and did not reproach Anninka for being an orphan, but patted her on her little head and tried to persuade her not to get upset. But even in bed Anninka could not calm down for a long time, she was trembling, tossing about and jumped up out of bed several times in the course of the night and talked to herself.

Then the years of schooling had arrived and after them the years of wandering. The former had been unremarkable, the latter painfully vulgar.

244

But even there, in the midst of the chaos of the actor's nomadic life, Anninka zealously singled out the "holy days" and sought out in her heart the echoes of the past which had enabled her to be moved so deeply and to sigh like a child. But now, when life had been completely laid bare, down to the final detail, when the past had put a curse on itself, and for the future there was no sign of repentance or forgiveness, when the source of deeper feeling had dried up, and together with it all tears had dried up as well,—the impression produced by the story of Christ's Calvary which she had just heard, was truly oppressive. Even then, in her childhood, the deep night had hung heavily over her, but beyond the darkness all the same there were premonitions of light. But now there were no premonitions, there was nothing on the horizon other than night, eternal, unrelenting night—and nothing more. Anninka no longer sighed, no longer grew upset, and it seemed that she was not even thinking about anything, but had simply fallen into a profound lethargy.

For his part, Porfiry Vladimirych had from his earliest years, respected the "holy days" with no lesser punctiliousness, but he did so exclusively for the sake of the ritual, like a true idolator. Each year, on the eve of Good Friday, he would invite the priest, listen to the Gospel story, sigh, raise his hands, strike his forehead against the ground, denote with wax pellets on the candle the number of Gospels read and still he comprehended exactly nothing. Only now, when Anninka had aroused in him the awareness of the "victims" did he comprehend for the first time that this story was talking about some incredible injustice which had delivered a bloody judgement on Truth...

Of course, it would be an exaggeration to say that this revelation had given rise in his heart to any actual comparisons, but no doubt, what had taken place in it was a kind of alarm practically bordering on desperation. This alarm was all the more agonizing for the reason that the past, which had given rise to it, had been such an unconscious process. There was something frightening in this past, but precisely what it was he found impossible to recall amid all the jumble. But it was impossible to forget. Something enormous, which until now had been standing there motionless, covered with an impenetrable curtain, had only now begun to advance, threatening to crush him at any minute. If it had genuinely crushed him—that would have been the best: but after all he was tenacious, he might manage to crawl out. No, it was leaving too much to chance to await the dénoument, in the natural course of things. He himself had to bring about the dénoument in order to have done with this unbearable sense of alarm. There was such a dénoument, indeed, there was. For a month he had been casting looks in its direction, and now it seemed that he would not pass it up. "On Sunday we'll take communion—we should go and pay our respects at mama's grave!" suddenly flashed through his head.

"Shall we go?" he turned to Anninka, putting his suggestion into words for her.

"If you like...we'll drive there together..."

"No, not together, but..." Porfiry Vladimirych was about to say and suddenly broke off as though realizing that Anninka might interfere.

"I'm the one who's guilty before my deceased mama... I'm the one who tormented her... I did it!" his thoughts were seething in the meanwhile, and the longing "to ask forgiveness" began to blaze hotter and hotter in his heart. Not "to ask forgiveness" the way people usually ask forgiveness, but to fall on her grave and grow numb with screams of mortal agony.

"So you say that Lyubinka died by her own hand?" he asked suddenly, apparently with the purpose of building up his courage.

At first Anninka seemed not to hear her uncle's question, but apparently it had reached her because in two or three minutes she herself felt a vague need to return to this death, to torment herself with it.

"So did she say: 'Drink... you vile creature!?' " he questioned her again when she had repeated her story with all the details.

"Yes... she said that."

"And so you were left? You didn't drink it?"

"Yes... here I am alive..."

He arose and paced back and forth in the room several times in obvious agitation. Finally he went up to Anninka and stroked her head.

"You poor thing! You poor thing of mine!" he uttered softly.

With this touch something unexpected happened inside her. At first she was amazed, but gradually her face grew distorted and more distorted, and suddenly a whole flood of hysterical, terrible sobbings burst out of her breast.

"Uncle! Are you good? Tell me, are you good?" she shouted almost in a scream.

"Did you hear what was being read at the evening service," he asked when she had finally settled down, "God, what sufferings those were! Only with sufferings of that sort is it possible... And yet He forgave! He forgave everyone forever!"

Once again he began with hurried steps to pace about the room, agonizing and suffering and not feeling that his face was covered with drops of perspiration.

"He forgave everyone," he said aloud to himself, "not only those who had *then* given Him vinegar and gall to drink, but those as well who both afterwards, right now, and forever, for all eternity, would raise vinegar mixed with gall to His lips... Terrible! God, how terrible it is!"

And suddenly, stopping in front of her he asked: "And what about you... have you forgiven?"

Instead of a reply she rushed to him and embraced him tightly.

"You have to forgive me," he continued, "for everyone... And for yourself... And for those who are no longer here... What has happened? What has happened?" he exclaimed, almost in distraction, peering all around, —where... is everyone?". . . . .
. . . .

Tormented and shaken, they went off to their rooms. But Porfiry Vladimirych could not sleep. He tossed from side to side in his bed and kept remembering the obligation that lay on him. And suddenly in his memory, with utter clarity, those words arose which had flashed through his head a few hours before. "I must go to mama's grave to ask her forgiveness..." At this recollection his entire being fell into the grip of a terrible, melancholy agitation...

Finally he could bear it no longer, arose from his bed and put on his housecoat. Outside it was still dark and not the slightest stirring came from any direction. Porfiry Vladimirych walked about his room for some time, stopping before the ikon of the Redeemer in the crown of thorns, illuminated by the ikon-lamp, and peering into his face. Finally he made up his mind. It's difficult to say to what degree he was conscious of his decision, but in several minutes, moving stealthily, he reached the front door and slipped the latch, unlocking the entry door.

Outside the wind was blowing and a wet March snowstorm was swirling, sending torrents of wet snow into his eyes. But Porfiry Vladimirych walked along the road, striding through the puddles without feeling either the snow or the wind and only instinctively drawing the skirts of his housecoat tighter.

* * *

The following day, early in the morning, from the village closest to the churchyard where Arina Petrovna was buried, a rider came galloping with the news that the frozen body of the master had been found a few steps from the road. Everyone rushed to Anninka, but she was lying in her bed unconscious, with all the signs of brain fever. Then a new rider was saddled up and sent off to Goryushkino to the "sister," Nadezhda Ivanovna Galkina (the daughter of auntie Varvara Mikhaylovna) who since the preceding autumn had been following keen-eyed everything that was going on at Golovlyovo.

BIBLIOGRAPHY

Secondary Sources in English, French and German

Foote, I.P. "Reaction or Revolution: The Ending of Saltykov's *History of a Town*." *Oxford Slavonic Papers*, New Series, Vol. 1 (1968).

Foote, I.P. "M.E. Saltykov-Shchedrin: *The Golovlyov Family*." *Forum for Modern Language Studies*. St. Andrews, Vol. 4 (1968), No. 1, pp. 53-63.

Foote, I.P. Introduction to M.E. Saltykov-Shchedrin, *Selected Satirical Writings*. Oxford: Clarendon Press, 1977, pp. 1-22.

Kramer, Karl D. "Satiric Form in Saltykov's *Gospoda Golovlevy*." *Slavic and East European Journal*, XIV (1970), No. 4, pp. 453-64.

Kuleshov, Catherine. "Saltykov-Shchedrin, Istoriia odnogo goroda *[The History of a Town]*: An Annotated Edition with an Introduction," Ph.D. dissertation, Indiana University, 1969. DA 30 (1970), 2973-A.

Lavretsky, Alexander. "Saltykov-Shchedrin—A Russian Satirist." *International Literature*. Moscow, 1939-June, pp. 72-78.

Lednicki, Waclaw. "Saltykov and the Russian Squire." [a review article]. *Slavonic and East European Review*, American Series, I (1941), pp. 347-54.

Makashin, S. "A Great Work of Russian Literature," preface to *The Golovlyovs*. Duddington translation, edited by O. Shartse. 2nd printing. Moscow: FLPH, 1975, pp. 7-16.

Strelsky, Nikander. *Saltykov and the Russian Squire*. New York: Columbia University Press, 1940. [Originally a Ph.D. thesis, Columbia University]. Book reviewed by Waclaw Lednicki, above.

Strelsky, Nikander. "A New Light on Saltykov's Philosophy." In *Slavic Studies: In Honour of George Rapall Noyes*. Ed. by A. Kaun and E.J. Simmons. Ithaca, NY: Cornell University Press, 1943.

Kupfer-Schmidt, H.G. *Saltykow-Stschedrin. Philosophisches Wollen und Schriftstellerische Tat*. Halle, 1958.

Sanine, Kyra. *Saltykow-Chtchedrine, sa vie et ses oeuvres*. Paris: Institut d'etudes slaves de l'université de Paris, 1955.

Anon. "Saltykov, M.I.—Sein Leben und Seine Werke." *Russische Geschichten und Satiren*, Vol. 3, pp. 1-47, Berlin, 190-.

Pezold, Theophil. "Michael Saltykov." *Deutsche Runschau*, Berlin, Vol. 85 (1895), pp. 273-293, 375-400.

Translations in English, French and German

Tchinovnicks. *Sketches of Provincial Life. From the Memoirs of the Retired Conseiller de Cour Stchedrin (Saltikov)*. Trans. F. Aston, London, 1861.

"The Fool." *Free Russia*, Vol. 1 (1890), No. 5, pp. 16-19.

"The Lost Conscience." *Short Stories*. New York, 1892, Vol. 9, pp. 33-42.

"Two Generals (Russian Fairy Tale)." *Free Russia*, Vol. 2 (1892), No. 6, pp. 14-16.

"Misha and Vania." *Free Russia*, Vol. 3 (1893), No. 6, pp. 13-15; No. 7, pp. 13-14.

"The Self-Sacrificing Rabbit"; "The Recollections of Onesime Chenapin"; "The Eagle as Mecaenas." Voynich, Ethel Lillian (Bull). *The Humor of Russia*. London: Scott, 1895.

"The Virtues and the Vices (A Fable)." *Free Russia*, Vol. 10 (1899), No. 11, pp. 76-78.

"Easter Eve." *Free Russia*, Vol 11 (1900), No. 4, pp. 42-44.

"Conscience." *Free Russia*, Vol. 13 (1902), No. 11, pp. 98-100.

"Beyond the Border," in *Anthology of Russian Literature*, ed. & tr. Leo Wiener. New York: Putnam, 1902-03. Vol. 2.

The Gollovlev Family. Trans. Athelstan Ridgway. London: Jarrold and Sons, 1916.

The Family of Noblemen. Trans. Avram Yarmolinsky. New York: Boni-Livewright, 1917.

The Village Priest and Other Stories. (from the Russian of Militsina and Saltikov). Trans. Beatrix L. Tollemache. London: Unwin Ltd., 1918.

"A Christmas Sermon"; "The Peasant and the Two Excellencies"; "The Lost Conscience"; "The Eagle"; "Patron of Learning." Ragozin, Z.A., *Little Russian Masterpieces*. New York: Putnam, 1920. 4 Vols.

The Death of Pazukhin; a Play in Four Acts. Trans. Julian Leigh. New York: Brentano's [1924].

The Golovlyov Family. Trans. Natalie Duddington. London: G. Allen & Unwin [1931]. Also: London & Toronto: J.M. Dent and Sons, 1934 [Everyman's Library]; reissued at London and New York, 1955 [Everyman's Library].

Fables by Shchedrin. Trans. Vera Volkhovsky. London: Chatto and Windus, 1931.

"The Self-Sacrificing Hare" and "The Sophisticated Gudgeon," *International Literature*. Moscow, 1939 (June), pp. 4-18.

"Boy in Pants and Boy Without." Trans. Gleb Struve. *Slavonic and East European Review*, London, 1939 (July), pp. 18-28.

"How a Mujik Fed Two Officials"; "Little Judas Speeds His Brother on His Way" [excerpt from *The Golovlyov Family*]. Trans. John Cournos. *A Treasury of Russian Life and Humor*. New York: Coward-McCann, 1943.

"Provincial Sketches" [excerpt], *The Russian Horizon*. Ed. N. Gangulee. London: Allen & Unwin, 1943.

"The Ideals of a Carp." Trans. Janko Lavrin. *Russian Humorous Stories*. London: Sylvan Press, 1946.

"Mr. and Mrs. Cheriozov." Trans. Janko Lavrin. *A Second Series of Representative Russian Stories: Leskov to Andreyev*. London: Westhouse, 1946.

"The Virtues and the Vices." Bernard Guilbert Guerney. *A Treasury of Russian Literature*. New York: Vanguard, 1943; London: Bodley Head, 1948.

Judas Golovlyov. Ed. Olga Shartse. [The unsuspecting reader should be warned that while Olga Shartse is listed as the translator, this is a Soviet edited version of Natalie Duddington's translation. It was reprinted in 1975 with the title *The Golovlyovs*.] Moscow: FLPH [1957].

The Golovlovs. Trans. Andrew R. MacAndrew. New York: New American Library [1961]. [Also in Signet Classics.]

"Zubatov." Trans. David Lapeza. *Russian Literature Triquarterly*, No. 10 (Fall 1974), pp. 67-76.

"Porfiry Petrovich." Trans. W.E. Brown. *Russian Literature Triquarterly*, No. 10 (Fall 1974), pp. 79-91.

Pazukhin's Death. Trans. Laurence Senelick. *Russian Literature Triquarterly*, No. 14 (Winter 1976), pp. 321-76.

Tales from M. Saltykov-Shchedrin. Trans. Dorian Rottenberg. Moscow: FLPH, 1956.

How a Muzhik Fed Two Generals. Trans. V. Volkhovsky. London: Chatto & Windus [n.d.].

* * *

L'Amie de l'ancien gouverneur; nouvelle de Chtchedrine. Traduit par E. O'Farell. Paris, 1881. 73 pp. [Extract from *Pompadours and Pompadouresses.*]

Trois contes russes de Chtchedrine. Traduit par E. O'Farell. Paris, 1881. 89 pp.

Berlin et Paris. Voyage satirique à travers l'Europe. La Conscience perdue. Traduit par M. Delines. 3-e edition. Paris, 1887.

Nos petits Bismarcks. Traduit par S. Nossoff. Paris: Weshausser [n.d.]. 271 pp.

Les Messieurs Golovleff. Traduit par M. Polonsky et G. Debesse. Paris, 1889.

Póchekhonie d'autrefois. Vie et aventures de Nikanor Zatrapezny. Traduit par Mme. M. Polonsky et G. Debesse. Paris, 1892.

Histoire d'une ville. Les Golovlev. Quatre contes. Deux recits. In: *Nicolas Leskov. M.E. Saltykov-Chtchedrine Oeuvres.* pp. 983-1668. Paris: Gallimard, 1967.

* * *

Skizzen aus dem Russischen Provinzialleben von Saltikow. Trans. A. Mecklenburg. Berlin: Springer, 1860. 2 vols.

Aus dem Volksleben Russlands. Skizzen aus dem Gouvernement. Berlin, 1863.

Die Herren Golowljew. Trans. von H. Moser. Leipzig: P. Reclam. [1886].

Die Herren Golowljew. Trans. F. Frisch. Munich: Müller, 1914.

Des Lebens Kleinigkeiten. Trans. von J. Eckardt. Hamburg. 1888.

Anon. *Russische Geschichten und Satiren,* Vol. 3, Berlin, 190-; pp. 47-154. This volume contains the following stories by Saltykov-Shchedrin: "Wie ein Muzhik zwei Generäle erhährte"; "Der verwilderte Gutsherr"; "Die Tugend und die Laster"; "Das Verlorene Gewissen"; "Eine lehrreiche Unterhaltung"; "Eine Episode Aus 'Wuhlhubers Leben' "; "Der Melancholische Widder."

"Knabe mit Hose und Knabe ohne Hose." *Süddeutsche Monatshefte*, München, 1915, Jahrg. 12, pp. 677-686.

Saltykow-Stschedrin, M.J. *M.J. Saltykow-Stschedrin über Kunst und Literatur.* [Ausgewählte Artikel, Rezensionen, Briefe.] Heidenau: Mitteldeutsche Kunstanstalt, 1956.